Lecture Notes in Computer Science 2536

Edited by G. Goos, J. Hartmanis, and J. van Leeuwen

T0226297

Springer
Berlin
Heidelberg
New York
Barcelona
Hong Kong
London
Milan
Paris
Tokyo

Manish Parashar (Ed.)

Grid Computing – GRID 2002

Third International Workshop
Baltimore, MD, USA, November 18, 2002
Proceedings

 Springer

Series Editors

Gerhard Goos, Karlsruhe University, Germany
Juris Hartmanis, Cornell University, NY, USA
Jan van Leeuwen, Utrecht University, The Netherlands

Volume Editor

Manish Parashar
Associate Professor
Department of Electrical and Computing Engineering
Rutger, The State University of New Jersey
94 Brett Road, Piscataway, NJ 08854-8058, USA
E-mail: parashar@caip.rutgers.edu

Cataloging-in-Publication Data applied for

Bibliographic information published by Die Deutsche Bibliothek

Die Deutsche Bibliothek lists this publication in the Deutsche Nationalbibliografie;
detailed bibliographic data is available in the Internet at <http://dnb.ddb.de>.

CR Subject Classification (1998): C.2, D.1-4, F.2

ISSN 0302-9743
ISBN 3-540-00133-6 Springer-Verlag Berlin Heidelberg New York

Springer-Verlag Berlin Heidelberg New York
a member of BertelsmannSpringer Science+Business Media GmbH

http://www.springer.de

© Springer-Verlag Berlin Heidelberg 2002
Printed in Germany

Typesetting: Camera-ready by author, data conversion by Steingräber Satztechnik GmbH, Heidelberg
Printed on acid-free paper   SPIN: 10871550   06/3142   5 4 3 2 1 0

Preface

The growth of the Internet and the availability of powerful computers and high-speed networks as low-cost commodity components are changing the way we do computing. These new technologies have enabled the clustering of a wide variety of geographically distributed resources, such as supercomputers, storage systems, data sources, and special devices and services, which can then be used as a unified resource. Furthermore, they have enabled seamless access to and interaction among these distributed resources, services, applications, and data. The new paradigm that has evolved is popularly termed "Grid computing". Grid computing and the utilization of the global Grid infrastructure have presented significant challenges at all levels, including application development, programming models, systems, infrastructures and services, networking, and security, and have led to the development of a global research community.

Grid 2002 is the third in a series of workshops developed to provide a forum for this growing Grid Computing research community. Grid 2000, the first workshop in the series, was chaired by Rajkumar Buyya and Mark Baker, and was held in conjunction with HiPC 2002 in Bangalore, India. Grid 2001 (Chair: Craig A. Lee) and Grid 2002 were held in conjunction with Supercomputing, the world's premier meeting for high-performance computing.

The Grid 2002 program committee consisted of a truly international group of experts representing 13 countries on 4 continents. Grid 2002 attracted 78 research papers. Each paper was thoroughly reviewed by the program committee and external reviewers, and 22 full papers and 6 "work-in-progress" papers were selected and presented at the workshop. We sincerely thank the program committee for the wonderful job they have done, the reviewers for their time and efforts, and specially the authors for their excellent submissions. It is because of you that the workshop was a success.

We also thank our sponsors, the ACM, the IEEE, the IEEE Computer Society, and Supercomputing 2002 for making the workshop and these proceedings possible. The WIMPE conference management software from Dartmouth College and system support at the CAIP Center at Rutgers University proved invaluable during the paper submission and review process. We also thank Jan van Leeuwen, Utrecht University (LNCS Series Editor) and Alfred Hofmann of Springer-Verlag (Executive Editor) for publishing the proceedings. Special thanks go to Anna Kramer of Springer-Verlag (Computer Science Editorial Assistant) and Sumir Chandra for helping perfect these proceedings. Finally, we wish to thank each one of you who attended Grid 2002 in Baltimore, MD. We do hope you find these proceedings interesting and informative.

November 2002   Manish Parashar

Grid 2002 Sponsoring Institutions

Association for Computing Machinery (ACM SIGARCH)
http://www.acm.org

Institute of Electrical and Electronics Engineers (IEEE)
http://www.ieee.org

IEEE Computer Society
http://www.computer.org

Supercomputing 2002
http://www.sc2002.org

Grid 2002 Organization

General Chair

Craig A. Lee   The Aerospace Corporation, CA, USA

Program Chair

Manish Parashar   Rutgers, State University of New Jersey, NJ, USA

Steering Committee

Mark Baker	University of Portsmouth, UK
Rajkumar Buyya	Monash University, Australia
Craig Lee	The Aerospace Corporation, USA
Manish Parashar	Rutgers, State University of New Jersey, NJ, USA
Heinz Stockinger	CERN, Switzerland

Publicity Chair

Ruth Aydt   University of Illinois, Urbana-Champaign, USA

Program Committee

David Abramson	Monash University, Australia
Gabrielle Allen	Max-Plank Institute, Germany
David Bader	University of New Mexico, USA
Kim Branson	CSIRO, Health Sciences and Nutrition, Australia
Henri Casanova	University of California, San Diego, USA
Steve Chapin	Syracuse University, USA
Francisco Curbera	IBM T.J. Watson Research Center, USA
Frederica Darema	National Science Foundation, USA
Jack Dongarra	University of Tennessee/ORNL, USA
Jonathan Giddy	Welsh e-Science Centre, Cardiff University, UK
Sergi Girona	Polytechnic University of Catalunya, Spain
Tomasz Haupt	Mississippi State University, USA
Ken Hawick	University of Wales, UK
Hai Jin Huazhong	University of Science and Technology, China
William Johnston	Lawrence Berkeley National Laboratory, USA
Domenico Laforenza	Institute of the Italian National Research Council, Italy
Gregor von Laszewski	Argonne National Laboratory, USA
Laurent Lefevre	RESAM/INRIA, France
Miron Livny	University of Wisconsin, USA

Satoshi Matsuoka	Tokyo Institute of Technology, Japan
Jarek Nabrzyski	Poznan Supercomputing and Networking Center, Poland
Lalit Patnaik	Indian Institute of Science, India
Marcelo Pasin	UFSM, Brazil
Thierry Priol	IRISA/INRIA, France
Alexander Reinefeld	ZIB, Germany
Mitsuhisa Sato	Real World Computing Partnership, Japan
Martin Schulz	Technische Universität München, Germany
Alan Sussman	University of Maryland, USA
Domenico Talia	ISI-CNR, Italy
Yoshio Tanaka	NIAIST, Japan
Brian Tierney	Lawrence Berkeley National Laboratory, USA
Putchong Uthayopas	Kasetsart University, Thailand
Jon Weissman	University of Minnesota, USA
Liang-Jie Zhang	IBM T.J. Watson Research Center, USA

Referees

M. Beck	S. Klasky	R. Raje
U. Bellur	K. Keahey	P. Reiher
V. Bhat	T. Kurc	C. Schmidt
S. Chandra	M. Ott	J. Sucec
Z. Juhasz	G. Popescu	
T. Kielmann	V. Putty	

Table of Contents

Resource Discovery and Management

Security and Policy Management

Scheduling

Grid Infrastructure and Services

Data Services

Framework for Peer-to-Peer Distributed Computing in a Heterogeneous, Decentralized Environment

Jerome Verbeke, Neelakanth Nadgir, Greg Ruetsch, and Ilya Sharapov

Sun Microsystems, Inc., Palo Alto, CA 94303

Abstract. This paper presents a framework for large-scale computations for problems that feature coarse-grained parallelization. The components of this framework are based on the Java^{TM1} programming language, which allows for a wide variety of platforms and components, and peer-to-peer communication is provided through the JXTA protocols, which allow for a dynamic and decentralized organization of computational resources.

1 Introduction

Parallel computation has been an essential component of scientific computing for decades. Such parallelization is typically fine-grained, which requires substantial inter-node communication utilizing protocols such as Message Passing Interface (MPI)[4,5] or Parallel Virtual Machine (PVM)[3]. Recently, however, there is an increasing demand for efficient mechanisms of computations which exhibit coarse-grained parallelism. Examples of this class of problems include throughput computations, where numerous independent tasks are performed to solve a large problem, or any solution which relies on ensemble averages, where a simulation is run under a variety of initial conditions which are then combined to form the result. This paper presents a framework for these types of computations.

The idea of achieving parallelization through performing many independent tasks is not new. One such realization is the Seti@Home[12,13] project, where data from astronomical measurements is farmed out to many PCs for processing, and upon completion returned to a centralized server for postprocessing. Other examples include solving the RSA cryptographic challenge on idle cycles of personal computers [1] and finding large Mersenne prime numbers [8].

While these examples do achieve coarse-grained parallelism, there are several issues which need to be addressed when building a generalized framework for distributed computing. In particular, running different simulations and decentralizing the tasks of job submission and result retrieval. The former property is addressed by the XtremWeb [2,9] platform that combines Java and native code for centralized control and job scheduling. We extend this approach to address

---

[1] Java is a trademark or registered trademark of Sun Microsystems, Inc. in the United States and other countries.

M. Parashar (Ed.): GRID 2002, LNCS 2536, pp. 1–12, 2002.
© Springer-Verlag Berlin Heidelberg 2002

other aspects that include (1) a dynamic grid, where nodes are added and removed during the lifetime of the jobs, (2) redundancy, such that the dynamic nature of the grid does not affect the results, (3) organization of computational resources into groups, such that inter-node communication does not occur in a one-to-all or all-to-all mode, thereby limiting the scalability of the system, and (4) heterogeneity, where a wide variety of computational platforms are able to participate.

The framework in this paper utilizes the JXTA[10] open peer-to-peer [11] communication protocols, which allow for the dynamic aspect (point 1 above) of the grid through peer discovery, in addition to the scalability aspect (point 3) through the use of peer groups. Heterogeneity (point 4) is achieved through Java's ability to run on various platforms. The decentralized aspect of the framework in addition to redundancy are discussed in the following sections.

Project JXTA was started at Sun Microsystems, Inc. in 2001. JXTA defines a set of protocols that can be implemented by peers to communicate and collaborate with peers implementing the JXTA protocols. It provides a means of standardizing messaging systems, specifically peer-to-peer systems, by defining protocols, rather than implementations. Currently Java and C implementations of the JXTA protocols are available.

In JXTA, every peer is identified by an ID, unique over time and space. Peer groups are user defined collections of entities (peers) who share a common interest. Peer groups are also identified by unique IDs. Peers can belong to multiple peer groups, can discover other entities (peers and peer groups) dynamically and can also publish themselves so that other peers can discover them. Three kinds of communication are supported in JXTA. The first kind is called unicast pipe and is similar to User Datagram Protocol (UDP) as it is unreliable. The second type is called secure pipe. The secure pipe creates a secure tunnel between the sender and the receiver, thus creating a secure, reliable transport. The third type is the broadcast pipe. When using the broadcast pipe, the message is broadcast to all the peers in the peer group.

2   Framework Peer Groups and Roles

In creating a framework for distributed computation, one needs to address the issue of reliability and scalability at the outset. Because we restrict the type of end-user applications to those that are embarrassingly parallel, a high potential for scalability is built into the system. The issue of efficiency then turns to the administration and coordination of tasks and resources. One advantage of building the framework utilizing the JXTA protocols is the concept of peer groups. By utilizing peer groups as a fundamental building block of the framework, one is able to group resources according to functionality, in the process building redundancy and restricting communication to relevant peers.

Our distributed computing framework contains the following peer groups: the monitor group, the worker group, and the task dispatcher group. The monitor group is a top-level group which coordinates the overall activity, including handling requests for peers to join the framework and their subsequent assignment of the node to peer groups, and high-level aspects of the job submission process. The worker group is responsible for performing the computations of a particular job, while the task dispatcher group distributes individual tasks to workers.

A single node can belong to several peer groups in the framework, likewise there can be many instances of each peer group within the framework. These interconnectivity and redundancy features are critical to handling the dynamic nature of the environment, where resources can be added and removed. In the following sections we discuss the interconnectivity of various peer groups in detail.

2.1   Code Repository

There are two parts to the submission of a job: the code used by the worker nodes which is common for all tasks within the global job, and the data used by the code which generally varies for each task within a global job. As with other aspects of this framework, the storage of the two elements for a job are distributed throughout the network in a decentralized fashion. The management of these components falls under the code repository manager, and example of which is given in Fig. 1.

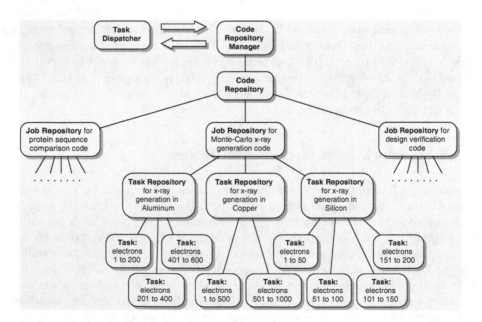

Fig. 1. Example of a Code Repository that contains three codes, each having its own job repository. The Monte-Carlo job repository has currently three jobs, each composed of a different number of tasks.

The interaction of the code repository manager with the rest of the framework is through the task dispatcher group. Upon receiving a job submission, the task dispatcher polls the repository to determine the status of the code within the code repository. If the repository is current, then the code is retrieved, otherwise it is uploaded and stored.

2.2   Distribution of Tasks amongst Workers

In this section we discuss the interaction of the task dispatcher and the worker groups. Within each worker group there is one task dispatcher group. Idle workers poll the task dispatcher group while relaying available resources, including codes the worker has cached. Based on this information, the task dispatcher polls the repository for tasks to be performed or codes to download. The worker then performs the task and returns the result to the task dispatcher. It is important to note that the task dispatcher does not keep track of which workers are performing which tasks.

No handshaking is being performed between the worker and the task dispatcher. Both are working in such a manner that lost messages do not affect the final completion of a job. The task dispatcher updates the repository with information about task completion and redundant tasks are performed to account for node failure.

2.3   Result Retrieval

Once a job has completed, that is, all the tasks in its task repository have completed, the results are sent back to the job submitter. The task dispatcher does not keep track of the job submitters, rather the job submitter initiates result retrieval.

The job submitter polls the task dispatcher inquiring whether the job it submitted has completed. This is facilitated through the unique ID associated with the task repository of each job obtained upon creation of the task repository.

The task dispatcher relays this request to the repository which returns with the tasks if the job has completed. These results are sent back to the job submitter.

2.4   Peer Redirection

Peers first joining the framework must make a request to the monitor peer group to either work or submit a job. The main role of the monitor group is to redirect incoming peers to other groups. A monitor has several subgroups and can redirect new peers to any of them. The choice of the group will depend on workload, code availability, etc. After the initial redirection to the correct worker group, no further communication is needed between the peer and the monitor group. The mechanism used to submit a job to the framework is illustrated in Fig. 2.

Monitors free task dispatchers from handling large number of requests coming from outside of the worker group. Task dispatchers communicate mainly with

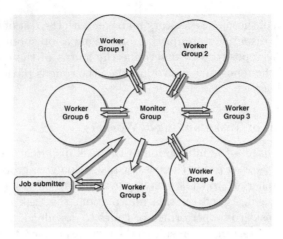

Fig. 2. Communications between monitor and other nodes.

their monitor, which allows them to reserve more bandwidth for communication with workers.

3   Reliability

Reliability is an important requirement for distributed computing. If the job is amenable to partitioning, it can benefit from the reliability features our framework implements. One of them is illustrated in Fig. 3. If only a single task dispatcher existed and consequently failed, the framework would be unreliable. With multiple task dispatchers keeping each other up to date with the latest results they have received, information is not lost if one of them incurs an outage.

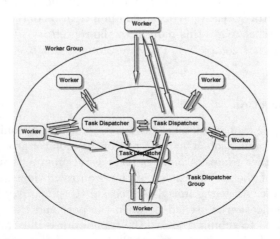

Fig. 3. Worker node assumes the role of task dispatcher when the latter is disrupted.

A new worker joining a worker group does not contact a particular task dispatcher, but the task dispatcher peer group. A task dispatcher replies to the incoming message. The question of which task dispatcher replies is discussed in the following section on scalability. The worker then establishes communication with the task dispatcher using a protocol illustrated by the worker at the top of Fig. 3. In this model, if a task dispatcher fails to respond to a worker, the worker backs out a level and contacts the task dispatcher peer group again. At this time, a different task dispatcher responds to his request. This protocol in case of a task dispatcher failure is illustrated by the worker at the bottom of Fig. 3.

Task dispatchers in a peer group communicate by sending each other messages. This regular exchange will be referred as the task dispatcher *heartbeat*. When task dispatchers receive new results from a worker, they send them to the other task dispatchers. To reduce the communication between task dispatchers, the implementation of the model could be such that they update each other with newest results only during heartbeats.

A few comments should be made regarding the sequence of events that happen if a member of a given task dispatcher peer group becomes unavailable. As soon as the other task dispatcher in the same peer group realizes that his redundant colleague is missing, it will invite a worker requesting a task to execute the task dispatcher code in his peer group, transforming a regular worker into a task dispatcher. This role interchange is simple to implement, because both the worker and task dispatcher codes implement a common interface, making them equally schedulable in this model. This role interchange is illustrated in Fig. 3 by the worker on the left side.

The number of task dispatchers in the task dispatcher peer group is not limited. We could easily have triple or higher redundancy. Also, because the communication protocols used do not limit us to working with peers in a small network, one can easily take advantage of the higher reliability offered by having redundant task dispatchers in various geographical locations. The same redundancy and role interchange mechanism exists in the monitor peer group as well.

4   Scalability

If too many worker groups are associated with the same monitor group, the communication bandwidth within that monitor group might become a bottleneck. Therefore, the model also enables one to have a hierarchy of monitor groups, with each monitor group monitoring a combination of worker groups and monitor groups. Whenever a monitor group becomes overloaded, it splits off a separate monitor group, and with it some of the load.

When a job submitter or worker contacts the top level monitor group, one of the peers in the group decides which subgroup to hand on the request to and forwards the request. If this subgroup is a monitor group, the message is forwarded until it reaches a worker group. A task dispatcher in the worker group then sends a reply to the job submitter/worker. The message contains the ID of

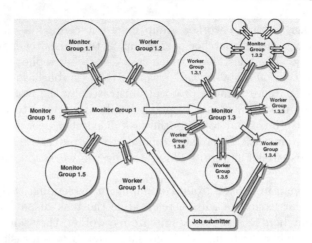

Fig. 4. Scalable network of worker groups and associated monitor groups.

the task dispatcher to contact, the task dispatcher peer group ID, as well as the IDs of the intermediate peer groups involved in passing down the message. The job submitter/worker at this stage has a point of contact in a new worker group. If it fails to contact the task dispatcher, it will contact the task dispatcher peer group, its parent, grand-parent, until it succeeds in contacting someone in the chain, with the last level being the top monitor group.

Because all the new peers joining the computing grid have to go through the top level monitor group, communication at that level might become a bottleneck. Numerous solutions exist to this problem. When a new peer contacts the top-level monitor group, all the monitors within this peer group receive the message. Each monitor in the monitor peer group has a subset of requests to which it replies. These subsets do not overlap and put together compose the entire possible set of requests that exist. Based on a feature of the request itself, a single monitor takes the request of the new peer and redirects it to a subgroup.

With two monitors in a monitor group, both monitors could determine without communicating whether replying to requests using a simple odd/even peer ID rule. This decision does not require any communication between the monitors. Another rule could be based on the geographical proximity of the requestor to the monitor.

5   Framework Performance Assessment on a Monte-Carlo Application

The implementation of the framework has been tested successfully on three different platforms: Sun Solaris^{TM2}, Microsoft Windows 2000 and RedHat Linux.

---

[2] Solaris is a trademark or registered trademark of Sun Microsystems, Inc. in the United States and other countries.

The code will become available as a developer community project named "JNGI" at http://jxta.org.

A simple Monte-Carlo application was used to determine how the framework scales with the number of peers in the framework. The application computes the distribution of x-rays generated by an electron beam incident on a vapor-deposited thin film on a metal substrate. The number of electron trajectories simulated was 38,400,000. The job was split into 384 tasks of 39 kbytes, each taking approximately 130 seconds. The total run time is shown as a function of the number of workers per task dispatcher in Fig. 5.

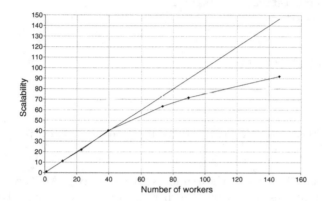

Fig. 5. Performance of the framework as a function of the number of peers.

The framework scales linearly to 40 workers. Scaling depends on the task granularity, larger problems with coarse granularity typically increase parallel efficiency[6,7]. For better processing power utilization, the number of workers per task dispatcher must vary dynamically based on the dispatcher workload.

6   Example of Usage of Peer-to-Peer Distributed Computing Framework

This section illustrates how to submit a job to the framework. The example used is trivial but illustrates the features required for the framework to work.

In this example, we compute the sum of all the integers between 1 and 1000. The calculation can easily be split into 10 tasks, the first task being the addition of all the integers between 1 and 100, etc.

6.1   Programs for Execution Kernel and for Job Submission

To use the framework to do this calculation on several machines, we first need to write the core of the calculation `AddNumbers.java` (see Fig. 6).

The `AddNumbers()` constructor is used to initialize the data, it takes arguments which must contain sufficient information for the code to run (in this case

```java
public class AddNumbers implements Runnable, Serializable {

    private int result, first, last;

    public AddNumbers(int first, int last) {
        result = 0;
        this.first = first;
        this.last = last;
    };

    public void run() {
        for (int i=first; i<=last; i++)
            result +=i;
    };

    public int getResult() {
        return result;
    };
};
```

Fig. 6. Sample computational program `AddNumbers.java`

the first and last indexes of the numbers to be added). An `AddNumbers` class instance differentiates itself from another instance only through the way they are constructed. The `run()` method is the core of the calculation. Since it will be invoked remotely on a machine unknown to the job submitter, it should not contain anything requiring user interaction or display any graphics. Once the `run()` method has been executed, the `AddNumbers` object contains the result of the calculation (in this case, the sum of all the integers from `first` to `last`).

We will now go over some details in this code that are implementation specific. First the `AddNumbers` class needs to implement `Serializable` and `Runnable` interfaces. The first interface is necessary for the class instances to be sent using Input/Output (IO) streams to the peers executing them. The second interface needs to be implemented for `AddNumbers` to be executable remotely using the `run()` method. The `RemoteThread` class is used by the job submitter to submit a job to the framework. It is an implementation specific class and similar to `java.lang.Thread`, but is executable remotely.

In this example, the job is split into ten tasks, which are created using the first and last indexes of the integers to be added. A `RemoteThread` is constructed with the array of `AddNumbers` and the directory containing the classes necessary to run the code. The bytecode transfer to remote peers uses XML messages which are sent to remote peers and stored locally.

After the `start()` method is called, the dispatcher checks with the repository to determine whether the `AddNumbers` code has previously been submitted. If not, the class files from the directory `AddNumbers` are sent to the dispatcher, which will create a job repository for this particular code in the repository. If it has previously been submitted (for example by someone who recently computed

```
public class exampleApp {

    public exampleApp() {
        AddNumbers [] tasks = prepareTasks(10); // Split the job into 10

        RemoteThread th = new RemoteThread(tasks, new File("AddNumbers"));
        th.start();
        th.join(10000);
        Runnable [] run = (Runnable []) remoteTh.getRunnable();

        if (run != null)
            postprocess(run);

        removeTh.remove();
        remoteTh.quit();
    };

    private AddNumbers [] prepareTasks(int numTasks) {
        /* Create the instances of AddNumbers class for each task */
        AddNumbers [] tasks = new AddNumbers [numTasks];
        for (int i=0; i<numTasks; i++)
            tasks [i] = new AddNumbers(1+(i*1000)/numTasks,
            ((i+1)*1000)/numTasks);
        return tasks;
    };

    private void postprocess(Runnable [] run) {
        int sum = 0;
        for (int i = 0; i<run.length; i++)
            sum += ((AddNumbers) run [i]).getResult();
        System.out.println("sum = '' + sum);
    };

    public static void main (String args[]) {
        exampleApp app = new exampleApp();
    };
};
```

Fig. 7. Example of pre- and post-processing for the application submitted to a distributed environment.

the sum of the integers between 2000 and 4000), we use the existing job repository for this code. The array of individual tasks is then sent to the dispatcher. A task repository is created for these tasks. Each of these task repositories has a unique ID that can be used by the job submitter to retrieve his results in the future.

Periodically, the job submitter polls the dispatcher to check whether its job has completed. The join() method only returns when all the tasks have completed. Once it returns, the individual tasks can be retrieved using the getRunnable() method of RemoteThread.

The `remove()` method removes all tasks belonging to this job from the task repository. If this method is not called, the memory requirements of the repository increase in time. The `quit()` method is called to interrupt the `RemoteThread` cleanly.

6.2   RemoteThread Class

The `RemoteThread` class is similar to the `java.lang.Thread` class and can be used by the application writer to submit a coarse-grained parallel application to the framework. It has the following methods:

- `public RemoteThread(java.lang.Runnable [] tasks, File directory)`:
  A `RemoteThread` object is constructed with an array of tasks implementing the `Runnable` interface and the directory where the classes containing the code to be transfered to remote peers is located.
- `public void start()`: Submits the code and the tasks to the framework.
- `public void join(int period)`: Checks every `period` milliseconds with the task dispatcher whether the job submitted has completed.
- `public java.lang.Runnable[] getRunnable()`: Once the job has completed, this method allows one to retrieve the results of the computations.
- `void remove()`: This method removes the `java.lang.Runnable` objects containing the results from the code repository.
- `void quit()`: This method cleans up the `RemoteThread` and should be used before quitting the application.

7   Conclusion

The model presented has all the features required for scalable, robust, efficient and dynamic grid computing. The peer-to-peer design of the grid limits communication to small peer groups that really require it. This enables the framework to scale to a very large numbers of peers. As pointed out earlier, the fact that task dispatchers can be redundant across large geographical locations, node outages in a single location will not affect the overall computational process. It also takes advantage of all the nodes willing to join the grid computing effort and is very efficient by this dynamicity. The RemoteThread class provides a set of APIs to harness the power of the framework by the application developers. One of the interesting features that has not been highlighted but which is a consequence of the features of this distributed computing model is the non-locality of the grid in the network. The grid could be composed of a few peers located in Europe today, and migrate to Asia tomorrow as more peers join the computing grid. This migration is directly dictated by the number of peer nodes joining the framework. Adding features to existing distributed computing models, this model pushes the boundary of grid computing to the global network.

References

1. distributed.net: Project RC5, RSA Labs Cryptographic Challenge.
   http://www.distributed.net/rc5/
2. C. Germain, V. Niri, G. Fedak and F. Cappello. XtremWeb: building an experimental platform for Global Computing, Grid2000, December 2000, IEEE Press.
3. A. Geist, A. Geguelin, J. Dongarra, W. Jiang, R. Manchek and V. Sunderam. PVM: Parallel Virtual Machine MIT Press, Cambridge, 1995.
4. W. Gropp, E. Lusk and A. Skjellum. Using MPI: Portable Parallel Programming with the Message-Passing Interface. MIT Press, Cambridge, 1999.
5. W. Gropp, E. Lusk and R. Thakur. Using MPI-2: Advanced Features of the Message Passing Interface. MIT Press, Cambridge, 2000.
6. J.L. Gustafson, G.R. Montry and R.E. Benner. Development Of Parallel Methods For A 1,024-Processor Hypercube. In SIAM Journal of Scientific and Statistical Computing, vol. 9, no.4, 1988.
7. J.L. Gustafson. Fixed Time, Tiered Memory, and Superlinear Speedup. In Proceedings of the Fifth Distributed Memory Computing Conference (DMCC5), October 1990.
8. The Great Internet Mersenne Prime Search. http://www.mersenne.org/
9. G. Fedak, C. Germain, V. Niri and F. Cappello. XtremWeb : A Generic Global Computing System, CCGRID2001, workshop on Global Computing on Personal Devices, May 2001, IEEE Press.
10. Project JXTA, http://www.jxta.org/
11. A. Oram, Editor. Peer-to-Peer, Harnessing the Power of Disruptive Technologies. O'Reilly & Associates, 2001.
12. SETI@home, The Search for Extraterrestrial Intelligence (SETI),
    http://setiathome.ssl.berkeley.edu/
13. W.T. Sullivan, D. Werthimer, S. Bowyer, J. Cobb, D. Gedye, D. Anderson. A new major SETI project based on Project Serendip data and 100,000 personal computers, in Astronomical and Biochemical Origins and the Search for Life in the Universe, Proc. of the Fifth Intl. Conf. on Bioastronomy. 1997.

Grid-Based Monte Carlo Application

Yaohang Li and Michael Mascagni

Department of Computer Science and School of Computational Science
and Information Technology
Florida State University
Tallahassee, FL 32306-4530, USA
{yaohanli, mascagni}@cs.fsu.edu

Abstract. Monte Carlo applications are widely perceived as computationally intensive but naturally parallel. Therefore, they can be effectively executed on the grid using the dynamic bag-of-work model. We improve the efficiency of the subtask-scheduling scheme by using an *N-out-of-M* strategy, and develop a Monte Carlo-specific lightweight checkpoint technique, which leads to a performance improvement for Monte Carlo grid computing. Also, we enhance the trustworthiness of Monte Carlo grid-computing applications by utilizing the statistical nature of Monte Carlo and by cryptographically validating intermediate results utilizing the random number generator already in use in the Monte Carlo application. All these techniques lead to a high-performance grid-computing infrastructure that is capable of providing trustworthy Monte Carlo computation services.

1. Introduction

Grid computing is characterized by large-scale sharing and cooperation of dynamically distributed resources, such as CPU cycles, communication bandwidth, and data, to constitute a computational environment [1]. In the grid's dynamic environment, from the application point of view, two issues are of prime import: performance – how quickly the grid-computing system can complete the submitted tasks, and trustworthiness – that the results obtained are, in fact, due to the computation requested. To meet these two requirements, many grid-computing or distributed-computing systems, such as Condor [2], HARNESS [3], Javelin [4], Globus [5], and Entropia [7], concentrate on developing high-performance and trust-computing facilities through system-level approaches. In this paper, we are going to analyze the characteristics of Monte Carlo applications, which are a potentially large computational category of grid applications, to develop approaches to address the performance and trustworthiness issues from the application level.

The remainder of this paper is organized as follows. In Section 2, we analyze the characteristics of Monte Carlo applications and develop a generic grid-computing paradigm for Monte Carlo computations. We discuss how to take advantage of the characteristics of Monte Carlo applications to improve the performance and trustworthiness of Monte Carlo grid computing in Section 3 and Section 4, respectively. Finally, Section 5 summarizes our conclusions and future research directions.

M. Parashar (Ed.): GRID 2002, LNCS 2536, pp. 13–24, 2002.

2.   Grid-Based Monte Carlo Applications

Among grid applications, those using Monte Carlo methods, which are widely used in scientific computing and simulation, have been considered too simplistic for consideration due to their natural parallelism. However, below we will show that many aspects of Monte Carlo applications can be exploited to provide much higher levels of performance and trustworthiness for computations on the grid. According to word of mouth, about 50% of the CPU time used on supercomputers at the U.S. Department of Energy National Labs is spent on Monte Carlo computations. Unlike data-intensive applications, Monte Carlo applications are usually computation intensive [6] and they tend to work on relatively small data sets while often consuming a large number of CPU cycles. Parallelism is a way to accelerate the convergence of a Monte Carlo computation. If N processors execute N independent copies of a Monte Carlo computation, the accumulated result will have a variance N time smaller than that of a single copy. In a distributed Monte Carlo application, once a distributed task starts, it can usually be executed independently with almost no inter-process communication. Therefore, Monte Carlo applications are perceived as naturally parallel, and they can usually be programmed via the so-called dynamic *bag-of-work* model. Here a large task is split into smaller independent subtasks and each are then executed separately. Effectively using the dynamic *bag-of-work* model for Monte Carlo requires that the underlying random number streams in each subtask be independent in a statistical sense. The SPRNG (Scalable Parallel Random Number Generators) library [11] was designed to use parameterized pseudorandom number generators to provide independent random number streams to parallel processes. Some generators in SPRNG can generate up to $2^{31}-1$ independent random number streams with sufficiently long period and good quality [13]. These generators meet the random number requirements of most Monte Carlo grid applications.

The intrinsically parallel aspect of Monte Carlo applications makes them an ideal fit for the grid-computing paradigm. In general, grid-based Monte Carlo applications can utilize the grid's *schedule service* to dispatch the independent subtasks to the different nodes [15]. The execution of a subtask takes advantage of the *storage service* of the grid to store intermediate results and to store each subtask's final (partial) result. When the subtasks are done, the *collection service* can be used to gather the results and generate the final result of the entire computation. Fig. 1 shows this generic paradigm for Monte Carlo grid applications.

The inherent characteristics of Monte Carlo applications motivate the use of grid computing to effectively perform large-scale Monte Carlo computations. Furthermore, within this Monte Carlo grid-computing paradigm, we can use the statistical nature of Monte Carlo computations and the cryptographic aspects of random numbers to reduce the wallclock time and to enforce the trustworthiness of the computation.

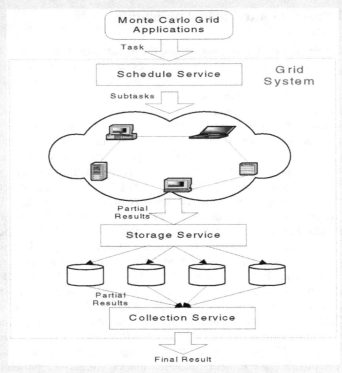

Fig. 1. Monte Carlo Application in a Grid System

3. Improving the Performance of Grid-Based Monte Carlo Computing

3.1 *N-out-of-M* Strategy

The nodes that provide CPU cycles in a grid system will most likely have computational capabilities that vary greatly. A node might be a high-end supercomputer, or a low-end personal computer, even just an intelligent widget. In addition, these nodes are geographically widely distributed and not centrally manageable. A node may go down or become inaccessible without notice while it is working on its task. Therefore, a slow node might become the bottleneck of the whole computation if the assembly of the final result must wait for the partial result generated on this slow node. A delayed subtask might delay the accomplishment of the whole task while a halted subtask might prevent the whole task from ever finishing. To address this problem, system-level methods are used in many grid or distributed-computing systems. For example, Entropia [7] tracks the execution of each subtask to make sure none of the subtasks are halted or delayed. However, the statistical nature of Monte Carlo applications provides a shortcut to solve this problem at the application level.

Suppose we are going to execute a Monte Carlo computation on a grid system. We split it into N subtasks, with each subtask based on its unique independent random number stream. We then schedule each subtask onto the nodes in the grid system. In this case, the assembly of the final result requires all the N partial results generated from the N subtasks. Each subtask is a "key" subtask, since the suspension or delay of any one of these subtasks will have a direct effect on the completion time of the whole task.

When we are running Monte Carlo applications, what we really care about is how many random samples (random trajectories) we must obtain to achieve a certain, predetermined, accuracy. We do not much care which random sample set is estimated, provided that all the random samples are independent in a statistical sense. The statistical nature of Monte Carlo applications allows us to enlarge the actual size of the computation by increasing the number of subtasks from N to M, where $M > N$. Each of these M subtasks uses its unique independent random number set, and we submit M instead of N subtasks to the grid system. Therefore, M bags of computation will be carried out and M partial results may be eventually generated. However, it is not necessary to wait for all M subtasks to finish. When N partial results are ready, we consider the whole task for the grid system to be completed. The application then collects the N partial results and produces the final result. At this point, the grid-computing system may broadcast abort signals to the nodes that are still computing the remaining subtasks. We call this scheduling strategy *the N-out-of-M strategy*. In the *N-out-of-M strategy* more subtasks than are needed are actually scheduled, therefore, none of these subtasks will become a "key" subtask and we can tolerate at most $M - N$ delayed or halted subtasks.

Fig. 2 shows an example of a distributed Monte Carlo computation using the "6-out-of-10" strategy. In this example, 6 partial results are needed and 10 subtasks are actually scheduled. During the computation, one subtask is suspended for some unknown reason. In addition, some subtasks have very short completion time while others execute very slowly. However, when 6 of the subtasks are complete, the whole computation is complete. The suspended subtask and the slow subtasks do not affect the completion of the whole computational task.

In Monte Carlo applications, N is determined by the application and it depends on the number of random samples or random trajectories needed to obtain a predetermined accuracy. The problem is thus how to choose the value M properly. A good choice of M can prevent a few subtasks from delaying or even halting the whole computation. However, if M is chosen too large, there may be little benefit to the computation at the cost of significantly increasing the workload of the grid system. The proper choice of M in the *N-out-of-M strategy* can be determined by considering the average job-completion rate in the grid system. Suppose p is the completion probability of subtasks up to time t in the grid system. Clearly, $M*p$ should be approximately N, i.e., the fraction of the M subtasks finished should equal to N. Thus a good choice is $M = \lceil N/p \rceil$. Note, if we know something about $p(t)$, the time-dependent completion probability, we can use this same reasoning to also help specify the approximate running time.

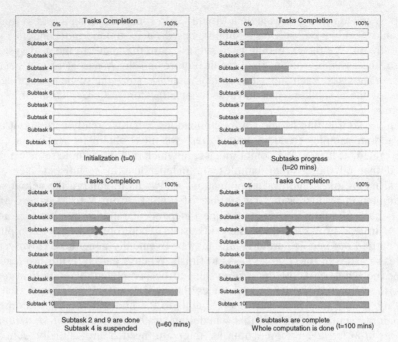

Fig. 2. Example of the "*6-out-of-10*" Strategy with 1 Suspended and 3 "Slow" Subtasks

We model the *N-out-of-M* strategy based on a binomial model. Assume that the probability of a subtask completing by time t is given $p(t)$. Also assume that $p(t)$ describes the aggregate probability over the pool of nodes in the grid, i.e., it could be measured by computing the empirical frequencies of the completion times over the pool. Then the probability that exactly N out of M subtasks are complete at time t is given by

$$P_{Exactly-N-out-of-M}(t) = \binom{M}{N} p^N(t) \times (1 - p(t))^{M-N}, \tag{1}$$

and so the probability that at least N subtasks are complete is given by

$$P_{N-out-of-M}(t) = \sum_{i=N}^{M} \binom{M}{i} p^i(t) \times (1 - p(t))^{M-i}. \tag{2}$$

The old strategy can be thought of as "*N-out-of-N*" which has probability given by

$$P_{N-out-of-N}(t) = p^N(t). \tag{3}$$

Fig. 3 shows an approximate sketch of $P(t)_{N\text{-}out\text{-}of\text{-}M}$, $p(t)$, and $P(t)_{N\text{-}out\text{-}of\text{-}N}$ ($p(t)$ can be either below $P(t)_{N\text{-}out\text{-}of\text{-}M}$ or above $P(t)_{N\text{-}out\text{-}of\text{-}M}$, depending on the value of N and M). As time goes on, the *N-out-of-M* strategy always has a higher probability of completion than the *N-out-of-N* strategy, although they all converge to 1.0 at large times.

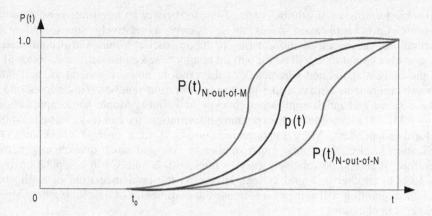

Fig. 3. Sketch of $P_{N\text{-}out\text{-}of\text{-}M}$, $p(t)$, and $P_{N\text{-}out\text{-}of\text{-}N}$

Also notice that the Monte Carlo computation using the *N-out-of-M strategy* is reproducible, because we know exactly which N out of M subtasks are actually involved and which random numbers were used. Thus each of these N subtasks can be reproduced later. However, if we want to reproduce all of these N subtasks at a later time on the grid system, the *N-out-of-N* strategy must be used!

One drawback of the *N-out-of-M* strategy is we must execute more subtasks than actually needed and will therefore increase the computational workload on the grid system. However, our experience with distributed computing systems such as Condor and Javelin shows that most of the time there are more nodes providing computing services available in the grid system than subtasks. Therefore, properly increasing the computational workload to achieve a shorter completion time for a computational task should be an acceptable tradeoff in a grid system.

3.2   Lightweight Checkpointing

A subtask running on a node in a grid system may take a very long time to finish. The *N-out-of-M* strategy is an attempt to mitigate the effect of this on the overall running time. However, if one incorporates checkpointing, he can directly attack reducing the completion time of the subtasks. Some grid computing systems implement a process-level checkpoint. Condor, for example, takes a snapshot of the process's current state, including stack and data segments, shared library code, process address space, all CPU states, states of all open files, all signal handlers, and pending signals [12]. On recovery, the process reads the checkpoint file and then restores its state. Since the process state contains a large amount of data, processing such a checkpoint is quite costly. Also, process-level checkpointing is very platform-dependent, which limits the possibility of migrating the process-level checkpoint to another node in a heterogeneous grid-computing environment.

Fortunately, Monte Carlo computation has a structure highly amenable to application-based checkpointing. Typically, a Monte Carlo application starts in an initial configuration, evaluates a random sample or a random trajectory, estimates a result, accumulates mean and variances with previous results, and repeats this process until some termination condition is met. Thus, to recover an interrupted computation, a Monte Carlo application needs to save only a relatively small amount of information. The necessary information to reconstruct a Monte Carlo computation image at checkpoint time will be the current results based on the estimates obtained so far, the current status and parameters of the random number generators, and other relevant program information like the current iteration number. This allows one to make a smart and quick application checkpoint in most Monte Carlo applications. Using XML [8] to record the checkpointing information, we can make this checkpoint platform-independent. More importantly, compared to a process checkpoint, the application-level checkpoint is much smaller in size and much quicker to generate. Therefore, it should be relatively easy to migrate a Monte Carlo computation from one node to another in a grid system. However, the implementation of application level checkpointing will somewhat increase the complexity of developing new Monte Carlo grid applications.

4.   Enhancing the Trustworthiness of Grid-Based Monte Carlo Computing

4.1   Distributed Monte Carlo Partial Result Validation

The correctness and accuracy of grid-based computations are vitally important to an application. In a grid-computing environment, the service providers of the grid are often geographically separated with no central management. Faults may hurt the integrity of a computation. These might include faults arising from the network, system software or node hardware. A node providing CPU cycles might not be trustworthy. A user might provide a system to the grid without the intent of faithfully executing the applications obtained. Experience with SETI@home has shown that users often fake computations and return wrong or inaccurate results. The resources in a grid system are so widely distributed that it appears difficult for a grid-computing system to completely prevent all "bad" nodes from participating in a grid computation. Unfortunately, Monte Carlo applications are very sensitive to each partial result generated from each subtask. An erroneous partial result will most likely lead to the corruption of the whole grid computation and thus render it useless.

The following Monte Carlo integration example illustrates how an erroneous computational partial result effects the whole computation. Let us consider the following hypothetical Monte Carlo computation. Suppose we wish to evaluate integral

$$\int_0^1 ... \int_0^1 \frac{4 x_1 x_3^2 e^{2 x_1 x_3}}{(1 + x_2 + x_4)^2} e^{x_5 + ... + x_{20}} x_{21} x_{22} ... x_{25} dx_1 ... dx_{25} \,. \tag{4}$$

The exact solution to 8-digits of this integral is 103.81372. In the experiment, we plan to use crude Monte Carlo on a grid system with 1,000 nodes. Table 1 tabulates the partial results from volunteer computers.

Table 1. Hypothetical Partial Results of Monte Carlo Integration Example

Subtask #	Partial Results
1	103.8999347
2	104.0002782
3	103.7795764
4	103.6894540
...	
561	89782.048998
...	
997	103.9235347
998	103.8727823
999	103.8557640
1000	103.7891408

Due to an error, the partial result returned from the node running subtask #561 is clearly bad. The fault may have been due to an error in the computation, a network communication error, or malicious activity, but that is not important. The effect is that the whole computational result ends 193.280805, considerably off the exact answer. From this example, we see that, in grid computing, the final computational result may be sensitive to each of the partial results obtained from nodes in the grid system. An error in a computation may seriously hurt the whole computation.

To enforce the correctness of the computation, many distributed computing or grid systems adapt fault-tolerant methods, like duplicate checking [10] and majority vote [16]. In these approaches, subtasks are duplicated and carried out on different nodes. Erroneous partial results can be found by comparing the partial results of the same subtask executed on different nodes. Duplicated checking requires doubling computations to discover an erroneous partial result. Majority vote requires at least three times more computation to identify an erroneous partial result. Using duplicate checking or majority vote will significantly increase the workload of a grid system.

In the dynamic *bag-of-work* model as applied to Monte Carlo applications, each subtask works on the same description of the problem, but estimates based on different random samples. Since the mean in a Monte Carlo computation is accumulated from many samples, its distribution will be approximately normal, according to the Central Limit Theorem. Suppose f_1, ..., f_i, ..., f_n are the n partial results generated from individual nodes on a grid system. The mean of these partial results is

$$\hat{f} = \frac{1}{n} \sum_{i=1}^{n} f_i, \tag{5}$$

and we can estimate its standard error, s, via the following formula

$$s = \sqrt{\frac{1}{n-1} \sum_{i=1}^{n} (f_i - \hat{f})^2}. \tag{6}$$

Specifically, the Central Limit Theorem states that $\hat{f}$ should be distributed approximately as a student-t random variable with mean $\hat{f}$, standard deviation $s/\sqrt{n}$, and n degrees-of-freedom. However, since we usually have n, the number of subtasks, chosen to be large, we may instead approximate the student-t distribution with the normal. Standard normal confidence interval theory states that with 68% confidence that the exact mean is within 1 standard deviation of $\hat{f}$, with 95% confidence within 2 standard deviations, and 99% confidence within 3 standard deviations. This statistical property of Monte Carlo computation can be used to develop an approach for validating the partial results of a large grid-based Monte Carlo computation.

Here is the proposed method for distributed Monte Carlo partial result validation. Suppose we are running n Monte Carlo subtasks on the grid, the ith subtask will eventually return a partial result, f_i. We anticipate that f_i are approximately normally distributed with mean, $\hat{f}$, and standard deviation, $\sigma = s/\sqrt{n}$. We expect that about one of the f_i in this group of n to lie outside a normal confidence interval with confidence $1 - 1/n$. In order to choose a confidence level that permits events we expect to see, statistically, yet flag events as outliers requires us to choose a multiplier, c, so that we flag events that should only occur in a group of size cn. The choice of c is rather subjective, but $c = 10$ implies that in only 1 in 10 runs of size n we should expect to find an outlier with confidence $1 - 1/10n$. With a given choice of c, one computes the symmetric normal confidence interval based on a confidence of $\alpha\% = 1 - 1/cn$. Thus the confidence interval is $[\hat{f} - Z_{\alpha/2}\sigma, \ \hat{f} + Z_{\alpha/2}\sigma]$, where $Z_{\alpha/2}$ is unit normal value such that $\int_0^{Z_{\alpha/2}} \frac{1}{\sqrt{2\pi}} e^{-\frac{x^2}{2}} dx = \frac{\alpha}{2}$. If f_i is in this confidence interval, we can consider this partial result as trustworthy. However, if f_i falls out of the interval, which may happen merely by chance with a very small probability, this particular partial result is suspect. We may either rerun the subtask that generated the suspicious partial result on another node for further validation or just discard it (if using the *N-out-of-M* strategy).

Let us now come back to the previous Monte Carlo integration example. We performed an experiment by running 1,000 subtasks for evaluating the integral described in the Monte Carlo integration example on a Condor pool [14]. Fig. 4 shows the distribution of all the generated partial results: 677 partial results are located within 1 standard deviation of the mean, 961 partial results within 2 standard deviations, and 999 of the 1,000 partial results within 3 standard deviations. If a hypothetical partial result happens as the one (#561) in the Monte Carlo integration example, the outlier lies 30 standard deviations to the right of the mean. As we know from calculating the confidence interval, we have • = 99.9999999999% within 7 standard deviations. A outlier falling outside of 7 standard deviations of the mean will be expected to happen by chance only once in 10^9 experiments. Therefore, the erroneous partial result of #561 in the Monte Carlo integration example will easily be captured and flagged as abhorrent.

This Monte Carlo partial result validation method supplies us with a way to identify suspicious results without running more subtasks. This method assumes that the majority of the nodes in grid system are "good" service providers, which can correctly and faithfully execute their assigned task and transfer the result. If most of the nodes are malicious, this validation method may not be effective. However, experience has shown that the fraction of "bad" nodes in volunteered computation is very small.

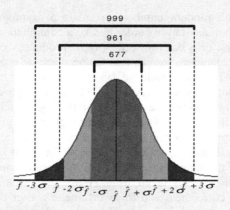

Fig. 4. Partial Result Distribution in Monte Carlo Integration Example

4.2   Intermediate Value Checking

Usually, a grid-computing system compensates the service providers to encourage computer owners to supply resources. Many Internet-wide grid-computing projects, such as SETI@home [9], have the experience that some service providers didn't faithfully execute their assigned subtasks. Instead they attempt to provide bogus partial result at a much lower personal computational cost in order to obtain more benefits. Checking whether the assigned subtask from a service provider is faithfully carried out and accurately executed is a critical issue that must be addressed by a grid-computing system.

One approach to check the validity of a subtask computation is to validate intermediate values within the computation. Intermediate values are some quantities generated within the execution of the subtask. To the node that runs the subtask, these values will be unknown until the subtask is actually executed and reaches a specific point within the program. On the other hand, to the clever application owner, certain intermediate values are either pre-known or are very easy to generate. Therefore, by comparing the intermediate values and the pre-known values, we can control whether the subtask is actually faithfully carried out or not. Monte Carlo applications consume pseudorandom numbers, which are generated deterministically from a pseudorandom number generator. If this pseudorandom number generator has a cheap algorithm for computing arbitrarily within the period, the random numbers are perfect candidates to be these cleverly chosen intermediate values. Thus, we have a very simple strategy to validate a result from subtasks by tracing certain predetermined random numbers in Monte Carlo applications.

For example, in a grid Monte Carlo application, we might force each subtask to save the value of the current pseudorandom number after every N (e.g., $N = 100,000$) pseudorandom numbers are generated. Therefore, we can keep a record of the Nth, $2N$th, ..., kNth random numbers used in the subtask. To validate the actual execution of a subtask on the server side, we can just re-compute the Nth, $2N$th, ..., kNth random numbers applying the specific generator with the same seed and parameters as used in this subtask. We then simply match them. A mismatch indicates problems during the execution of the task. Also, we can use intermediate values of the computation along with random numbers to create a cryptographic digest of the computation in order to make it even harder to fake a computational result. Given our list of random numbers, or a deterministic way to produce such a list, when those random numbers are computed, we can save some piece of program data current at that time in an array. At the same time we can use that random number to encrypt the saved data and incorporate these encrypted values in a cryptographic digest of the entire computation. At the end of the computation the digest and the saved values are then both returned to the server. The server, through cryptographic exchange, can recover the list of encrypted program data and quickly compute the random numbers used to encrypt them. Thus, the server can decrypted the list and compare it to the "plaintext" versions of the same transmitted from the application. Any discrepancies would flag either an erroneous or faked result. While this technique is certainly not a perfect way to ensure correctness and trustworthiness, a user determined on faking results would have to scrupulously analyze the code to determine the technique being used, and would have to know enough about the mathematics of the random number generator to leap ahead as required. In our estimation, surmounting these difficulties would far surpass the amount of work saved by gaining the ability to pass off faked results as genuine.

5.   Conclusions

Monte Carlo applications generically exhibit naturally parallel and computationally intensive characteristics. Moreover, we can easily fit the dynamic *bag-of-work* model, which works so well for Monte Carlo applications, onto a grid system to implement grid-based Monte Carlo computing. Furthermore, we may take advantage of the statistical nature of Monte Carlo calculations and the cryptographic nature of random numbers to enhance the performance and trustworthiness of this Monte Carlo grid-computing infrastructure at the application level.

The next phase of our research will be to develop a Monte Carlo grid toolkit, using the techniques described in this paper, to facilitate the development of grid-based Monte Carlo applications. At the same time, we will also try to execute more real-life Monte Carlo applications on our developing grid system.

References

1. I. Foster, C. Kesselman, and S. Tueske, "The Anatomy of the Grid," International Journal of Supercomputer Applications, **15**(3), 2001.
2. M. Litzkow, M. Livny, and M. Mutka, "Condor - A Hunter of Idle Workstations," Proceedings of the 8th International Conference of Distributed Computing Systems, pages 104-111, June, 1988.
3. Beck, Dongarra, Fagg, Geist, Gray, Kohl, Migliardi, K. Moore, T. Moore, P. Papadopoulous, S. Scott, and V. Sunderam, "HARESS: a next generation distributed virtual machine," Journal of Future Generation Computer Systems, (15), Elsevier Science B. V., 1999.

4. B. O. Christiansen, P. Cappello, M. F. Ionescu, M. O. Neary, K. E. Schauser, and D. Wu, "Javelin: Internet-Based Parallel Computing Using Java," Concurrency: Practice and Experience, **9**(11): 1139 - 1160, 1997.
5. I. Foster and C. Kesselman, "Globus: A metacomputing infrastructure toolkit," International Journal of Supercomputer Applications, **11**(2), 1997.
6. A. Srinivasan, D. M. Ceperley, and M. Mascagni, "Random Number Generators for Parallel Applications," to appear in Monte Carlo Methods in Chemical Physics, D. Ferguson, J. I. Siepmann and D. G. Truhlar, editors, Advances in Chemical Physics series, Wiley, New York, 1997.
7. Entropia website, http://www.entropia.com/entropia_platform.asp.
8. XML website, http://www.xml.org.
9. E. Korpela, D. Werthimer, D. Anderson, J. Cobb, and M. Lebofsky, "SETI@home-Massively distributed computing for SETI," Computing in Science and Engineering, **v3n1**, 81, 2001.
10. C. Aktouf, O.Benkahla, C.Robach, and A. Guran, "Basic Concepts & Advances in Fault-Tolerant Computing Design," World Scientific Publishing Company, 1998.
11. M. Mascagni, D. Ceperley, and A. Srinivasan, "SPRNG: A Scalable Library for Pseudorandom Number Generation," ACM Transactions on Mathematical Software, in the press, 2000.
12. M. Livny, J. Basney, R. Raman, and T. Tannenbaum, "Mechanisms for High Throughput Computing," SPEEDUP Journal, **11**(1), 1997.
13. SPRNG website, http://sprng.cs.fsu.edu.
14. Condor website, http://www.cs.wisc.edu/condor.
15. R. Buyya, S. Chapin, and D. DiNucci, "Architectural Models for Resource Management in the Grid," the First IEEE/ACM International Workshop on Grid Computing (GRID 2000), Springer Verlag LNCS Series, Germany, Bangalore, India, 2000.
16. L. F. G. Sarmenta, "Sabotage-Tolerance Mechanisms for Volunteer Computing Systems," ACM/IEEE International Symposium on Cluster Computing and the Grid (CCGrid'01), Brisbane, Australia, May, 2001.

A Grid Service-Based Active
Thermochemical Table Framework

Gregor von Laszewski[1], Branko Ruscic[2], Patrick Wagstrom[1], Sriram Krishnan[1],
Kaizar Amin[1], Sandeep Nijsure[1], Sandra Bittner[1], Reinhardt Pinzon[2],
John C. Hewson[3], Melita L. Morton[2], Mike Minkoff[1], and Al Wagner[2]

[1] Mathematics and Computer Science Division
[2] Chemistry Division
Argonne National Laboratory 9700 S. Cass Avenue, Argonne, IL 60439, U.S.A.
[3] Sandia National Laboratories, Livermore, CA 94551-0969, U.S.A.
gregor@mcs.anl.gov

Abstract. In this paper we report our work on the integration of existing scientific
applications using Grid Services. We describe a general architecture that provides
access to these applications via Web services-based application factories. Furthermore, we demonstrate how such services can interact with each other. These
interactions enable a level of integration that assists the scientific application architect in leveraging applications running in heterogeneous runtime environments.
Our architecture is implemented by using existing infrastructures and middleware,
such as Web services, the Globus Toolkit, and the Java CoG Kit. We test our architecture on a thermochemistry application that provides a number of requirements,
such as batch processing, interactive and collaborative steering, use of multiple
platforms, visualization through large displays, and access via a portal framework.
Besides the innovative use of the Grid and Web services, we have also provided
a novel algorithmic contribution to scientific disciplines that use thermochemical
tables. Specifically, we modified the original approach to constructing thermochemical tables to include an iterative process of refinement leading to increased
accuracy; we are now implementing this approach. We have designed a portal
for accessing the set of services provided, which include the display of network
dependencies between the reactions a chemist may be interested in and interactive
querying of associated species data.

1 Introduction

The study of energy changes that accompany chemical reactions and changes in the
physical states of matter is referred to as *thermochemistry*. The knowledge of thermochemical stability of substances is central to chemistry and critical in many industries,
since chemical reactions are ultimately governed by thermochemistry. Hence, thermochemistry finds applications in other disciplines such as earth science and engineering,
helping scientists to better understand processes such as climate and combustion [18,11]
and thus predict and verify them to a high degree of accuracy.

Until now, the thermochemical data necessary for such calculations has been available only in static table form, and the algorithms to derive accurate model descriptions
have been too imprecise to deal with the complex chemical reactions encountered in
state-of-the-art laboratory experiments or observed in nature. Our goal is to improve

M. Parashar (Ed.): GRID 2002, LNCS 2536, pp. 25–38, 2002.

this situation by delivering innovative algorithms to the scientists through an advanced collaborative environment.

Novel modalities of deriving new scientific results can be stimulated by enabling a collaborative environment in which scientists can publish and share their results with others, perform sophisticated calculations that are otherwise not feasible, and integrate newly developed algorithms.

The Grid [27,9,10] can provide the basic middleware infrastructure for bootstrapping this type of sophisticated collaborative environment. The Grid allows scientists to collaborate even though their resources may be controlled by different domains; access to these resources is enabled through the use and creation of "virtual organizations".

In this paper, we show how we provide advanced services that can be accessed collaboratively. Their integration as part of a workflow process enables the creation of services that can be easily reused by the community. Scientists are then in a position to concentrate on the science, while application developers can focus on the delivery of services that can be assembled as building blocks to create more elaborate services.

Our paper is structured as follows. First we give a short introduction to the problem domain and the terminology used in thermochemistry that is directly related to the work we perform. We analyze a current process to derive thermochemical tables, one of the most elementary building blocks in thermochemistry. Next we provide an improved technique for increasing the accuracy of this process. We introduce a scenario where our algorithm and the repeated use by the community will result in a highly accurate and elaborate thermochemistry table database. We outline our service-oriented architecture and discuss how services such as security, data transfer, registration, and scheduling assist in assembling such a sophisticated collaborative environment. We conclude our paper by summarizing the current state of the project and listing opportunities for further research.

2   Basic Thermochemistry

In this section we provide a minimal introduction to basic thermochemistry that is necessary to understand the services and scenarios presented later in this paper. A more complete account of the thermochemical development behind the concept of the active thermochemical tables will be published in the near future.

Elementary to the discipline of thermochemistry is *enthalpy* (ΔH_f°), which refers to the value of energy of a system when it is at constant pressure. The enthalpy relationships involved in examining thermochemical equations are easily visualized by means of enthalpy diagrams, such as that shown in Figure 1.

In this diagram the equations are expressed as a graph with horizontal lines representing different values of the enthalpy. Typically the differences between these values are determined experimentally or can be derived by using the thermodynamic laws from other enthalpy values. Values obtained from experiments, however, may contain errors (not shown in the diagram). Changes in the enthalpy are visualized by the distance between the lines. Based on the changes performed, different intermediate states (chemical species) may occur during the transition from one to the other final state. Thus, it is natural to visualize the transition with directed edges between the states. An alternative

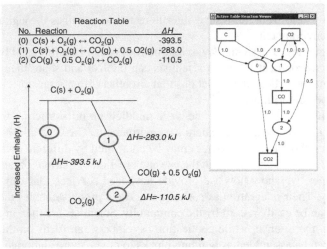

Fig. 1. Enthalpy diagrams and thermochemical reaction tables.

graph is displayed on the upper right-hand corner that emphasizes the possible states in which a chemical species (i.e., an ensemble of chemically identical molecular entities that can explore the same set of molecular energy levels on the time scale) can occur.

In traditional thermochemical tables the enthalpies of formation (ΔH_f^o) are developed with the help of an elaborate *sequential process*. In each step a new species is added while all ΔH_f^o values determined in previous steps are frozen. The enthalpy of the new species is determined at one temperature T from interconnecting measurements that are limited to those species already defined in previous steps. The temperature-dependent functions, $C_p^o, S^o, (H_T^o - H_o^o), \Delta H_{fT}^o, \Delta G_T^o$, are developed by determining the partition function $Q, lnQ, T\partial(lnQ)/\partial T$, and $T^2\partial^2(lnQ)/\partial T^2$ from the species-specified quantities and the newly selected single temperature enthalpy. (For more information about these terms, please see [20].)

The sequential process follows a *standard* order of chemical elements: $O \rightarrow H \rightarrow halogens \rightarrow noblegases \rightarrow chalcogens \rightarrow pnicogens \rightarrow carbonperiod \rightarrow$ etc. For every chemical element introduced, the sequence starts at the standard state for that element, for which $\Delta H_f^o = 0$ by convention. However, enthalpies of formation have complex hidden dependencies. These dependencies are backwards traceable, albeit with considerable manual effort, and in practice are not forwards traceable at all.

This sequential approach has several disadvantages. In particular, it results in ΔH_f^o and error bars that do not properly reflect the global relationships implied by the species-interconnecting data used. The values and error bars reflect, at best, only local relationships to nearest neighbors. A cumulative error is introduced based on the frozen enthalpies in previous steps. Furthermore, the hidden relationships in conventional tables produce thermodynamic tables that are static in its nature. Proper update with new knowledge is nearly impossible because forward relationships are nontransparent; hence, updating one species may improve things locally but increase the global inconsistencies.

We present a new approach, based on active tables, that circumvents these disadvantages.

3   Active Thermochemical Tables

The active table approach treats the information in the species-interdependent data from the viewpoint of a thermochemical network [20,19]. Every vertex (node) of this network represents the enthalpy of formation of one species. The species-interdependent data define the topology of the network graph by providing the edges (links) in the network. Competing measurements provide multiple (parallel) links in the network. The relational information defining the topology maps onto a set of equations, with the enthalpies of the involved species as unknowns, the stoichiometry of the reactions defining the coefficients, and the measurements and their error bars providing the free elements. Since the number of equations regularly exceeds the number of unknowns, the system is overdetermined. The best solution to the network is obtained in two steps.

The first step statistically analyzes the network with the goal of checking the error bars of individual data items for consistency. All inconsistencies are identified and proposals for their resolutions generated. The resolutions generally proceed through incrementing the error bars of the offending data items to their statistically indicated values, and the analysis is repeated. During subsequent steps the error bars of the offending data items usually oscillate up and down until self-consistency across the whole network is reached. The analysis is carried out in both unweighted and error-weighted space.

The second step occurs once the values and error bars of data items achieve consistency across the whole network. This step consists of finding simultaneously the optimal solution to all nodes by χ^2 minimization (in error-weighted space). The species-specific data is used to prepare the network for analysis by re-expressing all data items as reaction enthalpies at one common temperature. Once the optimal solution to the network has been found, the species-specific data is used to calculate the partition functions and hence develop the temperature dependence of the standard thermochemical functions.

We note that, as opposed to the simultaneous solution described above, in the traditional sequential approach the nodes are solved one at a time in a prescribed sequence. Each of the steps corresponds to selecting a particular path in the network leading from solved nodes to the next node, and ignoring all other possible paths. Both the fact that an overdetermined system of coupled equations is solved for one unknown at the time and that some of the equations are ignored contribute to the lack of global consistency in traditional tables.

4   Benefits of the Active Table Approach

Unlike the quantities found in a traditional table, the thermochemical quantities (and their error bars) obtained from the Active Table properly reflect the globalism of relationships implied by the underlying thermochemical network. All values and error bars are consistent in a global sense. An active table allows rapid update with new measurements (and possibly calculations) by globally propagating the new information through the table. Quality and integrity of the table are protected throughout the updates by error analysis, which runs in both directions: The error bar of the new experiment may shrink error bars in the table; however, the error bars of other experiments in the table might challenge, by means of the statistical analysis discussed above, the error bar assigned to the new experiment. In addition, an active table allows "what-if" tests. Such tests provide a critical evaluation of the tested data and its impact on prior thermochemical knowledge or, if the tests correspond to a new experiment, provide feedback on sensitivity of the network to various measurements. The approach has also potential to become an interesting learning and education tool. An active table can provide a ranked list of links that are missing or weak from a statistical viewpoint; in particular, it can provide pointers to the most useful new experiments or calculations.

5   Application Requirements

We have performed an initial requirements analysis that identified a number of important basic use cases that must be provided by our architecture. These use cases include

- the calculation of an active thermochemical reaction,
- the visualization of a set of active thermochemical reactions as a graph,
- the polynomial fitting (used in subsequent modeling) of a function based on data obtained either with standard or with active thermochemical tables from a variety of input sources,
- the display of the polynomial fitted functions, and
- the query of data needed for the polynomial fitting and the active tables.

In the next section we extend our requirements list beyond individual scientific applications needs and concentrate more on the modalities of using these applications in a shared and collaborative environment.

6   Grid Requirements

To decide on a computational environment that supports our proposed algorithmic solution, we first analyzed the requirements based on the modality of the scientific research to be performed. We identified the following requirements:

Collaborative environment that supports the interaction among scientists in geographically dispersed locations.
Secure environment that protects from the loss of intellectual property and allows restricted access to the data and compute resources.
Standardized environment that enables the scientist to use the tools in a straightforward fashion.
Adaptive environment that is flexible to future changes based on hardware and software.
Dynamic environment that allows the creation of transient services to enable adhoc collaboration and use of other application services.

These requirements are shared with many other scientific disciplines, and a large amount of research has been performed in the past few decades to develop frameworks that support such requirements.

We decided to base our architecture on a framework that is centered on the concept of the Grid. The Grid enables flexible resource sharing among a collection of resources that is maintained as part of different administrative domains. Middleware such as the Globus Toolkit can provide the foundation for an implementation of our architecture. Additionally, we need to develop advanced application specific services that build on basic Grid services so that scientists can use standardized Grids as defined by the Global Grid Forum [4].

Besides the integration of Grid standards we also need to take into account the availability of commodity tools and frameworks such as Web services that enable a bridge to commercially available middleware, thus simplifying our implementation. Examples of successful bridging initiatives include the Globus Project through the Java Commodity Grid Kit and, more recently, the Open Grid Service Architecture, which is currently under development. Drawing on this rich experience, we prototyped an architecture that can be supported by these commodity-integrating technologies.

Further analysis of our problem domain revealed that it is beneficial to build the framework based on a service-oriented architecture. Such an environment includes flexible design while still being able to integrate sophisticated security solutions. Additionally, we can design services that interact with each other and may operate at geographically dispersed locations. We have identified within our project the need to deliver the following services:

Grid Broker Service to deal with large numbers of calculations that are involved with future large-scale reactions and their real-time requirement for allowing interactive use [23,2].

Grid Workflow Service to enable the interplay of Grid services through workflow descriptions [24,25].

Grid Execution Factories to enable the execution of programs in a Grid while instantiating them in a hosting environment and making their results accessible to other services (the Globus Toolkit provides such services in Java and C) [24,14].

Grid Monitoring Service to monitor the state of the hosting environment so that feedback to Grid services is provided, enabling the environment to react to state changes [26].

Grid Migration Service to be able to migrate services and jobs executed with a Grid Execution Factory Service to a location that is better suited, based on performance and quality of service descriptions and policies [28].

Grid Logging Service to log and checkpoint services in order to enable migration and fault-tolerant behavior.

Grid Self-Healing Service to determine how and when it is necessary to change the dynamically instantiated Grid workflow applications (including preventive measurements such as service replication, service migration, service checkpointing, and service monitoring).

Collaborative Steering Service to collaboratively create data, thoughts, and ideas that will lead to new scientific findings.

Furthermore, we require a simple portal to interact with this sophisticated environment, so that scientists may concentrate on the science and not the environment [27]. Although many more services are needed, we decided to restrict our initial prototype on these sets of services.

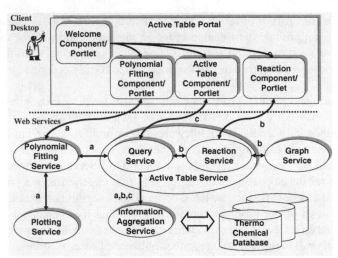

Fig. 2. The application-specific services to enable the scientist to access a convenient portal interfacing exposing active thermochemical tables, polynomial fitting of JANAF data, and their visualization. The letters a, b, and c refer to the corresponding use cases as explained in the text.

7   Architecture

We have identified that a service-oriented architecture with a discovery and binding mechanism can be used to deal with the dynamically changing nature of our collaborative environment. This architecture must enable to connect several functional services that perform the tasks demanded by the application. We depict these application specific services in Figure 2.

The scientist can interact with our computational programs via portal mechanisms. The functions currently supported by our portal are polynomial fitting of data based on thermochemical data provided in a standard format such as JANAF [17,22,29], the query of thermochemical data for species, the creation of a database based on species data, the calculation of an active table based on a number of reactions (currently under development), and the graphical display of the polynomial fitted data and the reactions.

The elegance of our architecture is based on the use of the service model that allows us to be flexible in many ways. First, we provide many of the algorithmic functions as services that can be placed in a geographically dispersed environment. Thus it is possible to maintain changes to the original algorithm by the application specialist, while at the same time minimizing the effort for reuse in a collaborative environment. Second, we are able to integrate new services into this architecture to extend it while being open to future requirements. Thus, we have created an architecture that is open and allows for expansion during the course of its development. Third, we are able to replace parts of our architecture with newly developed services, providing a customized functionality to disparate user communities.

In our first prototype we provide a Swing portal, as well as a Web-based portal based on the Jetspeed framework [5].

We have chosen intuitive names for our application-oriented services so that their functionality may be effectively communicated. Some of our services are as follows:

Polynomial Fitting Service that performs the polynomial fitting of data based on standard thermochemical tables such as JANAF

Active Table Service that performs the active table algorithms and the χ^2 minimization of the systems of linear equations obtained from a reaction table. This service is composed of two services:

    Query Service that returns information about the chemical species

    Reaction Service that allows the graphical display of the reactions to be analyzed

Plotting Service that allows the creation of two-dimensional data plots

Graph Service that allows the creation of two-dimensional visualization of augmented graphs (currently using the GraphViz engine [12,13])

Information Aggregation Service that allows querying multiple databases maintained in a distributed fashion. A caching mechanism minimizes the search latency for frequently asked queries.

8   Example Use Cases

Based on our instantiation of our architecture on a hosting environment, we provide a series of screenshots to illustrate the state of our implementation.

Use Case A: Requesting a polynomial approximation of the thermochemical characteristics of argon. The user starts up the polyfit client on his desktop and requests a mathematical approximation for the thermochemistry properties of a given species, for example, argon. The polyfit client then opens a communication channel to a polyfit Web service to send the request. To process the request, the polyfit service needs the basic thermo data for argon, which is requested and returned from the Active Table Service. Having the required information, the polyfit Web service calls the non Grid-aware FORTRAN application to process the table information and produce coefficients for equations. These equations are passed to the plotting Web service to generate a graphic image. This graphic image is then returned to the polyfit client, and the data can be viewed on the users terminal. The workflow for the components and services that are involved in this use case are indicated with the letter *a* in Figure 2. The portal interface is shown in Figure 3.

Use Case B: Visualizing a reaction graph and obtaining information on the species in the graph. The user starts up the reaction visualization client and submits a reaction file to this client. A reaction file can be as simple as one chemical reaction, or it can be hundreds of reactions all working together. The client then passes the information on to the graph service. The graph service takes this reaction file and parses it. It then calls some non-Grid-aware graphing service such as Dot [12] to create the graph. In order to provide more information on each of the species in the graph, the graph service also connects to the active table service for each of the species in the reaction file. This information is then passed back to the client and then the user for examination. The workflow for the

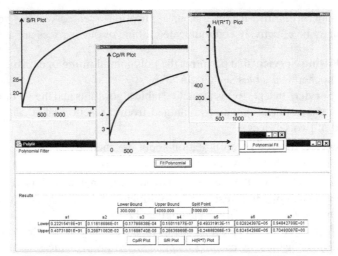

Fig. 3. The polynomial fitting of data based on JANAF tables.

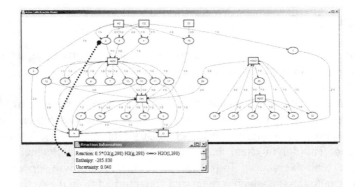

Fig. 4. A reaction graph visualization component.

components and services that are involved in this use case are indicated with the letter *b* in Figure 2. The portal interface is shown in Figure 4 with the reactions as depicted in Table 1.

Use Case C: Requesting the thermo table for carbon (graphite). The user starts an active tables client and enters a search string into the client, in this case *Graphite*. This data is then submitted to the active tables Web service. If the service does not contain enough information to process the request, it may request more information from a WebDAV [15] server or other Web services. That new information is returned to the active table services, where it is combined with the data obtained from the active tables program. This is then passed back to the client and then the user. The workflow for the components and services that are involved in this use case are indicated with the letter *c* in Figure 2. The portal interface is shown in Figure 5.

Table 1. A thermochemical reaction table

Equation	Enthalpy (kJ/mol)	Uncertainty		Equation	Enthalpy (kJ/mol)	Uncertainty
$O_2(g,0) \Leftrightarrow 2\,O(g,0)$	493.579	0.179		$H_2O(g,0) \Leftrightarrow OH+(g,0) + H(g,0)$	1748.101	0.482
$H_2(g,0) \Leftrightarrow 2\,H(g,0)$	432.071	0.012		$OH(g,0) \Leftrightarrow OH+(g,0)$	1255.947	0.024
$\frac{1}{2}O_2(g,298) + H_2(g,298) \Leftrightarrow H_2O(l,298)$	-285.830	0.040		$OH(g,0) \Leftrightarrow OH+(g,0)$	1255.274	0.965
$\frac{1}{2}O_2(g,298) + H_2(g,298) \Leftrightarrow H_2O(l,298)$	-285.795	0.040		$OH(g,0) \Leftrightarrow OH+(g,0)$	1254.309	9.649
$\frac{1}{2}O_2(g,298) + H_2(g,298) \Leftrightarrow H_2O(l,298)$	-285.850	0.330		$H_2O(g,0) \Leftrightarrow OH(g,0) + H(g,0)$	492.275	0.060
$H_2O(l,298) \Leftrightarrow H_2O(g,298)$	44.004	0.002		$\frac{1}{2}O_2(g,0) + \frac{1}{2}H_2(g,0) \Leftrightarrow OH(g,0)$	37.082	0.670
$H_2O(l,298) \Leftrightarrow H_2O(g,298)$	44.016	0.010		$H_2O_2(l,298) \Leftrightarrow H_2O_2(g,298)$	47.950	4.400
$H_2O(l,0) \Leftrightarrow H_2O(g,298)$	-2.093	0.001		$H_2O_2(l,298) \Leftrightarrow H_2O_2(g,298)$	51.920	0.150
$OH(g,0) \Leftrightarrow O(g,0) + H(g,0)$	423.717	0.179		$H_2O_2(l,298) \Leftrightarrow H_2O_2(g,298)$	47.510	3.100
$OH(g,0) \Leftrightarrow O(g,0) + H(g,0)$	424.076	1.196		$H_2O_2(l,298) \Leftrightarrow H_2O_2(g,298)$	51.750	0.160
$H_2O(g,0) \Leftrightarrow OH+(g,0) + H(g,0)$	1748.101	0.772		$H_2O_2(l,298) \Leftrightarrow H_2O_2(g,298)$	52.200	10.000
$H_2O(g,0) \Leftrightarrow OH+(g,0) + H(g,0)$	1748.207	0.338		$H_2O_2(l,298) \Leftrightarrow H_2O_2(g,298)$	51.925	0.073
$H_2O(g,0) \Leftrightarrow OH+(g,0) + H(g,0)$	1748.256	0.193		$H_2O_2(g,0) \Leftrightarrow H_2O_2(g,298)$	-5.990	0.001
				$H_2O_2(g,0) \Leftrightarrow 2\,OH(g,0)$	203.985	0.041

Fig. 5. Querying the species dictionary.

Use Case D (currently in planning): Using the active table in educational outreach projects. Because we use standard Grid security infrastructure [8] and the ability to flexibly assemble our services, it will be possible to create a customized portal access through the *Access Grid* [7]. This will allow us to share and display our interface through Active Murals among a set of participating institutions in an educational setting. The ongoing DOE-sponsored SciDAC projects [21] will enable the easy integration of our services in the near future, when we expect that Web services technologies are adopted within the Grid community. A cartoon of this use case is depicted in Figure 6.

9 Implementation

Our implementation follows the strict separation of backend services from rendering services as depicted in Figure 2. On the backend, we provide an application factory service, which is capable of launching non-Grid-aware applications, after initializing them with parameters and other command line arguments. We use such a service to export complex FORTRAN code (written by the chemists) as a Web service, without having to modifying it. In the future, clients will be able to retrieve a handle to such a service using standard mechanisms (e.g., UDDI [6]) and will be able to access the scientific codes, as shown in Figure 7. We prototyped a generic tool that exposes any non-Grid-aware code as a Grid service. This tool accepts the interfaces that the service

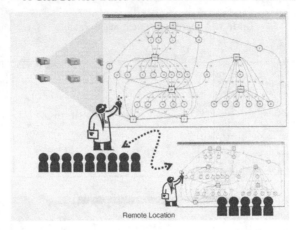

Fig. 6. Cartoon of the usage of an Active Mural in classroom settings.

should export (using some standard format, e.g., IDL, WSDL, Java interfaces) and the bindings from each method in such an interface to the actual calls to the non-Grid-aware application, and generates the required glue code to expose it as a service. The implementation is along the lines of the WSDL-to-Java converter tool provided by Axis [1] and, in fact, involved a slight modification of the code generation provided by Axis to suit our needs.

The graph service is also exported as a Web service, for the same reasons. The reactions that are fed into the graph service, in a format convenient to chemists, are then parsed and converted to a canonical XML format by using Castor [3], which is a data-binding framework for Java. The standard XML representation with corresponding Java bindings was a logical choice, as we can then plug in many different types of visualizers at the backend, without having to worry about conversions from the chemical format to the formats expected by the graphical packages. Currently, our visualization engine uses Dot to convert the XML representation into an SVG format, but we anticipate having several ways to visualize these graphs. The XML format also lends itself well to being transferred, and can be visualized locally, if need be, to save bandwidth.

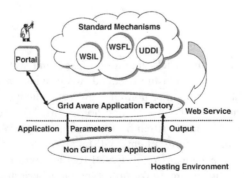

Fig. 7. Exporting a non-Grid-aware application as a Web service

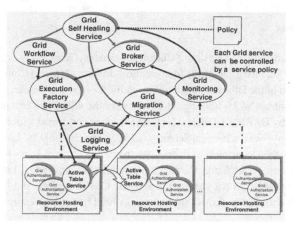

Fig. 8. Advanced Grid services enabling quality-of-service assurances.

Through the use of SWING applications and a Jetspeed portal we have shown that our services can be reused by a variety of frontend systems.

10   Future Developments

We will enhance our framework on multiple levels. First, we will enhance our Grid environment with more advanced services such as the ones listed in Section 6. These services allow us to create a sophisticated Grid environment that enables the creation of adaptive and self-healing Grid services. As our services can be assembled with each other using the Grid Workflow Service [16], we can provide application- and non-application-specific services with features currently not provided by the current generation of Grid software. Figure 8 shows an example of how we will use these services for reliable and flexible brokering of jobs in Grids with quality-of-service assurances. The goal is to investigate the design of a highly available service that can adapt itself to the disruptive nature of the Grid and the Internet.

11   Conclusion

In this paper we have shown that a service-oriented architecture can be used to provide access to collaborative application environments. We have demonstrated this feature by prototyping an application-oriented portal usable for thermochemical studies. We have developed an architecture that is flexible and open so that additional services can be integrated in our system at a later time. Because of the service-oriented design it will be possible to replace our services in the future with more advanced ones and to customize the behavior of the system with the help of a workflow engine. Because we combine the use of standard commodity technologies with Grid technologies, we are able to create a Grid infrastructure using commodity tools. This initial application has already led to the modification and enhancement of toolkits such as the Java CoG Kit providing access to the Grid.

Acknowledgments

This work was supported by the Division of Chemical Sciences, Geosciences and Biosciences, Office of Basic Energy Sciences, and by the Mathematical, Information, and Computational Science Division subprogram of the Office of Advanced Scientific Computing Research, U.S. Department of Energy, under Contract W-31-109-Eng-38. Funding for the Globus Project research and development is provided by DARPA, DOE, and NSF. The work is performed with help of the SciDAC Collaboratory for Multi-scale Chemical Sciences (CMCS) and the SciDAC Java Commodity Grid project sponsored by the Department of Energy. We thank Jim Meyers, Larry Rahn, David Leahy, David Montana, Karen Schuschardt, Carmen Pancerella, Christine Yang, Ian Foster, the other members of the SciDAC CoG Kit project, the SciDAC CMCS project, and the Globus Project. The Globus Toolkit and Globus Project are trademarks held by the University of Chicago.

References

1. Apache AXIS. http://xml.apache.org/axis/.
2. Condor home page. http://www.cs.wisc.edu/condor/.
3. The Castor Project. http://castor.exolab.org/.
4. The Global Grid Forum Web Page. http://www.gridforum.org.
5. The Jetspeed Webpage. http://jakarta.apache.org/jetspeed/.
6. Universal Description, Discovery and Integration of Business for the Web, June 2002. http://www.uddi.org/.
7. Access Grid. http://www-fp.mcs.anl.gov/fl/accessgrid/default.htm.
8. R. Butler, D. Engert, I. Foster, C. Kesselman, S. Tuecke, J. Volmer, and V. Welch. A National-Scale Authentication Infrastructure. *IEEE Computer*, 33(12):60–66, 2000.
9. I. Foster, C. Kesselman, and S. Tuecke. The Anatomy of the Grid: Enabling Scalable Virtual Organizations. *International Journal of Supercomputer Applications*, 15(3), 2001. http://www.globus.org/research/papers/anatomy.pdf.
10. Ian Foster, Carl Kesselman, Jeffrey Nick, and Steven Tuecke. The Physiology of the Grid: An Open Grid Services Architecture for Distributed Systems Integration. http://www.globus.org/research/papers/ogsa.pdf, February 2002.
11. M. Frenklach. *Combustion Chemistry*, chapter 7 Modeling, pages 423–453. Springer-Verlag, 1984.
12. GraphViz: A Graph Vizualization Package. AT&T Research, http://www.research.att.com/sw/tools/graphviz/.
13. Grappa, A Java Graph Package. AT&T Research, http://www.research.att.com/~john/Grappa/grappa.html.
14. International Symposium in High Performance and Distributed Computing. *High Performance and Grid Programming in Java and Python*, San Francisco, CA, 6 August 2001. http://www.cogkits.org.
15. E. J. Whitehead Jr. and M. Wiggins. WebDAV: IETF Standard for Collaborative Authoring on the Web. *IEEE Internet Computing*, 2(5):34, September-October 1998.
16. Sriram Krishnan, Patrick Wagstrom, and Gregor von Laszewski. GSFL: A Workflow Framework for Grid Services. In *Preprint ANL/MCS-P980-0802*, Argonne National Laboratory, 9700 S. Cass Avenue, Argonne, IL 60439, U.S.A., 2002.
17. Jr. M.W. Chase. NIST-JANAF Thermochemical Tables. Fourth Edition. *Journal of Physical and Chemical Reference*, (Monograph 9), 1998.

18. Carmen M. Pancerella, Larry Rahn, and Christine Yang. The Diesel Combustion Collaboratory: Combustion Researchers Collaborating over the Internet. In *Proceedings of SC99*, Portland, OR, November 13-19 1999. http://www.supercomp.org/sc99/.
19. B. Ruscic, M. Litorja, and R. L. Asher. Ionization Energy of Methylene Revisited: Improved Values for the Enthalpy of Formation of $CH2$ and the Bond Energy of $CH3$ via Simultaneous Solution of the Local Thermochemical Network. *J. Phys. Chem. A.*, 103:8625–8633, 1999.
20. B. Ruscic, J. V. Michael, P. C. Redfern, L. A. Curtiss, and K. Raghavachari. Simultaneous Adjustment of Experimentally Based Enthalpies of Formation of $CF3X$, $X = $ nil, H, Cl, Br, I, $CF3$, CN, and a Probe of G3 Theory. *J. Phys. Chem. A.*, 102:10889–10899, 1998.
21. SciDAC. http://www.scidac.org/.
22. Gregory P. Smith, David M. Golden, Michael Frenklach, Nigel W. Moriarty, Boris Eiteneer, Mikhail Goldenberg, C. Thomas Bowman, Ronald K. Hanson, Soonho Song, William, C. Gardiner, Jr., Vitali V. Lissianski, and Zhiwei Qin. Gri-Mech: Thermodynamic Data at 298 K, of the Standard Enthalpies of Formation for Radical Species. http://www.me.berkeley.edu/gri_mech/data/thermo_table.html.
23. Gregor von Laszewski and Ian Foster. Grid Infrastructure to Support Science Portals for Large Scale Instruments. In *Proceedings of the Workshop Distributed Computing on the Web (DCW)*, pages 1–16. University of Rostock, Germany, 21-23 June 1999. *(Invited Talk)*.
24. Gregor von Laszewski, Ian Foster, Jarek Gawor, and Peter Lane. A Java Commodity Grid Kit. *Concurrency and Computation: Practice and Experience*, 13(8-9):643–662, 2001.
25. Gregor von Laszewski, Ian Foster, Jarek Gawor, Peter Lane, Nell Rehn, and Mike Russell. Designing Grid-based Problem Solving Environments and Portals. In *34th Hawaiian International Conference on System Science*, Maui, Hawaii, 3-6 January 2001. http://www.mcs.anl.gov/~laszewsk/papers/cog-pse-final.pdf, http://computer.org/Proceedings/hicss/0981/volume%209/0981toc.htm.
26. Gregor von Laszewski, Jarek Gawor, Carlos J. Pe na, and Ian Foster. InfoGram: A Peer-to-Peer Information and Job Submission Service. In *Proceedings of the 11th Symposium on High Performance Distributed Computing*, Edinbrough, U.K., 24-26 July 2002.
27. Gregor von Laszewski, Gail Pieper, and Patrick Wagstrom. *Performance Evaluation and Characterization of Parallel and Distributed Computing Tools*, chapter Gestalt of the Grid. Wiley Book Series on Parallel and Distributed Computing. to be published 2002.
28. Gregor von Laszewski, Kazuyuki Shudo, and Yoichi Muraoka. Grid-based Asynchronous Migration of Execution Context in Java Virtual Machines. In Arndt Bode, Thomas Ludwig, Wolfgang Karl, and Roland Wismüller, editors, *Proceedings of EuroPar 2000*, volume 1900 of *Lecture Notes in Computer Science*, pages 22–34, Munich, Germany, 29 August - 1 September 2000. Springer. *(Invited Talk)*.
29. WebBook: A gateway to the data collections of the National Institute of Standards and Technology. NIST, http://webbook.nist.gov/.

GridLab: Enabling Applications on the Grid

Gabrielle Allen[1], Dave Angulo[2], Tom Goodale[1], Thilo Kielmann[3],
André Merzky[4] Jarek Nabrzysky[5], Juliusz Pukacki[5], Michael Russell[1],
Thomas Radke[1], Ed Seidel[1], John Shalf[6], and Ian Taylor[7]

[1] Albert Einstein Institute, Golm (AEI/MPG)
[2] Argonne National Lab (ANL)
[3] Vrije Universiteit, Amsterdam (VU)
[4] Zuse Institute, Berlin (ZIB)
[5] Poznań Supercomputing and Networking Center (PSNC)
[6] Lawrence Berkeley National Laboratory (LBNL)
[7] University of Wales, College of Cardiff (UWC)

www.GridLab.org

Abstract. Grid technology is widely emerging. Still, there is an eminent
shortage of real Grid users, due to the absence of two important catalysts:
First, a widely accepted vision on how applications can substantially
benefit from Grids, and second a toolkit of higher-level Grid services,
tailored to application needs. The GridLab project aims to provide fun-
damentally new capabilities for applications to exploit the power of Grid
computing, thus bridging the gap between application needs and existing Grid middleware. We present an overview of GridLab, a largescale,
EU-funded Grid project spanning over a dozen groups in Europe and the
US. We first outline our vision of Grid-empowered applications and then
discuss GridLab's general architecture.

1 Introduction

Computational Grids are becoming increasingly common, promising ultimately
to be ubiquitous and thereby change the way global resources are accessed and
used. However, presently there is a dearth of real Grid users, in part because
the whole concept is new, but also because there are few applications that can
exploit Grid resources. Although some application developers are interested in
writing Grid-enabled applications, there are few user-level tools, while tools for
application developers are nonexistent, and well-understood Grid usage scenarios
are unavailable.

It is therefore imperative to attract real users into the Grid community (for
example the Global Grid Forum (GGF)) and ultimately onto the Grid. The Applications Research Group (ARG) of the GGF (and formerly of the European
Grid Forum, EGrid) has been addressing questions about users requirements,
problems, and usage scenarios for several years now. In 2000, the group established a pan-European testbed [1], based on the Globus Toolkit, for prototyping
and experimenting with various application scenarios. These testbed experiences
gave inspiration for an application oriented project, called *GridLab*, funded by
the European Commission.

M. Parashar (Ed.): GRID 2002, LNCS 2536, pp. 39–45, 2002.

The primary aim of GridLab is to provide users and application developers with a simple and robust environment enabling them to produce applications that can exploit the full power and possibilities of the Grid. The GridLab project brings together computer scientists with computational scientists from various application areas to design and implement a *Grid Application Toolkit (GAT)*, together with a set of Grid services, in a production grid environment. The GAT will provide functionality through a carefully constructed set of generic high-level APIs, through which an application will be able to call the underlying grid services. The project will demonstrate the benefits of the GAT by developing and implementing real application scenarios, illustrating wild, exciting, new uses of the Grid. We will make extensive use of specific application frameworks, namely Cactus [2] and Triana [4], as powerful and broad reaching, real-world application examples for developing GridLab, but the GAT will be useful for applications and users of all types. Our aim is to make Grid computing accessible for the widest possible spectrum of applications and users. This paper first presents our vision of Grid-empowered application scenarios. Then we motivate and discuss the global architecture of the project.

2   A Vision of Grid-Empowered Application Scenarios

The advocates of Grid computing promise a world where large, shared, scientific research instruments, experimental data, numerical simulations, analysis tools, research and development, as well as people, are closely coordinated and integrated in "virtual organizations". This integration will be fostered through web-based portals, woven together into modular wide-area distributed applications. One hypothetical scenario in astrophysics, described in the following, illustrates such an integration. Although sounding futuristically, many individual components have already been prototyped, and through the GridLab project we are striving to make such a scenario a common-day occurrence.

Gravitational wave detectors will rely on results from large-scale simulations for understanding and interpreting the enormous amounts of experimental data they collect. The Grid infrastructure is used both to share expensive and centralized resources among many scientists, as well as to integrate experimental data sources with the simulation codes necessary to analyze them. For example, the GEO600 detector in Hanover detects an event characteristic of a black hole or neutron star collision, supernova explosion, or some other cosmic cataclysm. Astronomers around the world are alerted and stand by, ready to turn their telescopes to view the event before it fades, but the location of the event in the sky must first be found. This requires a time-critical data analysis with a number of templates created from full-scale simulations.

In a research institute in Berlin, an astrophysicist accesses the GEO600 portal and, using the performance tool, estimates the resources required for cross-correlating the raw data with the available templates. The brokering tool finds the fastest affordable machines around the world. Merely clicking to accept the portal's choice initiates a complex process by which executables and data files are automatically moved to these machines by the scheduling and data management tools. Then the analysis starts.

Twenty minutes later, on her way home, the astrophysicist's mobile phone receives an SMS message from the portal's notification unit, informing her that more templates are required and must be generated by a full-scale numerical simulation. She immediately contacts an international collaboration of colleagues who are experts in such simulations. Using a code composition tool in their simulation portal, her colleagues assemble a simulation code with appropriate physics modules suggested by the present analysis. The portal's performance prediction tool indicates that, due to memory constraints, the required simulation cannot be run on any single machine to which they have access. The brokering tool recommends that the simulation be run across two machines, one in the U.S. and the other in Germany, that are connected to form a large enough virtual supercomputer, to accomplish the job within the required time limit. The simulation begins, and after querying a Grid information server (GIS), the simulation decides by itself to spawn off a number of time-critical template generating routines, and to run asynchronously on various other machines around the world.

An hour later, the network between the two machines degrades and the simulation again queries the GIS, this time deciding to migrate to a new machine in Japan while still maintaining connections to the various template generators at other sites. All the while, the international team of collaborators monitor the simulation's progress from their workstations or wireless devices from an airport (where several team members happen to be), visualizing the physics results as they are computed. The template data are assembled and sent to the GEO600 experimenter in Germany for analysis, which finally yields the likely source location for the gravitational wave signal. This triggers an other Grid application which utilizes a different virtual organization and its infrastructure to direct the Hubble Space Telescope and various other available instruments at this source location. The entire process, which could not be performed on any single machine or at any supercomputing site available today, takes only a few hours.

3   Requirements for a Grid Software Environment

The main goal of GridLab is to provide a software environment for Grid-enabling scientific applications. In the advent of the Open Grid Service Architecture (OGSA) [3], GridLab's architecture will revolve around the notion of services.

It is our aim to provide an API through which applications access and use available resources. This API directly reflects application needs; among the intended functionality is the exploration of available resources (CPU, storage, visualization, etc.), remote data access, application migration, etc. The API will be concentrated in the *Grid Application Toolkit* (GAT). The functionality behind the API will be provided by interchangable service providers, being GridLab services as well as third-party services.

In this section, we will briefly define important types of services. We then summarize application requirements and constraints on a software architecture for a Grid Application Toolkit, and its service providers.

3.1   Service Categories

Service: "**A service is a network-enabled entity that provides a specific capability.** [...] A service is defined in terms of the protocol one uses to interact with it and the behavior expected in response to various protocol message exchanges (i.e., service = protocol + behavior)." [5]

Web Service: "The term **Web services describes an important emerging distributed computing paradigm** [with] **focus on simple, Internet-based standards** (e.g., eXtensible Markup Language: XML [...]) to address heterogeneous distributed computing. Web services define a technique for describing software components to be accessed, methods for accessing these components, and discovery methods that enable the identification of relevant service providers." [3]

Grid Service: "**A Web service that provides a set of well-defined interfaces and that follows specific conventions.** The interfaces address discovery, dynamic service creation, lifetime management, notification, and manageability; the conventions address naming and upgradeability." [3]

GridLab Service: A service provided by the GridLab project, normally a Grid Service.

Third-party Service: A service provided outside the scope of GridLab, either from underlying Grid middleware or from legacy software.

3.2   Application Requirements

The ultimate goal of the GridLab project is to provide application programmers and users with an environment which enables scenarios as the one from Section 2. From such scenarios, the main requirements to the GridLab architecture can be drawn.

One of the most important requirements of the GridLab user groups is that applications utilizing the GAT in order to become Grid applications are able to run in *all kinds* of real world environments, including *todays* Grid environments, disconnected environments (e.g. Laptops, developer machines), and firewalled resources.

Application execution inside a Grid installation or on isolated, disconnected resources should simply become two special cases of the same thing: an application running on whichever resources are available – without the need for both a "normal" and a "Grid-enabled" version of the application code. This requirement demands a single GAT API with which applications can be programmed. The actual service providers need to be instantiated at runtime.

Another user requirement is that of robustness, implying that "smart" adaptivity, complete control and fail safety are available on all levels.

3.3   Architecture Constraints

From the general design considerations for the GridLab project, the following constraints should apply to the GridLab architecture:

a) it must be cleanly layered,
b) it must incorporate security mechanisms on a global level,
c) all services should be dynamically swappable,
d) third-party services are to be easily incorporated.

3.4   Security Implications

It may not be obvious at first sight, but the above requirements and constraints partially contradict each other. In particular, the mandate to incorporate security mechanisms on a global level, for all components, is incompatible with respect to third-party services (one cannot mandate anything for those) and for disconnected environments. For third-party services, this could be solved by requiring access to any third-party service to be performed via a (secured) GridLab service. But that again is not possible if our application is running in a minimalistic environment, or just *deliberately chooses* to contact the suspicious (e.g., legacy) component on its own behalf – as applications need full control on all levels.

We assume that contradictions of this type are very natural in Grid environments: the middleware developer wants to have control over all aspects of the environment, in particular over security, but also over scheduling, network interfaces and so on. The end user in turn wants to be able to run an application in *any* environment – benefiting from a Grid infrastructure if available.

In our GridLab project, we learned to distinguish between these two cases. Our *"General Architecture"* reflects both variants: on the one hand it will allow the GAT and hence the applications to utilize whichever service provider they need, be it secure or not, be it in a Grid or not; on the other hand it strongly recommends a cleanly layered architecture for the actual scope of the project, which is to provide application-oriented services as an abstraction of Grid environments, including, e.g., global security.

4   The GridLab Architecture

As discussed above, the GridLab project distinguishes between GridLab services and third-party services (e.g. low-level Grid services like GIS or GRAM, system services, libraries). This section will describe the implications of this distinction for the actual architecture.

Figure 1 is divided into a user space and a service space, reflecting the possible boundary between the application programs and the network-enabled (thus possibly remote) services. Applications should be programmed using the GAT API, and the GAT itself uses *adapters* for all kinds of services it can make available through the GAT API.

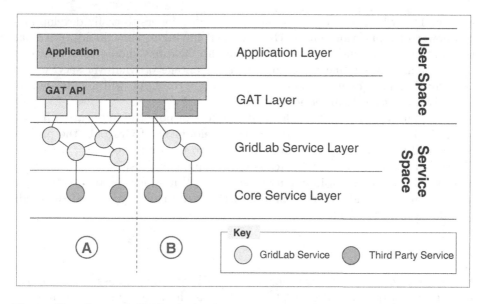

Fig. 1. The General GridLab Architecture: The GAT will be designed to interact with both types of service providers (cases A and B).

In addition to the GAT itself, GridLab will provide a large set of GridLab services, tailored to the needs of the GAT API. GridLab services will integrate lower-level services to build more powerful functionality (like smart adaptivity, control, and fail safety). In the recommended (Grid-enabled) case A in the figure, the GAT only uses adapters to GridLab services which in turn draw their functionality from lower-level, system services. In case B (for disconnected use or for legacy services), the GAT will also directly interface to third-party services, at the price of possibly sacrificing security concerns on the application's behalf.

5 Conclusions

In this paper we have briefly described the overall architecture of the GridLab project, which aims to provide application oriented Grid services for users and developers alike, covering the whole range of Grid capabilities as required by applications, such as resource brokering, monitoring, data management etc. These services will abstract lower level Grid functionality and will hence ease the development and deployment of Grid aware applications. This consistent service infrastructure will be the first major deliverable of the GridLab project.

These services will be made accessible to any applications running on the Grid through a Grid Application Toolkit (GAT), the second main project deliverable. The GAT will abstract those services needed by the Grid applications. In this way, applications can utilize service discovery at runtime, making use of whatever services are available, including different implementations of the same service. This will enable users and application developers to easily develop and run powerful applications on the Grid, without having to know in advance what the runtime environment will provide. Such applications should then run on a laptop or an intercontinental Grid, taking advantage of whatever services are actually available (or unavailable). In particular, the GAT will not depend on the existence of GridLab services.

Although we collaborate with the developers of powerful application frameworks such as Cactus and Triana for the development of GridLab, the project is designed to enable *any* application not only to run on the Grid (or without a Grid), but to endow it with new capabilities uniquely possible on a Grid, such as those described above in our usage scenario. With such an architecture, we expect many new and powerful applications to be developed to exploit the Grids of today and tomorrow alike.

Acknowledgments

We are pleased to acknowledge support of the European Commission 5th Framework program (grant IST-2001-32133), which is the primary source of funding for the GridLab project, but also the German DFN-Verein, Microsoft, the NSF ASC project (NSF-PHY9979985), and our local institutes for generous support for this work. We also thank Ewa Deelman, Thomas Dramlitsch, Ian Foster, Carl Kesselman, Jason Novotny, Gerd Lanfermann and various members of the Globus team for many discussions and support that have led to the current project.

References

1. G. Allen, T. Dramlitsch, T. Goodale, G. Lanfermann, T. Radke, E. Seidel, T. Kielmann, K. Verstoep, Z. Balaton, P. Kacsuk, F. Szalai, J. Gehring, A. Keller, A. Streit, L. Matyska, M. Ruda, A. Krenek, H. Frese, H. Knipp, A. Merzky, A. Reinefeld, F. Schintke, B. Ludwiczak, J. Nabrzyski, J. Pukacki, H.-P. Kersken, and M. Russell. Early experiences with the EGrid testbed. In *First IEEE/ACM International Symposium on Cluster Computing and the Grid*, pages 130–137, Brisbane, Australia, May 2001.
2. Cactus Computational Toolkit home page: http://www.cactuscode.org.
3. I. Foster, C. Kesselman, J. M. Nick, and S. Tuecke. The Physiology of the Grid: An Open Grid Services Architecture for Distributed Systems Integration. Draft Document, http://www.globus.org/research/papers/ogsa.pdf, June 2002.
4. Triana home page: http://www.triana.co.uk.
5. S. Tuecke, I. Foster, and C. Kesselman. The Anatomy of the Grid: Enabling Scalable Virtual Organizations. *International Journal of Supercomputer Applications*, 15(3), 2001.

Simulation of Dynamic Grid Replication Strategies in OptorSim

William H. Bell[1], David G. Cameron[1], Luigi Capozza[2], A. Paul Millar[1], Kurt Stockinger[3], and Floriano Zini[2]

[1] University of Glasgow, Glasgow, G12 8QQ, Scotland
[2] ITC-irst, Via Sommarive 18, 38050 Povo (Trento), Italy
[3] CERN, European Organization for Nuclear Research, 1211 Geneva, Switzerland

Abstract. Computational Grids normally deal with large computationally intensive problems on small data sets. In contrast, Data Grids mostly deal with large computational problems that in turn require evaluating and mining large amounts of data. Replication is regarded as one of the major optimisation techniques for providing fast data access.

Within this paper, several replication algorithms are studied. This is achieved using the Grid simulator: OptorSim. OptorSim provides a modular framework within which optimisation strategies can be studied under different Grid configurations. The goal is to explore the stability and transient behaviour of selected optimisation techniques.

1 Introduction

Within the Grid community much work has been done on providing the basic infrastructure for a typical Grid environment. Globus [4], Condor [1] and recently the EU DataGrid [3] have contributed substantially to core Grid middleware services software that are available as the basis for further application development. However, little effort has been made so far to optimise the use of Grid resources.

To use a Data Grid, users typically submit *job*s. In order for a job to be executed, three types of resources are required: computing facilities, data access and storage, and network connectivity. The Grid must make scheduling decisions for each job based on the current state of these resources (workload and features of Computing Elements, location of data, network load). Complete optimisation is achieved when the combined resource impact of all jobs is minimised, allowing jobs to run as fast as possible.

File replication (i.e. spread of multiple copies of files across the Grid) is an effective technique for reducing data access overhead. Maintaining an optimal distribution of replicas implies that the Grid optimisation service [7] must be able to modify the geographic location of data files. This is achieved by triggering both replication and deletion of data files. By reflecting the dynamic load on the Grid, such replica management will affect the migration of particular files toward sites that show increased frequency of file-access requests.

M. Parashar (Ed.): GRID 2002, LNCS 2536, pp. 46–57, 2002.

In order to study the complex nature of a typical Grid environment and evaluate various replica optimisation algorithms, a Grid simulator (called OptorSim) was developed. In this paper the design concepts of OptorSim are discussed and preliminary results based on selected replication algorithms are reported.

The paper is structured as follows. Section 2 describes the design of the simulator OptorSim. Various replication algorithms are discussed in Section 3. After setting the simulation configuration in Section 4, Section 5 is dedicated to a description of simulation results. Section 6 highlights related work. Finally, Section 7 concludes the paper and reports on future work.

2   Simulation Design

OptorSim [2] is a simulation package written in Java™. It was developed to study the effectiveness of replica optimisation algorithms within a Data Grid environment.

2.1   Architecture

One of the main design considerations for OptorSim is to model the interactions of the individual Grid components of a running Data Grid as realistically as possible. Therefore, the simulation is based on the architecture of the EU DataGrid project [14] as illustrated in Figure 1.

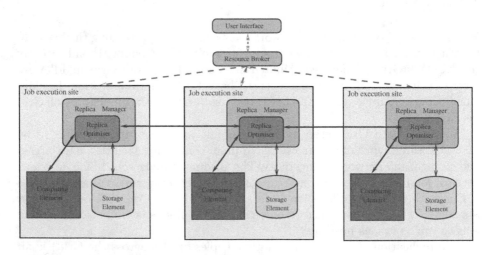

Fig. 1. Simulated DataGrid Architecture.

The simulation was constructed assuming that the Grid consists of several sites, each of which may provide computational and data-storage resources for submitted jobs. Each *site* consists of zero or more *Computing Elements* and zero or more *Storage Elements*. Computing Elements run jobs, which use the data in files stored on Storage Elements and a *Resource Broker* controls the scheduling of jobs to Computing Elements. Sites without Storage or Computing Elements act as network nodes or routers.

The decision about data movement associated with jobs between sites is performed by a component called the *Replica Manager*. Within the Replica Manager the decision to create or delete replicas is controlled by a *Replica Optimiser* called Optor. At the heart of Optor is a replica optimisation algorithm, the properties of which are discussed in Section 3.

2.2   Internals

In the simulation each Computing Element is represented by a thread. Job submission to the Computing Elements is managed by another thread: the Resource Broker. The Resource Broker ensures every Computing Element continuously runs jobs by frequently attempting to distribute jobs to all the Computing Elements. When the Resource Broker finds an idle Computing Element, it selects a job to run on it according to the policy of the Computing Element, i.e. which type of jobs it will run and how often it will run each job.

At any time, a Computing Element will be running at most one job. As soon as the job finishes, another is assigned by the Resource Broker. So, although there is no explicit job scheduling algorithm, all Computing Elements process jobs for the duration of the simulation but are never overloaded. Currently, optimisation only occurs after a job has been scheduled to a Computing Element. The more complex scenario of optimising both job scheduling and data access will be part of future work.

Each job has a set of files it may request. Two types of reference may be used for a file: a logical file name (LFN) and a physical file name (PFN). An LFN is an abstract reference to a file that is independent of both where the file is stored and how many replicas exist. A PFN refers to a specific replica of some LFN, located at a definite site. Each LFN will have one PFN for each replica in the Grid.

A job will typically request a set of LFNs for data access. The order in which those files are requested is determined by the access pattern. The following access patterns were considered: *sequential* (the set of LFNs is ordered, forming a list of successive requests), *random* (files are selected randomly from set with a flat probability distribution), *unitary random walk* (set is ordered and successive file requests are exactly one element away from previous file request, direction is random) and *Gaussian random walk* (as with unitary random walk, but files are selected from a Gaussian distribution centred on the previous file request).

When a file is required by a job, the file's LFN is used to locate the best replica via the Replica Optimiser function getBestFile(LFN, destinationStorage-Element), where destinationStorageElement is the Storage Element to which the replica may be copied. It is assumed the Computing Element on which the job is running and requested Storage Element are located at the same site.

getBestFile() checks the *Replica Catalogue* for copies of the file. The Replica Catalogue is a Grid middleware service currently implemented within the simulation as a table of LFNs and all corresponding PFNs. By examining the available bandwidth between `destinationStorageElement` and all sites on which a replica of the file is stored, `getBestFile()` can choose the PFN that will be accessed fastest and hence decrease the job running time.

The simulated version of `getBestFile()` partially fulfils the functionality as described in [7]. It is a blocking call that may cause replication to a Storage Element located in the site where the job is running. After any replication has completed, the PFN of the best available replica is returned to the job. If replication has not occurred, the best replica is located on a remote site and is accessed by the job using remote I/O.

Both the replication time (if replication occurs) and the file access time (if from a remote site) are dependent on the network characteristics over the duration of the connection. At any time, the bandwidth available to a transfer is limited by the lowest bandwidth along the transfer path. For transfers utilising a common network element, the bandwidth of that element is shared so each transfer receives an equal share.

3   Optimisation Algorithms

Replica optimisation algorithms are the core of the Replica Optimiser. Over the duration of a submitted job, PFNs for each LFN are requested by calling `getBestFile()`. Optimisation algorithms implement `getBestFile()` so that it may copy the requested file from the remote site to a Storage Element on the same site as the requesting Computing Element. If all Storage Elements on this site are full then a file must be deleted for the replication to succeed.

The strategy used to decide which file should be deleted differentiates optimisation algorithms. In the following, we briefly present three simple algorithms and a more sophisticated one in greater detail. These algorithms have been implemented into OptorSim.

3.1   Simple Algorithms

No replication. This algorithm never replicates a file. The distribution of initial file replicas is decided at the beginning of the simulation and does not change during its execution. This algorithm returns a PFN with the largest expected bandwidth. Since the network load varies during the simulation, the optimal PFN may change.

Unconditional replication, oldest file deleted. This algorithm always replicates a file to the site where the job is executing. If there is no space to accommodate the replication, the oldest file in the Storage Element is deleted.

Unconditional replication, least accessed file deleted. This algorithms behaves as the previous method, except the least accessed file in the past time interval δt is deleted.

3.2   An Economic Approach

This section presents a replication strategy based on an economic model for Grid resource optimisation. A general description of this economic approach can be found in [9].

The economic model we propose includes actors (autonomous goal-seeking entities) and the resources in the Grid. Optimisation is achieved via interaction of the actors in the model, whose goals are maximising the profits and minimising the costs of data resource management. Data files represent the goods in the market. They are purchased by Computing Elements for jobs and by Storage Elements in order to make an investment that will improve their revenues in the future. They are sold by Storage Elements to Computing Elements and to other Storage Elements. Computing Elements try to minimise the file purchase cost, while Storage Elements have the goal of maximising profits.

This economic model is utilised to solve two distinct problems: in deciding if replication should occur and in the selection of the expendable file(s) when creating space for a new replica.

When a job running on a Computing Element requests a file, the optimisation tries to locate the cheapest copy of it in the Grid by starting an auction. Storage Elements that have the file locally may reply, bidding a price that indicates the file transfer cost. A site that does not have a file locally may initiate its own auction to establish if, by replication, it can satisfy the file request. This mechanisms realises the global optimisation mentioned above. Currently, the auction protocol has still to be integrated into OptorSim. In the following discussion, we used the simpler protocol described in Section 2.2.

The mechanism for deciding if replication should occur is implemented in OptorSim. It is described the following section.

Replication Decision. Within our economic model the Replica Optimiser needs to make an informed decision about whether it should replicate a file to a local Storage Element. This decision is based on whether the replication (with associated file transfer and file deletion) will result in reduced expected future file access cost for the local Computing Element.

In order to make this decision, the Replica Optimiser keeps track of the file requests it receives and uses this history as input to an evaluation function $E(f, r, n)$. This function, defined in [9], returns the predicted number of times a file f will be requested in the next n requests based on the past r requests in the history.

After any new file request is received by the Replica Optimiser (say, for file f), the prediction function E is calculated for f and every file in the storage. If there is no file in the Storage Element that has a value less than the value of f then no replication occurs. Otherwise, the least valuable file is selected for deletion and a new replica of f is created on the Storage Element. If multiple files on the Storage Element share the minimum value, the file having the earliest last access time is deleted.

The evaluation function $E(f, r, n)$ is defined by the equation

$$E(f, r, n) = \sum_{i=1}^{n} p_i(f), \qquad (1)$$

with the following argument.

Assuming that requests for files containing similar data are clustered in spatial and time locality, the request history can be described as a random walk in the space of integer file identifiers[1]. In the random walk, the identifier of the next requested file is obtained from the current identifier by the addition of a step, the value of which is given by some probability distribution. Assuming a binomial distribution of the steps, the probability of receiving a request for file f at step i of the random walk is given by the equation

$$p_i(f) = \frac{1}{2^{2iS}} \binom{2iS}{id(f) - \bar{s} + iS}, \qquad |id(f) - \bar{s}| \leq iS \qquad (2)$$

where $\bar{s}$ is the mean value of the binomial distribution , S is the maximum value for the step, and $id(f)$ is a unique file identifier (for instance, the LFN). Then, the *most probable number of times file f will be requested during the next n requests* is given by (1).

A time interval δt describes how far back the history goes and thus determines the number r of previous requests which are considered in the prediction function. We assume that the mean arrival rate of requests is constant. Once δt has been decided, n is obtained by

$$n = r \frac{\delta t'}{\delta t} \qquad (3)$$

where $\delta t'$ is the future interval for which we intend to do the prediction.

The value for S in (2) depends on the value of r. The mean value $\bar{s}$ is obtained from the recent values of the step in the random walk. In particular, $\bar{s}$ is calculated as the weighted average of the last r steps, where weights decrease over past time.

4   Simulation Configuration

4.1   Grid Configuration

The study of optimisation algorithms was carried out using a model of EU DataGrid TestBed 1 sites and their associated network geometry as illustrated in Figure 2. Within this model, each site was allocated storage resources proportional to their actual hardware allocations. Each TestBed site, excluding CERN, was assigned a Computing and Storage Element. CERN was allocated a Storage Element to hold all of the master files but was not assigned a Computing

---

[1] We assume a mapping between file names and identifiers that preserve file content similarity.

Element. Routers, as previously stated, were described by creating a site without Computing or Storage Elements. The size of the Storage Elements for each TestBed site are given in Table 1.

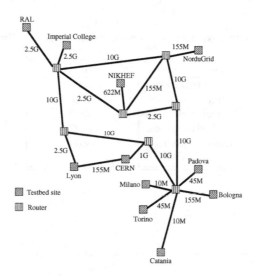

Fig. 2. The EU DataGrid TestBed 1 sites and the approximate network geometry. The numbers indicate the bandwidth between two sites.

Table 1. A list of resources allocated to the TestBed 1 sites, from which the results in this paper were generated.

Site Name	Bologna	Catania	CERN	Imperial College	Lyon
Storage Element (GBytes)	30	30	10000	80	50

Site Name	Milano	NIKHEF	NorduGrid	Padova	RAL	Torino
Storage Element (GBytes)	50	70	63	50	50	50

4.2   Job Configuration

Initially, all files were placed on the CERN Storage Element. Jobs were based on the CDF use-case as described in [12]. There were six job types, with no overlap between the set of files each job accessed. The total size of the file accessed by any job type were estimated in [12] and are summarised in Table 2. Each set of files was assumed to be composed of 10GByte files.

There will be some distribution of jobs each site performs. In the simulation, we modelled this distribution such that each site ran an equal number of jobs of each type except for a preferred job type, which ran twice as often. This job type was chosen for each site based on storage considerations; for the replication algorithms to be effective, the local storage on each site had to be able to hold all the files for the preferred job type.

Table 2. Estimated sizes of CDF secondary data sets (from [12])

Data Sample	Total Size (GBytes)
Central J/ψ	1200
High p_t leptons	200
Inclusive electrons	5000
Inclusive muons	1400
High E_t photons	5800
$Z^0 \to b\bar{b}$	600

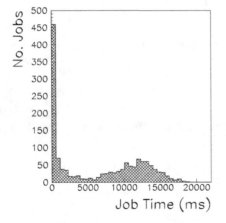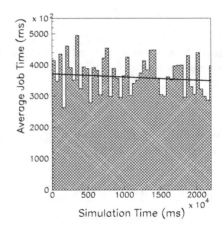

Fig. 3. A histogram of job duration (left) and the progression of job duration over course of the simulation (right).

5   Results

The left histogram in Figure 3 shows a typical spread of job duration for a single job type at a selected Computing Element over the course of a simulation run. The large spike near zero is due to the job requesting files that are available on the local site, hence no time-consuming file transfers need to take place. The longer durations are due to the job requesting some files not present at the local site. The spread is due to the network load, which can vary over time, affecting the file transfer times.

The variation of job duration over the simulation is shown in the right histogram in Figure 3 for the same job type and Computing Element as above. There is clearly a large variation in the job duration due to the factors already mentioned, but the general trend is for jobs to be executed more quickly over time, indicating the movement toward a more optimal replica configuration.

Further tests were conducted simulating 10000 jobs using each of the four algorithms:

1. *No replication*
2. *Unconditional replication, oldest file deleted*
3. *Unconditional replication, least accessed file deleted*
4. *Economic Model*

For each replication algorithm, each of the following four file access patterns (as defined in Section 2.2) was tested.

1. *Sequential*
2. *Random*
3. *Unitary random walk*
4. *Gaussian random walk*

Figure 4 shows the total time to complete 10000 jobs for each of the four access patterns using the four optimisation algorithms.

With no optimisation, the jobs take much longer than even the simplest optimisation algorithm as all the files for every job have to be transferred from CERN every time a job is run.

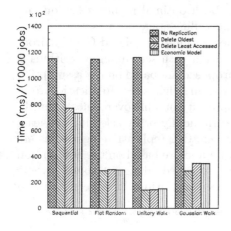 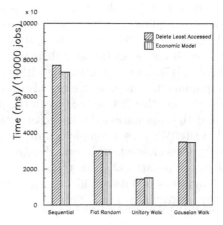

Fig. 4. Integrated running times for 10000 jobs using each access pattern and replica optimisation algorithm.

The three algorithms where replication is conducted all show a marked reduction in the time to execute 10000 jobs. This is not surprising as with no replication, all file requests from all jobs must come from CERN.

The three optimisation algorithms that implement replication show similar performance for Random, Unitary random walk and Gaussian random walk.

For sequential access patterns, the running time is at least 10% faster using the Economic Model optimiser than the other optimisers. These results were expected as the Economic Model assumes a sequential access pattern. However, this can be adjusted to match the observed distribution, if needed.

6   Related Work

Recently there has been great interest in modelling Data Grid environments. A simulator for modelling complex data access patterns of concurrent users in a distributed system is found in [13]. These studies were mainly conducted within the setting of scientific experiments such as the LHC, which finally resulted in the creation of the EU DataGrid project [3].

MicroGrid [18] is a simulation tool for designing and evaluating Grid middleware, applications and network services for the computational Grid. Currently, this simulator does not take data management issues into consideration. Further Grid simulators are presented in [11,6]

In [15] an approach is proposed for automatically creating replicas in a typical decentralised Peer-to-Peer network. The goal is to create a certain number of replicas on a given site in order to guarantee some minimal availability requirements.

In Nimrod-G [8,5] an economic model for job scheduling is introduced in where "Grid credits" are assigned to users that are proportional to their level of priority. In this model, optimisation is achieved at the scheduling stage of a job. However, our approach differs by including both optimal replica selection and automated replica creation in addition to scheduling-stage optimisation.

Various replication and caching strategies within a simulated Grid environment are discussed in [16] and their combination with scheduling algorithms is studied in [17]. The replication algorithms proposed are based on the assumption that popular files in one site are also popular in other sites. Replication from one site to another is triggered when the popularity of a file overcomes a threshold and the destination site is chosen either randomly or by selecting the least loaded site. We take a complementary approach. Our replication algorithms are used by Grid sites when they need data locally and are based on the assumption that in computational Grids there are areas (so called "data hot-spots") where particular sets of data are highly requested. Our algorithms have been designed to move data files toward "data hot-spots".

7   Conclusions and Future Work

In this paper we described the design of the Grid simulator OptorSim. In particular, OptorSim allows the analysis of various replication algorithms. The goal is to evaluate the impact of the choice of an algorithm on the throughput of typical Grid jobs. We have chosen two traditional cache management algorithms (oldest file deletion and least accessed file deletion) and compared them to a novel algorithm based on an economic model.

We based our analysis on several Grid scenarios with various work loads. Results obtained from OptorSim suggest that the economic model performs at least as well as traditional methods. In addition, there are specific realistic cases where the economic model shows marked performance improvements.

Our future work will extending the simulator by including the auction protocol proposed in [10]. This is motivated by the additional functionality of automatic replication to third party sites, allowing file migration to accurately match demand.

Acknowledgements

The authors thank Erwin Laure, Heinz Stockinger and Ekow Otoo for valuable discussions during the preparation of this paper.

William Bell and David Cameron thank PPARC for funding as part of the GridPP(EDG) project and as an e-Science student respectively; Paul Millar thanks SHEFC for funding under the ScotGRID project.

References

1. The condor project. http://www.cs.wisc.edu/condor/.
2. OptorSim - A Replica Optimiser Simulation. http://grid-data-management.web.cern.ch/grid-data-management/optimisati%on/optor/.
3. The DataGrid Project. http://www.eu-datagrid.org.
4. The Globus Project. http://www.globus.org.
5. D. Abramson, R. Buuya, and J. Giddy. A Computational Economy for Grid Computing and its Implementation in the Nimrod-G Resource Broker. In *Future Generation Computer Systems*, to appear.
6. K. Aida, A. Takefusa, H. Nakaka, S. Matsuoka, S. Sekiguchi, and U. Nagashima. Performance Evaluation Model for Scheduling in a Global Computing System. *International Journal of High Performance Applications*, 14(3), 2000.
7. W. H. Bell, D. G. Cameron, L. Capozza, P. Millar, K. Stockinger, and F. Zini. Design of a Query Optimisation Service. Technical report, CERN, 2002. WP2 - Data Management, EU DataGrid Project. http://edms.cern.ch/document/337977.
8. R. Buyya, H. Stockinger, J. Giddy, and D. Abramson. Economic Models for Management of Resources in Peer-to-Peer and Grid Computing. In *Commercial Applications for High-Performance Computing, SPIE's International Symposium on the Convergence of Information Technologies and Communications (ITCom 2001)*, Denver, Colorado, USA, August 2001.

9. L. Capozza, K. Stockinger, and F. Zini. Preliminary Evaluation of Revenue Prediction Functions for Economically-Effective File Replication, June 2002.
10. M. Carman, F. Zini, L. Serafini, and K. Stockinger. Towards an Economy-Based Optimisation of File Access and Replication on a Data Grid. In *International Workshop on Agent based Cluster and Grid Computing at International Symposium on Cluster Computing and the Grid (CCGrid 2002)*, Berlin, Germany, May 2002. IEEE Computer Society Press. Also appears as IRST Technical Report 0112-04, Istituto Trentino di Cultura, December 2001.
11. H. Casanova, G. Obertelli an F. Berman, and R. Wolski. The AppLeS Parameter Sweep Template: User-Level Middleware for the Grid. In *Proc. of Super Computing 2002*, Dallas, Texas, USA, November 2002.
12. B. T. Huffman et al. The CDF/D0 UK GridPP Project. CDF Internal Note. 5858.
13. I. C. Legrand. Multi-Threaded, Discrete Event Simulation of Distributed Computing Systems. In *Proc. of Computing in High Energy Physics (CHEP 2000)*, Padova, Italy, February 2000.
14. EU DataGrid Project. The DataGrid Architecture, 2001.
15. K. Ranganathan, A. Iamnitchi, and I. Foster. Improving Data Availability through Dynamic Model-Driven Replication in Large Peer-to-Peer Communities. In *Global and Peer-to-Peer Computing on Large Scale Distributed Systems Workshop*, Berlin, Germany, May 2002.
16. K. Ranganathana and I. Foster. Identifying Dynamic Replication Strategies for a High Performance Data Grid. In *Proc. of the International Grid Computing Workshop*, Denver, Colorado, USA, November 2001.
17. K. Ranganathana and I. Foster. Decoupling Computation and Data Scheduling in Distributed Data-Intensive Applications. In *International Symposium of High Performance Distributed Computing*, Edinburgh, Scotland, July 2002. To appear.
18. H. J. Song, X. Liu, D. Jakobsen, R. Bhagwan, X. Zhang, K. Taura, and A. Chien. The MicroGrid: a Scientific Tool for Modeling Computational Grids. *Scientific Programming*, 8(3):127–141, 2000.

Scheduling Independent Tasks with QoS Requirements in Grid Computing with Time-Varying Resource Prices*

Atakan Doğan and Füsun Özgüner

Department of Electrical Engineering, The Ohio State University,
2015 Neil Avenue, Columbus, OH 43210-1272
{dogana, ozguner}@ee.eng.ohio-state.edu

Abstract. This paper considers the problem of scheduling a set of independent tasks with multiple QoS requirements, which may include timeliness, reliability, security, version, and priority, in a Grid computing system in which resource prices can vary with time during scheduling time intervals. This problem is referred to as the *QoS-based scheduling problem with time-varying resource prices*. In order to solve this problem, a static scheduling algorithm (QSMTS_VP) is developed. The simulation studies carried out show that QSMTS_VP is capable of meeting diverse QoS requirements of many users simultaneously and that QSMTS_VP can react to the dynamics of the market. Thus, QSMTS_VP is a promising heuristic that can be deployed in a computational market.

1 Introduction

Computational Grids are emerging as a new computing platform for executing large-scale resource intensive applications. A challenging problem that needs to be solved so as to harness the computing power of the Grid is the *resource management and scheduling* (RMS) problem. Fortunately, there are already Grid toolkits, such as Globus [1] and Legion [2], developed to address this problem.

As noted in [3], Globus [1], Legion [4], and few other RMS systems developed adopt the *conventional style* of RMS where a scheduling component allocates computing resources to tasks with the goal of optimizing a certain objective function, e.g., minimizing the makespan of tasks. Such an objective function is typically defined in a way that optimizing the function results in better system throughput and utilization. In contrast to the conventional style is the *computational economy style* of RMS where users adopt the strategy of executing their tasks at low cost and resource providers pursue the strategy of maximizing their profits and resource utilization. In a Grid environment, a computational economy style of RMS has several advantages over a conventional one [3]. For example, in computational economy, users may be allowed to specify their resource requirements and preference parameters by a *utility model*. As a result,

---

* This material is based upon work supported by the National Science Foundation Award No. CCR-0100633.

M. Parashar (Ed.): GRID 2002, LNCS 2536, pp. 58–69, 2002.

a computational economy based Grid inherently supports users with diverse requirements for the execution of their tasks. In this paper, we model each of these diverse requirements as a quality of service (QoS) dimension of a task and design a QoS-based RMS system in which users are charged according to the quality of service provided to them by the Grid. For a more detailed discussion on the merits/demerits of these two RMS systems, we refer the reader to [3].

QoS-based resource management and scheduling has been the subject of many research studies. In [5], a taxonomy of QoS parameters composed of two groups, namely QoS metrics and QoS policies, is presented. *QoS metrics* are used to specify performance parameters, including timeliness, precision, and accuracy, security requirements, and the relative importance of applications. *QoS policies*, on the other hand, capture application specific policies that govern how an application will be treated by a RMS system. This taxonomy is followed in Section 3 for modeling the QoS requirements of independent tasks. QoS metrics of [5] are also recognized in [6] where an expression based on these metrics is developed to quantify the success of a resource management system.

Most of the QoS driven scheduling algorithms presented in the literature assume multimedia applications [7], [8], [9]. A QoS driven scheduling algorithm for independent tasks with QoS demands is proposed in [10] where each task is associated with a benefit function which depends on only the finish time of the task and a priority. The proposed algorithm in [10] is limited in that it accounts for only two QoS requirements for every task. A recent study [11] considers multiple QoS dimensions and proposes the GENITOR technique to produce high-quality QoS driven task allocations.

In [12], a QoS-based scheduling problem is formulated in the computational economy framework and an efficient heuristic is developed to solve this problem. However, the proposed heuristic assumes that the price of a resource does not change during a *scheduling time interval*, which is the interval from the start of a scheduling event to the completion of the last task scheduled in that event. However, it is possible that scheduling time intervals can be very large and that time-invariant pricing during large scheduling time intervals can put a crucial constraint on the pricing strategies that can be followed by resource owners. Motivated by this fact, in this paper, we relax this assumption and allow time-varying resource prices during scheduling time intervals. In order to solve the QoS-based scheduling problem with time-varying resource prices, we develop the QSMTS_VP (QoS-based meta-task scheduling for time-varying resource prices) algorithm, which can be deployed in an economy driven Grid resource management system.

2   Grid and Workload Models

A Grid computing environment is assumed to be composed of a set of computing sites where a *computing site* could be a single PC, a cluster of workstations, or a supercomputer; let $S = \{S_1, S_2, \cdots, S_h\}$ denote the set of these computing sites. This adopted model of the Grid is due to the Globus resource management architecture [1] where a GRAM (Globus Resource Allocation Manager) corresponds to a site that could comprise one or more computing resources; let $S_k = \{M_1^k, M_2^k, \cdots, M_{m_k}^k\}$ be a set of computing resources provided by site S_k for the Grid ($m_k = |S_k|$). Throughout the paper, it is assumed that the computing resources in site $S_k \in S$ can be *reserved* and *allocated* by a local resource manager on behalf of a centralized Grid scheduler so as to provide minimum performance guarantees for tasks with QoS requirements. Note that this assumption ensures that a resource can provide the requested QoS when required.

Suppose that there are n independent users and user i is associated with task T_i. Let $T = \{T_1, T_2, \cdots, T_n\}$ denote a set of independent tasks (a meta-task) and $t_{i,j,k}^E$ be the expected execution time of task T_i on computing resource (node) M_j^k in site S_k. It is assumed that the expected execution time $t_{i,j,k}^E$, $1 \leq i \leq n$, $1 \leq j \leq m_k$, and $1 \leq k \leq h$, is known. Fortunately, there are techniques available to estimate $t_{i,j,k}^E$ [13].

We split the time domain of node M_j^k into time-slots with equal size. Let $\mathcal{T}_j^k = \{\tau_j^k[1], \tau_j^k[2], \cdots, \tau_j^k[\kappa_j^k]\}$ denote the set of time-slots and κ_j^k denote the number of available time-slots of node M_j^k. Based on this splitting, the execution time of task T_i on a node is defined by two time-slots; the time-slot in which task T_i starts running, which is denoted by s_i, and the time-slot in which the execution of task T_i is completed, which is denoted by f_i. The time-slots between slots s_i and f_i, if any, will be occupied by task T_i. In addition, it is possible that the execution time of a task spans only one time-slot, in which case $s_i = f_i$.

3 Modeling QoS Requirements

In modeling the QoS requirements of tasks, each user is assumed to associate a distinct numbers of QoS requirements with its task. Thus, let d_i denote the number of QoS requirements of task T_i. In addition, let Q_i^j be a *finite* set of QoS choices for the jth QoS dimension of task T_i, $1 \leq j \leq d_i$, and $q_i^j \in Q_i^j$ denote a QoS choice available in the jth QoS dimension of task T_i. Thus, $Q_i = \{Q_i^1, Q_i^2, \cdots, Q_i^{d_i}\}$ defines a d_i dimensional space of the QoS choices of task T_i and a point in this space $q_i \in Q_i$ is given by $q_i = \{q_i^1, q_i^2, \cdots, q_i^{d_i}\}$. In the framework of this study, *timeliness* (**T**), *reliability* (**R**), *security* (**S**), or *version* (**V**) could be one of the QoS dimensions of a task. Priority, on the other hand, is exclusively treated in the computational economy framework as discussed in Section 4. As a result, it is possible for task T_i to have $Q_i = \{\mathbf{T}, \mathbf{R}, \mathbf{S}, \mathbf{V}\}$ where

$$\mathbf{T} = Q_i^1 = \{f_i|\ f_i = s_i + \lceil \frac{t_{i,j,k}^E}{|\tau_j^k|} \rceil - 1 \text{ and } s_i \text{ and } f_i \in \mathcal{T}_j^k\},$$

$$\mathbf{R} = Q_i^2 = \{e^{-\lambda_j^k f_i}|\ f_i = s_i + \lceil \frac{t_{i,j,k}^E}{|\tau_j^k|} \rceil - 1 \text{ and } s_i \text{ and } f_i \in \mathcal{T}_j^k\},$$

$$\mathbf{S} = Q_i^3 = \{\text{poor}, \text{low}, \text{medium}, \text{high}\}, \qquad \mathbf{V} = Q_i^4 = \{1, 2, 3, 4\}.$$

Note that the reliability of task T_i (**R** QoS dimension) is computed for each possible finish time f_i under the following assumptions; (1) failure of nodes are statistically independent, and (2) failure of each node follows a Poisson process and the failure rate of node M_j^k is denoted by λ_j^k.

Associated with each QoS dimension is a *utility function* which defines the benefit that will be perceived by a user with respect to QoS choices in that dimension. Formally, the utility function associated with the jth QoS dimension of task T_i is defined to be $U_i^j : Q_i^j \to R^+$, $1 \leq i \leq n$ and $1 \leq j \leq d_i$, where R^+ is the set of positive real numbers. Note that the domain of a utility function (Q_i^j) is discrete for each of the four QoS dimensions possible and utility functions are assumed to be *injective*. Such utility functions are known as *dimension-wise utility functions* [9]. For example, Fig. 1 shows dimension-wise utility functions for the timeliness dimension where a task has a hard deadline, a soft deadline, or no deadline, respectively (D_i is the deadline of task T_i). In this study, a task with no soft or hard QoS requirements in any of its QoS dimensions will be referred to as a *best-effort task* and a corresponding dimension-wise utility function will be referred to as a *best-effort utility function*.

Even though dimension-wise utility functions will sufficiently express users' accrued benefits in individual QoS dimensions, a scheduler needs a unique utility function for each task which maps the multi-dimensional QoS requirements of that task to a benefit value. However, defining such a utility function for a task with $d_i > 1$ is not trivial due to the fact that achieving a complete ordering among all possible QoS choices is usually impossible. This problem is circumvented by defining the utility function of a task as a weighted sum of its dimension-wise utility functions. Specifically, the utility function associated with task T_i, which is denoted by $U_i : Q_i \to R^+$, is defined to be [9]:

$$U_i(q_i) = \sum_{j=1}^{d_i} w_i^j U_i^j(q_i^j) \tag{1}$$

where $0 \leq w_i^j \leq 1$, $1 \leq j \leq d_i$, denotes the weight assigned to the jth QoS dimension of task T_i. It is natural that a dimension with hard QoS requirement will be heavily weighted as compared to one with soft QoS requirement or best-effort service, and so on.

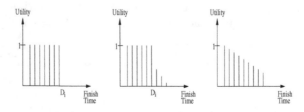

Fig. 1. Utility functions for the timeliness dimension.

4   QoS-Based Scheduling Problem

For each user in the Grid, we assume that the following optimization problem needs to be solved:

$$\max_{\mathcal{X}_{j,k,l}}\left\{J_i(\mathcal{X}_{j,k,l})\right\}$$

$$J_i(\mathcal{X}_{j,k,l}) = \alpha_i U_i(q_i(\mathcal{X}_{j,k,l})) - \beta_{i,j,k}P_i(\mathcal{X}_{j,k,l})$$

$$q_i^{min} \leq q_i(\mathcal{X}_{j,k,l}) \tag{2}$$

where $\mathcal{X}_{j,k,l}$ denotes a task assigment under which task T_i will start its execution in time-slot $\tau_j^k[l]$ on node M_j^k, $q_i(\mathcal{X}_{j,k,l})$ is the achieved QoS under $\mathcal{X}_{j,k,l}$, α_i is the maximum price per utility unit that will be paid by user i, P_i is the cost of executing task T_i under $\mathcal{X}_{j,k,l}$, $\beta_{i,j,k}$ is the priority of user i on node M_j^k, and $q_i^{min} \in Q_i$ denotes the minimum QoS demands of task T_i. A detailed explanation of the terms in (2) will be given in Section 4.1. With respect to (2), each user demands the maximum possible utility with the minumum cost to itself. In addition, each user must specify its minimum QoS requirements, since a scheduling decision that maximizes $J_i(\mathcal{X}_{j,k,l})$ may not meet all minimum QoS requirements of task T_i. Specifically, Definition 1 formalizes the conditions under which user i will accept scheduling decision $\mathcal{X}_{j,k,l}$.

Definition 1. *User i assumes scheduling decision $\mathcal{X}_{j,k,l}$ as a feasible one if and only if $q_i^{min} \leq q_i(\mathcal{X}_{j,k,l})$ and $J_i(\mathcal{X}_{j,k,l}) \geq 0$.*

A QoS-based Grid scheduler is assumed to find a solution to the following optimization problem subject to users' constraints.

$$\max_{\mathcal{X}}\left\{J(\mathcal{X})\right\}$$

$$J(\mathcal{X}) = \sum_{i=1}^{n} w_i^G J_i(\mathcal{X}_{j,k,l})$$

$$q_i^{min} \leq q_i(\mathcal{X}_{j,k,l}), \quad 1 \leq i \leq n \tag{3}$$

where $\mathcal{X}$ denotes a task assignment for all tasks, w_i^G is the weight assigned to task T_i by the Grid. With respect to (3), the *QoS-based scheduling problem* is to find a possible task assignment $\mathcal{X}$ that maximizes $J(\mathcal{X})$ subject to users' constraints. Note that each task is associated by two priorities; one is due to its user (α_i) and the other one is due to the system (w_i^G).

4.1   Computational Economy

According to the formulation of the QoS-based scheduling problem (3), a *computational economy* framework is adopted for the Grid in which users (consumers) pay for the Grid services and resource providers (producers) profit from being a part of the Grid. Among several economic models surveyed in [3], in this study, the *posted price* model is embraced as our Grid economy model. In this model, a Grid resource provider posts its price for each time-slot available on nodes in its site to a *Grid Market Directory* (GMD). A grid scheduler interacts with the GMD for finding out the cost of executing a task on a node. Specifically, this cost is computed as follows.

$$P_i(\mathcal{X}_{j,k,l}) = \sum_{r=s_i}^{f_i} p_j^k(r) \tag{4}$$

where $p_j^k(l)$ is the price of time-slot $\tau_j^k(l)$. Thus, we allow resource owners to have time-varying resource prices, which is the main difference from [12]. Resource owners will determine $p_j^k(l)$ based on a *pricing strategy* so as to maximize their profits and resource utilization. For the completeness of the paper, we assume that each owner agrees to follow the *derivative-following pricing strategy* [14]. For the details of this strategy, we refer reader to [14]. Owners can update their prices in the GMD only before a new scheduling event and they are not allowed to alter the prices until the next scheduling event.

The priority of user i on node M_j^k, $\beta_{i,j,k}$, in (2) is determined by Grid system managers for each user and node in the Grid. By introducing $\beta_{i,j,k}$ into (2), where $\beta_{i,j,k} \geq 0$, a Grid scheduler can market the same commodity at different prices to different consumers.

The first term in (2) ($\alpha_i U_i(q_i)$) simply corresponds to the budget of user i under the constraint that its minimum QoS requirements are met. In this study, a user is assumed to determine its budget as follows. Upon the submission of a task, a Grid scheduler will interact with the task owner and inform it about the average cost of meeting its minumum QoS requirements. Specifically, the average cost $\bar{P}_i$ is computed for task T_i as:

$$\bar{P}_i = \frac{1}{\Lambda_i} \sum_{k=1}^{h} \sum_{j=1}^{m_k} \frac{\beta_{i,j,k} P_i(\bar{\mathcal{X}}_{j,k,l})}{U_i(q_i(\bar{\mathcal{X}}_{j,k,l}))} \tag{5}$$

where $\bar{\mathcal{X}}_{j,k,l}$ denotes a task assignment for which $q_i^{min} \leq q_i(\bar{\mathcal{X}}_{j,k,l})$ is met with the cheapest cost to the user on node M_j^k and Λ_i is the number of nodes for which $q_i^{min} \leq q_i(\bar{\mathcal{X}}_{j,k,l})$ is satisfied. Then, the user submits its budget for per utility unit as $\alpha_i = \bar{P}_i \hat{\alpha}_i$ to the scheduler, where $\hat{\alpha}_i \geq 0$.

Finally, in order to maximize resource owners' profits, weights w_i^G, $1 \leq i \leq n$, in (3) are set as follows:

$$w_i^G = \frac{\frac{\alpha_i}{\Lambda_i} \sum_{k=1}^{h} \sum_{j=1}^{m_k} U_i(q_i(\bar{\mathcal{X}}_{j,k,l}))}{\max_{T_i \in T} \left\{ \frac{\alpha_i}{\Lambda_i} \sum_{k=1}^{h} \sum_{j=1}^{m_k} U_i(q_i(\bar{\mathcal{X}}_{j,k,l})) \right\}} . \tag{6}$$

5   QSMTS_VP Algorithm

The QSMTS_VP (QoS-based meta-task scheduling for time-varying resource prices) algorithm is shown in Fig. 2, where time-varying resource prices means

1. Split set T into three disjoint lists, namely LIST_1, LIST_2, and LIST_3;
2. **for** each list LIST_b, $1 \leq b \leq 3$
3.   **while** ($\text{LIST}_b \neq \emptyset$)
4.   **for** each task $T_i \in \text{LIST}_b$
5.   **for** each node $M_j^k \in S$
6.   **for** each time-slot $\tau_j^k[l] \in \mathcal{T}_j^k$
7. $s_i = l$ and $f_i = s_i + \lceil \frac{t_{i,j,k}^E}{|\tau_j^k|} \rceil - 1$;
8.   **if** ($f_i \leq \kappa_j^k$ and all time-slots $\tau_j^k[l]$, $s_i \leq l \leq f_i$, are free)
9.   **if** ($q_i(\mathcal{X}_{j,k,l}) \geq q_i^{min}$)
10.   Compute
$$J(\mathcal{X}_{j,k,l}) = w_i^G \Big[\alpha_i U_i(q_i(\mathcal{X}_{j,k,l})) - \beta_{i,j,k} P_i(\mathcal{X}_{j,k,l}) \Big];$$
11.   **else** $J(\mathcal{X}_{j,k,l}) = -\infty$;
12.   **else** $J(\mathcal{X}_{j,k,l}) = -\infty$;
13.   **endfor**.
14.   **if** ($J(\mathcal{X}_{j,k,l}) < 0$ for all $\tau_j^k[l] \in \mathcal{T}_j^k$)
15.   Node M_j^k is not feasible for task T_i;
16.   **endfor**.
17.   **if** (No feasible node exists for task T_i)
18.   Remove task T_i from LIST_b;
19.   **endfor**.
20.   Find task $\hat{T}_i$ and node $\hat{M}_j^k$ that maximizes $J(\mathcal{X}_{j,k,l})$;
        Assign $\hat{T}_i$ to $\hat{M}_j^k$ and remove $\hat{T}_i$ from LIST_b;
21.   **endwhile**.
22. **endfor**.

Fig. 2. The QSMTS_VP algorithm.

that the cost of running task T_i on node M_j^k is dependent on the start time of the execution of task T_i on node M_j^k.

In the first step, set T is split into three disjoint lists: LIST_1 (LIST_2) is composed of tasks with hard (soft) QoS requirements in the timeliness or reliability dimension and LIST_3 includes tasks with best-effort service in both dimensions. Note that a task with a hard QoS requirement in one dimension and a soft QoS requirement in the other one will be in list LIST_1. Tasks in lists LIST_1 and LIST_2 are required to specify their worst-case execution times.

Steps between 2 and 22 will be repeated for each list, namely LIST_1, LIST_2, and LIST_3, separately until no task is left in the corresponding list. Specifically, QSMTS_VP will allocate tasks in list LIST_1 first, then tasks in list LIST_2, and finally tasks in list LIST_3. Note that LIST_b is the list of tasks that are currently being considered for scheduling. A task will be removed from list LIST_b if it is *scheduled* or *dropped*. QSMTS_VP will drop task T_i if there is no feasible node in the Grid on which task T_i can be executed. We consider a node M_j^k as a *feasible node* for task T_i if (1) all of the minimum QoS requirements of task T_i can be met on node M_j^k, and (2) the owner of task T_i have enough money or credit to pay for the services of node M_j^k.

Inside the *while* loop, there are three *for* loops; the first *for* loop (4-19) is to account for all unscheduled tasks in LIST_b, the second one (5-16) is to consider each node in the Grid for executing these unscheduled tasks, and the third one (6-13) is to find time-slots on nodes that optimize users' and Grid's objectives. At step 7, s_i and f_i are computed for task T_i on M_j^k. Note that, while computing f_i, the worst case execution time of task T_i on M_j^k must be used if $T_i \in \text{LIST}_1$ or $T_i \in \text{LIST}_2$. At step 8, it is checked if time-slots between s_i and f_i are available for executing task T_i; otherwise, at step 12, $J(\mathcal{X}_{j,k,l})$ is set to minus infinity. At step 9, it is checked if the current scheduling decision for task T_i ($\mathcal{X}_{j,k,l}$) meets the minimum QoS requirements of task T_i. If $q_i(\mathcal{X}_{j,k,l}) \geq q_i^{min}$, at step 10, the net utility $J(\mathcal{X}_{j,k,l})$ due to the current scheduling decision is computed; otherwise, at step 11, $J(\mathcal{X}_{j,k,l})$ is set to minus infinity. At steps 14 and 15, it is checked if node M_j^k is feasible for task T_i. At steps 17 and 18, task T_i will be excluded from scheduling if there is no feasible node in the Grid to execute task T_i. At step 20, the task-node pair $(\hat{T}_i, \hat{M}_j^k)$ that maximizes the net utility $J(\mathcal{X}_{j,k,l})$ is found and task $\hat{T}_i$ is assigned to machine $\hat{M}_j^k$.

We should note that a best effort task can far exceed its expected execution time which may result in $J(\mathcal{X}_{j,k,l}) < 0$. In such a case, the node executing the task will suspend the task. In addition, the time complexity of QSMTS_VP is $O(|T| \times |S| \times |\mathcal{T}| + |T|^2 \times \kappa_{max})$, where $|S| = \sum_{k=1}^{h} m_k$, $|\mathcal{T}| = \sum_{k=1}^{h} \sum_{j=1}^{m_k} \kappa_j^k$, and $\kappa_{max} = \max_{M_j^k \in S} \kappa_j^k$.

6   Experiments

Simulation studies were carried out to evaluate the performance of QSMTS_VP. In these simulations, a Grid computing environment with 10 computing sites is considered, each with a random number of nodes uniformly distributed between 1 and 8. It is assumed that all nodes in a site are the same and nodes in different sites are dissimilar in terms of their computational capabilities.

In the simulation, computational economy of the Grid is modeled as follows. It is assumed that there are four different market and price ratings, namely *cheap* (C), *normal* (N), *expensive* (E), *excessive* (X); the *market rating* (*price rating*) reflects the most probable price of a time-slot in the Grid market (at a site in the Grid). In order to create a Grid market of expensive market rating, for example, half of all sites are assumed to have expensive price rating and the others have cheap, normal, or excessive price rating with equal probability. Once the price ratings of all sites are set, time-slots associated with each node are priced according to the price rating of its computing site. Before determining the price of a time-slot, we assume that each node in the Grid provide 100 time-slots with equal size of 10 time units, e.g., $\kappa_j^k = 100$ and $|\tau_j^k[l]| = 10$ for all $M_j^k \in S_k$ and $1 \leq l \leq \kappa_j^k$. In addition, since QSMTS_VP is specifically designed for time-varying resource prices, time-slots of a node are *equally* grouped into a random number of *time-slot blocks* uniformly distributed between 2 and 5, where each time-slot block has a different price and all time-slots in a time-slot block have the same price. Finally, a time-slot $\tau_j^k[l]$ is considered to be cheap if its price $p_j^k(l)$ is between 5 and 15 G\$ (G\$ is from [3]), normal if $15 \leq p_j^k(l) < 25$, expensive if $25 \leq p_j^k(l) < 45$, and excessive if $50 \leq p_j^k(l) < 80$. Then, the price of a time-slot block is determined based on the price rating of its site and Table 1. For example, if the price rating of the site is expensive, the price of a time-slot block will be cheap (uniformly distributed between 5 and 15) 10% of the time, normal 20% of the time, expensive 60% of the time, and so on.

Table 1. Determining the price of a time-slot according to the price rating of its site.

Price rating	C	N	E	X
C	0.6	0.3	0.1	-
N	0.2	0.6	0.2	-
E	0.1	0.2	0.6	0.1
X	-	0.1	0.3	0.6

In the simulation, the security level and failure rates of nodes in a site are set based on the price rating of the site as well. Basically, a site with a more expensive price per time-slot is made more likely to offer higher security levels and less failure probability for tasks. In this framework, each site is randomly associated with a security level (poor, low, medium, or high) and a failure rate per unit time uniformly distributed between 0.001 and 0.005.

In the economy Grid architecture outlined above, it is assumed that there are 100 users (tasks), each task T_i with d_i QoS dimensions (randomly set to an integer number between 1 and 4). Thus, timeliness, reliability, security, and version are the only available QoS dimensions. If $d_i = 1$, the timeliness dimension is assumed to be the fixed QoS dimension of task T_i. For each QoS dimension of task T_i, a service type among three possible service types, namely best-effort, soft, and hard, is randomly chosen. Specifically, the service type of the jth QoS dimension of task T_i (Q_i^j) is determined as follows: (1) A random number uniformly distributed between 0 and 1 is generated. If the random number generated is less than V_Q ($0 \leq V_Q \leq 1$), the service type of Q_i^j is set to *hard*. (2) Otherwise, a second random number is generated. If this number is less than 0.5, the service type of Q_i^j is set to *soft*, otherwise chosen to be *best-effort*.

A task is offered four distinct security levels and may have up to four different versions (uniformly distributed between 1 and 4). A soft or hard QoS requirement in the security (version) dimension is randomly set to one of the available choices in the dimension. On the other hand, a soft or hard QoS requirement in the timeliness (reliability) dimension is determined as follows. First, each task in lists $LIST_1$ and $LIST_2$ is assigned to a machine where its finish time is minimized. Let SL denote the schedule length of this task assignment, $rand()$ be a function which generates a uniformly distributed random number between 0 and 1, and $V_D \geq 0$ be a variable used for assigning deadlines and reliability requirements to tasks. Then, the deadline of task T_i (D_i) is $D_i = (0.5 + 0.5 \times rand()) \times SL \times V_D$, and the reliability requirement of task T_i (R_i) is $R_i = (0.5 + 0.5 \times rand()) \times e^{(-0.001 \times SL \times V_D)}$.

While modeling expected execution times, a site is assumed to have *slow* (110-130), *normal* (80-100), *fast* (50-70), or *superb* (20-40) nodes in terms of their computing speed. That is, a site can only have one of the four possible *computing power ratings*. Note that the numbers in parentheses, for example (50-70), show that a task will take between 50 and 70 time units (uniformly distributed) to complete on a fast node. Furthermore, it is assumed that a site with higher price rating is more likely to have higher computing power rating. Based on this, in order to determine the computing power rating of a site, Table 1 is used with the exception that columns are named slow, normal, fast, and superb, respectively. We should also note that the expected execution time of the ith version of a task is assumed to be between 50% and 90% of the expected execution time of the (i+1)th version of that task [11].

In the simulation, the financial rating of users is modeled as follows. There are four possible *financial ratings*, namely *poor*, *normal*, *rich*, and *royal*, assumed. For example, if the financial rating of users is rich, at least half of the users are made rich and the others can be poor, normal, or royal with equal probability. Since the financial rating of user i is related to its budget and the budget of the user is determined by $\hat{\alpha}_i$, $\hat{\alpha}_i$ is uniformly set between 0.25 and 0.75 for a poor user, 0.75 and 1.25 for a normal user, 1.25 and 2.75 for a rich user, and 2.75 and 4.25 for a royal user. Finally, $\beta_{i,j,k}$ is taken to be one for each task T_i and node M_j^k in the Grid (every user is treated equally).

The results of our simulation studies are shown in Tables 2-3, where each number is the average of the data obtained over 100 experiments. In these tables, we report the following important figures: average number of users whose minimum QoS requirements are met (# tasks scheduled), average makespan, average user net utility, average user budget, and average site profit. In # tasks scheduled column, the numbers in parentheses show how many of poor, normal, rich, or royal rated user tasks are scheduled, respectively. In addition, in profit column, average system profit is reported in terms of average profit of sites with cheap, normal, expensive, and excessive price rating, respectively.

According to Table 2 and 3, while the financial rating of users gets higher, average user budget increases (from 154 to 758 G$ in Table 2 and from 140 to 799 G$ in Table 3) as expected. Increasing average user budget has positively helped QSMTS_VP to schedule more tasks (70 vs. 93 in Table 2 and 73 vs. 93 in Table 3) simply because more users can now afford the Grid services. As a result, QSMTS_VP is shown to react to the changes in the financial status of Grid users, which is an essential feature for a computational economy based resource management system. In parallel to the increase in the number of scheduled tasks, average makespan increases as well.

With the increase in the financial rating of users, average amount of G$ spent by users, which is the difference between average budget and average net utility, increases from 47 to 64 G$ in Table 2 and from 53 to 68 G$ in Table 3. That is, a wealthier population of users tends to spend more, which is typical in a real-world. More spending by users, on the other hand, positively affects average profit of sites, e.g., the average profit of a site with expensive price

Table 2. Results for cheap market rating, $V_Q = 0.25$, and $V_D = 1$.

User rating	# tasks scheduled	Makespan	Net utility	Budget	Profit (C, N, E, X)
Poor	70 (42, 14, 14, -)	350	107	154	(1753, 403, 580, 700)
Normal	86 (9, 63, 14, -)	392	143	199	(2307, 544, 819, 1018)
Rich	89 (7, 10, 61, 11)	409	337	396	(2416, 591, 956, 1248)
Royal	93 (-, 14, 14, 65)	420	694	758	(2612, 629, 1106, 1447)

Table 3. Results for excessive market rating, $V_Q = 0.25$, and $V_D = 1$.

User rating	# tasks scheduled	Makespan	Net utility	Budget	Profit (C, N, E, X)
Poor	73 (44, 14, 15, -)	308	87	140	(719, 479, 617, 2010)
Normal	88 (10, 63, 15, -)	335	157	216	(912, 626, 767, 2699)
Rich	90 (7, 10, 61, 11)	341	363	426	(938, 670, 867, 2970)
Royal	93 (-, 14, 14, 65)	346	731	799	(963, 720, 943, 3388)

rating increased from 580 to 1106 G\$ in Table 2. As a result, users with big budgets are shown to be great from the point of resource providers in terms of maximizing their resource utilization and profit.

When we compare Table 2 against Table 3, we observe the following. Even though the market rating is changed from cheap to excessive, average number of scheduled tasks did not virtually change. This is due to the fact that the financial rating of users are only related to the current market rating. Thus, a poor user in a market with excessive rating might correspond to a royal user in a market with cheap rating. Average makespan is less in Table 3 simply because a Grid market with excessive rating provides more powerful computing resources. Average budget and average spending of users, on the other hand, are more in Table 3 due to higher resource prices. According to Table 2 and 3, computing sites with cheap and excessive price rating made the most profit, respectively. The reason is that there are plenty of sites with cheap (excessive) price rating in a market with cheap (excessive) rating which forces users to use cheaply (excessively) priced resources.

7 Conclusions

In this paper, we first presented a formulation of the QoS-based scheduling problem with time-varying resource prices based on utility functions and resource price functions. The formulation of the QoS-based scheduling problem is general enough to account for as many QoS dimensions as available in a Grid system. In order to solve this challenging problem, we developed the QSMTS_VP algorithm. According to the simulation results presented in the previous section, QSMTS_VP is a promising heuristic that can be a part of an economy based Grid resource management system.

References

1. Foster, I., Kesselman, C.: Globus: A metacomputing infrastructure toolkit. Int. Journal of Supercomputer Applications **11(2)** (1997) 115–128.
2. Grimshaw, A. S., Wulf, W. A., French, J. F., Weaver, A. C., Reynolds, P. F.: Legion: The next logical step toward a nationwide virtual computer. Technical Report CS-94-21, University of Virgiana (1994).
3. Buyya, R., Abramson, D., Giddy, J., Stockinger, H.: Economic models for resource management and scheduling in Grid computing. The Journal of Concurrency and Computation: Practice and Experience (2002).
4. Chapin, S., Karpovich, J., Grimshaw, A.: The Legion resource management system. Proc. of the IPPS/SPDP Workshop on Job Scheduling Strategies for Parallel Processing (1999) 162–178.
5. Sabata, B., Chatterjee, S., Davis, M., Sydir, J., Lawrence, T.: Taxonomy for QoS specifications. Proc. of WORDS (1997) 100–107.
6. Kim, J.-K., et al.: A QoS performance measure framework for distributed heterogeneous networks. Proc. of the 8th Euromicro Workshop on Parallel and Distributed Processing (2000) 18–27.
7. Chatterjee, S.: A quality of service based allocation and routing algorithm for distributed, heterogeneous real time systems. Proc. of the Int. Conf. Distributed Computing Systems (1997) 235–243.
8. Chatterjee, S., Sydir, J., Sabata, B., Lawrence, T.: Modeling applications for adaptive QoS-based resource management. Proc. of the 2nd IEEE High Assurance Systems Engineering Workshop (1997).
9. Lee, C., Lehoczky, J., Siewiorek, D., Rajkumar, R., Hansen, J.: A scalable solution to the multi-resource QoS-problem. Proc. of the IEEE Real-Time Systems Symposium (1999) 315–326.
10. Maheswaran, M.: Quality of service driven resource management algorithms for network computing. Proc. of the Int. Conf. Parallel and Distributed Processing Techniques and Applications (1999) 1090–1096.
11. Braun, T. D, Seigel, H. J., Maciejewski, A. A.: Static mapping heuristics for tasks with dependencies, priorities, deadlines, and multiple versions in heterogeneous environments. Proc. of the Int. Parallel and Distributed Processing Symposium (2002).
12. Doğan, A., Özgüner, F.: On QoS-based scheduling of a meta-task with multiple QoS demands in heterogeneous computing. Proc. of the Int. Parallel and Distributed Processing Symposium (2002).
13. Iverson, M. A., Özgüner, F., Potter, L.: Statistical prediction of task execution times through analytic benchmarking for scheduling in a heterogeneous environment. IEEE Trans. Computers **48(12)** (1999) 1374–1379.
14. Sairamesh, J., Kephart, J. O.: Price dynamics of vertically differentiated information markets. Proc. of the Int. Conf. Information on Information and Computational Economy (1998).

A Theoretical Approach to Load Balancing of a Target Task in a Temporally and Spatially Heterogeneous Grid Computing Environment

Soo-Young Lee and Jun Huang

Department of Electrical and Computer Engineering
Auburn University
Auburn, AL 36849
{sylee,junhuang}@eng.auburn.edu

Abstract. One of the distinct characteristics of computing platforms shared by multiple users such as a computational grid is heterogeneity on each computer and/or among computers. Temporal heterogeneity refers to variation, along the time dimension, of computing power (or communication bandwidth) available for a task on a computer, and spatial heterogeneity represents the variation among computers. In minimizing the average parallel execution time of a target task on a spatially heterogeneous computing system, it is not optimal to distribute the target task linearly proportional to the average computing powers available on computers. In this study, based on a theoretical model of heterogeneous computing environment, an approach to load balancing for minimizing the average parallel execution time of a target task is discussed. The approach of which validity has been verified through simulation considers temporal and spatial heterogeneities in addition to the average computing power on each computer.

1 Introduction

A cluster of computers or a computational grid is often employed for high performance computing these days [1] [2]. Such a system is usually shared by multiple users, and computers in the system may not be all identical. One of the most distinct characteristics of a grid or cluster computing environment compared to a dedicated multiprocessor system is its heterogeneity [3] which may be classified into two types: *temporal* ("variation with time on a computer") and *spatial* ("variation with computer") heterogeneity.

Heterogeneity of such systems has been addressed from various viewpoints of high performance computing, including modeling (heterogeneity of) the system [4], performance estimation [5], reliability [6], scheduling and load balancing [7], etc. Much of the efforts has gone into scheduling a stream of tasks (i.e., from the system's viewpoint) [8]-[11]. One of the important issues is how to utilize a heterogeneous computing system to optimize performance of a *target* task.

In [7], a "stochastic scheduling" strategy where the performance variability is considered in partitioning a data parallel application to be executed on a heterogeneous computing platform is described. The mean and standard deviation

M. Parashar (Ed.): GRID 2002, LNCS 2536, pp. 70–81, 2002.
© Springer-Verlag Berlin Heidelberg 2002

of the predicted completion time of a task are used in scheduling, along with a "tuning factor" which specifies how "conservative" the scheduling is to be. However, how the tuning factor should be set is not discussed.

In order to develop an effective load balancing scheme for heterogeneous computing environments, how heterogeneity affects performance of a target task is to be well understood. In our early study [12], effects of temporal and spatial heterogeneities on the average parallel execution time of a target task has been thoroughly analyzed. Also, it has been shown that it is not optimal to partition a task over computers linearly proportional to their average computing powers in order to minimize the average parallel execution time. In this paper, a load balancing strategy for minimizing the average parallel execution time of a target task in a spatially heterogeneous computing environment is described in order to provide a theoretical foundation for developing a practical load balancing scheme. The strategy takes into account the standard deviation of available computing power in addition to the average computing power available on each computer. It has been shown that the average parallel execution time of a target task can be significantly reduced by the strategy. This strategy has a good potential to be applicable to real heterogeneous computing environments.

In Section 2, some of the early results [12] are reviewed. In Section 3, a strategy for load balancing of a target task is described. In Section 4, simulation results are discussed in detail, followed by a summary in Section 5.

2   Heterogeneity

In this section, models, heterogeneity, and certain performance measures are briefly reviewed from [12].

2.1   Models

Task model: A target task is assumed to be linearly partitionable over N computers. Many data-parallel applications such as low-level image processing, (Monte Carlo) simulations, matrix computation, etc. would fit to this model well. In this paper, in order to focus on effects of heterogeneous computing power on performance of a target task, communication is not considered in the task model. Also, it has been shown through simulation that heterogeneity in communication bandwidth has similar effects on target task's performance.

System Model: All hardware and software components collectively affect the effective computing power (and communication bandwidth) available for tasks on each computer. It is the available computing power (and communication bandwidth) for a target task, that eventually determine execution time of the task. Hence, in this study, "availability" of computing power is adopted in defining heterogeneity. The system consists of N computers where the availability varies with time and shows a different behavior on a different computer.

2.2   Temporal and Spatial Heterogeneities

Availability: Let the maximum computing power of computer C_i be denoted by α_i for $i = 1, \cdots, N$ where N is the number of computers. Then, the computing power available for a task at time t may be expressed by $\alpha_i A_i(t)$ where $A_i(t)$ is "availability" of C_i for the task at time t and $0 \leq A_i(t) \leq 1$. The mean and standard deviation of $A_i(t)$ are denoted by a_i and σ_{A_i}, respectively. In the steady state, a_i and σ_{A_i} are fixed, not varying with time while $A_i(t)$ varies with time. In the time-varying state, not only $A_i(t)$ but also a_i and/or σ_{A_i} vary with time, i.e., one needs to use the notations $a_i(t)$ and $\sigma_{A_i}(t)$. The time-varying state is not considered in this paper.

When a heterogeneous computing system is shared by multiple independent users, workload on each computer would vary with time and computer. Therefore, workload coupled with the heterogeneous hardware and software components makes availability vary spatially and temporally. *Temporal heterogeneity* refers to variation of availability along the time dimension on a computer while *spatial heterogeneity* refers to the variation among computers as illustrated in Figure 1.

With the notations in the definition of availability above, a computer C_i is said to exhibit temporal heterogeneity when $A_i(t)$ is a non-uniform function of time. Temporal heterogeneity is defined on an individual computer, which indicates variation of computing power available for a task along the time dimension. Therefore, the standard deviation of availability may be used to quantify temporal heterogeneity on each computer. Noting that load balancing for computer-dependent *average* availability is straightforward (i.e., distribute a task over computers proportional to their average availability), temporal heterogeneity, to be denoted by TH_i, on C_i is defined to be the normalized standard deviation of availability.

$$TH_i \stackrel{\triangle}{=} \bar{\sigma}_{A_i} = \frac{\sigma_{A_i}}{a_i} \tag{1}$$

The notation TH will be used when TH_i is the same for all i (computers), i.e., spatially homogeneous, or the mean of TH_i among computers is to be referred to.

A system consisting of multiple computers shows spatial heterogeneity when $a_i \neq a_j$ and/or $\sigma_{A_i} \neq \sigma_{A_j}$ for some i, j. Spatial heterogeneity is defined for a group of computers to be employed to execute a target task. It represents variation of computing power among the computers. Let's denote the mean and maximum of $\bar{\sigma}_{A_i}$ among C_i by $\bar{\sigma}_A^{mean}$ and $\bar{\sigma}_A^{max}$, respectively, i.e., $\bar{\sigma}_A^{mean} = \frac{1}{N} \sum_{i=1}^{N} \bar{\sigma}_{A_i}$ and $\bar{\sigma}_A^{max} = max_i\{\bar{\sigma}_{A_i}\}$. Spatial heterogeneity denoted by SH for a set of computers $\{C_i\}$ (the notation $\{\ \}$ refers to a set) is defined as

$$SH \stackrel{\triangle}{=} \bar{\sigma}_A^{max} - \bar{\sigma}_A^{mean} \tag{2}$$

That is, SH quantifies variation of temporal heterogeneity among computers.

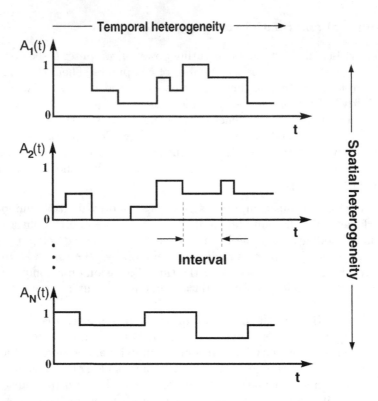

Fig. 1. Temporal and spatial heterogeneity. $A_i(t)$ is availability of computing power on C_i for a target task where $i = 1, \cdots, N$.

2.3   Parallel Execution Time

Let X and X_i denote the size of a target task and the portion of the target task assigned to the computer C_i, respectively. The execution time of X_i on C_i is represented by T_i which is a random variable, and its mean and standard deviation are denoted by t_i and σ_{T_i}, respectively. In this paper, the same notation is used for a random variable and its observation in order to minimize the number of variables.

It is not difficult to show that $t_i = \frac{X_i}{\alpha_i a_i}$ and

$$\sigma_{T_i} = \sqrt{t_i} \frac{\sigma_{A_i}}{a_i} \tag{3}$$

in the steady state assuming the uncorrelatedness between $A_i(t)$ and $A_i(t')$.

The parallel execution time of X in a run on $\{C_i\}$, to be denoted by T which is also a random variable, is given by $T = max_i \{ T_i \}$. The mean and standard deviation of T are denoted by τ and σ_T, respectively.

For a spatially homogeneous system, τ can be analytically derived in a simple form, from which effects of temporal heterogeneity can be appreciated. On such a system, $\alpha_i = \alpha$, $a_i = a$, and $\sigma_{A_i} = \sigma_A$ for all i since all computers are "identical." It would be reasonable to partition X such that $X_i = X$ for all i. When there are N homogeneous computers, τ can be derived analytically [5], [13]. Omitting the derivation steps,

$$\tau = \frac{X'}{\alpha a} + K(N)\sqrt{\frac{X'}{\alpha a}}\frac{\sigma_A}{a} \tag{4}$$

where $K(N)$ is an increasing function of N and $K(1) = 0$.

Notice that the average parallel execution time of a target task consists of two components, one depending on the mean of availability and the other on the standard deviation of availability, i.e., temporal heterogeneity. It is to be noted that temporal heterogeneity makes the average parallel execution time increase beyond the average sequential execution time on each computer. The increase is larger when the number of computers employed is greater. Also, as will be shown later in Section 4, a higher spatial heterogeneity leads to a longer average parallel execution time.

3   Load Balancing

The load balancing strategy described in this paper assumes that the size (execution time) of a target task is sufficiently large such that the system can be considered to be in the steady state. Recall that the analytic formulas reviewed in Section 2.3 were derived for the steady state. This assumption is valid since tasks requiring a high performance computing platform such as a computational grid would be normally of large scale. Also, the assumption is necessary to extract system parameters such as a_i and σ_{A_i}. Let an *interval* be the period during which availability remains constant or does not vary more than a certain threshold. Then, parallel execution time of a target task is to be much longer than the average interval of a system, in order to benefit from the load balancing strategy.

Let's denote the computing power (*speed*) of C_i at t by $S_i(t)$ which has the mean s_i and the standard deviation σ_{S_i}. Then, noting that $S_i(t) = \alpha_i A_i(t)$, $s_i = \alpha_i a_i$ and $\sigma_{S_i} = \alpha_i \sigma_{A_i}$. When $\sigma_{S_i} = 0$ for all i, a target task is to be partitioned proportional to s_i, in order to achieve the minimum τ. However, such partitioning does not lead to the minimum τ in general when $\sigma_{S_i} \neq 0$ for some i.

Let's consider cases where $\sigma_{S_i} \neq 0$ for some i. Suppose that X is partitioned such that X_i is linearly proportional to s_i. Then, t_i (the average execution time on C_i) would be the same for all i, but σ_{T_i} (the standard deviation of execution time on C_i) would not be. It is to be pointed out that σ_{T_i} is linearly proportional to $\bar{\sigma}_{A_i}$ (or TH_i). Noting that τ is given by $E[max_i\{T_i\}]$ rather than $max_i\{T_i\}$ or $max_i\{t_i\}$ where $E[\ ]$ is the expectation operator, it is possible to further reduce τ by taking $\{\sigma_{T_i}\}$ into account. Therefore, load balancing may be carried out in two steps as follows:

(1) X is partitioned over $\{C_i\}$ such that X_i is proportional to s_i,

(2) $\{X_i\}$ is further adjusted considering $\{\sigma_{T_i}\}$ and $\{s_i\}$.

In the following, this two-step load balancing approach is elaborated for different cases.

When $s_i = s_j$ for all i, j:

Consider the case of $N = 2$ (two computers). In Step (1) of the two-step load balancing approach, X is divided equally between C_1 and C_2 since $s_1 = s_2$. That is, after Step (1), $X_1 = X_2 = \frac{X}{2}$ and $t_1 = t_2$. Suppose that $\sigma_{T_1} > \sigma_{T_2}$ after Step (1). Then, it is possible to reduce τ further by transferring a certain amount of work ($\Delta X \geq 0$) from C_1 to C_2 in Step (2), i.e., $X_1' = X_1 - \Delta X$ and $X_2' = X_2 + \Delta X$, where X_i' is X_i after Step (2). Then,

$$t_1' = t_1 - \frac{\Delta X}{s_1} \overset{\triangle}{=} t_1 - \Delta t_1 \quad \text{and} \quad t_2' = t_2 + \frac{\Delta X}{s_2} \overset{\triangle}{=} t_2 + \Delta t_2 \tag{5}$$

where t_i' is t_i after Step (2).

Note that $\Delta t_1 = \Delta t_2$ since $s_1 = s_2$. Also, from Equation 3, it can be shown that

$$\sigma_{T_1}' = \sigma_{T_1}\sqrt{1 - \frac{\Delta X}{s_1 t_1}} \quad \text{and} \quad \sigma_{T_2}' = \sigma_{T_2}\sqrt{1 + \frac{\Delta X}{s_2 t_2}} \tag{6}$$

where σ_{T_i}' is σ_{T_i} after Step (2).

A heuristic scheme, to be referred to as *equalization scheme*, that can be employed in Step (2) equalizes the sum of the mean and standard deviation of execution time between two computers. That is, it determines ΔX such that

$$t_1' + \sigma_{T_1}' = t_2' + \sigma_{T_2}' \tag{7}$$

where t_i and σ_{T_i}' are given by Equations 5 and 6, respectively.

The equalization scheme is illustrated in Figure 2. The scheme attempts to reduce the probability that the parallel execution time of a target task, $T = max_i\{T_i\}$, is large, in order to minimize its average parallel execution time. This heuristic can be generalized for cases where $N > 2$, i.e., X_i is determined such that $t_i' + \sigma_{T_i}'$ is the same for all i.

When $s_i \neq s_j$ for some i, j:

Again, consider the case of $N = 2$, and suppose that $s_1 < s_2$. After Step (1), $X_1 = \frac{s_1 X}{s_1 + s_2}$ and $X_2 = \frac{s_2 X}{s_1 + s_2}$. What is to be done in Step (2) to further reduce τ depends on $\{\sigma_{T_i}\}$ and $\{s_i\}$, as discussed below, and can be generalized for cases where $N > 2$.

(a) $\sigma_{T_1} > \sigma_{T_2}$: In this case, ΔX is to be moved from C_1 to C_2 and the equalization scheme may be employed in determining ΔX. One difference is that

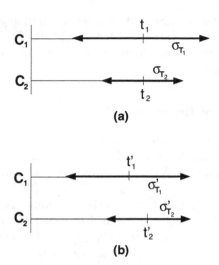

Fig. 2. Equalization scheme: (a) after Step (1) where a target task is partitioned such that the average execution time is the same on all computers and (b) after Step (2) where the partitioning is adjusted such that $t'_i + \sigma'_{T_i}$ is equalized for all computers.

$\Delta t_1 > \Delta t_2$. In other words, for the same increase in t_2 (by moving ΔX from C_1 to C_2), a larger decrease in t_1 results in, leading to a larger reduction in τ, compared to the case where $s_1 = s_2$.

(b) $\sigma_{T_1} < \sigma_{T_2}$ and $s_1 \ll s_2$: It is still possible to reduce τ by transferring ΔX from C_1 to C_2 though the equalization scheme may not be used since the condition, $t'_1 + \sigma'_{T_1} = t'_2 + \sigma'_{T_2}$, cannot be satisfied. Reduction in τ would be smaller than that in (a).

(c) $\sigma_{T_1} < \sigma_{T_2}$ and $s_1 \simeq s_2$: In this case, ΔX is to be moved from C_2 to C_1 and the equalization scheme can be used. Reduction in τ would be smaller than that in (a) and (b).

It should be clear that transferring ΔX in the other direction than specified above would result in a longer τ.

4   Simulation Results and Discussion

Simulation

Some of the early simulation results [12] are reviewed to highlight effects of spatial and temporal heterogeneity on performance of a target task, and then effectiveness of the two-step load balancing approach is discussed with simulation results for load balancing. First, simulation results for cases where $A_i(t)$ has a uniform distribution are presented (it was observed that other distributions such as a "truncated" Gaussian distribution lead to the similar results). The resulting T_i has a distribution similar with a Gaussian or Gamma distribution which was adopted also in other study [4]. Second, a_i is set to 0.5 in most cases, to maximize the range of variation of σ_{A_i} (note that $0 \leq a_i \leq 1.0$). Then, the maximum σ_{A_i} ($\bar{\sigma}_{A_i}$) is $\frac{1}{2\sqrt{3}}$ ($\frac{1}{\sqrt{3}}$). Third, the maximum computing power α_i on C_i is set to 1.0 for normalization purpose.

Spatial and Temporal Heterogeneities

In Figure 3, dependency of τ and $\bar{\sigma}_T$ on SH and TH is shown when N is fixed to 8. In these graphs, when SH is zero (i.e., on the TH axis), $\bar{\sigma}_{A_i}$, which is TH_i, is the same for all computers. When SH is greater than zero, distribution of $\bar{\sigma}_{A_i}$ among computers is *linear* such that $\bar{\sigma}_{A_i} = \bar{\sigma}_A^{mean} + 2(\frac{i-1}{N-1} - 0.5)(\bar{\sigma}_A^{max} - \bar{\sigma}_A^{mean})$ for $i = 1, \cdots, N$. That is, $TH = \bar{\sigma}_A^{mean}$ in these graphs. As SH increases, τ and $\bar{\sigma}_T$ increase significantly, especially when $TH(= \bar{\sigma}_A^{mean})$ also increases (going diagonally from the origin on the $SH - TH$ plane). Therefore, it is necessary to take temporal and spatial heterogeneities into account in load balancing in order to minimize the average parallel execution time and its variation of a target task.

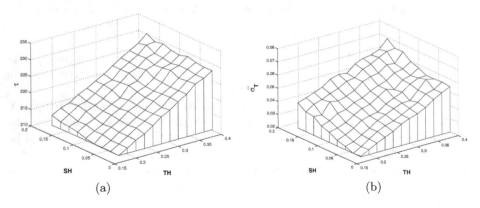

(a)   (b)

Fig. 3. (a) Average parallel execution time and (b) normalized standard deviation of parallel execution time, $\bar{\sigma}_T = \frac{\sigma_T}{\tau}$, when SH and TH are varied with N fixed at 8 where $X_i = 100$ for $i = 1, \cdots, 8$.

Load Balancing

Let's first consider a case where the average computing speed is the same for all computers, i.e., $s_i = s_j$ for all i, j. In Figure 4, τ and *percentage standard deviation* of $(t'_i + \sigma'_{T_i})$ are shown as functions of $Slope_T$ which specifies how a target task is distributed over N computers when $N = 10$. Since s_i is the same for all i, $X_i = X_j$ for all i, j in Step (1) of the two-step load balancing approach described in Section 3. It is assumed that $t_i = 100$ and $\sigma_{T_i} = \frac{i-1}{N-1}\sigma_{max}$, for $i = 1, \cdots, N$, after Step (1). In Step (2), X_i is adjusted such that $t'_i = $

$t_i + Slope_T (i - \frac{N-1}{2})$ for $i = 1, \cdots, N$. $Slope_T = 0$ corresponds to the case where X_i' is proportional to s_i (the *average* computing speed or power), i.e., Step (1) only. A negative $Slope_T$ indicates that a computer with a larger σ_{T_i} is assigned a larger ΔX_i (refer to Section 3) in Step (2) in addition to X_i allocated in Step (1). First of all, it is to be noted from Figure 4 that it is not optimal to distribute a target task linearly proportional to the *average* computing power of computers. In Figure 4-(a), it is clear that the performance improvement (reduction in τ) achieved by Step (2) over Step (1) is significant, and is larger for a larger $\Delta \sigma_T$ (equivalently, a higher spatial heterogeneity). Comparing Figures 4-(a) and (b), it can be seen that the equalization scheme employed in Step (2) works well, i.e., the distribution of X minimizing τ closely matches with that minimizing variation in $t_i + \sigma_{T_i}$.

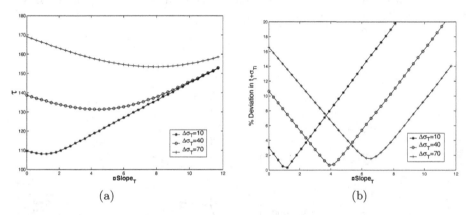

(a)   (b)

Fig. 4. (a) Average parallel execution time and (b) Percentage standard deviation of $t_i' + \sigma_{T_i}'$ after Step (2) in the load balancing, when the number of computers, N, is 10. After Step (1), $t_i = 100$ and $\Delta \sigma_T = \sigma_{T_N} - \sigma_{T_1}$ where $\sigma_{T_i} = \frac{i-1}{N-1} \sigma_{Tmax}$, where $i = 1, \cdots, 10$.

In Figure 5, a system of two computers where $s_1 < s_2$ is considered. In these graphs, τ is plotted as a function of ΔX. Again, $\Delta X = 0$ corresponds to the cases where X is divided between two computers proportional to their average computing powers (s_1 and s_2). It can be observed that reduction in τ, which can be achieved by Step (2), is larger for a larger s or a larger $\Delta \sigma_T$. Let's define the percentage error (ε) of the equalization scheme as $\frac{\Delta \tau_{max} - \Delta \tau}{\Delta \tau_{max}} \times 100$ where $\Delta \tau_{max}$ and $\Delta \tau$ are the maximum possible and achieved (by the heuristic) reductions in τ, re spectively. In this set of results, the average ε was 5.1%.

In Figure 6, percentage reduction in τ, which is achieved by Step (2), is analyzed with the number of computers (N) varied. In this simulation , s_i increases and σ_{T_i} decreases linearly proportional to i, i.e., a faster computer has a smaller variation of execution time. The *percentage reduction in* τ is defined to be $\frac{\tau_{(1)} - \tau_{(2)}}{\tau_{(1)}} \times 100$ where $\tau_{(1)}$ and $\tau_{(2)}$ are τ achieved by Steps (1) and (2), respecti

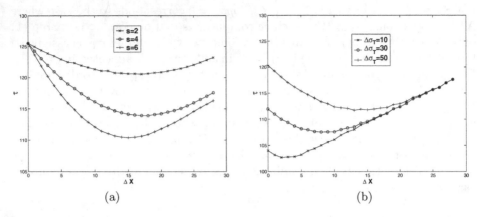

Fig. 5. Average parallel execution time on two computers (a) with a fixed $\Delta\sigma_T = \sigma_{T_1} - \sigma_{T_2} = 50$ ($\sigma_{T_2} = 10$) and (b) with a fixed $s = 4$, where $s = \frac{s_2}{s_1}$ ($s_1 = 1$) and $\Delta\sigma_T = \sigma_{T_1} - \sigma_{T_2}$ ($\sigma_{T_2} = 0$).

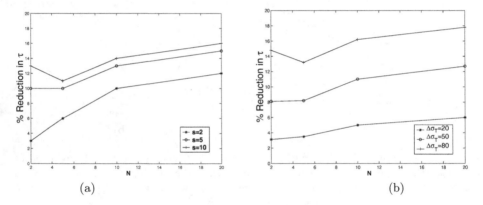

Fig. 6. Percentage reduction in average parallel execution time as a function of the number of computers (a) with a fixed $\Delta\sigma_T = \sigma_{T_1} - \sigma_{T_N} = 60$ ($\sigma_{T_N} = 0$) and (b) with a fixed $s = 5$, where $s = \frac{s_N}{s_1}$ ($s_1 = 1$) and $\Delta\sigma_T = \sigma_{T_1} - \sigma_{T_N}$ ($\sigma_{T_N} = 0$). After Step (1), $t_i = 100$ for all i.

vely. It can be seen that the percentage reduction increases as N increases. That is, the performance improvement by Step (2) becomes greater when a larger number of computers are employed. In Figure 6-(a), $\Delta\sigma_T$ is fixed independent of N. However, in reality, $\Delta\sigma_T$ would usually increase as N increases. Therefore, in such a case, one may expect a larger reduction in τ. Note that for a larger $\Delta\sigma_T$ leads to a greater reduction in τ as shown in F igure 6-(b).

5   Summary

In this paper, effects of the spatial and temporal heterogeneity on performance of a target task have been briefly reviewed first. Then, an approach to partitioning a target task for minimizing its average parallel execution time is described with a theoretical model, and performance improvement by the approach has been demonstrated. Results may be summarized as follows:

- The average parallel execution time of a target task on a given number of computers significantly increases as one or both types of heterogeneity (SH and TH) increase while its average sequential execution time is not affected by temporal heterogeneity (note that spatial heterogeneity is not defined for a single computer).
- A shorter average parallel execution time can be achieved by a careful load balancing where a fraction of target task, which is larger than the fraction determined proportional to the average computing power, is assigned to a computer with a smaller temporal heterogeneity or a higher average computing power.
- Reduction in the average parallel execution time is greater (i) when variation of the average computing power among computers is larger, (ii) when variation of the standard deviation of computing power among computers is larger, or (iii) when the number of computers employed is greater.

The current and future work includes developing an efficient load balancing scheme for heterogeneous cluster or grid computing environments, and application to channel bandwidth allocation in mobile computing.

References

1. R. Buyya, "High Performance Cluster Computing," Prentice Hall, 1999.
2. Ian Foster and Carl Kesselman (ed.), "The Grid: Blueprint for a New Computing Infrastructure," Morgan Kaufmann, 1998.
3. R.F. Freund and H. J. Siegel "Heterogeneous Processing", *Computer*, vol. 26, no.6, pp13-17, June 1993.
4. S. Ali, H. Siegel, M. Maheswaran, D. Hensgen and S. Ali, "Task Execution Time Modeling for Heterogeneous Computing Systems," *IEEE 9th Heterogeneous Computing Workshop*, pp185-199, May 2000.
5. C.-Z. Xu, L. Y. Wang, and N.-T. Fong, "Stochastic Prediction of Execution Time for Dynamic Bulk Synchronous Computations," *Proceedings of International Parallel and Distributed Processing Symposium*, San Francisco, April 2001.
6. Atakan Dogon and Fusun Ozguner, "Trading off Execution Time for Reliability in Scheduling Precedence-Constrained Tasks in Heterogeneous Computing," *Proceedings of International Parallel and Distributed Processing Symposium*, San Francisco, April 2001.
7. J. Schopf and F. Berman, "Stochastic Scheduling," *CS Dept. Technical Report*, #CS-99-03, University of California, San Diego.

8. X. Zhang and Y. Yan, "Modeling and Characterizing Parallel Computing Perfor-
    mance On Heterogeneous Networks of Workstations", *Proc. Seventh IEEE Symp.
    Parallel and Distributed Processing*, pp25-34, October 1995.
9. M. Maheswaran and H. Siegel, "A Dynamic Matching and Scheduling Algo-
    rithm for Heterogeneous Computing Systems", *Proc. Heterogeneous Computing
    '98*, pp57-69, 1998.
10. T. Thanalapati and S. Dandamudi, "An Efficient Adaptive Scheduling Scheme for
    Distributed Memory Multicomputers," *IEEE Transactions on Parallel and Dis-
    tributed Systems*, vol. 12, no. 7, pp758-768, July 2001.
11. Y. Zhang, A. Sivasubrmaniam, J. Moreira and H. Franke, "Impact of Workload
    and System Parameters on Next Generation Cluster Scheduling Mechanisms,"
    IEEE Transactions on Parallel and Distributed Systems, vol. 12, no. 9, pp967-985,
    September 2001.
12. J. Huang and S.-Y. Lee, "Effects of Spatial and Temporal Heterogeneity on Per-
    formance of a Target Task in Heterogeneous Computing Environments," to be
    presented at *the 15th ISCA International Conference on Parallel and Distributed
    Computing Systems*, September 19-21, 2002.
13. H. David, "Order Statistics," John Wiley and Sons Inc., 1970.

Source Code Transformations Strategies to Load-Balance Grid Applications*

Romaric David, Stephane Genaud, Arnaud Giersch,
Benjamin Schwarz, and Eric Violard

LSIIT-ICPS, Université Louis Pasteur, Bd S. Brant, F-67400 Illkirch (France)
Tel: +33 3 90 24 45 42 / Fax: +33 3 90 24 45 47
{david,genaud,giersch,schwarz,violard}@icps.u-strasbg.fr
http://grid.u-strasbg.fr/

Abstract. We present load-balancing strategies to improve the performances of parallel MPI applications running in a Grid environment. We analyze the data distribution constraints found in two scientific codes and propose adapted code transformations to load-balance computations. Experimental results confirm that such source code transformations can improve Grid application performances.

1 Introduction

With the growing popularity of middleware dedicated at making so-called *Grids* of processing and storage resources, network based computing will soon offer to users a dramatic increase in the available aggregate processing power. However, parallel applications have traditionally been designed for parallel computers and their executions on a Grid show poor performances. There are two major reasons for the lack of performance: first, the processors available are heterogeneous and hence the work assigned to processors is often unbalanced, and secondly the network links are orders of magnitude slower on the Grid than in a parallel computer.

Much work has been carried out to take into account such heterogeneous environments for distributed computing. However, few research works concern load-balancing strategies specifically guided by the application to be run. The well-known AppLeS project [1] uses information drawn from a specific application to schedule the execution of the application processes, but they do not modify the application source code to improve its execution. Thus, our project is original in the sense that we study how *source code transformations* may impact on the performances obtained when running applications on Grids, and eventually systematically operate these transformations so as to produce programs permanently adapted to heterogeneous environments. To validate our ideas, we work on some real scientific MPI applications.

---

* This work is supported by the French Ministry of Research through the ACI-GRID program.

M. Parashar (Ed.): GRID 2002, LNCS 2536, pp. 82–87, 2002.

This paper presents preliminary results concerning load-balancing techniques we designed to improve performances of two scientific applications. The two codes differ by their constraints on data distribution. The first one is unconstrained, it is possible to send any chunk of data to any process. The second one contains data dependencies, which implies a constrained data distribution. The next two sections describe each of the test applications. We discuss their constraints and expose the code transformation we applied to load-balance computations. We finish with some experimental results. The last section comments on the code transformations operated and discusses future work.

2   Load-Balancing for Unconstrained Data Distribution

2.1   Motivating Example: A Geophysical Application

We consider for our first experiment a geophysical code in the seismic tomography field. The parallelization of the application, presented in [2], assumes that all available processors are homogeneous (the implicit target for execution is a parallel computer). Consequently, an MPI_Scatter instruction was used, in which the root process distributes equal shares of data to each process.

We examine two methods of load-balancing this kind of application. The first one, a classical master/slave scheme, is *dynamic*. Slave processes ask a master process for a small chunk of the whole data set to compute. After computing it, the slaves ask for a new chunk and repeat this scheme until the master sends a termination message. The second one is *static*: the root process distributes the whole data set in a single communication round, except that it sends unequal shares of data whose sizes are statically computed on the basis of the processors and network performances.

We have implemented and tested both program transformations, but we focus in this study on the conditions the application must meet to implement the second load-balancing technique, and which performance results can be obtained with it.

2.2   Static Load-Balancing of Computations and Communications

The static load-balancing technique applies for SPMD programs made of rounds of simultaneous communications between all processes, followed by local computations ended by a global synchronization (which may be another communication round). Moreover, we must state further assumptions the programmer must verify before the load-balancing may take place. First, the data items in the input data set are *independent*, and secondly the number of data-items is *the only factor in time complexity*. Hence, giving any equal-size part of the domain to a given process will result in the same computation time.

Our objective is to minimize the elapsed time between two synchronization points. We consider the full overlap, single-port model of [3] in which a processor node can simultaneously receive data, send data to at most one destination, and perform some computation. As in this model the root process sends data to processes in turn, a receiving process actually begins its communication after all previous processes have been served. The root process starts its computation after all the processes have received their data. This leads to what we call a *"stair effect"*.

We explain in [4] how to compute, given the processors and network links speeds, the number of data items that should be allocated to each processor, so as to reach a load-balanced execution. Once this static load-balance computed, the MPI_Scatter instruction of the original program is replaced with an MPI_Scatterv.

2.3   Experimental Results

Our experiment consists in the computation of 827,000 data units on 16 processors. Processors are heterogeneous and located at two geographically distant sites. All machines run Globus with MPICH-G2 [5]. We made a series of benchmarks to measure processor and network performances.

The first experiment (fig. 1(a)) evaluates performances of the original program in which each process receives an equal amount of data. Non-surprisingly the processes end times largely differ, thus exhibiting an important imbalance. The second experiment (fig. 1(b)) shows the master/slave version behavior which appears well-balanced after we have finely tuned the size of data chunk sent to slaves[1].

Next, we experiment the load-balance of the scatter operation. To assess important parameters, we have first tried to load-balance using the relative processors speed ratings only (fig. 1(c)). Omitting the network parameters leaves important imbalances and gives unsatisfactory results as compared to the master/slave implementation. The last experiment (fig. 1(d)) computes the load-balance using all parameters. We obtain here the best balance, which confirms the importance of all parameters, especially to take into account the "stair effect" that clearly appears on figures 1(a,c,d). In the master/slave implementation the total communication time is short as compared to the computation time. We conclude that in the scatter implementations only a small part of the measured total time is spent in true communications of data.

3   Load-Balancing with Constrained Data Distribution

3.1   Motivating Example: An Application in Plasma Physics

Our example is an application devoted to the numerical simulation of problems in Plasma Physics and particle beams propagation. The application implements the PFC resolution method discretizing the Vlasov equation. The parallel code [6] works with any number of processors and uses a classical data decomposition

---

[1] Note that there are only 15 computation processes in this implementation since the master process only handles data distribution.

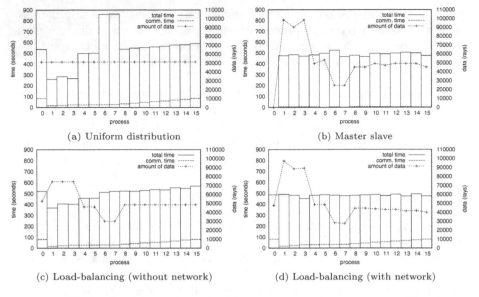

(a) Uniform distribution   (b) Master slave

(c) Load-balancing (without network)   (d) Load-balancing (with network)

Fig. 1. Experimental results (the root process is on processor 0)

technique. Matrices are split into blocks of equal size distributed by row on the processors. The code consists in a succession of computation-communication phases where the communication steps are global block matrix transpositions.

3.2 Load-Balancing through Process Emulation

In such applications where data structure must be preserved, but computations can still be spread over any number of processes, a naive solution to achieve load balancing is to make the operating system run more than one process per processor on fastest processors. Such a procedure implies a lot of system overhead, due to inter-process communications and time-sharing mechanisms. An idea to avoid this, is to rewrite the code in such a way that only one real process will compute all data given to the processes we intended to run on the given processor. In other words we *emulate* several processes by a single one.

The original program must meet the following conditions : *(i) the code works with any number of processors, (ii) the workload is evenly spread over the processors* and *(iii)* the workload *only depends on the amount of data* to be processed.

The emulation of several processes by one process consists in serializing the computations of the computation phases and changing the communication scheme. The MPI calls have to be modified in order to map emulated processes onto real processes and perform memory copy instead of communications when sender and receiver are on the same processor.

Moreover, blocking point-to-point communications such as MPI_Send have to be replaced by their non-blocking versions (e.g. MPI_Isend) in order to avoid deadlock situations. Calls to a collective communication have to be performed only once on a processor, no matter the number of emulated processes it holds. Some collective communications such as MPI_Barrier do not require any other changes whereas some others do. For example MPI_Scatter instances should be replaced by MPI_Scatterv to distribute chunks of data proportionally to the number of emulated processes on each processor. A more detailed description of the transformation process can be found in [4].

3.3   Experimental Results

For our experiments, we use our code in Plasma Physics and a subset of our test Grid made of four heterogeneous processors. We approximate the number of emulated process from speed ratings obtained from benchmarks[2]. The results show significant gains in performance.

In order to validate our code transformation, we measured the wall clock time of: (a) the initial application with one process per processor, (b) the initial application with a basic load balancing using the system to run several processes on a single processor and (c) the transformed application with a load-balancing using emulated processes. For (b) and (c), we distributed 11 processes on the four processors. Experiments were conducted for 32^4, 48^4, and 64^4 data points. Results are reported in table 1. The modified algorithm is always better than the original one, may there be or not system load-balancing.

Table 1. Elapsed time (seconds)

Size	(a) No load balancing	(b) System load balancing	(c) Emulated processes
32^4	342	525	301
48^4	2005	2223	1874
64^4	5380	4752	4404

4   Related Work

The study carried out in [8] compares dynamic versus static load-balancing strategies in an image rendering ray-tracing application. They conclude that no one scheduling strategy is best for all load conditions, and recommend to investigate further the possibilities of switching from static to dynamic load-balancing. Our experiments confirm that static load-balancing requires precise information about parameters to be efficient whereas the master/slave model naturally adapts to heterogeneous conditions. Therefore, the variance of conditions could be taken into account to request static or dynamic load-balance during execution. Providing a dedicated library to implement load-balancing is also

---

[2] Work is under progress to use theoretical results from [7] so as to find the optimal number of emulated processes.

proposed by George [9] with the `DParLib`, who addresses the problem of dynamic load-balancing via array distribution for the class of iterative algorithms with a SPMD implementation. The statistics about load-balance produced dynamically during the execution can be used to redistribute arrays from one iteration to the other. However, the library does not take into account possible communication-computation overlaps that we need in our second test application.

5 Conclusion

It appears from this study, that the source code must be finely analyzed to choose which load-balancing solution matches best the problem. In the first example, we have put forward influent parameters for static load-balancing. In the second example we have shown that a possible transformation strategy to overcome the constraints on data-distribution and keep a good communication-computation overlap can be the process emulation technique.

Future work should be done in several directions. We first need to further investigate the communication schemes used in real applications and how they perform in a Grid environment. A classification of the communication types may be used by a software tool to select appropriate transformation strategies. We also believe the programmer should interact with the tool to guide program transformations as he can bring useful information about the application.

References

1. Berman, F., Wolski, R., Figueira, S., Schopf, J., Shao, G.: Application-level scheduling on distributed heterogeneous networks. In: Proceedings of SuperComputing '96. (1996)
2. Grunberg, M., Genaud, S., Mongenet, C.: Parallel seismic ray-tracing in a global earth mesh. In: Proceedings of PDPTA'02. (2002) 1151–1157
3. Beaumont, O., Carter, L., Ferrante, J., Legrand, A., Robert, Y.: Bandwidth-centric allocation of independent tasks on heterogeneous platforms. Technical Report 4210, INRIA, Rhône-Alpes (2001)
4. David, R., Genaud, S., Giersch, A., Schwarz, B., Violard, E.: Source code transformations strategies to load-balance grid applications. Technical Report 02-09, ICPS-LSIIT, University Louis Pasteur, Pôle API, Bd. S. Brant,F-67400 Illkirch (2002)
5. Foster, I., Karonis, N.: A grid-enabled MPI: Message passing in heterogeneous distributed computing systems. Supercomputing (1998)
6. Violard, E., Filbet, F.: Parallelization of a Vlasov solver by communication overlapping. In: Proceedings of PDPTA'02. (2002)
7. Boulet, P., Dongarra, J., Robert, Y., Vivien, F.: Static tiling for heterogeneous computing platforms. Parallel Computing **25** (1999) 547–568
8. Shao, G., Wolski, R., Berman, F.: Performance effects of scheduling strategies for master/slave distributed applications. Technical Report CS98-598, UCSD CSE Dept., University of California, San Diego (1998)
9. George, W.: Dynamic load-balancing for data-parallel MPI programs. In: Message Passing Interface developers and users conference. (1999) 95–100

A Parallel CORBA Component Model for Numerical Code Coupling*

Christian Pérez, Thierry Priol, and André Ribes

IRISA/INRIA, PARIS research group
Campus de Beaulieu - 35042 Rennes Cedex, France
{Christian.Perez, Thierry.Priol, Andre.Ribes}@irisa.fr

Abstract. The fast growth of high bandwidth wide area networks has allowed the building of computational grids, which are constituted of PC clusters and/or parallel machines. Computational grids enable the design of new numerical simulation applications. For example, it is now feasible to couple several scientific codes to obtain a multi-physic application. In order to handle the complexity of such applications, software component technology appears very appealing. However, most current software component models provide no support to transparently and efficiently embed parallel codes into components. This paper describes a first study of GridCCM, an extension to the CORBA Component Model to support parallel components. The feasibility of the model is evaluated thanks to its implementation on top of two CCM prototypes. Preliminary performance results show that bandwidth is efficiently aggregated.

1 Introduction

The fast growth of high bandwidth wide area networks (WAN) allows to build computing infrastructures, known as computational grids [10]. Such infrastructures, like the TeraGrid project [3], allow the interconnection of PC clusters and/or parallel machines with high bandwidth WAN. For example, the bandwidth of the French VTHD WAN [4] is 2.5 Gb/s while TeraGrid targets 40 Gb/s bandwidth.

Thanks to the performance of grid infrastructure, new kinds of applications are enabled in the scientific numerical simulation field. In particular, it is now feasible to couple scientific codes, each code simulating a particular aspect of a physical phenomenon. For example, it is possible to perform more realistic simulation of the behavior of a satellite by incorporating all aspects of a simulation: dynamic, thermal, optic and structural mechanic. Each of these aspects is simulated by a dedicated code, which is usually a parallel code, and is executed on a set of nodes of the grid. Because of the complexity of the phenomena, these codes are developed by independent specialist teams. So, one may expect to have to couple codes written in different languages (C, C++, FORTRAN, etc) using different communication paradigms (MPI, PVM, etc).

* This work was supported by the Incentive Concerted Action "GRID" (ACI GRID) of the French Ministry of Research.

M. Parashar (Ed.): GRID 2002, LNCS 2536, pp. 88–99, 2002.

The evolution of scientific computing requires a programming model including technologies coming from both parallel and distributed computing. Parallelism is needed to efficiently exploit PC clusters or parallel machines. Distributed computing technologies are needed to control the execution and to handle communications between codes running in heterogeneous grids.

The complexity of such applications is very high with respect to design issue but also with respect to deployment issue. So, it appears that it is required to consider adequate programming models. Software component [23] appears as an appealing solution because a code coupling application can be seen as an assembly of components; each component embeds a simulation code. However, most software component models such as COM+ [20], Enterprise Java Bean [22] or CORBA Component Model [16] only support sequential component. With these models, a component is associated to a unique address space: the address space of the process where the component is created. Communication between components consists in transferring data from one address space to another one using communication mechanism such as port.

The embedding of parallel codes in sequential components raises some problems. Usually, parallel codes are executed by processes. Each process owns its private address space and uses a mechanism like MPI to exchange data with other processes (SPMD model). A first solution consists in allowing only one process to handle the component port to talk with others components. This solution leads, first, to a bottleneck in the communication between two parallel components and, second, it leads to a modification of the parallel code to introduce this master/slave pattern: the node handling the port is a kind of master, the others nodes are the slaves. A second solution would be to require that all communications have to be done through the software component model. This does not seem to be a good solution: first, it is a huge work to modify existing codes. Second, parallel oriented communication paradigm like MPI are much more tailored to parallelism while component communication paradigm is oriented toward distributed computing.

A better solution appears to let parallel components choose their communication paradigm and to allow all processes belonging to a parallel component to participate to inter-parallel component communications. Hence, a data transfer from the address spaces of the source parallel component to the address spaces of the destination component can generate several communication flows. It should include a data redistribution as the source and the destination data distribution may be different.

The only specification that we are aware with respect to high-performance components is the work done by the CCA Forum [6] (Common Component Architecture). The CCA Forum objectives are *"to define a minimal set of standard interfaces that a high-performance component framework has to provide to components, and can expect from them, in order to allow disparate components to be composed together to build a running application"*. The model, currently being developed, does not intentionally contain an accurate definition of a CCA component. It only defines a set of APIs. It is a low level mechanism: only point to point communications are defined. There is also a notion of collective ports, that allows a component to broadcast data to all the components connected to this port. While CCA's goal is to define a model specifically targets high performance computing, we aim to adapt existing standards to high performance computing.

There are several works about parallel objects like PARDIS [13] or PaCO [21]. OMG has started a normalization procedure to add data parallel features to CORBA. The adopted specification [17] requires modifications to the ORB (the CORBA core). Another work, PaCO++ [9], is an evolution of PaCO that targets efficient and portable parallel CORBA objects.

The contribution of this paper is to study the feasibility of defining and implementing parallel components within the CORBA Component Model (CCM). We choose to work with CCM because it inherently supports the heterogeneity of processors, operating system and languages; it is an open standard and there are several implementations being available with an Open Source license. Moreover, the model provides a deployment model. CORBA seems to have some limitation but it appears possible to overcome most of them. For example, we have shown that high performance can be achieved [8]. The problems related with IDL can be solved by defining and using domain specific types or valuetypes to handle complex number or graph types.

Our objective is to obtain both parallelism transparency and high performance. Transparency is required because a parallel component needs to look like a standard component at the assembly phase. The effective communications between parallel components needs to be hidden to the application designer. To obtain high performance, we propose to apply a technique that allows all processes of a parallel component to be involved in inter-component communications. Thus, inter-parallel component communications are able to remain efficient when increasing the number of node of a parallel component.

The remaining of this paper is divided as follows. Section 2 presents a brief discussion about objects and components. The CORBA component model is presented in Section 3. GridCCM, our parallel extension to the CORBA component model, is introduced in Section 4. Some preliminary experiment results are reported in Section 5. Section 6 concludes the paper.

2   From Objects to Components

Object-oriented programming has provided substantial advantages over structured programming. Recently, software component technology is expected to bring a similar evolution to software technology. While object-oriented programming targets application design, component software technology emphasizes component composition and deployment. Before introducing the software component technology, the object-oriented programming model is briefly reviewed.

2.1   Object-Oriented Programming

Object is a powerful abstraction mechanism. It has demonstrated its benefits, in particular in application design, in a very large number of applications.

However, objects have failed some of their objectives. Code reuse and maintenance are not satisfactory mainly because object dependences are not very explicit. For example, it is very difficult to find object dependences in a large application involving hundreds of objects using inheritance and delegation. Experience has shown that it is better to use an approach only based on delegation [11] that allows objects to be "composed".

For distributed applications, objects do not intrinsically provide any support for deployment. For example, neither JAVA RMI [12] nor CORBA 2 provide a way to remotely install, create or update an object.

Despite its benefits, object oriented programming lacks some important features for distributed applications. Software components aim at providing them.

2.2 Software Component

Software component technology [23] has been emerging for some years [7] even though its underlying intuition is not very recent [15]. Among all the definition of software components, here is Szyperski's one [23]: *A software component is a unit of composition with contractually specified interfaces and explicit context dependencies only. A software component can be deployed independently and is subject to composition by third parties.*

First, the main component operation is the composition with other components. This composition is done through well-defined interfaces: components need to agree on the contract related to their connected interfaces. This agreement brings a lot of advantages: it explicits the abstraction of the service. In particular, interfaces are strongly typed so that checks such as type conformance can be performed at connection time.

Second, a component inherently embeds deployment capabilities. All the information like the binary code (i.e. the code of the component), the dependencies in term of processors, operating systems and libraries are embedded into the component. A component may also embed binary codes for different processors or operating systems. The right version of the binary is automatically selected by the deployment tool. So, deployment in a heterogeneous environment is easier.

Building an application based on components emphasizes programming by *assembly*, i.e. manufacturing, rather than by *development*. Some goals are to focus expertise on domain problems, to improve software quality and to decrease the time to market thanks to reuse of existing code.

Components exhibit advantages over objects. Applications are naturally more modular as each component represents a functionality. Code reuse and code maintainability are ease as component are well-defined and independent. Last, components provide mechanisms to be deployed and to be connected in a distributed infrastructure. Thus, they appear very well suited for grid computing.

3 CORBA Component Model

The CORBA Component Model [16] (*CCM*) is going to be added to the next CORBA [18] version (version 3). The CCM specifications allow the deployment

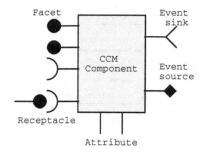

Fig. 1. A CCM component

```
foo ref =
    ServerComp->provide_FacetExample();
ClientComp->connect_FacetExample(ref);
```

Fig. 2. Example of code to connect two components.

of components into a distributed environment, that is to say that an application can deploy interconnected components on different servers.

A CORBA component is represented by a set of ports described in IDL3, an extension of CORBA's IDL2 language. There are five kinds of ports as shown in Figure 1. Facets are distinct named interfaces provided by the component for client interaction. Receptacles are named connection points that describe the component's ability to use a reference supplied by some external agent. Event sources are named connection points that emit events of a specified type to one or more interested event customers, or to an event channel. Event sinks are named connection points into which events of a specified type may be pushed. Attributes are named values exposed through accessor and mutator operations. Attributes are primarily intended to be used for component configuration, although they may be used in a variety of other ways.

Each component's life cycle is managed by an entity named *home*. To create a component, a client calls a **create** method of the component home interface.

Figure 2 shows how a component **ServerComp** is connected to component **ClientComp** through the facet **FacetExample**. First, a reference is obtained from the facet. Second, this reference is given to a receptacle. This connection is dynamically done by a third party, usually the deployment tool. Consequently, connexions can be changed during component's life.

4   A Parallel CORBA Component Model: GridCCM

The CORBA component model is an interesting component model mainly because its deployment model. However, it provide no efficient support to embed parallel codes into components. This section presents GridCCM, a parallel extension to the CORBA Component Model (CCM). A GridCCM's goal is to study the concept of parallel component.

4.1   Overview

Our objective is to encapsulate parallel codes into CORBA components with as few modifications to parallel codes as possible. Similarly, we target to extend

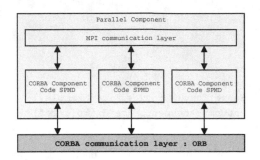

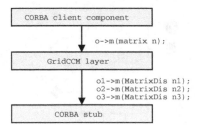

Fig. 3. Parallel component concept

Fig. 4. The user invokes a method on a remote component. The Grid-CCM layer actually invokes the distributed version of this method.

CCM but not to introduce deep modifications in the model. That's why, we don't allow ourselves to modify the CORBA's Interface Definition Language (IDL).

We currently restrict ourselves to embed SPMD (*Single Program Multiple Data*) codes into a parallel component. In a SPMD code, each process executes the same program but on different data. This choice stems from two considerations. First, many parallel codes are indeed SPMD. Second, SPMD codes bring a manageable execution model.

Figure 3 shows our vision of a parallel component in the CORBA framework. The SPMD code continues to be able to use MPI for its inter-process communications but it uses CORBA to communicate with other components. In order to avoid bottlenecks, all processes of a parallel component participate to inter-component communications. This scheme has been successfully demonstrated with parallel CORBA object [9]: an aggregated bandwidth of 103 MB/s (820 Mb/s) has been obtained on VTHD [4], a French high-bandwidth WAN, between two 11-nodes CORBA parallel objects.

GridCCM's objective is to extend CCM to allow an efficient encapsulation of SPMD codes. For example, GridCCM has to be able to aggregate bandwidth when two parallel components exchange data. As data may need to be redistributed during communications, GridCCM model has to support it as transparently as possible. The client should only have to describe how its data are locally distributed and the data should be automatically redistribute accordingly to the server's preferences. A GridCCM component should appear as close as possible to a *sequential* component. For example, a sequential component should connect itself to a parallel component without noticing it is a *parallel* component.

To achieve these objectives, GridCCM introduces the notion of parallel component. Our definition of a parallel component is: *a parallel component is a collection of identical sequential components. It executes in parallel all or some parts of its services.*

The designer of a parallel component needs to describe the parallelism of the component in an auxiliary XML file. This file contains a description of the parallel methods of the component, the distributed arguments of these methods and the expected distribution of the arguments. An example is given in section 4.4.

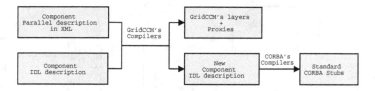

Fig. 5. The different compilation phase to generate a parallel component

4.2   Introducing Parallelism Support into CCM

To introduce parallelism support, like data redistribution, without requiring modifications to the ORB, we choose to introduce a new software layer between client's code and stub's code as illustrated in Figure 4. This scheme has been successfully used with PaCO++ [9] for a similar problem: the management of parallel CORBA objects.

The role of the GridCCM layer is to allow a transparent management of the parallelism. A call to a parallel method of a parallel component is intercepted by this new layer. The layer sends the distributed data from the client nodes to the server nodes. The data redistribution can actually be performed on the client side, on the server side or during the communication between the client and the server. The decision depends on several constraints like feasibility (mainly memory requirements) and efficiency (client network performance versus server network performance). Another goal is to manage parallel exceptions [14].

The parallel management layer is generated by a compiler specific to Grid-CCM, as illustrated in Figure 5. This compiler uses two files: an IDL description of the component and a XML description of the component parallelism. In order to have a transparent layer, a new IDL description is generated during the generation of the component. GridCCM layer internally uses an interface derived from the original interface. The new IDL interface is the interface that is remotely invokes on the server side. The original IDL interface is used between the user code and the GridCCM layer on the client and the server sides.

In the new IDL interface, the user arguments described as distributed have been replaced by their equivalent distributed data types. Because of this transformation, there are some constraints about the types that can be distributed. The current implementation requires the user type to be an IDL **sequence** type, that is to say a 1D array. So, one dimension distribution can automatically be applied. This scheme can easily be extended for multidimensional arrays: a 2D array can be mapped to a sequence of sequences. It is worthwhile to note that IDL type do not allow a direct mapping of "scientific" types like multidimensional arrays or complex number. However, CORBA is just a communication technology. Higher level environments, like code coupling environments such as HLA [5] or MpCCI [2], should be able to overcome the CORBA type system limitation as described in the introduction.

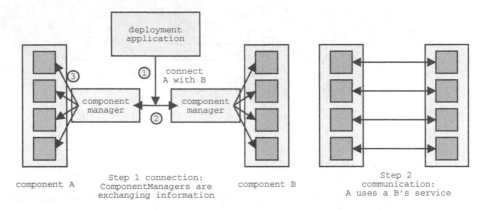

Fig. 6. Connection between two parallel components

4.3 Home and Component Proxies

One of our objectives is to allow a parallel component to be seen as a sequential component. So, the nodes of a parallel component and the nodes of the component homes are not directly exposed to other components. We introduced two entities, named the *HomeManager* and the *ComponentManager*. They are proxies respectively for the nodes homes and for the parallel component's nodes.

An application that needs to create a parallel component interacts in the CCM standard way with the *HomeManager* instead of using each nodes home. The *HomeManager* is configured during the deployment phase. The references to all the nodes homes are given through a specific interface to the *HomeManager*. Then, the *HomeManager* calls the homes on all the nodes.

Similarly, when a client gets a reference to a parallel component, it actually has a reference to the *ComponentManager*. When two parallel components are connected, the *ComponentManager*s transparently exchange information about the parallel components so as to configure GridCCM's layers.

Figure 6 shows an example of connection between two parallel components: A and B. First, the deployment tool connects A with B using the standard CCM protocol (see Figure 2). Second, A's *ComponentManager* asks B's *Component-Manager* for information. For example, component B gives the references of all B's nodes to component A. Third, A's *ComponentManager* configures the layers of all A's nodes. Fourth, when component A performs a call to a B's service, all A's nodes may participate to the communication with B's nodes.

4.4 Example

This example illustrates the definition and the use of a parallel component.

A component, named *A*, provides a port of name *myPort* which contains an operation that computes the average of a vector. Figure 7 shows the IDL description of the component and the IDL description of the *Average* interface. The facet and the interface are described without CCM's IDL modifications.

```
// Average definition
typedef sequence<long> Vector;
interface Average {
  long compute(in Vector v);
};
// ExParComponent definition
component A {
  provides Average myPort;
};
```

Fig. 7. A component IDL definition

```
// Parallelism definition
Component: A
Port     : myPort
Port Type: Average
Operation: compute
Argument1: bloc
Result   : noReduction
```

Fig. 8. Parallelism description of the facet

```
// Get a reference to the facet myPort
Average avg = aComponent.get_connection_myPort();
// Configure it with a GridCCM API
avg.init_compute('bloc',0); // 1st arg is bloc distributed
// ''Standard'' CCM call
avg.compute(MyMatrixPart);
```

Fig. 9. A client initializes and uses a parallel operation

The component implementer needs to write an XML file to describe the parallelism of component *A*. This file, shown in figure 8, is not presented in XML for the sake of clarity. An important remark is that this file is not seen by the client. In this example, the operation *compute* is declared parallel and its first argument is block distributed.

Standard clients normally use the *myPort* facet. A parallel client has to specify how the data to be sent are locally distributed. Figure 9 shows an example of the API. Its specification is not yet stable mainly because we work at allowing external redistribution library [1] to be plugged. In the example of Figure 9, the client gets a reference of the facet *myPort*. Then, it configures its local GridCCM layer with the method *init_compute* before invoking the *compute* operation.

5   Preliminary Experiments

This section presents some preliminary experiments that evaluate the feasibility and the scalability of GridCCM. They also show that the model is generic with respect to two different CCM implementations. First, the experimental protocol is presented and, second, some performance measurements are reported.

5.1   Experimental Protocol

The experimental setup, shown in Figure 10, contains two parallel components (*Customer* and *Server*), a GridCCM-aware sequential component and a standard sequential CORBA client. First, the standard CORBA client creates a vector and sends it to the sequential component. Second, the vector is sent to *Customer* with

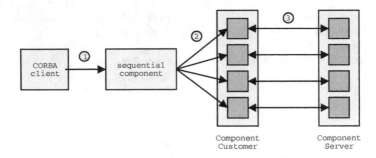

Fig. 10. Experimental protocol

Number of nodes of	Aggregate bandwidth in MB/s	
parallel components	Java compiled (JIT)	C++
1	8.3	9.8
2	16.6	19.6
4	33.2	39.2
8	66.4	78.4

Fig. 11. Bandwidth between component *Customer* and component *Server*. The two parallel components have with the same cluster size.

an automatic distribution in *Customer*'s nodes according to a bloc distribution. Third, *Customer* invokes a *Server*'s service which takes the distributed vector as an in-out argument. The *Server* method implementation contains only a MPI barrier. Then, the vector is sent back to *Customer*. In this example, the two parallel components use MPI. *Customer* uses MPI for barriers and reductions. *Server* only uses MPI for barriers.

There is no modification in the sequential component code to call a *Customer*'s parallel service. The parallel service is transparent for the sequential code. With regard to the connection, the deployment application complies with the CCM specification. The *ComponentManager*s perform their role correctly since the parallel component nodes are connected without user intervention.

5.2   Performance Measurements

We have implemented a preliminary prototype of GridCCM on top of two CCM implementations: OpenCCM [24] and MicoCCM [19]. Our first prototype has been derived from OpenCCM [24]. OpenCCM is made by the research laboratory LIFL (*Laboratoire Infomatique Fondamentale de Lille*). It is written in Java. The second prototype has been derived from MicoCCM [19]. MicoCCM is an *OpenSource* implementation based on the Mico ORB. It is written in C++.

The test platform is a cluster of 16 dual-pentium III 1 Ghz with 512 MB of memory interconnected with a Fast Ethernet network and a gigabit switch. For OpenCCM, the Java Runtime Environment is the SUN JDK 1.3 and ORBacus 4.0.5 is the used ORB.

The measures have been made in the first parallel component (*Customer*). After a MPI barrier to synchronize all *Customer*'s nodes, the start time is measured. *Customer* performs 1000 calls to *Server*. Then, the end time is taken.

The aggregated bandwidth between the two parallel components is shown in Figure 11 for different sizes of the parallel components. First, bandwidth is efficiently aggregated. Second, as expected C++ implementation is more efficient than the Java one. Last, the latency for the 8-node to 8-node case is 215 μs for MicoCCM. This is the latency observed for plain MicoCCM over a Fast Ethernet network. The GridCCM layer, without data redistribution, does not add a significant overhead.

In conclusion, these preliminary experiments show that parallel components can be achieved without exhibiting overhead on classical networks. In the future, we plan to evaluate more accurately GridCCM overhead using PadicoTM [8] to have a high performance CORBA environment. With PadicoTM, a point-to-point latency of 20 μs and a point-to-point bandwidth of 240 MB/s have been measured on a Myrinet-2000 network. On such network, MPI has a latency of 11 μs and a bandwidth of 240 MB/s.

6   Conclusion

Computing grids allow new kinds of application to be developed. For example, code coupling applications can benefit a lot from grids because grids provide very huge computing, networking and storage resources. However, the distributed and heterogeneous nature of grids raises many problems to application designer. Software component technology appears to be a very promising technology to handle such problems. However, software component models do not offer a transparent and efficient support to embed parallel codes into components.

The first contribution of this paper is to describe a first study of the extension of the CORBA Component Model in order to introduce parallel components. Another contribution is to have successfully integrated the proposed model into two existing CCM prototypes. With both prototypes, the preliminary performance results have shown that the model is able to aggregated bandwidth without introducing noticeable overhead. However, more experiments need to be done.

The next step of our work is to finalize the GridCCM model, in particular with respect to parallel component exceptions. Regarding to security issue, a parallel component should behave as a standard CORBA component. Supporting fault tolerance feature is a more complex issue that needs to be further investigated. Moreover, the prototype needs to be finalized. In particular, the current GridCCM layer is mainly hand-written. A dedicated compiler will soon be operational. Last, we plan to test the model with real applications. One of them will be an EADS code coupling application which involves five MPI codes.

References

1. The DARPA data reorganization effort. http://www.data-re.org.
2. MpCCI - mesh-based parallel code coupling interface. http://www.mpcci.org.
3. The TeraGrid project. http://www.teragrid.org.
4. The VTHD project. http://www.vthd.org.
5. IEEE standard for modeling and simulation (M&S) high level architecture (HLA)—federate interface specification. IEEE Standard 1516, September 2000.
6. R. Armstrong, D. Gannon, A. Geist, K. Keahey, S. Kohn, L. McInnes, S. Parker, and B. Smolinski. Toward a common component architecture for high-performance scientific computing. In *Proceeding of the 8th IEEE International Symposium on High Performance Distributed Computation*, August 1999.
7. L. Barroca, J. Hall, and P. Hall. *Software Architectures: Advances and Applications*, chapter An Introduction and History of Software Architectures, Components, and Reuse. Springer Verlag, 1999.
8. A. Denis, C. Pérez, and T. Priol. Towards high performance CORBA and MPI middlewares for grid computing. In Graig A. Lee, editor, *Proc of the 2nd International Workshop on Grid Computing*, number 2242 in LNCS, pages 14–25, Denver, Colorado, USA, November 2001. Springer-Verlag.
9. A. Denis, C. Pérez, and T. Priol. Portable parallel CORBA objects: an approach to combine parallel and distributed programming for grid computing. In *Proc. of the 7th Intl. Euro-Par'01 conf.*, pages 835–844, Manchester, UK, 2001. Springer.
10. I. Foster and C. Kesselman, editors. *The Grid: Blueprint for a New Computing Infracstructure*. Morgan Kaufmann Publishers, Inc, 1998.
11. Erich Gamma, Richard Helm, Ralph Johnson, and John Vlissides. *Design Patterns*. Addison Wesley, 1995.
12. William Grosso. *Java RMI*. O'Reilly & Associates, 2001.
13. K. Keahey and D. Gannon. PARDIS: A Parallel Approach to CORBA. In *Supercomputing'97*. ACM/IEEE, November 1997.
14. Hanna Klaudel and Franck Pommereau. A concurrent semantics of static exceptions in a parallel programming language. In J.-M. Colom and M. Koutny, editors, *Applications and theory of Petri nets*, volume 2075 of *Lecture Notes in Computer Science*, pages 204–223. Springer, 2001.
15. M. D. McIlroy. Mass Produced Software Components. In P. Naur and B. Randell, editors, *Software Engineering*, pages 138–155, Brussels, 1969. Scientific Affairs Division, NATO.
16. OMG. Corba 3.0 new components chapters, nov 2001. Document ptc/2001-11-03.
17. OMG. Data parallel CORBA. Technical report, 2001. Document orbos/01-10-19.
18. OMG. The Common Object Request Broker: Architecture and Specification (Revision 2.5). OMG Document formal/01-09-34, September 2001.
19. Frank Pilhofer. The MICO CORBA component project. http://www.fpx.de/MicoCCM.
20. David S. Platt. *Understanding COM+*. Microsoft Press, 1999.
21. C. René and T. Priol. MPI code encapsulating using parallel CORBA object. In *Proceedings of the Eighth IEEE International Symposium on High Performance Distributed Computing*, pages 3–10, August 1999.
22. E. Specification and S. June. Enterprise JavaBeans Specification, 1999.
23. C. Szyperski. *Component Software - Beyond Object-Oriented Programming*. Addison-Wesley / ACM Press, 1998.
24. M. Vadet, P. Merle, R. Marvie, and J.-M. Geib. The OpenCCM platform. http://corbaweb.lifl.fr/OpenCCM/.

Meaning and Behaviour
in Grid Oriented Components

Anthony Mayer, Stephen McGough, Murtaza Gulamali,
Laurie Young, Jim Stanton, Steven Newhouse, and John Darlington

London e-Science Centre, Imperial College of Science, Technology and Medicine,
London, SW7 2BZ, UK
icpc-sw@doc.ic.ac.uk
http://www.lesc.ic.ac.uk/

Abstract. The ICENI middleware utilises information captured within
a component based application in order to facilitate Grid-based scheduling. We describe a system of application related meta-data that features
a separation of concerns between meaning, behaviour and implementation, which allows for both communication and implementation selection
at run-time, while providing the user with a flow-based programming
model. It is shown that this separation enables a flexible approach to
scheduling, and eases the integration of components with disparate control flow patterns or data types, by means of converters and tees for collective communication. By explicitly recording application information
and supporting multiple scheduling approaches, communication protocols and component applications, while retaining OGSA compatibility,
the ICENI component model is ideally suited to Grid computing.

1 Introduction

ICENI, the Imperial College e-Science Networked Infrastructure, is an experimental framework for Grid computing that supports the complete top-down
utilisation of grid resources for scientific applications. The application framework within ICENI features the use of component based technology to capture
information regarding an application's structure.

In this paper we describe the incremental development of this system, and a
second generation component description language which features a separation
of component meaning, behaviour and implementation. This separation isolates
meaning, based upon typed dataflow between components, from the associating
flow of control. User construction of an application relies exclusively upon the information in the meaning level. The behaviour and implementation information
are used to build performance models to facilitate scheduling and implementation, and to inform communication selection.

2 Meta-data

In previous works [1,2], we have made the observation that information is key to
the successful exploitation of the Grid - information about the resources them-

M. Parashar (Ed.): GRID 2002, LNCS 2536, pp. 100–111, 2002.
© Springer-Verlag Berlin Heidelberg 2002

selves, information regarding the user's requirements, and information about the applications that are to operate upon the Grid. The ICENI component framework captures information relating to the application, its structure and the inter-component data and control flow.

2.1 Separation: Meaning, Behaviour and Implementation

We identify three concerns within the grid-oriented component model, all of which are independent, and through their interaction suffice to define the nature of the application. Each of these three categories of meta-data has a role to play in the grid deployment of a component.

Meaning From the user's perspective it is essential that a software component is endowed with meaning, in particular its composability with other components. As components are defined principally through their interactions with each other we attach meaning to the flow of data between components. Thus the highest level of abstraction is that of typed dataflow, shorn of control flow information.

Behaviour Separate from the component's meaning in terms of dataflow is *how* the data is passed from one component to another, and what dependencies exist between the dataflow relations described in the component's meaning. Thus the component's *behaviour* is a distinct concern, but necessary for scheduling and other grid-oriented tasks.

Implementation The implementation of the component also possess meta-data, in the form of the concrete format of data passed through the ports, performance characteristics of the computation that occurs when control is passed to the component, and the platform and operating system that this particular implementation may be deployed upon.

These three concerns are independent, though overlapping. Every component instance will have a single meaning, behaviour and implementation. On the other hand, a single meaning may have multiple behaviours, and a single behaviour may have multiple implementations. While the user manipulates components in terms of their meaning, behaviours and implementations may be selected by the Grid middleware, providing a flexibility necessary for effective application deployment on the Grid.

2.2 Meta-data Representation

A component is described by a set of documents that capture its meaning, behaviour and implementation. These documents use three different XML realisations, a Component Definition Language (CDL), Behaviour Definition Language (BDL) and Implementation Definition Language (IDL) for meaning, control concerns and software issues respectively.

Each component possess a set of ports, through which all communication passes. The meaning document captures the abstract dataflow through the ports, the behaviour document records the control flow through the same ports, while the implementation description document specifies the actual data format of passed messages, together with the performance characteristics associated with the port's behaviour.

Each XML document provides annotations for the same port, which has a unique name (within the component definition). The port characteristics are as follows:

CDL A port represents the production or consumption of data. As such at the meaning level a port has an associated dataflow, **in**, **out**, or **exchange**. An inport represents the consumption of data, an outport its production, while exchange represents a port which performs both. Inports and outports possess an abstract data type, which identify the type consumed or produced, respectively. Exchanges possess two types, indicating the flow in and out of the port.

BDL The BDL document provides additional control information for the ports - each port must correspond to a CDL port. Control flow is specified as being **in** or **out**. Any of the dataflow directions may possess either of the control-flow directions. The various combinations may be interpreted as different forms of message passing behaviour as indicated in Table 1. Those components which possess control flow in also possess a **dependency**, which indicates which other component ports are accessed following the arrival of control flow.

IDL The IDL defines concrete data types, including the precise format of the data, for all of the component's ports. Additionally the IDL includes performance characteristics for those ports which have a control flow **in**.

These markup languages are designed to be extensible. In the future we may extend the CDL with additional "meaning" information, regarding a component's mathematical properties for example, or augment the IDL performance metadata with information regarding the implementation's security characteristics, or fault tolerance, for example.

Table 1. Interpretations of the Data and Control Flow Annotations

	Dataflow In	Dataflow Out	Exchange
Control Flow In	Message Receive *push*	Method Offered (no arguments) *pull*	Method Offered (arguments) *pull*
Control Flow Out	Method Call (no arguments) *pull*	Message Send *push*	Method Call (arguments) *push*

2.3   Example: Finite Difference Method

The Finite Difference Method solves sets of partial differential equations in n dimensions over a given region of space where the final state of the boundary is known. Figure 1 illustrates the construction of the Finite Difference Method solver as a component architecture within ICENI. The solver component requires two inputs, the stencil operation (derived from the partial differential equations) and a description of the space that the differential operator is to be applied to. The latter includes such information as the portion of space that is to be solved, the boundary conditions for the space and the initial grid resolution. A display component is also attached to display the final result.

Example CDL, BDL and IDL documents for the FDM solver component are shown in Table 2.

2.4   User Level Application Composition

An application is composed by the user from component instances by using information at the 'meaning' meta-data level. The end-user making the composition ideally avoids all reference to corresponding behaviour and implementation annotations for their component types. An application consists of a set of component instances, together with a set of links, defined as an ordered pair of component ports. The types of the component ports (in terms of their abstract meaning-level type) must be the same, and the dataflow directions must be compatible, i.e. a dataflow in port must be connected to a dataflow out port, while an exchange must be connected to an exchange.

The links thus represent channels of data flow passing between concurrently existing components. At this level of abstraction the component composition is an example of *Flow Based Programming* [3]. This means that all control flow issues are hidden from the end-user, simplifying the task of connecting components with different control flow patterns. As long as the data types and direction of information flow is correct, components can be composed. Each link connects only two ports, and each port may only have one attached link. Collective communication between multiple ports is discussed in Section 3.1.

The details of binding different components together, in terms of behaviour and their software, is left to the middleware (see Section 2.7). This delegation to the middleware is made possible by the encapsulation of the control issues, and the isolation of the meaning (in terms of dataflow) as relevant to the user.

2.5   Application Description Document

Application composition produces an application description document, which is passed to the scheduling system. This document consists of specifications to create new component instances, and to establish links between component instances, either those newly created or currently executing. Though application description document is an XML document, we represent it as a flow diagram, as it is intended that composition will take place using visual programming

Table 2. Meta-Data and Derived Java Interfaces for the FDM Solver

CDL: Meaning	BDL: Behaviour	IDL: Implementation
`<componentDefinitionDocument name="FDM Meanings">`	`<behaviourDescriptionDocument>`	`<implementationDescriptionDocument name="FDM implementations">`
`<componentTypeDefinition>`	`<behaviour ComponentDescriptionDocument ="FDM_cdl.xml">`	`<implementation ComponentDescriptionDocument ="FDM_cdl.xml">`
`<componentTypeName> FDMSolver </componentTypeName>`	`<componentName> FDMSolver </componentName>`	`<componentName> FDMSolver </componentName>`
`<port> <name>stencil</name> <portTypeDefinition> <ddl:adt> StencilOperation </ddl:adt> </portTypeDefinition> <dataflow>in</dataflow> </port>`	`<behaviourName> Pull Model </behaviourName>` `<software>idl.xml</software>` `<portBehaviour> <name> stencil </name> <controlFlowOut/> </portBehaviour>`	`<implementationName> DefaultImplementation </implementationName>` `<portImplementation> <name>stencil</name> <dataStruct> icpc.FDM.Stencil </dataStruct> </portImplementation>`
`<port> <name>spaceDescriptionIn </name> <portTypeDefinition> <ddl:adt> SpaceDescription </ddl:adt> </portTypeDefinition> <dataflow>in</dataflow> </port>`	`<portBehaviour> <name> spaceDescriptionIn </name> <controlFlowOut/> </portBehaviour>`	`<portImplementation> <name>spaceDescriptionIn</name> <dataStruct> icpc.FDM.SpaceDescription </dataStruct> </portImplementation>`
`<port> <name>matrixOut</name> <portTypeDefinition> <ddl:adt> matrix </ddl:adt> </portTypeDefinition> <dataflow>out</dataflow> </port>`	`<portBehaviour> <name> matrixOut </name> <controlFlowIn> <dependency> <sequential> <call portName="stencil"/> <call portName="spaceDescriptionIn"> </sequential> </dependency> </controlFlowIn> </portBehaviour>`	`<portImplementation> <name>matrixOut</name> <dataStruct> icpc.matrix.DgeRCj </dataStruct> </portImplementation>`
`</componentTypeDefinition>` `<componentTypeDefinition>` `... other components ...` `</componentDefinitionDocument>`	`</behaviour>` `</behaviourDescriptionDocument>`	`</implementation>` `... other components ...` `</implementationDescriptionDocument>`

Required Interface (Component)	Middleware Interface (Context Object)

`public interface FDM_Interface`
`                extends GridComponent {`
 	
`    public icpc.matrix.DgeRCj matrixOut();`
`}`
	`public interface FDM_Middleware`
	`                extends ContextObject {`
	
	`    public icpc.FDM.stencil stencil();`
	
	`    public icpc.FDM.spaceDescriptor`
	`                spaceDescriptionIn();`
	`}`

tools. Indeed, the current ICENI version includes a functional visual composition tool [1].

Figure 1 below shows the application description document for the Finite Difference Method application. In this, and other figures, each application description document is represented by a dotted box surrounding component instances

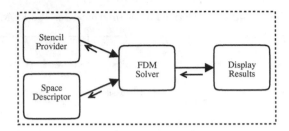

Fig. 1. The Finite Difference Method Applicaton Structure

and links. Documents can refer to existing components in other documents by a unique identifier. Links are represented by arrows with solid heads, indicating the direction of dataflow. Control flow is also indicated with additional annotation arrows with hollow heads. Control flow directions would not be visible to the user, but are shown here for illustrative purposes.

2.6   Software Bindings

The XML annotations that describe the component are used to construct the software bindings that allow the component to interact with the middleware and hence the grid environment. The XML may be mapped to more than one set of bindings - our current system can create both Java interfaces and WSDL (Web Service Definition Language) documents for a given component definition. This extensibility is a key strength of the annotation technique. If one were to define the component with Java interfaces directly, OGSA compatibility via web services would be lost, while restricting to the WSDL document forces one into a particular paradigm. (See Section 4 for further discussion on this point).

Where Java software bindings are created, two interfaces are produced for each component definition. These automatically generated interfaces form a contract for the component developer. The first Java interface, relating to the software component, must be implemented by the component developer. The second Java interface defines a context object which is provided by the middleware at run-time. In order to access the middleware functions or communicate with other components, the user code may call the provided methods of the context object. Thus there is a fair trade for the component developer - in exchange for implementing an interface (which grants access to the middleware and hence other components) the user code is provided with the means to itself access the middleware and other components.

A similar situation results with the automatically generated GSDL (Grid Services Definition Language) documents, in that they define a component as a GridService, and as such they may utilise the OGSA tools to access and be accessed by other OGSA compliant entities.

2.7   Behaviour and Implementation Selection

Once the application description document is submitted for execution, it is necessary to match the available BDL and IDL information for the specified component types. Typically a behaviour will have many implementations (the component code compiled for different architecture options), while an implementation will have only one corresponding behaviour. The middleware must choose between implementations, each with their associated behaviour.

The choice of implementation is made by analysing the control flow paths between the the components, as discussed in our previous works on the subject [2,4]. With the enhanced XML, the dependency information used to build the call graph of the application is not stored in "outports", but is attached to any port with control flow **in**. Thus while pull mode methods have dependency where data flows out, push mode messages have dependency attached when they arrive.

Where legacy codes are used, they will possess only a single behaviour and implementation, and in as such there is no selection at this stage. Nevertheless the annotations provided in the CDL, BDL and IDL are used during scheduling (see Section 4).

2.8   Communication Selection

From the component developer's point of view, implementing communication features ends with the satisfaction of the automatically generated software bindings. The actual connections between the run-time components are decided and instantiated by the middleware according to the relative positions of the endpoints. For example, where two components are scheduled to execute on the same machine, the middleware can use conventional procedure calls, or low-latency MPI [5] libraries. For distributed execution remote procedure calls, Java RMI or SOAP [6] may be employed. This system's strength is its flexibility. The scheduler can schedule according to the available resources and requirements, and as long as the software bindings are adhered to, any convenient protocol may be used.

3   Advanced Issues and Case Studies

While the separation of concerns and static component model outlined above prove extremely flexible in terms of middleware selection and application construction, a number of applications require more sophisticated structures. These aspects are the subject of ongoing research within the London e-Science Centre. The research uses the ICENI component system to support practical applications. These serve as case studies that illustrate various features of the model, and deal with ongoing areas of our research.

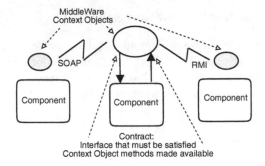

Fig. 2. Communication Selection via Middleware

3.1   Collective Communication

While each link only connects two ports, and each port may only have one
attached link, collective communication between multiple ports is facilitated by
means of tees. Examples of some possible tees are given in Figure 3, though this
list is by no means exhaustive.

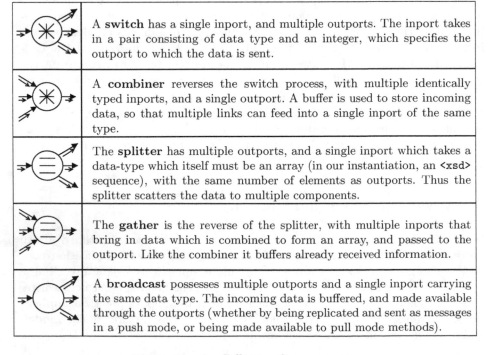

	A **switch** has a single inport, and multiple outports. The inport takes in a pair consisting of data type and an integer, which specifies the outport to which the data is sent.
	A **combiner** reverses the switch process, with multiple identically typed inports, and a single outport. A buffer is used to store incoming data, so that multiple links can feed into a single inport of the same type.
	The **splitter** has multiple outports, and a single inport which takes a data-type which itself must be an array (in our instantiation, an `<xsd>` sequence), with the same number of elements as outports. Thus the splitter scatters the data to multiple components.
	The **gather** is the reverse of the splitter, with multiple inports that bring in data which is combined to form an array, and passed to the outport. Like the combiner it buffers already received information.
	A **broadcast** possesses multiple outports and a single inport carrying the same data type. The incoming data is buffered, and made available through the outports (whether by being replicated and sent as messages in a push mode, or being made available to pull mode methods).

Fig. 3. Tees for Collective Communication

These tees are created using automatic code generation, which takes in the specified data type, together with a given number of ports, and produces the tee code together with the associated component description XML. From the user perspective control flow remains concealed - it is generated automatically along with the code for the tee. Hence while the user selects the tee manually to satisfy their requirements at the level of meaning, the behaviour and implementation of the tee are middleware generated.

3.2   Tees Case Study: GENIE

Grid Enabled Integrated Earth system model (GENIE) [1] aims to simulate the long term evolution of the Earth's climate, by coupling together individual models of the climate system. The constituents may include models for the Earth's atmosphere, ocean, sea-ice, marine sediments, land surface, vegetation and soil, hydrology, ice sheets and the biogeochemical cycling within and between components. GENIE aims to be a modular and scalable simulation of the Earth's climate, allowing for individual models in the system to be easily added or replaced by alternatives.

Figure 4 illustrates the organisation of the application. The simulation components communicate with each other through an integration component. This component also performs tasks requiring data from all the simulation components (e.g. describing the heat exchange between the surface of the ocean and the base of the atmosphere), and is designed to be extendable to allow further simulation components to be added to the system in future.

A control component manages the flow of information between each of the components in the GENIE framework. It also allows communication of the simulation data with external resources such as visualisation and steering components (see Section 3.3).

This particular case study demonstrates the flexibility of the component system at design time. Multiple simulation components may be attached to the integration component by the application builder as she sees fit. This requires no change to the integration component itself: as long as it can handle multiple simulation components (with a parameter passed as data by the setup component), the actual collective communication is organised using tees.

3.3   Factories

While the composition and deployment system outlined above is essentially static, in that a complete application is composed and deployed as a single unchanging unit, it may be extended to realise dynamic programming by making multiple submissions of connected applications to the scheduling system.

A *factory* component is a component capable of creating an XML application description document and submitting it to the middleware's scheduling

[1] a recently funded Natural Environment Research Council e-Science pilot project

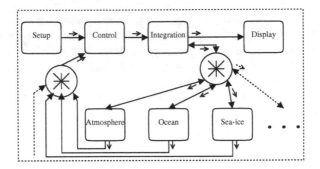

Fig. 4. GENIE Application Structure

system. This is done at run-time, and thus the created application may be data dependent. An example of this form of behaviour is given in Section 3.4.

The links in an application description document may refer to either a port on a new component instance (specified within the application description document), or to any already existing component instance. Thus the factory can create a new subset of components at run-time, and connect them to the already existing components (such as itself), given that it can access the middleware to identify them.

As a port can only possess one attached link, the scheduling of a new link replaces the pre-existing one. Thus factories may rewire the network of existing components as well as generating new components. In this way completely dynamic behaviour is expressible, while at the same time restricting all component creation to occur through the middleware scheduling system.

A factory component accesses the middleware through methods made available through the context object (for Java software bindings), or by being declared as a Factory (for the OGSA-WSDL bindings).

3.4   Factories Case Study:
Parameter Sweep of Acoustic Scattering Application

This application is a parameter study, in which the the acoustical back scatter from a number of different submarines is computed across a range of designs, and the optimal design is subsequently identified according to some user defined criteria. The acoustical simulation is performed with an independently written application, DRACS [7], while other components extend the single application to a full parameter study. A Design Generator component produces design specifications for a number of submarines. Each submarine design is then converted to a three dimensional unstructured mesh (the required input to DRACS) by a Mesh Generation component. DRACS then runs inside a component wrapper to perform the analysis and the back scatter data is passed to an analysis component, which may request that the Design Generator produces a new generation of submarines if none of the results are acceptable, within the user's tolerance range. This is shown in Figure 5.

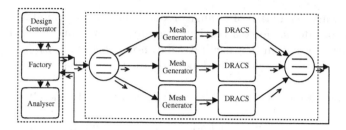

Fig. 5. Acoustic Scattering Parameter Study

This application highlights dynamic component creation, as the number of submarines analysed per generation is data dependent. As such, an analysis factory component launches a secondary application (containing the parameter sweeps) and connects to it during the execution cycle of the primary application.

4   Related and Further Work

The ICENI component model is complimentary to the Open Services Grid Architecture [8], which is rapidly becoming the accepted standard for gird based development. The ICENI model deliberately adopts the notion of standard grid life cycle interfaces within its software bindings and the notion of factory components, which may be realised by the OGSA FactoryServices. Thus an executing component may be exposed as a service within the OGSA model. Component software services may be discovered and utilised using a Service Oriented Architecture lookup process. We have described how ICENI components may be exposed as both Jini and OCSA services in a companion paper [9]. What the ICENI model adds to the Service Oriented Architecture design is information, beyond the software bindings provided by OGSA and the underlying Web Services technology, which remains immature in terms of control flow descriptions.

The explicit meta-data provided by the ICENI system allows implementation and communication selection as described above. Additionally it enables the constuction of dataflow and control flow graphs that facilitate scheduling on the distributed resources made available by ICENI [1].

5   Conclusion

The ICENI component model has been extended to include a separation of concerns between meaning and behaviour, as well as implementation. This gives the ICENI grid user the following added value:

- Flow based programming model hides control and thread issues from the end-user, easing application development. Tees explicitly enable collective communication within this model.

- Enables easy generation of a range of 'contract' software bindings - the XML annotations do not force a particular model on the component developer.
- Provides information that facilitates dataflow scheduling, while retaining the control- and dependency-based performance modelling of previous ICENI work [4].
- The model is OGSA compatible, but not restricted to the OGSA view.

In effect the component model adds value by adding information to existing or novel applications. This information, in terms of meaning and behaviour, provides a greater handle on the code and its composition than a standard 'interface' or simple software binding can produce. It allows a range of automated composition and selection techniques at various levels of abstraction - costing the user or component developer nothing, but enabling exploitation of the grid resources.

Acknowledgements

This work is funded by the UK DTI/EPSRC e-Science Core Programme (THBB/C/008/00023) and by EPSRC grants GR/R74505/01 and GR/R67699/01. The equipment used in this work was funded through HEFCE JREI awards GR/R04034/01 and GR/M92355/01.

References

1. N. Furmento, A. Mayer, S. McGough, S. Newhouse, and J. Darlington. A Component Framework for HPC Applications. In *Euro-Par 2001, Parallel Processing*, volume 2150 of *LNCS*, pages 540–548. Springer-Verlag, 2001.
2. A. Mayer. *Composite Construction of High Performance Scientific Applicaitons.* PhD thesis, Imperial College of Science, Technology and Medicine, University of London, 2001.
3. J. Paul Morrison. *Flow-Based Programming : A New Approach to Application Development.* Van Nostrand Reinhold, July 1994.
4. Nathalie Furmento, Anthony Mayer, Steven McGough, Steven Newhouse, Tony Field, and John Darlington. Optimisation of Component-based Applications within a Grid Environment. In *SuperComputing 2001*, Denver, USA, November 2001.
5. Message Passing Interface Forum. MPI: A message-passing interface standard. Technical Report UT-CS-94-230, University of Tennessee, 1994.
6. W3C Consortium, May 2000. http://www.w3.org/TR/2000/NOTE-SOAP20000508.
7. Steven Newhouse. *Adaptive error analysis with hierarchical shape functions for three dimensional rigid acoustic scattering.* PhD thesis, Imperial College of Science, Technology and Medicine, April 1995.
8. I. Foster, C. Kesselman, J. Nick, and S. Tuecke. The physiology of the grid: An open grid services architecture for distributed systems integration. http://www.globus.org/research/papers/ogsa.pdf.
9. N. Furmento, W. Lee, A. Mayer, S. Newhouse, and J. Darlington. ICENI: An Open Grid Service Architecture Implemented with Jini. accepted for SuperComputing 2002, Baltimore, November 2002.

Trustless Grid Computing in ConCert *

Bor-Yuh Evan Chang, Karl Crary, Margaret DeLap, Robert Harper,
Jason Liszka, Tom Murphy VII, and Frank Pfenning

Department of Computer Science
Carnegie Mellon University
Pittsburgh, PA, USA
{bechang,crary,mid,rwh,jliszka,tom7,fp}@cs.cmu.edu

Abstract. We believe that fundamental to the establishment of a grid
computing framework where all (not just large organizations) are able to
effectively tap into the resources available on the global network is the
establishment of trust between grid application developers and resource
donors. Resource donors must be able to trust that their security, safety,
and privacy policies will be respected by programs that use their systems.

In this paper, we present a novel solution based on the notion of *certified code* that upholds safety, security, and privacy policies by examining
intrinsic properties of code. Certified code complements authentication
and provides a foundation for a safe, secure, and efficient framework that
executes native code. We describe the implementation of such a framework known as the ConCert software.

1 Introduction

In recent years, numerous organizations have been vying for donated resources
for their grid applications. Potential resource donors are inundated with worthwhile grid projects such as discovering a cure for AIDS, finding large prime
numbers, and searching for extraterrestrial intelligence. Part of the difficulty in
obtaining resources is establishing trust between the grid application developer
and the resource donors. Because resource donors often receive little or no direct
reward for their contributions, they demand assurances of safety, security, and
privacy to protect themselves from malicious as well as simply unreliable software. In an ideal grid framework, as proposed in Legion [18], users are provided
the abstraction of a single virtual machine that automatically distributes work
and gathers results. In such a framework, this issue is even more salient because
the exchange of code happens automatically.

Most current grid frameworks, such as the Globus toolkit [13], focus on *authentication* to provide the basis for security on computational grids. Authentication provides a means for one entity to verify the identity of another. If this
is combined with some form of *access control*, then resource donors are able
to control *who* can access their resources. In essence, this seeks to address the

---

* The ConCert Project is supported by the National Science Foundation under grant ITR/SY+SI
0121633: "Language Technology for Trustless Software Dissemination".

M. Parashar (Ed.): GRID 2002, LNCS 2536, pp. 112–125, 2002.

question "how do I identify those I trust?"; however, there seems to be a more fundamental question: "whom can I trust?" Currently, resource donors are limited to relying on the reputation of the developer or possibly the reputation of some quality assurance team that endorses him. While this is a reasonable solution for large well-known projects, we would like a more automated means that would enable more people to utilize the grid.

To address this issue, the ConCert project [9] enforces safety, security, and privacy policies by verifying *intrinsic* properties of code. This is realized through the use of *certifying compilers* that allow software developers to produce efficient machine code along with checkable certificates that can be easily and automatically verified on behalf of code recipient. Our vision is to empower *all* programmers to utilize donated resources by establishing trust via rigorous, mathematical proof of the intrinsic safety, security, and privacy properties of software.

Our report proceeds as follows. We compare several existing techniques for code certification, briefly introduce the specific technologies on which our framework is built, then explain the properties that can be certified. We then discuss the design and implementation of our peer-to-peer architecture, and finally describe our first application, a grid ray tracer.

2 Certification and Security

In this section, we discuss current means of ensuring safety and security without authentication, provide an overview of the certified code technologies we employ, and discuss properties that can be certified.

2.1 Related Safety and Security Ideas

Mechanisms for safeguarding against faulty code produced by trusted users have been needed in systems long before the concern over malicious mobile code. For example, one method to safeguard memory between threads of computation is to simply place the processes in separate address spaces, as is done in most modern-day operating systems. This and other operating system mechanisms provide a very coarse level of safety or fault isolation both for individual systems and any grid framework. The problem with basing safety solely on these coarse mechanisms is that there is very little control on what properties are enforced and there is often a significant runtime overhead associated with these mechanisms (*e.g.* frequent context switching and copying between addresses spaces). Several technologies have been developed to lower the cost of fault isolation and provide finer control over which safety, security, and privacy properties are ensured. This, in essence, is also the goal of certified code. In this section, we describe a few of these related technologies, namely virtual machine techniques and methods that interpose between the process and the operating system, along with some shortcomings that we believe certified code addresses.

Virtual Machine Methods. The most prominent use of a virtual machine environment for providing a secure execution space is in the Java Development

Kit (JDK). At the core of the JDK 1.2 security model [15] is the ability to type-check Java Virtual Machine (JVM) bytecode [21]. It is critical that untrusted code cannot bypass the runtime checks that enforce the high-level security policy. In addition, the JDK has authentication-based mechanisms for identifying the origin of code and restricting access based on this information.

Several grid frameworks have been developed using Java as a secure host for mobile code, such as IceT [17], Javelin [5], and Bayanihan [33]. The IceT project aims at allowing processes running in the IceT environment to freely flow among available sites. IceT code primarily consists of Java *application* bytecode that is dynamically loaded into a governing environment with some optional policy-based means to link with native code. Javelin focuses on creating a grid framework using Java-enabled web browsers to minimize the technical expertise needed to participate in grid computing. Code for Javelin must be in the form of Java *applets* rather than Java applications. Project Bayanihan also aims to utilize Java applets to make it easier to participate but also supports the loading of Java applications. Further, it investigates preventing *sabotage* by nodes who submit erroneous results.

At the same time, despite the additional safety and security guarantees afforded by a virtual machine environment for loading code, a number of grid frameworks load native code for performance reasons. Although concerns about the performance of interpreted Java bytecode are somewhat relieved by just-in-time (JIT) compilers, JIT compilation to native code occurs *after* bytecode verification, so errors in the JIT compiler may lead to security holes. In addition, since the JIT compiler is run at execution time, its compilation process must be fast, which limits the quality of code it is able to produce.

Interposition Methods. Even prior to grid computing, interposition mechanisms between an untrusted process and the operating system were used to provide finer control of safety properties. Interposition gives control of execution to a watchdog whenever the untrusted process performs a possibly unsafe operation. One interposition method is known as Software-based Fault Isolation (SFI) [35], which is exhibited in the Omniware system for mobile code [22]. One striking issue with interposition mechanisms is that they are limited in what properties they ensure. For example, SFI only ensures memory safety. As with virtual machine methods, performance of interposition methods is often also a concern. In grid applications where we seek to make the best use of donated resources, avoiding the overhead of these methods is desirable.

Proof-Carrying Code. *Proof-carrying code* (PCC) is a form of certified code with arbitrary certification properties written as logic statements [28]. In PCC, a *certifying compiler* generates a proof along with the object code, and this proof is verified by a simple proof-checker on the code recipient's computer. PCC has very little runtime overhead because many properties can be verified before the program is ever run. For instance, Necula and Lee show that PCC handily outperforms SFI on a network packet filter application [29].

Because the certified properties are, in principle, arbitrary, PCC is highly flexible. However, this flexibility also means that it can be difficult for programmers to know when the certifying compiler will be able to generate proofs. One response to this problem is to encode desired safety properties in a *type system* for the source programming language. In this sense, a type system is simply a syntactic realization of specific properties such that a well-formed program is guaranteed to have those properties. Verification then consists of type-checking rather than proof-checking. A well-designed type system makes it easy for the programmer to understand which properties are certifiable by a compiler.

Many properties can be encoded in a type system; however, all type systems rely on the basic notion of *type safety*. Type safety means that the program will not "go wrong" by violating abstraction boundaries, accessing memory outside its address space, or branching into unsafe code. Therefore, for our first version of a grid framework with certified code, we choose languages with just this basic property.

2.2   Enabling Technologies

In this section, we provide some background on the enabling technologies that allow us to develop a grid framework based on the notion of certified code. The implementation of our grid framework builds on the TALx86 [24] realization of the Typed Assembly Language (TAL) [26, 25] developed by Morrisett *et al.* A certifying compiler for a type-safe C-like language called Popcorn that compiles to TALx86 has also been developed as part of the TAL project. These tools serve as a foundation for an implementation of the ConCert grid software and applications that run on it.

An Overview of Popcorn. Popcorn is a programming language similar to C, except that unsafe features like the unrestricted address-of operator, pointer arithmetic, and pointer casts have been left out. At the same time, it has a number of advanced features akin to modern high-level programming languages like Java [16] and Standard ML (SML) [23], such as exceptions, garbage collection, tagged unions, and parametric polymorphism that mitigate the need for these unsafe features.

The primitive types supported by Popcorn include bool, char, short, int, float, double, string, and unsigned forms of the numeric types. Unlike C, arrays carry their size for bounds checking, and strings are not null-terminated. Instead, strings are treated like arrays of chars, and a special size construct is used to extract the size of an array or string. Popcorn's basic control flow constructs (if, for, while, do, break, and continue) behave identically to their C counterparts except that test expressions must have type bool.

The aggregate data structures in Popcorn are similar to ones in high-level languages like Java and SML. First, Popcorn supports tuple types in addition to structs and unions. Tuples (as well as structs and unions) are created using the new construct and projected using .1, .2, ... as shown in Fig. 1A. There are two forms of structure definitions: `struct` and `?struct`. Values of types defined with `struct` cannot be `null` (a primitive in Popcorn) whereas values of types defined with `?struct` may. A value of a type defined with `?struct` is checked for `null` upon access to a field. If it is `null`, the program aborts immediately. Unions in Popcorn resemble SML datatypes more than C unions in that each variant has a tag and an associated type. In Fig. 1B, we declare a full binary tree with integer data at the leaves.

```
(A)     *(int,int) p   = new (0,1);
        int        sum = p.1 + p.2;
(B)     union tree { int Leaf; *(tree,tree) Node; }
(C)     int numleaves(tree t) {
          switch (t) {
            case Leaf(x):       return 1;
            case Node *(l,r):  return numleaves(l) + numleaves(r);
          }
        }
(D)     *(t2,t1) swap<t1,t2>(*(t1,t2) x) {
          return new (x.2,x.1);
        }
```

Fig. 1. Popcorn examples

Notice that `union` types may be recursive. We often utilize values of a type defined with `union` by `switch`ing on them. For example, we can write a function that counts the number of leaves in a binary tree (Fig. 1C).

Parametric polymorphism provides a means to write data structures or algorithms where the use of values is independent of the types. The syntax of parametric polymorphism in Popcorn resembles that of templates in C++ or generic types in GJ [4]. In Fig. 1D, we use parametric polymorphism to write a generic swap of the components of a pair. The symbols `t1` and `t2` are type variables that represent arbitrary types.

From this overview, we see the similarity of Popcorn to Java in that it has the look and feel of C but with strictures that enable the demonstration of safety properties. However, Popcorn differs from Java in that the output of the Popcorn compiler is machine code able to be run at full speed rather than bytecode that is interpreted or that requires just-in-time compilation upon execution.

An Overview of TALx86. TALx86 is a statically-typed assembly language for the Intel IA-32 architecture. Since it is not feasible to fully describe TALx86 here, we simply provide an overview of TALx86 in order to appreciate our grid framework's underlying technology. Further details about TALx86 can be found in Morrisett *et al.* [24] as well as about its theoretical basis in related works [26, 25].

From the high-level source language, the Popcorn compiler (or potentially other certifying compilers) produce `.tal` files that contain TALx86 assembly with all the typing annotations for each source file along with a number of other files that are generated by the TALx86 assembler `talc`. Some of these files are shipped to the code recipient. These contain information such as the imports, exports,

Table 1. TALx86/Popcorn Files for `main`

File	Produced By	Description	Shipped
main.pop	developer	the Popcorn source file for `main`	
main.tal	popcorn	typed assembly language output	
main_i.tali	talc	main's imports (any `extern` declarations)	√
main_e.tali	talc	main's exports (non-static types and values)	√
main.to	talc	binary file with the typing annotations	√
main.o	talc	native object file in ELF	√

and typing annotations that are used for link-time verification. A `.tal` file is a realistic assembly language that is, in fact, compatible with the Microsoft Macro Assembler (MASM). Table 1 summarizes these files for an example program called `main` that is written in Popcorn.

The TALx86 assembler `talc` translates a `.tal` file into a native object file in either COFF (for Windows) or ELF (for Unix variants) and a `.to` file that contains typing annotations from the original `.tal` file in a binary format. The `talc` assembler is actually composed of a TALx86 type-checker, a link-verifier, a code assembler, and a code linker. Upon reading of `.tal` files, `talc` first type-checks each file individually. This type-check should never fail provided that the implementation of the certifying compiler is correct; however, by type-checking, we no longer need to assume the correctness of the certifying compiler. Contrast this with using the JVM with just-in-time compilation for ensuring type-safety where we have to assume that the JIT compiler is implemented correctly. Before creating the native object file, the link-verifier ensures that the multiple `.tal` files are safe after being linked together by verifying that they have the same assumptions about the values and types that they share. Technical details about link verification can be found in Glew and Morrisett [14].

The ConCert grid software simply ships the native object, `.to`, `_i.tali`, and `_e.tali` files. Before dynamically loading the code on the donor host, the grid software type-checks the code using a TAL verification library on the received files.

Certifiable Properties. Type safety is the key property that allows us to control how a program behaves. As a baseline, a type-safe program must be memory safe (no illegal reads or writes) and control-flow safe (no jumps to illegal addresses). In addition, it cannot violate abstraction boundaries that could lead to such errors. We are further able to provide the distributed code with an arbitrary "safe" subset of the system library. It is simple, for instance, to allow the code to modify or delete only files that it created (without run-time checks), or to simply not allow access to any files at all. The grid volunteer can be given a choice of several policies on these sorts of issues, each of which is enforced by verifying that the candidate code type-checks with the supplied view of the system library.

There are, however, other properties that we may wish to certify that cannot be enforced this way. These properties are a subject of current research. To express these, we enhance our type systems so that type safety implies adherence to the property in question. For instance, one primary concern for grid computing is the resource usage of the distributed code. Much work is in progress regarding *resource bound certification* [30, 10], which allows the type system to include bounds on how much CPU, memory, and disk resources a piece of code may use.

Finally, users may wish to give code access to private information (such as the computer's configuration), so long as this information does not, for instance, make its way back onto the network. Such requirements are known as *information-flow* properties, and work is being carried out on type systems that certify them [19, 36, 27].

3   ConCert Architecture

A chief property of our architecture is decentralization. A decentralized grid allows us to use idle resources while avoiding bottlenecks that could overload hosts or networks and degrade performance—possibly even for users who are not involved in grid computation. Another driving principle is fault tolerance; we expect nodes in the network to fail frequently, and this has a significant impact on our programming and scheduling model.

Our current design is entirely peer-to-peer and symmetric (each node both serves code and runs it). Every participating node has three components: a *locator*, a *worker*, and a *conductor*. The *locator* finds a host's peers at runtime as is necessitated by the decentralized architecture. The *conductor* component keeps track of what work is available to be done and bundles files as necessary to provide work to peers. The *worker* acquires code from a peer (perhaps itself), verifies it using the TAL verifier, and runs it. We now provide an overview of each of these components. Further details can be found in DeLap's honors thesis [12].

Node Discovery. Because of the system is decentralized, participants should find their peers dynamically. In our current implementation of the *locator* component, we use a protocol similar to Gnutella's [8] to discover nodes. Using this protocol, hosts build tables of peers as they run. A host that wishes to participate joins the network by sending an initial ping message to some number of predetermined peers. If any of these peers are participating, they will forward that message to the peers of which they are aware, and so forth within a limited number of hops. Anyone receiving a ping message notifies the originating host that it is alive by sending a response.

We do not share all of Gnutella's privacy goals, so we are able to reduce network traffic for certain exchanges. Nonetheless, since it is known that Gnutella may have scalability issues [31], we may wish to change our method of node discovery in the future. Components other than the locator remain unaware of how the list of contacts is found. Therefore, it would be feasible for us to change our entire network topology without affecting the serving and running of work itself.

Parallelism Model. Since the grid is likely to contain slow, unreliable network links and hosts, we do not support the use of either fine-grained, high-communication threads or shared memory, both for performance reasons and for failure tolerance. At the same time, our model of parallelism should allow for inexpensive scheduling. We therefore base our model of parallelism on that of Cilk-NOW [3] and, more generally, dataflow computer architectures [11]. In our model, programs are split into segments called *cords*, on which we impose certain invariants to simplify scheduling tasks.[1]

First, once a cord is ready to run, it is able to execute continuously to completion without waiting for data from other cords or otherwise blocking. In other words, a cord does not communicate with other cords while executing. This restriction simplifies scheduling greatly.

Second, any execution of a cord is, as far as the developer is concerned, "as good as" any other. This is evident for deterministic cords. Nondeterministic or randomized algorithms may also be acceptable, as long as a re-execution (due to the failure of a node) still produces a valid result.

Finally, cords do not produce outside effects that other cords rely on. For example, it would be unsound for one cord to write to a file on a participating machine and another cord to depend upon the contents of that file. Such effects are forms of "out-of-band" communication with other cords. As such, they would be hidden from the scheduler; if any cords were later rescheduled, they would almost certainly not behave correctly.

How, then, does information travel between the parts of a program? Each cord's I/O consists of the entire set of *arguments* it needs and the *result* it produces. We may therefore represent a program as a graph in which nodes denote cords and edges indicate the data flowing into them as arguments. A cord is not ready to run until its inward edges have the necessary data available. Fig. 2(A) gives a simple example of this model. This form of "communication" may seem rudimentary, but by creating new cords at run-time with appropriate dependencies we are able to implement more sophisticated forms of control flow. For instance, with a process similar to Continuation-Passing Style [1], we are able to implement fork-join parallelism.

To make our model more powerful, we collect sets of dependencies into groups of *and-* and *or*-dependencies. In an *and*-dependency set, all of the dependencies are required—they must all contain data before the set of dependencies is considered complete. Alternatively, in an *or*-dependency set, only one dependency result is necessary. As soon as any one of the dependencies is filled, that set is considered completed. Such sets can be chained into trees of dependencies that are to be simplified and collapsed as dependency data (results) are filled in. Fig. 2(B) provides a simple example of a dependency tree.

---

[1] Adherence to these invariants is not presently certified, however, programs that do not meet them do not pose any danger to the resource donor; the programs simply do not work properly. It would be desirable that a grid programming language assist the programmer in verifying these properties.

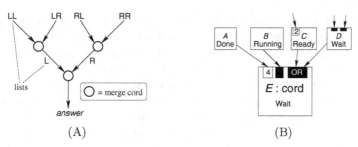

(A)   (B)

Fig. 2. (A) A simple cord graph example. This graph represents an execution of a program that mergesorts four sorted list segments into one sorted list. The list segments, which are themselves results of cords, are arguments to the cords. Merged list segments travel downward in the graph until the final result (the entire sorted list) is obtained. (B) Dependency resolution. Here, cord A has recently terminated; its result, 4, becomes one of the arguments to E. Cord E now awaits results from B and either C or D. Meanwhile, cord C is ready to run, having received the result 2 from the cord on which *it* depends. To summarize, the set $C + D$ is a set of *or*-dependencies for E; $AB(C + D)$ is its overall set of *and*-dependencies.

Work Stealing. Whenever a participating workstation becomes idle, it may pull work from its peers. Hosts never actively foist work on others. We choose to use the work-stealing model for three reasons. First, the worker node knows best when the host it is running on is idle, and when it is in need of more work. Second, the worker is likely to know better *how much* work it will need (depending on its number of processors, etc.). Third, the worker is able to send with its request a description of its security policy. This allows the code producer to find or generate a matching cord and send only the certification information that the worker needs to be satisfied.

Work stealing has major implications for scheduling. In our case, it means the conductor's scheduler can run *on demand only*, that is, whenever it receives a work request or result from a worker. Since users may wish to serve cords even when their machines are not idle, reducing the scheduler's use of resources is especially advantageous.

To steal work from a conductor, a worker initiates a sequence of messages to acquire the appropriate cord and its arguments. It then verifies and runs the code, sending the result back to the conductor. If, on the other hand, the code fails to verify, the worker does not run it.

Failure Tolerance and Recovery. Of course, computation will not always proceed smoothly on a failure-prone network such as the grid. Given that grid computing attempts to solve large problems on possibly unreliable networks and often on non-dedicated, consumer-level hardware, tolerance of failure is critical. In particular, we need to be able to checkpoint programs at some reasonable granularity and to restart them with partial results, so that earlier computation is not lost if some part of the program fails (*e.g.* due to a downed node). Since cords do not communicate among themselves as they run, restarting them is not especially difficult provided the code for the cord in question is kept. With respect to checkpointing, results are cached on conductors so that if a cord *is* rescheduled, preceding cords on which it depends do not have to be re-run.

Failure detection is also an issue. If a worker notices and notifies the corresponding conductor that its cord has died or failed to match its host's security policy, the conductor can simply reschedule it and hand it off to any subsequent requester. Otherwise, we need to decide if and when to reschedule apparently failed cords. In some cases, grid programmers may wish to approximate the result of a failed cord rather than reschedule the cord itself. We expect that failure detection will involve some form of heartbeat between cords and originating conductors, but further work on implementation is required. Related work has already been done on failure detection for distributed computing, including [6].

Our framework also entails a new mode of failure, where a binary does not pass the type-checking phase once transmitted to the worker's hosts. There are several reasons such failure may occur. For example, it may fail because the certificate does not match the code, due to corruption of the files, a bad copy of the certifying compiler, malice, or similar causes. Second, it may fail because, while correct, it does not match the host's security policy. Presumably this would occur only if the conductor serving the code did not check the worker's policy against it in advance, or if the worker host's policy changed in the midst of the negotiation. In those cases, however, explicit failure notices can be generated to reduce the impact on the overall grid performance.

Grid Clients. External clients can connect to conductors on local machines to submit work and view or interpret results. To do this, they use a socket interface to send messages to the conductor specifying the cord and the arguments with which to run it. If all goes well, the conductor will return a handle to that cord, which may be used to query its status and retrieve its result through the same socket interface. Using a socket allows for easy interaction with clients written in various languages—we have written demonstration clients in C and Standard ML. The ConCert *protocol* software is also language-independent. Note, however, that the cords themselves must be available in the TAL-produced format of an object file and typing annotations, and the verifier clearly must check this format.

4   Sample Application: Ray Tracer

Because of the strong interplay between certification technology and the source programming language, we are interested in how applications are developed for the grid and especially in what programming issues arise. Therefore we have developed a sample application for our grid framework: a parallel ray tracer called Lightharp. The ray tracer back-end, which does the actual tracing work (and is distributed across the grid), is written in the Popcorn language described in section 2.2. The front-end, which divides the scene into small chunks, submits the tracing jobs, and displays the results, is a separate program written in Standard ML.

Lightharp implements the specification for the ICFP 2000 Programming Contest [20]. Scenes to be rendered are described by a simple stack-based language called GML. GML supports basic diffuse and specular lighting, constructive solid geometry, and several advanced features such as procedural textures. The GML representation of a scene is typically quite compact because it can create named objects and duplicate them to populate the scene. Therefore, rather than create an intermediate representation of the scene we communicate a (slightly) modified version of the original GML code on the grid.

The back-end is a function of type `string -> string`, which takes a GML program as input, and returns the rendered scene as a sequence of RGB colors. The color of a particular pixel is computed by shooting a "ray" from the point of view through the image plane and recursively tracing its path through the scene using standard ray-tracing algorithms. Note that the color of each pixel or block of pixels can be calculated independently, which is the only source of parallelism in our implementation.

The front-end works by parsing the GML scene and modifying it to instruct the back-end to render only a small part of the image, that is, only trace rays through a certain range of pixels. It then submits cords into the grid to cover the entire image, and simply waits for the results to arrive (currently by polling the ConCert software).

For an application with such a simple parallelism model as a ray tracer, we found that this implementation strategy was adequate. Popcorn is a powerful enough language to implement the back-end tracing functions without much pain. It is also relatively easy to manage the cords from the front-end and only mildly tedious to manually marshal between strings and RGB data.

Our ray tracer application's parallel behavior is extremely simple; for instance, the back-end cords have no need to spawn other cords, nor do they have any dependencies. Work is currently under way to tackle some more difficult parallel computations, such as parallel game tree search in chess. We hope to push the limits of what is possible with cords, and discover interesting research problems in programming techniques for the grid.

5   Conclusion

We have presented a framework and technologies for grid computing in a trustless setting based on the idea of certified code. Certification compares favorably to similar technology; it verifies rich properties of native code with low run-time overhead. We have also described a peer-to-peer network for fetching and running work, and presented a sample ray-tracing application that runs on the grid.

We believe that our trustless peer-to-peer strategy is the most effective way to lower the barriers to universal utilization of the grid, while maintaining a secure and robust network. However, code certification can be applied to other mobile code scenarios in grid computing. For instance, manually-installed native code applications like used for SETI@home [34] could benefit from the improved security and potential for automatic updates afforded by certification. Untrusted systems based on virtual machines could use certified native code to improve performance.

Future Work. At present, we certify only type safety (which entails memory safety and control flow safety). In section 2.2, we discussed other properties that might be certified. When more certification options are available, we will need to encode policies in such a way that code can be tested against them easily and efficiently. We also plan to provide an accessible interface for users to specify their security policies in a transparent manner.

Our framework protects cycle donors from broken or malicious code, but it does not protect developers from false answers. Malicious workers might, instead of actually running the code presented, return a fabricated result. We plan to investigate how techniques proposed elsewhere [32, 33] can be adapted to the ConCert architecture.

So far, we have concentrated on certification of safety properties. In practice, this should be combined with methods for peer-to-peer authentication. Here, again, the ideas behind proof-carrying code provide novel solutions [2]. We plan to investigate how they may be applied in the ConCert framework.

Although we have implemented a ray tracer application using the ConCert grid software, we noted in section 4 that the parallel structure of Lightharp is exceedingly simple. To support more sophisticated uses of parallelism, we will need a high-level programming model for supporting some notion of starting remote computation and gathering of results *within* a grid application. Consequently, we will need the means to map high-level programming languages to the simple low-level interface provided by ConCert. Although it has yet to be demonstrated, we believe we can leverage several programming language techniques to achieve this goal. Preliminary work in this direction is discussed in Chang's honors thesis [7].

Acknowledgments

Our implementation and protocols, especially the work-stealing protocol and code to support TAL verification, are based largely on Joshua Dunfield's initial implementation of the ConCert framework. We would also like to acknowledge the other members of the ConCert project and Guy Blelloch for their helpful comments.

References

1. Andrew Appel. *Compiling With Continuations*. Cambridge University Press, Cambridge, 1992.
2. Andrew W. Appel and Edward W. Felten. Proof-carrying authentication. In G. Tsudik, editor, *Proceedings of the 6th Conference on Computer and Communications Security*, pages 52–62, Singapore, November 1999. ACM Press.

3. Robert D. Blumofe and Philip A. Lisiecki. Adaptive and reliable parallel computing on networks of workstations. In *USENIX 1997 Annual Technical Conference on UNIX and Advanced Computing Systems*, pages 133–147, Anaheim, California, 1997.

4. Gilad Bracha, Martin Odersky, David Stoutamire, and Philip Wadler. Making the future safe for the past: Adding genericity to the Java™ programming language. In *Object Oriented Programming: Systems, Languages, and Applications (OOPSLA)*, pages 183–200, Vancouver, British Columbia, October 1998.

5. Peter Cappello, Bernd Christiansen, Mihai F. Ionescu, Michael O. Neary, Klaus E. Schauser, and Daniel Wu. Javelin: Internet-based parallel computing using Java. In *ACM Workshop on Java for Science and Engineering Computation*, Las Vegas, Nevada, June 1997.

6. Tushar Deepak Chandra and Sam Toueg. Unreliable failure detectors for reliable distributed systems. *Journal of the ACM*, 43(2):225–267, March 1996.

7. Bor-Yuh Evan Chang. Iktara in ConCert: Realizing a certified grid computing framework from a programmer's perspective. Technical Report CMU-CS-02-150, Carnegie Mellon University, June 2002. Undergraduate honors thesis.

8. Clip2 Distributed Search Services. The Gnutella protocol specification v0.4, September 2000. URL: http://www.gnutella.co.uk/library/pdf/gnutella_protocol_0.4.pdf.

9. ConCert. Certified code for grid computing, project webpage, 2001. URL: http://www.cs.cmu.edu/~concert.

10. Karl Crary and Stephanie Weirich. Resource bound certification. In *Twenty-Seventh ACM SIGPLAN-SIGACT Symposium on Principles of Programming Languages*, pages 184–198, Boston, Massachusetts, January 2000.

11. David E. Culler, Jaswinder Pal Singh, and Anoop Gupta. *Parallel Computer Architecture: A Hardware/Software Approach*. Morgan Kaufmann, San Francisco, California, 1999.

12. Margaret DeLap. Implementing a framework for certified grid computing. Technical Report CMU-CS-02-151, Carnegie Mellon University, June 2002. Undergraduate honors thesis.

13. Ian Foster and Carl Kesselman. The Globus toolkit. In Ian Foster and Carl Kesselman, editors, *The Grid: Blueprint for a New Computing Infrastructure*, chapter 11, pages 259–278. Morgan Kaufmann, San Francisco, California, 1999.

14. Neal Glew and Greg Morrisett. Type-safe linking and modular assembly language. In *Twenty-Sixth ACM SIGPLAN-SIGACT Symposium on Principles of Programming Languages*, pages 250–261, San Antonio, Texas, January 1999.

15. Li Gong, Marianne Mueller, Hemma Prafullchandra, and Roland Schemers. Going beyond the sandbox: An overview of the new security architecture in the Java Development Kit 1.2. In *USENIX Symposium on Internet Technologies and Systems*, Monterey, California, December 1997.

16. James Gosling, Bill Joy, Guy Steele, and Gilad Bracha. *The Java™ Language Specification*. Addison-Wesley, second edition, 2000.

17. Paul A. Gray and Vaidy S. Sunderam. Metacomputing with the IceT system. *International Journal of High Performance Computing Applications*, 13(3):241–252, 1999.

18. Andrew S. Grimshaw and William A. Wulf. Legion: The next logical step toward the world-wide virtual computer. *Communications of the ACM*, 40(1):39–45, January 1997.

19. Nevin Heintze and Jon G. Riecke. The SLam calculus: Programming with secrecy and integrity. In *Twenty-Fifth ACM SIGPLAN-SIGACT Symposium on Principles of Programming Languages*, pages 365–377, San Diego, California, January 1998.

20. ICFP. The third annual ICFP programming contest, 2000. URL: http://www.cs.cornell.edu/icfp/.

21. Tim Lindholm and Frank Yellin. *The Java™ Virtual Machine Specification*. Addison-Wesley, second edition, 1999.

22. Steven Lucco, Oliver Sharp, and Robert Wahbe. Omniware: A universal substrate for web programming. In *Fourth International World Wide Web Conference*, pages 359–368, Boston, Massachusetts, December 1995.

23. Robin Milner, Mads Tofte, Robert Harper, and David MacQueen. *The Definition of Standard ML (Revised)*. MIT Press, Cambridge, Massachusetts, 1997.

24. Greg Morrisett, Karl Crary, Neal Glew, Dan Grossman, Richard Samuels, Frederick Smith, David Walker, Stephanie Weirich, and Steve Zdancewic. TALx86: A realistic typed assembly language. In *1999 ACM SIGPLAN Workshop on Compiler Support for System Software*, pages 25–35, Atlanta, Georgia, May 1999.

25. Greg Morrisett, Karl Crary, Neal Glew, and David Walker. Stack-based typed assembly language. *Journal of Functional Programming*, 12(1):43–88, January 2002.

26. Greg Morrisett, David Walker, Karl Crary, and Neal Glew. From System F to typed assembly language. *ACM Transactions on Programming Languages and Systems*, 21(3):527–568, May 1999.

27. Andrew C. Myers. Jflow: Practical mostly-static information flow control. In *Twenty-Sixth ACM SIGPLAN-SIGACT Symposium on Principles of Programming Languages*, pages 228–241, San Antonio, Texas, January 1999.

28. George C. Necula. Proof-carrying code. In *Twenty-Fourth ACM SIGPLAN-SIGACT Symposium on Principles of Programming Languages*, pages 106–119, Paris, France, January 1997.

29. George C. Necula and Peter Lee. Safe kernel extensions without run-time checking. In *Second Symposium on Operating Systems Design and Implementation*, pages 229–243, Seattle, Washington, October 1996.

30. George C. Necula and Peter Lee. Safe, untrusted agents using proof-carrying code. In Giovanni Vigna, editor, *Special Issue on Mobile Agent Security*, volume 1419 of *Lecture Notes in Computer Science*, pages 61–91. Springer-Verlag, October 1997.

31. Jordan Ritter. Why Gnutella can't scale. No, really., February 2001. URL: http://www.darkridge.com/~jpr5/doc/gnutella.html.

32. Luis F. G. Sarmenta. Bayanihan: Web-based volunteer computing using Java. In *Second International Conference on World-Wide Computing and its Applications*, pages 444–461, March 1998.

33. Luis F. G. Sarmenta and Satoshi Hirano. Bayanihan: Building and studying web-based volunteer computing systems using Java. *Future Generation Computer Systems*, 15(5-6):675–686, 1999. Special Issue on Metacomputing.

34. SETI@home. The search for extraterrestrial intelligence, 2001. URL: http://setiathome.ssl.berkeley.edu.

35. Robert Wahbe, Steven Lucco, Thomas E. Anderson, and Susan L. Graham. Efficient software-based fault isolation. In *Fourteenth ACM Symposium on Operating Systems Principles*, pages 203–216, December 1993.

36. Steve Zdancewic and Andrew C. Myers. Confidentiality and integrity with untrusted hosts. Technical Report 2000-1810, Cornell University, 2000.

A Unified Peer-to-Peer Database Framework for Scalable Service and Resource Discovery

Wolfgang Hoschek

CERN IT Division
European Organization for Nuclear Research
1211 Geneva 23, Switzerland
wolfgang.hoschek@cern.ch

Abstract. In a large distributed system spanning many administrative domains such as a Data Grid, it is desirable to maintain and query dynamic and timely information about active participants such as services, resources and user communities. However, in such a database system, the set of information tuples in the universe is partitioned over many distributed nodes, for reasons including autonomy, scalability, availability, performance and security. It is not obvious how to enable general-purpose discovery query support and collective collaborative functionality that operate on the distributed system as a whole, rather than on a given part of it. Further, it is not obvious how to allow for search results that are fresh, allowing dynamic content. It appears that a Peer-to-Peer (P2P) database network may be well suited to support dynamic distributed database search, for example for service discovery. In this paper, we devise the *Unified Peer-to-Peer Database Framework (UPDF)*, which allows to express specific applications for arbitrary query languages (e.g. XQuery, SQL) and node topologies, and a wide range of data types, query response modes (e.g. Routed, Direct and Referral Response), neighbor selection policies, pipelining characteristics, timeout and other scope options.

1 Introduction

Grid technology attempts to support flexible, secure, coordinated information sharing among dynamic collections of individuals, institutions and resources. This includes data sharing but also includes access to computers, software and devices required by computation and data-rich collaborative problem solving [1]. Grids are cooperative distributed Internet systems characterized by large scale, heterogeneity, lack of central control, multiple autonomous administrative domains, unreliable components and frequent dynamic change. These and other advances of distributed computing are necessary to increasingly make it possible to join loosely coupled people and resources from multiple organizations.

For example, the next generation Large Hadron Collider project at CERN, the European Organization for Nuclear Research, involves thousands of researchers and hundreds of institutions spread around the globe. A massive set of com-

M. Parashar (Ed.): GRID 2002, LNCS 2536, pp. 126–144, 2002.

puting resources is necessary to support it's data-intensive physics analysis applications, including thousands of network services, tens of thousands of CPUs, WAN Gigabit networking as well as Petabytes of disk and tape storage [2]. To make collaboration viable, it was decided to share in a global joint effort - the European Data Grid (EDG) [3,4,5,6] - the data and locally available resources of all participating laboratories and university departments.

An enabling step towards increased Grid software execution flexibility is the (still immature and hence often hyped) *web services* vision [3,7] of distributed computing where programs are no longer configured with static information. Rather, the promise is that programs are made more flexible, adaptive and powerful by querying Internet databases (registries) at runtime in order to discover information and network attached third-party building blocks. Services can advertise themselves and related metadata via such databases, enabling the assembly of distributed higher-level components. For example, a data-intensive High Energy Physics analysis application sweeping over Terabytes of data looks for remote services that that exhibit a suitable combination of characteristics, including appropriate interfaces, operations and network protocols as well as network load, available disk quota, access rights, and perhaps Quality of Service and monetary cost. It is thus of critical importance to develop capabilities for rich service discovery as well as a query language that can support advanced resource brokering.

More generally, in a distributed system, it is often desirable to maintain and query dynamic and timely information about active participants such as services, resources and user communities. As in a data integration system [8,9,10], the goal is to exploit several independent information sources as if they were a single source. However, in a large distributed database system spanning many administrative domains, the set of information tuples in the universe is partitioned over one or more distributed nodes, for reasons including autonomy, scalability, availability, performance and security. It is not obvious how to enable powerful discovery query support and collective collaborative functionality that operate on the distributed system as a whole, rather than on a given part of it. Further, it is not obvious how to allow for search results that are fresh, allowing time-sensitive dynamic content. Distributed (relational) database systems [11] assume tight and consistent central control and hence are infeasable in Grid environments, which are characterized by heterogeneity, scale, lack of central control, multiple autonomous administrative domains, unreliable components and frequent dynamic change. It appears that a Peer-to-Peer (P2P) database network may be well suited to support dynamic distributed database search, for example for service discovery.

The overall P2P idea is as follows. Rather than have a centralized database, a distributed framework is used where there exist one or more autonomous database nodes, each maintaining its own data. Queries are no longer posed to a central database; instead, they are recursively propagated over the network to some or all database nodes, and results are collected and send back to the client. A node holds a set of tuples in its database. Nodes are interconnected with links in any arbitrary way. A link enables a node to query another node. A *link topology* describes the link structure among nodes. The centralized model has a single node only. For example, in a service discovery system, a link topology can tie together a distributed set of administrative domains, each hosting a registry node holding descriptions of services local to the domain. In other examples, nodes may support replica location [12], replica management and optimization [13,14], interoperable access to grid-enabled relational databases [15], gene sequencing or multi-lingual translation, actively using the network to discover services such as replica catalogs, remote gene mappers or language dictionaries. Several link topology models covering the spectrum from centralized models to fine-grained fully distributed models can be envisaged, among them single node, star, ring, tree, graph and hybrid models [16]. Figure 1 depicts some example topologies.

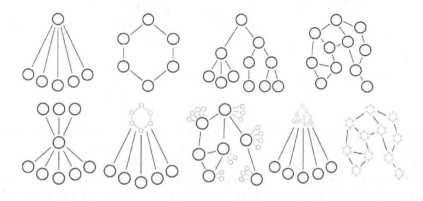

Fig. 1. Example Link Topologies [16].

In any kind of P2P network, nodes may publish themselves to other nodes, thereby forming a topology. In a P2P network for service discovery, a *node* is a service that exposes *at least* interfaces for publication and P2P queries. Here, nodes, services and other content providers may publish (their) service descriptions and/or other metadata to one or more nodes. Publication enables distributed node topology construction (e.g. ring, tree or graph) and at the same time constructs the database to be searched. For example, based on our *Web Service Discovery Architecture (WSDA)* [17], we have introduced a registry node [18] for service discovery that allows to publish and query dynamic tuples, which are annotated multi-purpose soft state data containers that may contain a piece of arbitrary *content* and allow for refresh of that content at any time. Examples of content include a service description expressed in WSDL [19], a Quality of Service description, a file, file replica location, current network load, host information, stock quotes, etc. For a detailed discussion of a wide range of discovery queries, their representation in the XQuery [20] language, as well as detailed motivation and justification, see our prior studies [3]. In other examples, a node may support replica management optimization, gene sequencing or multi-lingual

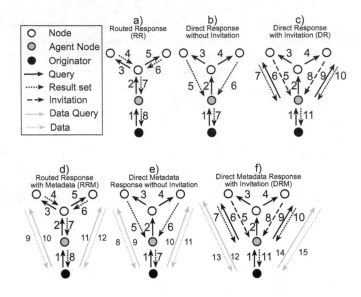

Fig. 2. Peer-to-Peer Response Modes [21].

translation, actively using the network to discover services such as replica catalogs, remote gene mappers or language dictionaries.

When any *originator* wishes to search the P2P network with some query, it sends the query to an *agent node*. The node applies the query to its local database and returns matching results; it also forwards the query to select *neighbor nodes*. These neighbors return their local query results; they also forward the query to select neighbors, and so on. In [21] four techniques to return matching query results to an originator are characterized, namely Routed Response, Direct Response, Routed Metadata Response, and Direct Metadata Response (see Figure 2). Under *Routed Response*, results are fanned back into the originator along the paths on which the query flowed outwards. Each (passive) node returns to its (active) client not only its own local results but also all remote results it receives from neighbors. Under *Direct Response*, results are not returned by routing through intermediary nodes. Each (active) node that has local results sends them directly to the (passive) agent, which combines and hands them back to the originator. Interaction consists of two phases under *Routed Metadata Response and Direct Metadata Response*. In the first phase, routed responses or direct responses are used. However, nodes return only small metadata results. In the second phase, the originator selects which data results are relevant. The originator directly connects to the relevant data sources and asks for data results.

Simple queries for lookup by key are assumed in most P2P systems such as Gnutella [22], Freenet [23], Tapestry [24], Chord [25] and Globe [26], leading to highly specialized *content-addressable* networks centered around the theme of distributed hash table lookup. Simple queries for exact match (i.e. given a flat set of attribute values find all tuples that carry exactly the same attribute values) are assumed in systems such as SDS [27] and Jini [28]. Others such as LDAP [29] and MDS [30] consider simple queries from a hierarchical namespace. None support rich and expressive general-purpose query languages such as XQuery [20] and SQL [31]. The key problems then are:

- *What are the detailed architecture and design options for P2P database searching? How should a P2P query processor be organized? What query types can be answered (efficiently) by a P2P network? What query types have the potential to immediately start piping in (early) results? How can a maximum of results be delivered reliably within the time frame desired by a user, even if a query type does not support pipelining? How can loops be detected reliably using timeouts? How can a query scope be used to exploit topology characteristics in answering a query?*

- *Can we devise a unified P2P database framework for general-purpose query support in large heterogeneous distributed systems spanning many administrative domains? More precisely, can we devise a framework that is unified in the sense that it allows to express specific applications for a wide range of data types, node topologies, query languages, query response modes, neighbor selection policies, pipelining characteristics, timeout and other scope options?*

In this paper, we take the first steps towards unifying the fields of database management systems and P2P systems, which so far have received considerable, but separate, attention. We extend database concepts and practice to cover P2P search. Similarly, we extend P2P concepts and practice to support powerful general-purpose query languages such as XQuery [20] and SQL [31]. As a result, we answer the above questions by proposing the *Unified Peer-to-Peer Database Framework (UPDF)*.

This paper is organized as follows. Section 2 unifies query processing in centralized, distributed and P2P databases. A theory of query processing for queries that are (or are not) *recursively partitionable* is proposed, which directly reflects the basis of the P2P scalability potential. We discusses for which query types the originator has the potential to immediately start piping in results (at moderate performance rate). Other query types must wait for a long time until the first result becomes available (the full result set arrives almost at once, however). Section 3 and 4 discuss loop and abort timeouts, as well as query scoping. Section 5 compares our work with existing research results. Finally, Section 6 concludes this paper.

2   Query Processing

In a distributed database system, there exists a single local database and zero or more neighbors. A classic centralized database system is a special case where there exists a single local database and zero neighbors. From the perspective of query processing, a P2P database system has the same properties as a distributed

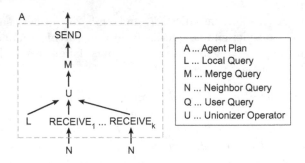

Fig. 3. Template Execution Plan.

database system, in a recursive structure. Hence, we propose to organize the P2P query engine like a general distributed query engine [32,11]. A given query involves a number of operators (e.g. SELECT, UNION, CONCAT, SORT, JOIN, SEND, RECEIVE, SUM, MAX, IDENTITY) that may or may not be exposed at the query language level. For example, the SELECT operator takes a set and returns a new set with tuples satisfying a given predicate. The UNION operator computes the union of two or more sets. The CONCAT operator concatenates the elements of two or more sets into a list of arbitrary order (without eliminating duplicates). The IDENTITY operator returns its input set unchanged. The semantics of an operator can be satisfied by several operator implementations, using a variety of algorithms, each with distinct resource consumption, latency and performance characteristics. The query optimizer chooses an efficient query execution plan, which is a tree plugged together from operators. In an execution plan, a parent operator consumes results from child operators.

Template Query Execution Plan.   *Any* query Q within our query model can be answered by an agent with the *template execution plan* A depicted in Figure 3. The plan applies a local query L against the tuple set of the local database. Each neighbor (if any) is asked to return a result set for (the same) neighbor query N. Local and neighbor result sets are unionized into a single result set by a unionizer operator U that must take the form of either UNION or CONCAT. A merge query M is applied that takes as input the result set and returns a new result set. The final result set is sent to the client, i.e. another node or an originator.

Centralized Execution Plan.   To see that indeed any query against any kind of database system can be answered within this framework we derive a simple *centralized execution plan* that always satisfies the semantics of any query Q. The plan substitutes specific subplans into the template plan A, leading to distinct plans for the agent node (Figure 4-a) and neighbors nodes (Figure 4-b). In the case of XQuery and SQL, parameters are substituted as follows:

XQuery	SQL
A: M=Q, U=UNION, L="RETURN /", N'=N N: M=IDENTITY, U=UNION, L="RETURN /", N'=N	A: M=Q, U=UNION, L="SELECT *", N'=N N: M=IDENTITY, U=UNION, L="SELECT *", N'=N

In other words, the agent's plan A fetches all raw tuples from the local and all remote databases, unionizes the result sets, and then applies the query Q. Neighbors are handed a rewritten neighbor query N that recursively fetches all raw tuples, and returns their union. The neighbor query N is recursively partitionable (see below).

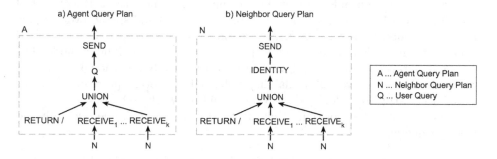

Fig. 4. Centralized Execution Plan.

The same centralized plan works for routed and direct response, both with and without metadata. Under direct response, a node does forward the query N, but does not attempt to receive remote result sets (conceptually empty result sets are delivered). The node does not send a result set to its predecessor, but directly back to the agent.

The centralized execution plan can be inefficient because potentially large amounts of base data have to be shipped to the agent before locally applying the user's query. However, sometimes this is the only plan that satisfies the semantics of a query. This is always the case for a complex query. A more efficient execution plan can sometimes be derived (as proposed below). This is always the case for a simple and medium query.

Recursively Partitionable Query. A P2P network can be efficient in answering queries that are recursively partitionable. A query Q is *recursively partitionable* if, for the template plan A, there exists a merge query M and a unionizer operator U to satisfy the semantics of the query Q assuming that L and N are chosen as L = Q and N = A. In other words, a query is recursively partitionable if the very same execution plan *can* be recursively applied at every node in the P2P topology. The corresponding execution plan is depicted in Figure 5.

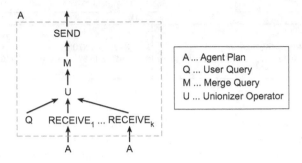

Fig. 5. Execution Plan for Recursively Partitionable Query.

The input and output of a merge query have the same form as the output of the local query L. Query processing can be parallelized and spread over all participating nodes. Potentially very large amounts of information can be searched while investing little resources such as processing time per individual node. The recursive parallel spread of load implied by a recursively partitionable query is the basis of the massive P2P scalability potential. However, query performance is not necessarily good, for example due to high network I/O costs.

Now we are in the position to clarify the definition of simple, medium and complex queries.

– *Simple Query.* A query is *simple* if it is recursively partitionable using M = IDENTITY, U = UNION. Examples are *(1) Find all (available) services. (2) Find all services that implement a replica catalog service interface and that CMS members are allowed to use, and that have an HTTP binding for the replica catalog operation "XML getPFNs(String LFN)".*

– *Medium Query.* A query is a *medium* query if it is not simple, but it is recursively partitionable. Examples are *(1) Return the number of replica catalog services. (2) Find the two CMS execution services with minimum and maximum CPU load and return their service descriptions and load.*

– *Complex Query.* A query is *complex* if it is not recursively partitionable. Examples are *(1) Find all (execution service, storage service) pairs where both services of a pair live within the same domain. (2) Find all domains that run more than one replica catalog with CMS as owner.*

For simplicity, in the remainder of this paper we assume that the user explicitly provides M and U along with a query Q. If M and U are not provided as part of a query to any given node, the node acts defensively by assuming that the query is not recursively partitionable. Choosing M and U is straightforward for a human being. Consider for example the following medium XQueries.

– *Return the number of replica catalog services.* The merge query computes the sum of a set of numbers. The unionizer is CONCAT.

```
Q = RETURN <tuple>
               count(/tupleset/tuple/content/
                                    service[interface/@type="repcat"])
           </tuple>
M = RETURN <tuple> sum(/tupleset/tuple) </tuple>
U = CONCAT
```

– *Find the service with the largest uptime.*

```
Q=M= RETURN (/tupleset/tuple[@type="service"]
                               SORTBY (./@uptime)) [last()]
U =  UNION
```

Note that the query engine always encapsulates the query output with a `tupleset` root element. A query need not generate this root element as it is implicitly added by the environment.

Pipelining. The success of many applications depends on how fast they can start producing initial/relevant portions of the result set rather than how fast the entire result set is produced [33]. Often an originator would be happy to already do useful work with one or a few *early results*, as long as they arrive quickly and reliably. Results that arrive later can be handled later, or are ignored anyway. This is particularly often the case in distributed systems where many nodes are involved in query processing, each of which may be unresponsive for many reasons. The situation is even more pronounced in systems with loosely coupled autonomous nodes.

Operators of any kind have a uniform iterator interface, namely the three methods `open()`, `next()` and `close()`. For efficiency, the method `next()` can be asked to deliver several results at once in a so-called *batch*. Semantics are as follows: *"Give me a batch of at least N and at most M results"* (less than N results are delivered when the entire query result set is exhausted). For example, the SEND and RECEIVE network communication operators typically work in batches.

The monotonic semantics of certain operators such as SELECT, UNION, CONCAT, SEND, RECEIVE allow that operator implementations consume just one or a few child results on `next()`. In contrast, the non-monotonic semantics of operators such as SORT, GROUP, MAX, some JOIN methods, etc. require that operator implementations consume *all* child results already on `open()` in order to be able to deliver a result on the first call to `next()`. Since the output of these operators on a subset of the input is not, in general, a subset of the output on the whole input, these operators need to see all of their input before they produce the correct output. This does not break the iterator concept but has important latency and performance implications. Whether the root operator of an agent exhibits a short or long latency to deliver to the originator the first result from the result set depends on the query operators in use, which in turn depend on the given query. In other words, for some query types the originator has the potential to immediately start piping in results (at moderate performance rate), while for other query types it must wait for a long time until the first result becomes available (the full result set arrives almost at once, however).

A query (an operator implementation) is said to be *pipelined* if it can already produce at least one result tuple before all input tuples have been seen. Otherwise, a query (an operator) is said to be *non-pipelined*. Simple queries do support pipelining (e.g. Gnutella queries). Medium queries may or may not support pipelining, whereas complex queries typically do not support pipelining.

3   Static Loop Timeout and Dynamic Abort Timeout

Clearly there comes a time when a user is no longer interested in query results, no matter whether any more results might be available. The query roaming the network and its response traffic should fade away after some time. In addition, P2P systems are well advised to attempt to limit resource consumption by defending against *runaway* queries roaming forever or producing gigantic result sets, either unintended or malicious. To address these problems, an absolute *abort timeout* is attached to a query, as it travels across hops. An abort timeout can be seen as a deadline. Together with the query, a node tells a neighbor *"I will ignore (the rest of) your result set if I have not received it before 12:00:00 today."* The problem, then, is to ensure that a maximum of results can be delivered reliably within the time frame desired by a user. The value of a *static timeout* remains unchanged across hops, except for defensive modification in flight triggered by runaway query detection (e.g. infinite timeout). In contrast, it is intended that the value of a *dynamic timeout* be decreased at each hop. Nodes further away from the originator may time out earlier than nodes closer to the originator.

Dynamic Abort Timeout. A static abort timeout is entirely unsuitable for non-pipelined result set delivery, because it leads to a serious reliability problem, which we propose to call *simultaneous abort timeout*. If just one of the many nodes in the query path fails to be responsive for whatever reasons, all other nodes in the path are waiting, eventually time out and attempt to return at least a partial result set. However, it is impossible that any of these partial results ever reach the originator, because all nodes time out *simultaneously* (and it takes some time for results to flow back).

To address the simultaneous abort timeout problem, we propose dynamic abort timeouts. Under *dynamic abort timeout*, nodes further away from the originator time out earlier than nodes closer to the originator. This provides some safety time window for the partial results of any node to flow back across multiple hops to the originator. Intermediate nodes can and should adaptively decrease the timeout value as necessary, in order to leave a large enough time window for receiving and returning partial results subsequent to timeout.

Observe that the closer a node is to the originator, the more important it is (if it cannot meet its deadline, results from a large branch are discarded). Further, the closer a node is to the originator, the larger is its response and bandwidth consumption. Thus, as a good policy to choose the safety time window, we propose *exponential decay with halving*. The window size is halved at each hop, leaving large safety windows for important nodes and tiny window sizes for nodes that contribute only marginal result sets. Also, taking into account network latency and the time it takes for a query to be locally processed, the timeout is updated at each hop N according to the following recurrence formula:

$$timeout_N = currenttime_N + \frac{timeout_{N-1} - currenttime_N}{2} \qquad (1)$$

Consider for example Figure 6. At time t the originator submits a query with a dynamic abort timeout of t+4 seconds. In other words, it warns the agent to ignore results after time t+4. The agent in turn intends to safely meet the deadline and so figures that it needs to retain a safety window of 2 seconds, already starting to return its (partial) results at time t+2. The agent warns its own neighbors to ignore results after time t+2. The neighbors also intend to safely meet the deadline. From the 2 seconds available, they choose to allocate 1 second, and leave the rest to the branch remaining above. Eventually, the safety window becomes so small that a node can no longer meet a deadline on timeout. The results from the unlucky node are ignored, and its partial results are discarded. However, other nodes below and in other branches are unaffected. Their results survive and have enough time to hop all the way back to the originator before time t+4.

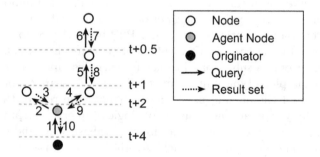

Fig. 6. Dynamic Abort Timeout.

Static Loop Timeout. The same query may arrive at a node multiple times, along distinct routes, perhaps in a complex pattern. For reliable loop detection, a query has an identifier and a certain life time. To each query, an originator attaches a *loop timeout* and a different *transaction identifier*, which is a universally unique identifier (UUID). A node maintains a state table of transaction identifiers and returns an error when a query is received that has already been seen and has not yet timed out. On loop timeout, a node may "forget" about a query by deleting it from the state table. To be able to reliably detect a loop, a node must not forget a transaction identifier before its loop timeout has been reached. Interestingly, a static loop timeout is required in order to fully preserve query semantics. Otherwise, a problem arises that we propose to call *non-simultaneous loop timeout*. The non-simultaneous loop timeout problem is caused by the fact that some nodes still forward the query to other nodes when the destinations have already forgotten it. In other words, the problem is that loop timeout does not occur simultaneously everywhere. Consequently, a loop timeout must be static (does not change across hops) to guarantee that loops can reliably be detected. Along with a query, an originator not only provides a dynamic abort timeout, but also a static loop timeout. Initially at the originator, both values must be identical (e.g. t+4). After the first hop, both values become unrelated.

To summarize, we have `abort timeout` $\leq$ `loop timeout`. To ensure reliable loop detection, a loop timeout must be static whereas an abort timeout may be static or dynamic. Under non-pipelined result set delivery, dynamic abort timeout using *exponential decay with halving* ensure that a maximum of results can be delivered reliably within the time frame desired by a user. We speculate that dynamic timeouts could also incorporate sophisticated cost functions involving latency and bandwidth estimation and/or economic models.

4   Query Scope

As in a data integration system [8,9,10], the goal is to exploit several independent information sources as if they were a single source. This is important for distributed systems in which node topology or deployment model change frequently. For example, cross-organizational Grids and P2P networks exhibit such a character. However, in practice, it is often sufficient (and much more efficient) for a query to consider only a subset of all tuples (service descriptions) from a subset of nodes. For example, a typical query may only want to search tuples (services) within the scope of the domain `cern.ch` and ignore the rest of the world. To this end, we cleanly separate the concepts of (logical) query and (physical) query scope. A query is formulated against a global database view and is insensitive to link topology and deployment model. In other words, to a query the set of tuples appears as a single homogenous database, even though the set may be (recursively) partitioned across many nodes and databases. This means that in a relational or XML environment, at the global level, the set of all tuples appears as a single, very large, table or XML document, respectively. The query scope, on the other hand, is used to navigate and prune the link topology and filter on attributes of the deployment model. Conceptually, the scope is the input fed to the query. The query scope is a set and may contain anything from all tuples in the universe to none. Both query and scope can prune the search space, but they do so in a very different manner. A query scope is specified either *directly* or *indirectly*. One can distinguish scopes based on neighbor selection, timeout and radius.

Neighbor Selection. For simplicity, all our discussions so far have implicitly assumed a *broadcast* model (on top of TCP) in which a node forwards a query to all neighbor nodes. However, in general one can select a subset of neighbors, and forward concurrently or sequentially. Fewer query forwards lead to less overall resource consumption. The issue is critical due to the snowballing (epidemic, flooding) effect implied by broadcasting. Overall bandwidth consumption grows exponentially with the query radius, producing enormous stress on the network and drastically limiting its scalability [34,35].

Clearly selecting a neighbor subset can lead to incomplete coverage, missing important results. The best policy to adopt depends on the context of the query and the topology. For example, the scope can select only neighbors with a service description of interface type "Gnutella". In an attempt to explicitly exploit topology characteristics, a virtual organization of a Grid may deliberately organize global, intermediate and local job schedulers into a tree-like topology. Correct operation of scheduling may require reliable discovery of all or at least most relevant schedulers in the tree. In such a scenario, random selection of half of the neighbors at each node is certainly undesirable. A policy that selects all `child` nodes and ignores all `parent` nodes may be more adequate. Further, a node may maintain statistics about its neighbors. One may only select neighbors that meet minimum requirements in terms of latency, bandwidth or historic query outcomes (`maxLatency, minBandwidth, minHistoricResult`). Other node properties such as hostname, domain name, owner, etc. can be exploited in query scope guidance, for example to implement security policies. Consider an example where the scheduling system may only trust nodes from a select number of security domains. Here a query should never be forwarded to nodes not matching the trust pattern.

Further, in some systems, finding a single result is sufficient. In general, a user or any given node can guard against unnecessarily large result sets, message sizes and resource consumption by specifying the maximum number of result tuples (`maxResults`) and bytes (`maxResultsBytes`) to be returned. Using sequential propagation, depending on the number of results already obtained from the local database and a subset of the selected neighbors, the query may no longer need to be forwarded to the rest of the selected neighbors.

Neighbor Selection Query.   For flexibility and expressiveness, we propose to allow the user to specify the selection policy. In addition to the normal query, the user defines a *neighbor selection query* (XQuery) that takes the tuple set of the current node as input and returns a subset that indicates the nodes selected for forwarding. For example, a neighbor query implementing broadcasting selects all services with registry and P2P query capabilities, as follows:

```
RETURN /tupleset/tuple[@type="service"
  AND content/service/interface[@type="Consumer-1.0"]
  AND content/service/interface[@type="XQuery-1.0"]]
```

A wide range of policies can be implemented in this manner. The neighbor selection policy can draw from the rich set of information contained in the tuples published to the node. Further, recall that the set of tuples in a database may not only contain service descriptions of neighbor nodes (e.g. in WSDL [19]), but also other kind of (soft state) content published from any kind of content provider. For example, this may include the type of queries neighbor nodes can answer, descriptions of the kind of tuples they hold (e.g. their types), or a compact summary or index of their content. Content available to the neighbor selection query may also include host and network information as well as statistics that a node periodically publishes to its immediate neighbors. A neighbor selection query enables group communication to all nodes with certain characteristics (e.g. the same group ID or interfaces). One can implement domain filters and security filters (e.g. `allow/deny` regular expressions as used in the Apache HTTP server if the tuple set includes metadata such as hostname and node owner. To summarize, a neighbor selection query can be used to implement *smart dynamic routing*.

Radius. The *radius* of a query is a measure of path length. More precisely, it is the maximum number of hops a query is allowed to travel on any given path. The radius is decreased by one at each hop. The roaming query and response traffic must fade away upon reaching a radius of less than zero. A scope based on radius serves similar purposes as a timeout. Nevertheless, timeout and radius are complementary scope features. The radius can be used to indirectly limit result set size. In addition, it helps to limit latency and bandwidth consumption and to guard against runaway queries with infinite lifetime. In Gnutella and Freenet, the radius is the primary means to specify a query scope. The radius is termed *TTL (time-to-live)* in these systems. Neither of these systems support timeouts.

For maximum result set size limiting, a timeout and/or radius can be used in conjunction with neighbor selection, routed response, and perhaps sequential forward, to implement the *expanding ring* [36] strategy. The term stems from IP multicasting. Here an agent first forwards the query to a small radius/timeout. Unless enough results are found, the agent forwards the query again with increasingly large radius/timeout values to reach further into the network, at the expense of increasingly large overall resource consumption. On each expansion radius/timeout are multiplied by some factor.

5   Related Work

Pipelining. For a survey of adaptive query processing, including pipelining, see the special issue of [37]. [38] develops a general framework for producing partial results for queries involving any non-monotonic operator. The approach inserts update and delete directives into the output stream. The Tukwila [39] and Niagara projects [40] introduce data integration systems with adaptive query processing and XML query operator implementations that efficiently support pipelining. Pipelining of hash joins is discussed in [41,42,43]. Pipelining is often also termed *streaming* or *non-blocking* execution.

Neighbor Selection. *Iterative deepening* [44] is a similar technique to *expanding ring* where an optimization is suggested that avoids reevaluating the query at nodes that have already done so in previous iterations. Neighbor selection policies that are based on randomness and/or historical information about the result set size of prior queries are simulated and analyzed in [45]. An efficient neighbor selection policy is applicable to simple queries posed to networks in which the number of links of nodes exhibits a power law distribution (e.g. Freenet and Gnutella) [46]. Here most (but not all) matching results can be reached with few hops by selecting just a very small subset of neighbors (the neighbors that themselves have the most neighbors to the n-th radius). Note, however, that the policy is based on the assumption that not all results must be found and that all query results are equally relevant. These related works discuss in isolation neighbor selection techniques for a particular query type, without the context of a framework for comprehensive query support.

JXTA. The goal of the JXTA P2P network [47,48,49] is to have peers that can cooperate to form self-organized and self-configured peer groups independent of their position in the network, and without the need of a centralized management infrastructure. JXTA defines six stateless best-effort protocols for ad hoc, pervasive, and multi-hop P2P computing. These are designed to run over uni-directional, unreliable transports. Due to this ambitious goal, a range of well-known higher level abstractions (e.g. bi-directional secure messaging) are (re)invented from first principles.

The Endpoint Routing Protocol allows to discover a route (sequence of hops) from one peer to another peer, given the destination peer ID. The Rendezvous Protocol offers publish-subscribe functionality within a peer group. The Peer Resolver Protocol and Peer Discovery Protocol allow for publication of advertizements and *simple* queries that are unreliable, stateless, non-pipelined, and non-transactional. We believe that this limits scalability, efficiency and applicability for service discovery and other non-trivial use cases. Lacking expressive means for query scoping, neighbor selection and timeouts, it is unclear how chained rendezvous peers can form a search network. We believe that JXTA Peer Groups, JXTA search and publish/subscribe can be expressed within our UPDF framework, but not vice versa.

DNS. Distributed databases with a hierarchical name space such as the Domain Name System (DNS) [50] can efficiently answer *simple* queries of the form *"Find an object by its full name"*. Queries are not forwarded (routed) through the (hierarchical) link topology. Instead, a node returns a *referral* message that redirects an originator to the next closer node. The originator explicitly queries the next node, is referred to yet another closer node, and so on. To support neighbor selection in a hierarchical name space within our UPDF framework, a node could publish to its neighbors not only its service link, but also the name space it manages. The DNS referral behavior can be implemented within UPDF by using a radius scope of zero. The same holds for the LDAP referral behavior (see below).

X.500, LDAP and MDS. The hierarchical distributed X.500 directory [51] works similarly to the DNS. It also supports referrals, but in addition can forward queries through the topology (*chaining* in X.500 terminology). The query language is simple [3]. Query scope specification can support maximum result set size limiting. It does not support radius and dynamic abort timeout as well as pipelined query execution across nodes. LDAP [29] is a simplified subset of X.500. Like DNS, it supports referrals but not query forwarding. The Metacomputing Directory Service (MDS) [30] inherits all properties of LDAP. MDS additionally implements a simple form of query forwarding that allows for multi-level hierarchies but not for arbitrary topologies. Here neighbor selection forwards the query to LDAP servers overlapping with the query name space. The query is forwarded "as is", without loop detection. Further, MDS does not support radius and dynamic abort timeout, pipelined query execution across nodes as well as direct response and metadata responses.

6   Conclusions

Traditional distributed systems assume a particular type of topology (e.g. hierarchical as in DNS, LDAP). Existing P2P systems are built for a single application and data type and do not support queries from a general-purpose query language. For example, Gnutella, Freenet, Tapestry, Chord, Globe and DNS only support lookup by key (e.g. globally unique name). Others such as SDS, LDAP and MDS support simple special-purpose query languages, leading to special-purpose solutions unsuitable for multi-purpose service and resource discovery in large heterogeneous distributed systems spanning many administrative domains. LDAP and MDS do not support essential features for P2P systems such as reliable loop detection, non-hierarchical topologies, dynamic abort timeout, query pipelining across nodes as well as radius scoping. None introduce a unified P2P database framework for general-purpose query support.

We propose the *Unified Peer-to-Peer Database Framework (UPDF)* for general-purpose query support in large heterogeneous distributed systems spanning many administrative domains. UPDF is unified in the sense that it allows to express specific applications for arbitrary query languages (e.g. XQuery, SQL) and node topologies, and a wide range of data types, query response modes (e.g. Routed, Direct and Referral Response), neighbor selection policies, pipelining characteristics, timeout and other scope options. The uniformity, wide applicability and reusability of our approach distinguish it from related work, which individually addresses some but not all problem areas.

We are starting to build a system prototype with the aim of reporting on experience gained from application to an existing large distributed system such as the European Data Grid.

References

1. Ian Foster, Carl Kesselman, and Steve Tuecke. The Anatomy of the Grid: Enabling Scalable Virtual Organizations. *Int'l. Journal of Supercomputer Applications*, 15(3), 2001.
2. Large Hadron Collider Committee. Report of the LHC Computing Review. Technical report, CERN/LHCC/2001-004, April 2001. http://cern.ch/lhc-computing-review-public/Public/Report_final.PDF.
3. Wolfgang Hoschek. *A Unified Peer-to-Peer Database Framework for XQueries over Dynamic Distributed Content and its Application for Scalable Service Discovery.* PhD Thesis, Technical University of Vienna, March 2002.
4. Ben Segal. Grid Computing: The European Data Grid Project. In *IEEE Nuclear Science Symposium and Medical Imaging Conference*, Lyon, France, October 2000.
5. Wolfgang Hoschek, Javier Jaen-Martinez, Asad Samar, Heinz Stockinger, and Kurt Stockinger. Data Management in an International Data Grid Project. In *1st IEEE/ACM Int'l. Workshop on Grid Computing (Grid'2000)*, Bangalore, India, December 2000.
6. Dirk Düllmann, Wolfgang Hoschek, Javier Jean-Martinez, Asad Samar, Ben Segal, Heinz Stockinger, and Kurt Stockinger. Models for Replica Synchronisation and Consistency in a Data Grid. In *10th IEEE Symposium on High Performance and Distributed Computing (HPDC-10)*, San Francisco, California, August 2001.
7. Ian Foster, Carl Kesselman, Jeffrey Nick, and Steve Tuecke. The Physiology of the Grid: An Open Grid Services Architecture for Distributed Systems Integration, January 2002. http://www.globus.org.
8. J.D. Ullman. Information integration using logical views. In *Int'l. Conf. on Database Theory (ICDT)*, Delphi, Greece, 1997.
9. Daniela Florescu, Ioana Manolescu, Donald Kossmann, and Florian Xhumari. Agora: Living with XML and Relational. In *Int'l. Conf. on Very Large Data Bases (VLDB)*, Cairo, Egypt, February 2000.
10. A. Tomasic, L. Raschid, and P. Valduriez. Scaling access to heterogeneous data sources with DISCO. *IEEE Transactions on Knowledge and Data Engineering*, 10(5):808–823, 1998.
11. M. Tamer Özsu and Patrick Valduriez. *Principles of Distributed Database Systems.* Prentice Hall, 1999.
12. Ann Chervenak, Ewa Deelman, Ian Foster, Leanne Guy, Wolfgang Hoschek, Adriana Iamnitchi, Carl Kesselman, Peter Kunszt, Matei Ripeanu, Bob Schwartzkopf, Heinz Stockinger, Kurt Stockinger, and Brian Tierney. Giggle: A Framework for Constructing Scalable Replica Location Services. In *Proc. of the Int'l. IEEE/ACM Supercomputing Conference (SC 2002)*, Baltimore, USA, November 2002. IEEE Computer Society Press.
13. Leanne Guy, Peter Kunszt, Erwin Laure, Heinz Stockinger, and Kurt Stockinger. Replica Management in Data Grids. Technical report, Global Grid Forum Informational Document, GGF5, Edinburgh, Scotland, July 2002.
14. Heinz Stockinger, Asad Samar, Shahzad Mufzaffar, and Flavia Donno. Grid Data Mirroring Package (GDMP). *Journal of Scientific Programming*, 2002.
15. William Bell, Diana Bosio, Wolfgang Hoschek, Peter Kunszt, Gavin McCance, and Mika Silander. Project Spitfire - Towards Grid Web Service Databases. Technical report, Global Grid Forum Informational Document, GGF5, Edinburgh, Scotland, July 2002.

16. Nelson Minar. Peer-to-Peer is Not Always Decentralized. In *The O'Reilly Peer-to-Peer and Web Services Conference*, Washington, D.C., November 2001.

17. Wolfgang Hoschek. The Web Service Discovery Architecture. In *Proc. of the Int'l. IEEE/ACM Supercomputing Conference (SC 2002)*, Baltimore, USA, November 2002. IEEE Computer Society Press.

18. Wolfgang Hoschek. A Database for Dynamic Distributed Content and its Application for Service and Resource Discovery. In *Int'l. IEEE Symposium on Parallel and Distributed Computing (ISPDC 2002)*, Iasi, Romania, July 2002.

19. E. Christensen, F. Curbera, G. Meredith, and S. Weerawarana. Web Services Description Language (WSDL) 1.1. *W3C Note 15*, 2001. http://www.w3.org/TR/wsdl.

20. World Wide Web Consortium. XQuery 1.0: An XML Query Language. *W3C Working Draft*, December 2001.

21. Wolfgang Hoschek. A Comparison of Peer-to-Peer Query Response Modes. In *Proc. of the Int'l. Conf. on Parallel and Distributed Computing and Systems (PDCS 2002)*, Cambridge, USA, November 2002.

22. Gnutella Community. Gnutella Protocol Specification v0.4. dss.clip2.com/GnutellaProtocol04.pdf.

23. I. Clarke, O. Sandberg, B. Wiley, and T. Hong. Freenet: A distributed anonymous information storage and retrieval system. In *Workshop on Design Issues in Anonymity and Unobservability*, 2000.

24. B. Zhao, J. Kubiatowicz, and A. Joseph. Tapestry: An infrastructure for fault-resilient wide-area location and routing. Technical report, U.C. Berkeley UCB//CSD-01-1141, 2001.

25. I. Stoica, R. Morris, D. Karger, M. Kaashoek, and H. Balakrishnan. Chord: A scalable peer-to-peer lookup service for internet applications. In *ACM SIGCOMM*, 2001.

26. M. van Steen, P. Homburg, and A. Tanenbaum. A wide-area distributed system. *IEEE Concurrency*, 1999.

27. Steven E. Czerwinski, Ben Y. Zhao, Todd Hodes, Anthony D. Joseph, and Randy Katz. An Architecture for a Secure Service Discovery Service. In *Fifth Annual Int'l. Conf. on Mobile Computing and Networks (MobiCOM '99)*, Seattle, WA, August 1999.

28. J. Waldo. The Jini architecture for network-centric computing. *Communications of the ACM*, 42(7), July 1999.

29. W. Yeong, T. Howes, and S. Kille. Lightweight Directory Access Protocol. *IETF RFC 1777*, March 1995.

30. Karl Czajkowski, Steven Fitzgerald, Ian Foster, and Carl Kesselman. Grid Information Services for Distributed Resource Sharing. In *Tenth IEEE Int'l. Symposium on High-Performance Distributed Computing (HPDC-10)*, San Francisco, California, August 2001.

31. International Organization for Standardization (ISO). Information Technology-Database Language SQL. *Standard No. ISO/IEC 9075:1999*, 1999.

32. Donald Kossmann. The state of the art in distributed query processing. *ACM Computing Surveys*, September 2000.

33. T. Urhan and M. Franklin. Dynamic Pipeline Scheduling for Improving Interactive Query Performance. *The Very Large Database (VLDB) Journal*, 2001.

34. Jordan Ritter. Why Gnutella Can't Scale. No, Really. http://www.tch.org/gnutella.html.

35. Matei Ripeanu. Peer-to-Peer Architecture Case Study: Gnutella Network. In *Int'l. Conf. on Peer-to-Peer Computing (P2P2001)*, Linkoping, Sweden, August 2001.

36. S.E. Deering. *Multicast Routing in a Datagram Internetwork.* PhD Thesis, Stanford University, 1991.
37. IEEE Computer Society. *Data Engineering Bulletin*, 23(2), June 2000.
38. Jayavel Shanmugasundaram, Kristin Tufte, David J. DeWitt, Jeffrey F. Naughton, and David Maier. Architecting a Network Query Engine for Producing Partial Results. In *WebDB 2000*, 2000.
39. Zachary G. Ives, Alon Y. Halevy, and Daniel S. Weld. Integrating Network-Bound XML Data. *IEEE Data Engineering Bulletin*, 24(2), 2001.
40. J. F. Naughton, D. J. DeWitt, D. Maier, A. Aboulnaga, J. Chen, L. Galanis, J. Kang, R. Krishnamurthy, Q. Luo, N. Prakash, R. Ramamurthy, J. Shanmugasundaram, F. Tian, K. Tufte, S. Viglas, Y. Wang, C. Zhang, B. Jackson, A. Gupta, and R. Chen. The Niagara Internet Query System. *IEEE Data Engineering Bulletin*, 24(2), 2001.
41. Annita N. Wilschut and Peter M. G. Apers. Dataflow query execution in a parallel main-memory environment. In *First Int'l. Conf. on Parallel and Distributed Information Systems*, December 1991.
42. Zachary G. Ives, Daniela Florescu, Marc T. Friedman, Alon Y. Levy, and Daniel S. Weld. An adaptive query execution system for data integration. In *ACM SIGMOD Conf. On Management of Data*, 1999.
43. Tolga Urhan and Michael J. Franklin. Xjoin, A reactively-scheduled pipelined join operator. *IEEE Data Engineering Bulletin*, 23(2), June 2000.
44. Beverly Yang and Hector Garcia-Molina. Efficient Search in Peer-to-Peer Networks. In *22nd Int'l. Conf. on Distributed Computing Systems*, Vienna, Austria, July 2002.
45. Adriana Iamnitchi and Ian Foster. On Fully Decentralized Resource Discovery in Grid Environments. In *Int'l. IEEE Workshop on Grid Computing*, Denver, Colorado, November 2001.
46. L. Adamic, R. Lukose, A. Puniyani, and B. Huberman. Search in power-law networks. *Phys. Rev*, E(64), 2001.
47. Bernard Traversat, Mohamed Abdelaziz, Mike Duigou, Jean-Christophe Hugly, Eric Pouyoul, and Bill Yeager. Project JXTA Virtual Network, 2002. White Paper, http://www.jxta.org.
48. Steven Waterhouse. JXTA Search: Distributed Search for Distributed Networks, 2001. White Paper, http://www.jxta.org.
49. Project JXTA. JXTA v1.0 Protocols Specification, 2002. http://spec.jxta.org.
50. P. Mockapetris. Domain Names - Implementation and Specification. *IETF RFC 1035*, November 1987.
51. International Telecommunications Union. Recommendation X.500, Information technology – Open System Interconnection – The directory: Overview of concepts, models, and services. *ITU-T*, November 1995.

Grid Resource Discovery
Based on a Routing-Transferring Model

Wei Li[1], Zhiwei Xu[1], Fangpeng Dong[1], and Jun Zhang[1]

Institute of Computing Technology of CAS,
Beijing China, 100080
{liwei, zxu, fpdong, zhjun}@ict.ac.cn

Abstract. The Grid technology emerges with the need of resource sharing and cooperation in wide area. Compared with the traditional single computer system, effective resource locating in Grid is difficult because of huge amount and wide-area distribution of dynamical resources. In this paper, we propose a Routing-Transferring resource discovery model, which includes three basic roles: the resource requester, the resource router and the resource provider. The provider sends its resource information to a router, which maintains this information in routing tables. When a router receives a resource request from a requester, it checks routing tables to choose a route for it and transfer it to another router or provider. We give the formalization of this model and analyze the complexity of the SD-RT (Shortest Distance Routing-Transferring) algorithm. The analysis shows that the resource discovery time depends on topology (the longest path in the graph) and distribution of resources. When topology and distribution are definite, the SD-RT algorithm can find a resource in the shortest time. Our experiments also show that when topology is definite, the performance is determined by resource distribution, which includes two important factors: resource frequency and resource location. The testing result shows that high frequency and even location of resources can reduce the resource discovery time significantly.

1 Introduction

During the development of computer architecture, the basic idea is to share computational resources efficiently. Fundamental techniques such as time-sharing, multi-user and multi-process are all designed to realize this goal. With the distribution of computational resources in wide area network and the maturity of the Internet, the demand for resource sharing in wide area increases continually, which causes the emergence of computational Grid [3]. We think the kernel of computational Grid is resource sharing and cooperation in wide area, which could improve resource utilization and obtain much higher computational powers.

A precondition of resource sharing and cooperation is discovering resource efficiently. In traditional computing environments, the resource discovery problem is easy to solve because resource types and numbers are few and resources are

M. Parashar (Ed.): GRID 2002, LNCS 2536, pp. 145–156, 2002.

under central control. In a Grid environment, the characteristic of computational resource has changed drastically: the type and number of resources are very huge; resources are distributed in wide area and interconnected by WAN such as the Internet; resources are owned by different organizations and these organizations have various resource management policies. Because of these new properties, traditional resource discovery methods can not search and locate resources efficiently in a Grid environment. In this paper, we propose a Routing-Transferring resource discovery model in which the key component is the *resource router*, which can transfer resource requests one by one from resource requesters to resource providers.

This paper is organized as follows: Section 2 gives related work on resource discovery in a Grid environment. Section 3 introduces the classification of Grid resources, the Routing-Transferring resource discovery model and the SD-RT algorithm. Section 4 describes the formalization of our model and the complexity analysis. Section 5 gives experiments and results.

2   Related Work

Resource discovery in a Grid environment is different from the name-based resource discovery, as the latter one is not feasible in computational Grid [4]. Several research projects have made their efforts to solve this problem. Condor's Matchmaker [6] uses a centralized architecture to discover the computational resource. Matchmaker is a central server with responsibility for matching the advertisement between resource requesters and resource providers. Globus's MDS-2 [2] uses a distributed architecture to provide resource information services. A resource provider can use a registration protocol to register resource information to GIIS [2], and a user can use a query protocol to access resource information from GIIS and GRIS [2]. Legion uses Collections [1] to search and locate resources in Grid. When a user requests a resource, Legion will query resource information in multiple Collections; If finding out such resources, Legion's resource scheduler will randomly choose one of them. The research of Iamnitchi [4] uses a peer-to-peer architecture for resource discovery. It is a fully distributed architecture providing four request-forwarding algorithms. Their results show that a decentralized approach is suited for resource discovery in a Grid environment. Our model also uses a distributed architecture and we construct a resource network via resource routers, which maintain resource information about Grid and perform resource discovery tasks.

3   Routing-Transferring Model

3.1   Classification of Grid Resources

In a Grid environment, we can divide computational resource into two classes. The first one is the static resource with only two states: existent or non-existent, such as operating system, software and etc., which does not change often and can be measured by two values such as 0 for existent and 1 for non-existent. The second one is the dynamical resource, whose state can change often and linearly, for example, the CPU load. We can measure the dynamical resource by a linear number such as 50% CPU load. When discovering dynamical resources, we must give the resource type and the value at the same time.

To distinguish various resource types, we assign each resource type a unique *resource type ID* and a *resource type value*. The coding of resource types is a challenge problem because Grid resources have so many types and are always expanding. In our model we just simply assign a unique integer for a resource type. The assignment of resource value for static resources and dynamical resources is also different. The static resource has only two values: 0 or 1. But the dynamical resource has linear values.

We also use different methods to locate static resources and dynamical resources. The reason is as follows: when we search a static resources of a special type, if there are many resources of the same type (resource type ID), we regard these resources as same and we select one of them randomly. But when we search dynamical resources of a given resource type value, although there are many resources of this type, we can not randomly select one because they may have different values. For example, if we want to search a computer that can provide 128MB memory, then a computer providing 100MB memory can not satisfy the request, but a computer with 256MB memory will meet.

3.2 Framework

There are three basic roles in our model: the resource requester, the resource router and the resource provider. Every provider must link itself to a router. Every router must link at least one other router. Each requester may link one or several routers. A requester sends a resource request to a router and the request will contain a resource type and a resource type value. The request may contain multiple resource types and values, for example, a Linux OS and a 256MB memory. The router always waits on requests coming from requesters or neighbor routers. It maintains multiple *resource routing tables* (discussed later) recording resource information about its neighbors (routers or providers). When a router receives a request from a requester, it checks routing tables and chooses a neighbor to transfers the request. A request may be transferred by several routers until it arrives at a provider satisfying the requirement. If the time-to-live (TTL) of a request expires, the router will discard it. Another work of the router is maintaining resource information about its neighbors. The router periodically receives resource information sent by its neighbors and updates relevant routing tables. On the other hands, the router also sends local resource information to neighbor routers periodically. A resource provider is a computer supplying static or dynamical resources. It first registers its resources to a router and periodically sends its up-to-date resource information to the router. When a provider receives a request, it checks the resource requirement of this request and decides whether accepting it or not.

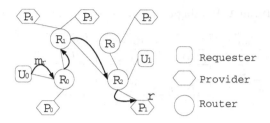

Fig. 1. The Routing-Transferring model and the process of locating a resource

Figure 1 illustrates the structure of our model and the process of locating a resource. A resource r locates at a provider P_1. A request m_r asking for r is sent from U_0 to R_0. R_0 knows that if transferring the request to R_1, the request can find r. Then R_0 sends m_r to R_1. Similarly, R_1 and R_2 will choose a route and transfer the request until m_r arrives at P_1.

3.3   The Nature of Resource Routers

The resource router is the backbone of our model, which is a transfer station for resource requests. It collects resource information of Grid and gives a path for a resource request. It is also a bridge linking all providers and requesters together. All providers and requesters can dynamically join or leave Grid by connecting or disconnecting to routers. When more and more routers are linked together, Grid can expand to huge scale. The resource router is something like the IP router in the Internet [5].

Resource Routing Table. In a resource router, routing tables are used to record resource information about subgrid, a sub partition of Grid. A router can connect several subgrids and it is the common joint of these subgrids.

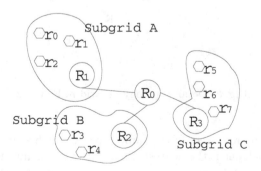

Fig. 2. R_0 connects the subgrid A, B and C and R_1, R_2, R_3 are entry points

Table 1. Routing tables in the resource router R_0

Router	Resource Type			
R_1	$t(r_0)$	$t(r_1)$	$t(r_2)$	...
R_2	$t(r_3)$	$t(r_4)$	...	
R_3	$t(r_5)$	$t(r_6)$	$t(r_7)$	...

In Figure 2, the router R_0 connects the subgrid A, B and C. Table 1 gives routing tables of R_0. In order to determine which subgrid can provide a special resource, the router R_0 collects up-to-date resource information about these subgrids and records them in routing tables. For a given subgrid, there is a router which collects resource information of this subgrid and it is the entry point of this subgrid. For the router R_0, the router R_1, R_2 and R_3 are entry points of the subgrid A, B and C, respectively. In other words, a router will maintain a table for every other router or provider connected with it because they each represent a subgrid. In each routing table, each resource type has one and only one entry indicating whether there is such a resource type in this subgrid. In our model, we choose to record the "direction" and the "distance" of resource types but not the physical location of resources (such as the IP address). That is, the router knows that there is a path with certain length along which a request can reach the resource required. Here, the length of a path is the hops when a request passes through this path. If we record location information of every resource, the space cost is huge because the number of resources will be infinite although the type of resources may be finite. In fact, we need not to record physical location information and recording the path is enough. When R_0 receives a request, it checks these tables and determines where to transfer the request. For example, if the request is $t(r_4)$, the router will transfer it to the neighbor R_2.

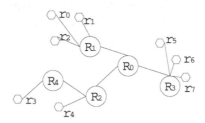

Fig. 3. Detail topology of Grid in Figure 2

If there are many resources of the same type, when choosing a route, a router needs to know which one is the nearest. So another important function of routing tables is recording the distance from a router to a resource type. Figure 3 gives the detail topology of Grid in Figure 2. For the resource r_0, its distance to R_1 is 1, which means finding a request for r_0 from R_1 needs 1 hop. Similarly, the distance from r_0 to R_0 is 2 and to R_2 or R_3 is 3. In Table 2, we add distance

Table 2. Routing tables in the resource router R_3 with distance information

Router	Resource Type/Distance					
R_0	$t(r_0)/3$	$t(r_1)/3$	$t(r_2)/3$	$t(r_3)/4$	$t(r_4)/3$	...
Local	$t(r_5)/1$	$t(r_6)/1$	$t(r_7)/1$	...		

information to routing tables in Table 1. In Table 2, if r_3 and r_5 have same resource type such as $t(r_3) = t(r_5) = t'$, when a request for resource of type t' arrives at R_3, R_3 knows that resource r_5 is nearer. So it will transfer the request to r_5.

Routing Table Updating Policy. To transfer resource requests correctly, a router maintains up-to-date resource information about its neighbors. Every router and provider sends resource information of local subgrid to its neighbors periodically. If one subgrid contains multiple subgrids, resource information of this subgrid is created by aggregating resource information of these subgrids. Here two things are needed: aggregation of resource types and aggregation of resource values.

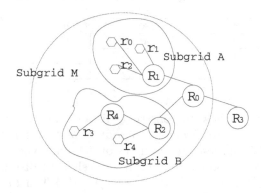

Fig. 4. The subgrid A and B merge into subgrid M

First we will talk about how to aggregate resource types. Figure 4 is another view of Grid in Figure 2. For the router R_3, subgrid A and B merge into subgrid M and the entry point of M is R_0. When R_0 updates resource information of M to R_3, it aggregates routing information of A and B. In other words, resource information sent to R_3 is the aggregation of the routing table of R_1 and R_2 in the router R_0. Consider routing tables in Table 1, if r_0 and r_3 have a same type t', then R_0 will send t' to R_3 but not both r_0's type and r_3's type. Table 3 gives the routing table of R_3, in which r_0 and r_3 have a same type t'. In routing tables of R_3, the routing table for R_0 records t' only once as well as the shortest distance from R_3 to t'. For R_3, it only needs to know whether there have such resource in M. It does not care for where it is.

Table 3. Routing tabless in the router R_3, in which r_0 and r_3 have a same type t'

Router	Resource Type/Distance				
R_0	$t(r_1)/3$	$t(r_2)/3$	$t'/3$	$t(r_4)/3$	...
Local	$t'/1$	$t(r_6)/1$	$t(r_7)/1$	...	

Now consider the aggregation of multiple resource values. For static resources in routing tables, they are marked with 1 to represent existent. When we aggregate multiple static resources, the new value will also be 1. But for multiple dynamical resources, because their resource values are different, so we should map these multiple values into one value. For different resource types, mapping methods are different. For example, when mapping multiple memory resources, we choose the maximum one as the new value. That is, if there are two memory resources with the value of 256MB and 128MB respectively, we will choose the value of 256MB. This mapping method can guarantee that we can find a memory resource satisfying the resource request, but it is hard to find a resource best matching.

Table 4. Routing tables in the resource router R_0 with distance information

Router	Resource Type/Distance			
R_1	$t'/2$	$t(r_1)/2$	$t(r_2)/2$	...
R_2	$t'/3$	$t(r_4)/2$	...	
R_3	$t'/2$	$t(r_6)/2$	$t(r_7)/2$	...

Another problem is how to construct distance information. The distance information is updated from routers to routers and plus 1 whenever passing through a router. When there are resources of the same type in different routing tables, the router will choose a router with the shortest distance. Table 4 gives routing tables of R_0. Here $t(r_0) = t(r_3) = t(r_5) = t'$. When R_0 updates distance information to R_3, it will choose a shortest distance from the table of R_1 and R_2 (excluding R_3), which is 2, and sends it to R_3. So in routing tables of R_3, the shortest distance from R_3 to the resource of type t'(which is $t(r_0), t(r_3)$ or $t(r_5)$) is 3.

Resource Request Routing Policies. Another issue in our model is how to determine the destination of resource requests, namely the problem of routing policies. It is very important because it will influence the efficiency of resource discovery significantly. Here we present an efficient algorithm called Shortest Distance Routing-Transferring. This algorithm is designed to locate resources as soon as possible. When a router receives a request, the SD-RT algorithm will choose a route by which the resource is nearest to this router. Especially when distance is 1, it means that the provider is a neighbor of this router. Using the SD-RT algorithm, a request can arrive at the resource provider as soon as possible. If there are more than one provider supplying resources of the same type, the SD-RT algorithm can guarantee the request being able to arrive at the provider nearer to the requester. In Table 4, if a request arriving at R_0 is for the resource of type t', the SD-RT algorithm will choose R_1 or R_3 but not R_2 to transfer the request.

4   Formalization and Complexity

In this section, we give the formalization of our model on condition that there are only static, single-resource requests. We don't consider dynamical resource requests and multiple-resource requests because of the complexity. We also suppose all routing information in a router is valid.

Our model can be defined as a undirected weight graph without loops, denoted by $G = (V, E)$, V is the aggregation of all nodes and E is the aggregation of all edges; where $|V| = n$, n is the number of nodes; $|V| = m$, which is the number of edges. For every node v_i we give it the weight $w(v_i)$, which is the time cost when a request passes through v_i. We don't consider the time cost on edges here. The aggregation of nodes connecting to node v_i is denoted by $Neighbor(v_i)$. The nodes of G can be divided into two classes: provider nodes and router nodes, denoted by V_P and V_R. When a request passes through these nodes, we need to check resource information in them. We suppose the checking time is constant.

The aggregation of resources is denoted by R and the number of resources is $|R|$. We assume $|R| \geq |V_P|$. We suppose R can be divided into various types and denote the type of R by t. For every resource r, we denote its type by $t(r)$. If there are several resources $r_0, r_1, \ldots, r_i$, $i \leq |R|$ of the same type, we have the equation $t(r_0) = t(r_1) = \ldots = t(r_i)$. If the resource r locates in a node $v_i \in V_P$, we have the equation $at(v_i, t(r)) = 1$. That means there is a resource of type $t(r)$ on the node $v_i \in V_P$. If there are no resources of type $t(r)$ on the node $v_i \in V_P$, we have the equation $at(v_i, t(r)) = 0$.

In a router node, we use routing tables to record direction and distance information of resources. In our model, we use a routing function to calculate the destination of requests, which is denoted by $Route(v_i, t(r)) = v_n$, $v_n \in Neighbor(v_i)$.

In the SD-RT algorithm, we also provide a distance function to calculate the shortest distance from the router v_i to $t(r)$, which is denoted by $Shortest(v_i, t(r)) = v_n$, $v_n \in Neighbor(v_i)$. The process of discovering the resource r can be regarded as a request going from the router node v_0 until reaching the provider node v_i where there is $at(v_i, t(r)) = 1$. All nodes excepting v_i are router nodes. We denoted this process as a search path by $P = v_0 e_0 v_1 e_1 \ldots v_{i-1} e_{i-1} v_i$, $1 \leq i \leq n$, $v_i \in V_P$ and $v_j \in V_R$, $0 \leq j \leq i$ and $at(v_i, t(r)) = 1$ and $Shortest(v_{i-1}, t(r)) = v_i$. The weight of P is denoted by W_P and the longest discovery path as P_{max}, whose weight is W_{max}. So, the time cost of SD-RT resource discovery algorithm is W_P, the weight of P. Then the time complexity is $O(W_{max})$ at worst. Also because the distance function determines the exact length of P, which reflects the resource distribution of G, so $O(W_{max})$ depends on distribution of resources firstly. On the other hand, because there are no loops in G, the length of P can not exceed the length of P_{max}, so $O(W_{max})$ also depends on topology of routers. No matter what distribution it is, a request can always find the resource if it exists and the length of its path will not exceed the length of P_{max}.

5 Experiments

In our experiment, we construct a test network and make various distributions to test the performance of the SD-RT algorithm. Our experiment starts after constructing all routing tables successfully.

5.1 Topology

We know that the network topology will influence the performance greatly. So we should avoid the special condition such as the star-topology network. Using the Minimum Spanning Tree algorithm, we create a network consisting of 5000 nodes to simulate the real network. In our network all nodes are resource routers. We do not allocate nodes for resource providers and just record their resource information in neighbor routers.

5.2 Resource Distribution

In addition to the network topology, we find that there are two other factors responsible for the performance of our algorithm: the resource frequency (the ratio of the valid number of resources to the scale of the network, for example, the frequency of 1/1000 means there are 5 resources of the same type in our network) and the resource location. Also because resources of different types are irrelevant, we just distribute one type of resource in our network. According to our algorithm, multiple resources of the same type distributed in one node will be treated as one resource. So, to make full use of resources, multiple resources of the same type will not be placed on one node.

We distribute resources by two different policies: one is even, the other is uneven. First, we distribute different number of resources of the same type to a same network in order to validate the effect of the resource frequency. The values are 1, 10, 50, 100 and 500, so the frequencies are 1/5000, 1/500, 1/100, 1/50 and 1/10 respectively. The resource location is random in order to simulating the real world. Secondly, according to our algorithm, we can draw a conclusion that once the topology of the network and the frequency of resources are definite, there is an optimizing location for these resources, which can make the value of

$$\sum_{i=1}^{5000} Shortest\,(v_i, t) \tag{1}$$

minimum. Under this distribution, we say the overall performance is best. Unfortunately it is unpractical to find this distribution for its tremendous complexity. It is obvious that when every node has a resource, the performance is best. This fact enlightens us that we can divide the whole network into a number of subnet-works according to the amount of resources. The more the resources, the more subnetworks we use. These subnetworks are similar in scale and the number of resources they have. We call this as even distribution. On the other hand, re-sources may be deployed on neighboring nodes centralized in one subnetwork, and we call this as uneven distribution. We notice that when distribution trends to be even, the performance goes along a better direction. In our experiment, we distribute resources in above two ways.

5.3   User Request

To estimate the performance of the whole system, we assume user requests are from every one of 5000 nodes. Because we only distribute one resource type, so the request only contains this resource type. Also because every router records the shortest path to this resource type, we need not to send multiple requests to a same router and just send one request to each router.

5.4   Result

As we know, the topology of the network has fatal effect to the performance of our model. But in our experiment, we concern about the effect of resource distribution more than the topology. So we just assume the topology is fixed. In our network the length of the longest path is 261 hops, that is, the P_{max} is 261.

Table 5. The average discovery time for different resource frequencies

Resource Frequency	1/5000	1/500	1/100	1/50	1/10
Average Hops	101	41	21	13	5

Figure 5 highlights the influence to discovery performance by different re-source frequency. It shows that the higher the frequency, the better the per-formance. But as the ratio increases, the improvement of performance is slowed down. As we can see, the longest path is about 200 hops, less than P_{max}. Table 5 show the average discovery time for various resource frequency.

Figure 6 shows the influence by resource locations. The performance is better when resources are distributed evenly. When these resources are centralized, the number of resources has little influence on the performance. However, when these resources are distributed more evenly, the number of the resources affects the performance significantly. That means when resources are located more evenly and their frequency are higher, the resource discovery performance is better.

6   Conclusion and Future Works

In this paper we introduce a Routing-Transferring resource discovery model. The experiment result show that when network topology and resource distribution is

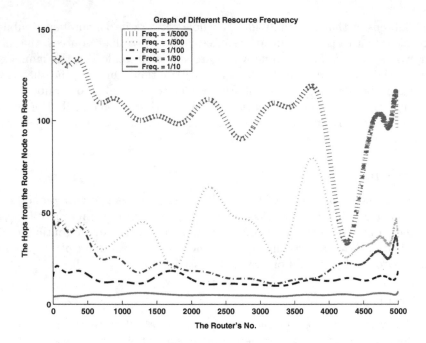

Fig. 5. The discovery time for different resource frequencies

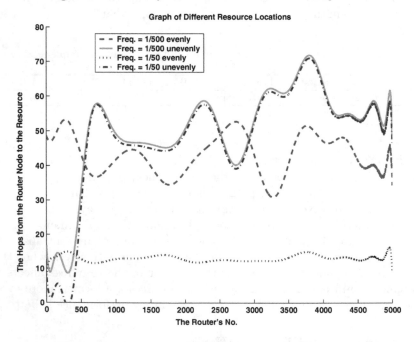

Fig. 6. The discovery time for different resource locations

definite, the SD-RT algorithm can find a resource in shortest time. The result also show that change of network topology and resource distribution will influence the resource discovery performance. When topology is definite, the performance is determined by resource distribution. Higher frequency and more even location of resource can improve the resource discovery performance significantly.

We have developed a prototype of resource router in our Vega Grid project [7][8][9]. In next step, we will improve our model and algorithms to support the discovery of dynamical-resource and multiple-resource.

Acknowledgement

We are grateful to Bingchen Li, Yili Gong, Hua Huang and Haiying Tang for their helpful works on developing prototype of resource router.

References

1. S. J. Chapin, D. Katramatos, J. Karpovich, A. Grimshaw: Resource Management in Legion. Future Generation Computer Systems, Vol. 15, No. 5, pp. 583594, 1999.
2. K. Czajkowski, S. Fitzgerald, I. Foster, C. Kesselman: Grid Information Services for Distributed Resource Sharing. Proc. of the 10th IEEE Int'l Symp. on High Performance Distributed Computing(2001).
3. I. Foster, C. Kesselman (ed.): The Grid: Blueprint for a New Computing Infrastructure. Morgan Kaufmann Publishers(1998).
4. A. Iamnitchi, I. Foster: On Fully Decentralized Resource Discovery in Grid Environments. International Workshop on Grid Computing, Denver, CO, 2001.
5. J. Postel (ed.): Internet Protocol: DARPA internet program protocol specification. RFC791, September 1981.
6. R. Raman,M. Livny, M. Solomon: Matchmaking: Distributed Resource Management for High Throughput Computing. Proc. of IEEE Intl. Symp. on High Performance Distributed Computing, Chicago, USA(1998).
7. Z. Xu, W. Li: HPC Research in China and the Vega Grid Project. Keynote Speech, Proc. HPC Asia 2002, Bangalore, India, 2002.
8. Z. Xu, W. Li, H. Fu, Z. Zeng: The Vega Grid and Grid-Based Education. The 1st International Conference on Web-Based Learning, HK, China, 2002.
9. Z. Xu, N. Sun, D. Meng, W. Li: Cluster and Grid Superservers: The Dawning Experience in China. Proc. of the 3rd IEEE International Conference on Cluster Computing(2001).

Resource Allocation
for Steerable Parallel Parameter Searches*

Marcio Faerman[1], Adam Birnbaum[2], Henri Casanova[1,2], and Fran Berman[1,2]

[1] Department of Computer Science and Engineering, University of California, San Diego
mfaerman@cs.ucsd.edu
[2] San Diego Supercomputer Center
{birnbaum, casanova, berman}@sdsc.edu

Abstract. Computational Grids lend themselves well to parameter sweep applications, in which independent tasks calculate results for points in a parameter space. It is possible for a parameter space to become so large as to pose prohibitive system requirements. In these cases, *user-directed steering* promises to reduce overall computation time. In this paper, we address an interesting challenge posed by these user-directed searches: how should compute resources be allocated to application tasks as the overall computation is being steered by the user? We present a model for user-directed searches, and then propose a number of resource allocation strategies and evaluate them in simulation. We find that prioritizing the assignments of tasks to compute resources throughout the search can lead to substantial performance improvements.

1   Introduction

An increasingly common class of scientific applications is that of *Parameter Sweep Applications*: applications that consist of large sets of *independent* computational tasks. Each task typically evaluates a multi-dimensional *objective function* at a point in a multi-dimensional parameter space. Parameter Sweep Applications arise in many domains (e.g. Computational Fluid Dynamics [17], Bioinformatics [2]). From a parallel computing perspective, these applications present many advantages. They can tolerate high network latencies due to the lack of inter-task communications. They can benefit from simple fault-detection/restart mechanisms due to the lack of hard task synchronization requirements. Therefore, they are ideally suited to emerging *Computational Grids* where resources are widely distributed and loosely coupled. Nevertheless they pose interesting challenges in terms of scheduling and deployment, some of which we have addressed in our previous work [3,8].

Based on our experience, we have seen that parameter spaces often become too large to be entirely computed even on large-scale platforms. This is due both to extensive parameter value ranges, and to high dimensionality of the parameter space itself. Furthermore, even though exhaustively computing values over an entire parameter space would be ideal, users are often mostly interested in finding certain patterns in a parameter space (e.g. a set of parameter values that leads to certain values of the objective

---

* This work was supported by the National Science Foundation under Award ACI-0086092.

M. Parashar (Ed.): GRID 2002, LNCS 2536, pp. 157–168, 2002.

function). Therefore, an appealing approach is to *search* the parameter space for these patterns, in order to save both time and compute resources. We denote such applications as *Parameter Search Applications*. A large number of algorithms have been developed and used successfully for such searches [4,5,11,13,19]. These algorithms, often called guided-search algorithms, can be very effective when the user's objectives are clearly specified (e.g. minimize a given function).

In this work we focus on scenarios in which the user *interactively steers* the search. In many real-world applications, the user's objectives cannot be precisely specified, or are not even known at the onset of the search (e.g. users are looking for something "interesting"). This subjectivity makes it impossible to automate the search process, and it is necessary to involve the user directly. For instance, one can let the user periodically indicate which regions of the parameter space seem more or less likely to contain solutions or features of interest, so that the search can concentrate on promising regions. We denote such search scenarios as *user-directed searches*. In this paper we make the following contribution. We propose and evaluate a resource allocation approach that improves the performance of user-directed parallel parameter space searches on distributed computing platforms. Our goal is *not* to develop novel search/optimization algorithms, but rather to investigate techniques to allocate appropriate computing resources to tasks of a user-directed search.

Our work is in the context of the Virtual Instrument (VI) project [7,21]. The project focuses on a computational neuroscience application, MCell [15], which is used by scientists to explore large parameter spaces for subjectively "interesting features". Due to space constraints, we give details about the implication of our results on the Virtual Instrument software in [9].

2   Background

2.1   Methodology

Evaluation of resource allocation strategies for user-directed searches faces an inherent difficulty: specific behaviors are unknown until users have access to production software. Steering in the VI will be based on iterative feedback from the user. The user will begin running the application with a small set of parameter space points. As the application runs and results are returned, the user may add new points for evaluation, and may also assign different levels of importance to each point. Once the VI software has been released to a large community of MCell users and is being used in a production environment, we will be able to evaluate different resource allocation strategies in real steering scenarios that make use of this user input. However, for the time being we chose to *simulate* user behavior.

In order to simulate user behavior, we replace the search for subjective "interesting" features with an iterative search for the minimum of the well-known, "hard-to-optimize", Griewank function [12]. The Griewank function we use in this paper, g_σ, is defined as:

$$g_\sigma(x_1, ..., x_D) = 1 + \frac{\sigma}{4000} \sum_{i=1}^{i=D} x_i^2 - \prod_{i=1}^{i=D} \cos(\frac{x_i}{\sqrt{i}}), \qquad (1)$$

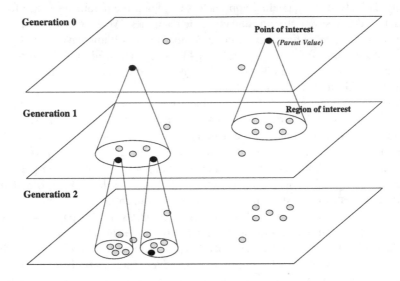

Fig. 1. Overall User-directed Search Strategy

where σ is a real that parameterizes the overall shape of the function. In the rest of the paper we use the 2-D Griewank function for experiments and simulations.

There is a large number of existing algorithms for performing guided searches [4,5], [11,13,19]. Our goal is to test resource allocation strategies that will enable user steering, allowing users to reach useful results more quickly by allocating more compute resources to promising areas of parameter space. We are not trying to develop novel search algorithms, since the searches in question will ultimately involve subjective user goals and criteria. Based on discussions with MCell researchers, we have developed a search procedure that is representative of what a user may do when exploring an MCell parameter space. We believe that this search procedure, described in the next section, provides a useful basis for evaluating steering and resource allocation techniques.

2.2   Search Strategy

We present here the overall process for a user-directed search. The search starts with the evaluation of the objective function for an arbitrary number of points uniformly scattered over the parameter space of interest. These evaluations present the user with an initial, very sparse, view of the parameter space. Based on these results, the user can assign *levels of importance* to regions on the parameter space. The levels of importance indicate which regions are more promising than others, if any, and should thus be explored sooner. The search proceeds by evaluating the objective functions at several points within regions with high levels of importance. In effect, this increases the search resolution within these regions. This process is repeated iteratively until the user has found a (small enough) region or a parameter space point that meets his/her subjective criteria. In effect, the search consists of a hierarchy of sub-searches that progressively prune search regions and refine the search resolution. This is depicted in Figure 1 for a 2-D parameter space. We show three levels of search, where points with high levels of importance are shown in black.

In the instantiation of the search procedure used in this paper, the search starts with 4 points at coordinates $(100, 100)$, $(100, -100)$, $(-100, -100)$, and $(-100, 100)$ in the x-y plane. These 4 points form generation 0 of the search. Each point is associated with an objective function *value* (in our case-study, the Griewank value evaluated at that point). At each generation, local random searches are conducted in neighboring regions of points from the previous generations. These regions are spherical and of decreasing radius at each generation. For the sake of simplicity, we call the objective function value of the point that has triggered the exploration of a region the *parent value* of new tasks in this region. In each region, the local search consists in evaluating 10 random points. At most the 2 points with the best objective function evaluations are propagated to the next generation. If such a local search does not return any point that has a lower objective function value than the parent value, then the local search is repeated up to a maximum number of times: $maxTrials$. If $maxTrials$ is reached and no improvement has been seen, then we use a standard random restart mechanism by selecting a new, random, parameter space point. A smaller $maxTrials$ leads to a more random and exploratory search, whereas a larger $maxTrials$ leads to a more thorough search.

The goal of this work is to quantify the benefit, if any, of allocating more compute resources to areas of parameter space that the user judges to be more promising. Since our user simulation is built to minimize the Griewank function, we assign levels of importance to points in the parameter space inversely correlated to the parent values. The scheduler will then assign compute resources to regions of parameter space based on their importance. The search algorithm presented here combines global and local search strategies, similarly to other well known search strategies [11,13,14]. Our search model is configurable, allowing us to adjust the accuracy and resolution of the search process, using the parameter $maxTrials$. Moreover the "bumpiness" of the Griewank function is configurable as well: the parameter σ controls the relative height between the bottoms of basins of attraction. In the rest of the paper, we will use the above algorithm with different values of $maxTrials$ to minimize Griewank functions with different values of σ in order to simulate a range of user-directed search scenarios.

2.3   Assumptions

We make a number of important assumptions in this paper. In the search strategy described in the previous section, we use objective function values to determine the levels of importance for the search. This assumes that there is some spatial correlation of the objective function, meaning that function values and parameter space point locations are in some way correlated. Without such correlation, the most effective strategy would be a purely random search. For MCell, and many other applications, the assumption of spatial correlation is valid.

In addition, our resource allocation strategy assumes that each function evaluation, or task, requires the same amount of computation and that compute resources are homogeneous. This assumption allows us to test a resource allocation strategy in which the order of task assignments is equivalent to the order of task completion. It is straightforward to extend this strategy to account for tasks with various execution times and resources with various capabilities (see Section 3). Note that in this work we currently ignore issues pertaining to application data movement and location: we focus solely on the steerability of the application. We have addressed data location issues in our previous work [8], in which we developed a number of scheduling heuristics. We will integrate this work with these heuristics in future work.

Another assumption implied here, is that the execution time of all function evaluations is known a-priori. In other words, given a point in the parameter space, we assume that we know how much computation is needed for evaluating the objective function at that point. This assumption holds for MCell, and is therefore justified for our work on the VI project. However, for some applications, there can be some degree of uncertainty. In addition, prediction errors for task execution times are often due to dynamic changes in resource load. This is especially common in Grid environments where resources are distributively owned and shared among users. These considerations imply that resource allocation decisions will be based on possibly inaccurate predictions for task execution times. A number of authors, including ourselves, have investigated the impact of such prediction inaccuracies on scheduling, and at the moment we leave this issue for future work. Our assumptions in this work are substantial, but necessary to gain initial understanding of the principles of resource allocation for steerable parameter search applications.

3   Priority-Based Resource Allocation

3.1   Task Priorities

We claim that an important factor impacting the performance of the search is the **fraction of resources** allocated to search regions. Thus, we conjecture that a resource allocation strategy that assigns fractions of compute resources to regions based on their levels of importance may reduce overall search time. The alternative is to simply sort regions by level of importance and to compute regions sequentially, using all available resources for each region. We have seen experimentally that such a strategy is not effective [9]. An intuitive rationale for the former approach is that letting several tasks share compute resources concurrently may lead to a broader exploration of the search space, in a shorter period time.

To test this conjecture, we developed a model in which different fractions of compute resources can be allocated to tasks. We then used this model to evaluate the effectiveness of several resource allocation strategies that map regional levels of importance to resource fractions. We have implemented a simulator that uses the Simgrid toolkit [6,18] to simulate the execution of the search procedure of Section 2.2 with resources that can be continuously divided among tasks. We describe this approach in the next section.

Simulation Model. We present results for an *ideal platform* that consists of a single, "continuously partitionable" processor. In other words, it is possible to assign any fraction of the computing platform to a given task. Larger resource fractions correspond to more computing power enabling a task to complete earlier. As we will see in our results, this model allows us to gain basic understanding of the potential of priority-based resource allocation for parallel searches. We discuss extensions to this model model in Section 3.3.

We make the initial assumption that it is possible to achieve fine-grain, accurate job control over our distributed computing platform. Larger fractions of the compute platform allocated to a task could be interpreted in practice as:

- more time slices assigned to a task sharing a processor with other tasks and/or,
- longer time slices and/or,
- task allocated to faster processor and/or,
- task allocated to less loaded processor.

Nevertheless, our model is ideal in that we ignore the overhead of such fine-grain job control, which we discuss in Section 3.4. In summary, our results provide us with a "best-case" scenario.

Resource Allocation Strategies. The resource allocation strategies we investigate are *priority-based*: tasks within search regions with higher levels of importance are assigned higher priorities. The higher the task priority, the larger the fraction of resources that will be allocated to the task. Let us illustrate how priority-based resource allocation could be easily employed for the user-directed search described in Section 2.2.

The user identifies regions and assigns them levels of importance. For instance, if the user has identified 3 regions that should be explored and assigned levels of importance 2, 2, and 1, then the first two regions should each get 40% of the resources, and the last region should get 20%. Our approach is to assign a priority to each point of the parameter space, corresponding to the level of importance of the region to which the point belongs. If each of the current n points being computed has a priority $Priority_i$, then point i should get a fraction of the entire compute resource equal to $Priority_i / \sum_{j=1}^{n} Priority_j$. This allows many tasks to use the compute resource concurrently, but at different rates.

In our simulated user scenario we seek to minimize the Griewank function (see Section 2.1). Therefore high task priorities are associated with low objective function values. The priority of a task in computed according to its *parent value* (recall from Section 2.2 that the search strategy proceeds in generations – new tasks are the offspring of parameter space evaluations in a previous search generation). We investigate the relationship between parent values and task priorities by using a conventional no-priority policy:

Policy 0 – **No-priority** policy:
$$Priority_{task} = 1,$$

as a basis for comparison with the following three priority-based policies:

Policy 1 – Inverse **linear** policy:
$$Priority_{task} = Value_{parent}^{-1},$$
Policy 2 – Inverse **sub-linear** policy:
$$Priority_{task} = Value_{parent}^{-1/2},$$
Policy 3 – Inverse **super-linear** policy:
$$Priority_{task} = Value_{parent}^{-2},$$

where $Priority_{task}$ is the priority assigned to a task, and $Value_{parent}$ is the parent value (in our case it is a Griewank value).

Table 1. Speedup due to priority-based scheduling where $Priority_{task} = Feedback_{parent}^{-1}$

$maxTrials$	σ								
	10^{-2}	10^{-1}	10^{0}	10^{1}	10^{2}	10^{3}	10^{4}	10^{5}	10^{6}
1	0.94	0.96	0.93	0.79	**1.03**	0.51	0.65	**1.05**	**1.68**
4	0.69	0.25	0.60	0.13	**7.90**	**9.66**	**6.74**	**10.79**	**22.83**
16	0.40	0.56	0.18	0.13	**7.38**	**7.85**	**6.84**	**11.46**	**22.26**
32	**1.18**	0.55	0.26	0.16	**7.31**	**6.71**	**5.90**	**10.05**	**19.01**
64	**1.36**	0.77	0.25	0.17	**7.35**	**6.12**	**5.64**	**9.69**	**18.21**

Table 2. Speedup due to priority-based scheduling where $Priority_{task} = Feedback_{parent}^{-1/2}$

$maxTrials$	σ								
	10^{-2}	10^{-1}	10^{0}	10^{1}	10^{2}	10^{3}	10^{4}	10^{5}	10^{6}
1	0.84	**1.03**	0.93	0.76	0.91	**1.06**	0.92	**3.43**	**4.65**
4	0.75	0.47	0.36	0.61	**4.12**	**5.77**	**8.44**	**13.96**	**27.34**
16	**1.53**	**2.15**	**1.22**	**1.71**	**4.08**	**5.12**	**7.83**	**13.55**	**24.70**
32	**1.15**	0.97	**1.14**	**1.69**	**4.05**	**5.00**	**7.80**	**13.73**	**25.07**
64	**1.37**	**1.05**	**1.25**	**1.69**	**4.06**	**5.00**	**7.76**	**13.71**	**25.03**

3.2 Simulation Results

In the simulation results presented here, we assumed that each function evaluation would require 1 second of computation if it could be performed on the entire computing platform by itself. Therefore, if a task, due to its priority, were assigned 1% of the compute resources, it would take 100 seconds to complete.

Figure 2 show results comparing the use of the four priority policies for several values of σ and of $maxTrials$. The search is run until a Griewank value below some threshold (in this case 0.01) is found. The average time to reach this threshold is plotted on the y-axis with a logarithmic scale. We show plots for $maxTrials$ values of 1, 4, 16, 32 and 64. On each plot, σ is on the x-axis and we show bars for the search time for the four priority policies. Since our search algorithm is randomized, each data point is obtained as an average over 100 repetitions.

We present speed-up results in Tables 1, 2, and 3. Those results show the ratios between the overall search time with no priorities and the overall search time with the linear, sub-linear, and super-linear priority policies. Therefore values over 1.0 mean that priority-based resource allocation leads to a performance improvement. We show these values in boldface in the tables.

The first observation we can make is that the use of priorities leads to drastic improvements for large σ for all three priority-based policies. Furthermore, the sub-linear policy ($Priority_{task} = Value_{parent}^{-1/2}$) appears to be very promising – if $maxTrials > 4$, it performs better than the no-priority policy, even when σ is small (see Table 2).

For $maxTrials \leq 4$ the local search over a region is less accurate, since local basins are sampled with lower density and it is harder to detect local minima. Therefore, biasing search regions with priorities is not as effective as it is when $maxTrials$ is larger. Larger $maxTrials$ provides more thorough local searches and hence more accurate information

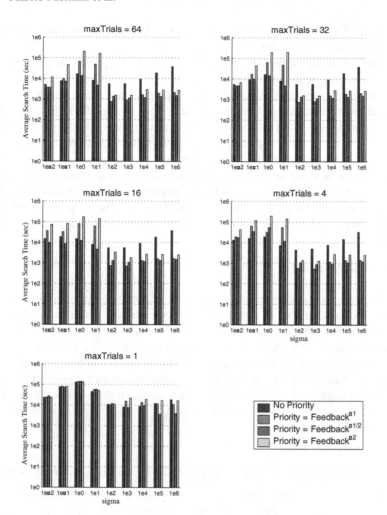

Fig. 2. Average simulated search times vs. σ for the four priority policies and for $maxTrials = 1, 4, 16, 32, 64$. Both axes are logarithmic scales.

Table 3. Speedup due to priority-based scheduling where $Priority_{task} = Feedback_{parent}^{-2}$

$maxTrials$	σ								
	10^{-2}	10^{-1}	10^{0}	10^{1}	10^{2}	10^{3}	10^{4}	10^{5}	10^{6}
1	0.99	0.95	0.94	0.87	0.98	0.36	0.46	0.72	**1.08**
4	0.31	0.14	0.10	0.05	**3.27**	**3.95**	**2.83**	**5.69**	**12.76**
16	0.20	0.22	0.09	0.06	**1.60**	**3.04**	**3.37**	**7.07**	**14.93**
32	0.81	0.21	0.08	0.04	**3.49**	**3.65**	**3.26**	**6.88**	**14.33**
64	0.44	0.16	0.08	0.05	**3.61**	**3.66**	**3.13**	**6.61**	**14.03**

about local minima. In this case the biasing property of priority-based strategies improves search performance significantly.

One curious factor is that for small σ the linear and super-linear priority policies performed much worse than the no-priority policy (see Tables 1 and 3). We suspect that these two policies *over-bias* the search regions. When σ is small the values at the bottom of the local basins of attraction become similar making it more difficult to use objective function evaluations to interpret how close the search process is to the global minimum. Therefore we think that in this context many low objective function results erroneously indicated a "false" proximity to the global minimum. The linear and super-linear policies increase the priority in the neighborhood of such misleading results more drastically than the sub-linear policy, thereby wasting a lot of computational power which could be used for exploring other (more useful) search regions. This over-biasing phenomenon may be due to our use of the Griewank function, but is certainly worth studying in other cases.

3.3   Multiple Processors

We wish to evolve our platform model to account for more realistic assumptions. Our first step is to simulate a number of distinct, but still continuously partitionable, processors. In these experiments, tasks are assigned to processors in a round-robin fashion. Each processor is divided among tasks assigned to it according to their priorities.

Table 4 and table 5 show speed-up results for the sub-linear priority policy for a platform with 8 and 512 processors. We observe that priorities are more effective when there is more contention for resources, i.e. when there are more tasks per resource. More processors reduce contention and consequently the priority speedup decreases, as can be observed in the tables.

Table 4. Speedup for platform with 8 processors, where $Priority_{task} = Feedback_{parent}^{-1/2}$

$maxTrials$	σ								
	10^{-2}	10^{-1}	10^{0}	10^{1}	10^{2}	10^{3}	10^{4}	10^{5}	10^{6}
1	**1.08**	**1.25**	**1.11**	0.89	0.93	0.88	**1.62**	0.81	**2.70**
4	**1.04**	0.46	0.33	0.71	**3.95**	**5.49**	**8.17**	**13.96**	**24.72**
16	0.70	**1.89**	0.94	**1.46**	**4.03**	**4.73**	**7.52**	**13.77**	**25.14**
32	0.49	**1.03**	**1.26**	**1.38**	**4.07**	**4.80**	**7.54**	**13.86**	**25.58**
64	**1.37**	**1.18**	**1.28**	**1.38**	**4.08**	**4.79**	**7.58**	**13.95**	**25.76**

Table 5. Speedup for platform with 512 processors, where $Priority_{task} = Feedback_{parent}^{-1/2}$

$maxTrials$	σ								
	10^{-2}	10^{-1}	10^{0}	10^{1}	10^{2}	10^{3}	10^{4}	10^{5}	10^{6}
1	0.97	0.98	0.96	**1.04**	1.00	**1.01**	1.00	**1.02**	**1.04**
4	**1.15**	0.86	0.51	**1.10**	**1.08**	**1.16**	**1.32**	**1.91**	**2.96**
16	0.95	**1.08**	**1.31**	**1.12**	**1.13**	**1.19**	**1.45**	**2.09**	**3.07**
32	0.92	0.96	**1.26**	**1.16**	**1.13**	**1.19**	**1.46**	**2.06**	**3.02**
64	0.97	**1.07**	**1.27**	**1.16**	**1.13**	**1.19**	**1.46**	**2.06**	**3.02**

These preliminary results indicate that an environment with multiple resources can benefit from priority-based policies, provided that the number of tasks per compute resource is high (which is reasonable for large parameter space searches). Also, note that for these results we used the simplistic round-robin strategy to map tasks to processors. We are currently evaluating mapping strategies that assign tasks to processors while taking into account priority information.

3.4 Discussion

We conjectured that a resource allocation approach that allocates fractions of the compute resources to tasks concurrently would be effective. We confirmed this conjecture in simulation for a sub-linear priority policy when the search is marginally thorough (i.e. for $maxTrials > 4$).

However, our simulation results were obtained with an ideal platform model. Indeed, we assumed fine-grain job control with no overhead, which allows the allocation of fractions of resources precisely corresponding to priorities dictated by the resource allocation strategy. In practice, such a strategy can be implemented by assigning time slices of compute resources to tasks. This could be done at the level of the operating system (e.g. with process priorities). This is possible if tasks do not consume large amounts of RAM and the behavior of the operating system scheduler is well understood, which is debatable with current systems. Alternatively, tasks could be explicitly context-switched by checkpoint/restart. This can be done at various granularity levels. The lower the granularity, the closer the schedule will be to the one evaluated in our simulation results, at the cost of higher overhead. We are currently developing a cost model for the context-switching overheads and will perform simulations in order to answer the following questions: What is the best granularity for explicit context-switching? How does the overall performance of the search compare with a simple non-prioritized resource allocation? In other terms, how much of the improvement due to using priorities, as shown in our simulation, will withstand the context-switching overhead?

Note that in order to implement priority-based resource allocation in a practical setting, it is required that application tasks be checkpointed on demand. The MCell application provides on-demand checkpointing already, which will make it possible for the VI to context-switch MCell tasks during a search. We will present experimental results obtained with MCell in a future paper.

4 Related Work

Our work is related to parallel search algorithms [4,5,11,19]. However, our work focuses on the improvement of the performance of search algorithms *from the perspective of computing resource allocation*. Land [13] and Hart [11] investigate search algorithms that combine local and global search methodologies. Their search algorithm biases the search in favor of more promising regions of the parameter space. Our approach is complementary to their work since we use biasing strategies to determine resource allocations.

This work is also related to a number of computational steering efforts [10,16,20]. The VI project itself is related to projects that provide software for deploying large scale applications onto the Computational Grid. In particular, it is related to projects that target parameter sweep applications [1,8]. The VI software builds on these efforts in order to enable parameter space searches.

5   Conclusion and Future Work

In this paper we have investigated resource allocation approaches that can improve the performance of user-directed parallel parameter space searches on distributed computing platforms. Our goal was *not* to develop novel search/optimization algorithms, but rather to develop techniques to allocate appropriate compute resources to tasks of a user-directed search. We instantiated a search strategy that is representative of user-directed searches and that we used to simulate a range of user behaviors. Our fundamental idea for resource allocation is that "promising" regions of the parameter space should be explored more intensively. In our model, promising regions are defined as ones that have high "levels of importance". We conjectured that a resource allocation approach that defines priorities to allocate fractions of compute resources to tasks concurrently should be effective. We verified that conjecture in simulation and thereby made a good case for priority-based resource allocation.

To further validate our approach we will perform experiments in a broader context: we will evaluate priority-based resource allocation for several other representative search strategies over a variety of objective functions. We will investigate the questions raised in Section 3.4 and develop a model for the overhead involved for context-switching of application tasks. We will then re-evaluate our approach both in simulation and with the VI software using MCell as a case-study. We will also evaluate the use of priority-based resource allocation for a number of platform models that are more realistic than the ones used in this work. Our ultimate goal is to produce a version of the VI software that improves the performance of parameter space searches while using a Computational Grid platform.

Acknowledgement

We wish to thank the members of the MCell and the Virtual Instrument team for their help. We are also grateful to the NPACI Rocks team for allowing us to use their cluster for experiments. Finally, the authors wish to thank Rick Belew, Charles Elkan, and Andrew Kahng for their help with understanding search applications.

References

1. J. Abramson, D. Giddy and L. Kotler. High Performance Parametric Modeling with Nimrod/G: Killer Application for the Global Grid? In *Proceedings of the International Parallel and Distributed Processing Symposium (IPDPS), Cancun, Mexico*, pages 520–528, May 2000.
2. S. Altschul, W. Gish, W. Miller, E. Myers, and D. Lipman. Basic Local Alignment Search Tool. *Journal of Molecular Biology*, 215:403–410, 2990.
3. APST Webpage. http://grail.sdsc.edu/projects/apst.
4. T. Back. *Evolutionary Algorithms in Theory and Practice*. Oxford University Press, 1996.

5. S. Baluja. An empirical comparison of seven iterative and evolutionary function optimization heuristics. Technical report, Carnegie Mellon University, 1995.
6. H. Casanova. Simgrid: A Toolkit for the Simulation of Application Scheduling. In *Proceedings of the IEEE/ACM International Symposium on Cluster Computing and the Grid*, May 2001.
7. H. Casanova, T. Bartol, F. Berman, A. Birnbaum, J. Dongarra, M. Ellisman, M. Faerman, E. Gockay, M. Miller, G. Obertelli, S. Pomerantz, T. Sejnowski, J. Stiles, and R. Wolski. The Virtual Instrument: Support for Grid-enabled Scientific Simulations. Technical Report CS2002-0707, Dept. of Computer Science and Engineering, University of California, San Diego, June 2002.
8. H. Casanova, G. Obertelli, H. Berman, and R. Wolski. The AppLeS Parameter Sweep Template: User-level middleware for the Grid. In *Proceedings of SC'00*, November 2000.
9. M. Faerman, A. Birnbaum, H. Casanova, and F. Berman. Resource Allocation for Steerable Parallel Parameter Searches: an Experimental Study. Technical Report CS2002-0720, Dept. of Computer Science and Engineering, University of California, San Diego, 2002.
10. G. Geist, J. Kohl, and P. Papadopoulos. CUMULVS: Providing Fault Tolerance, Visualization, and Steering of Parallel Applications. *The International Journal of Supercomputer Applications and High Performance Computing*, 11(3):224–235, 1997.
11. W. Hart. *Adaptive Global Optimization with Local Search*. PhD thesis, University of California, San Diego, 1994.
12. W. Hart and R. Belew. *Adaptive Individuals in Evolving Populations, Models and Algorithms*, chapter Optimization with Genetic Algorithm Hybrids that Use Local Search, pages 483–494. Addison-Wesley Publishing Company, Inc., 1996.
13. M. Land. *Evolutionary Algorithms with Local Search for Combinatorial*. PhD thesis, University of California, San Diego, 1998.
14. R. Leary and J. Doye. Tetrahedral global minimum for the 98-atom lennard-jones cluster. *Physical Review E*, 60(6), December 1999.
15. MCell Webpage at the Salk Institute. http://www.mcell.cnl.salk.edu.
16. S. Parker, M. Miller, C. Hansen, and C. Johnson. An integrated problem solving environment: The SCIRun computational steering system. In *Proceedings of the 31st Hawaii International Conference on System Sciences (HICSS-31), vol. VII*, pages 147–156, January 1998.
17. S. Rogers and D. Ywak. Steady and Unsteady Solutions of the Incompressible Navier-Stokes Equations. *AIAA Journal*, 29(4):603–610, Apr. 1991.
18. Simgrid Webpage. http://grail.sdsc.edu/projects/simgrid.
19. P.J.M. van Laarhoven and E.H.L. Aarts. *Simulated Annealing: Theory and Applications*. D. Reidel Publishing Company, 1987.
20. J. Vetter and K. Schwan. PROGRESS: A Toolkit for Interactive Program Steering. In *Proceedings of the 1995 International Conference on Parallel Processing*, pages 139–149, 1995.
21. Virtual Instrument Webpage. http://grail.sdsc.edu/projects/vi_itr.

An Authorization Framework
for a Grid Based Component Architecture

Lavanya Ramakrishnan[1], Helen Rehn[2], Jay Alameda[2],
Rachana Ananthakrishnan[1], Madhusudhan Govindaraju[1],
Aleksander Slominski[1], Kay Connelly[1], Von Welch[2],
Dennis Gannon[1], Randall Bramley[1], and Shawn Hampton[2]

[1] Department of Computer Science, Indiana University, Bloomington, IN 47404, USA
{laramakr, ranantha, mgovinda , aslom, connelly, gannon, bramley}@cs.indiana.edu,
[2] National Center for Supercomputer Applications, Champaign, IL 61820, USA
{hrehn, jalameda, shawn}@ncsa.uiuc.edu, welch@mcs.anl.gov

Abstract. This paper[1] presents an architecture to meet the needs for
authentication and authorization in Grid based component systems.
While Grid Security Infrastructure (GSI) [1] is accepted as the standard for authentication on the Grid, distributed authorization is still an
open problem being investigated by various groups [2],[3],[4]. Our design
provides authentication and fine-grained authorization at the interface,
method and parameter levels. We discuss the ways in which internal and
external authorization services can be used in a component framework.
The design is flexible to allow the use of various existing policy languages
and authorization systems. Our prototype is based on XCAT, an implementation of the Common Component Architecture (CCA) specification.

1 Introduction

Computational grids combine computational and data resources across organi-
zational boundaries. The sharing of code and data on the Grid gives rise to the
need for security. Desired characteristics of Grid security include:

- The ability to verify the identity of an individual. Authentication ensures
  that the individual is who he/she claims to be.
- The capacity to allow or restrict access to some or all resources on the Grid,
  i.e. authorization.

The specific problem that this paper addresses is how does one provide secure
authorization mechanisms for controlling access to distributed scientific applications that are executing as Grid Services. This question is motivated by the
emergence of two Grid technologies. The web services model that has been developed recently by industry has now been recognized as the logical architecture
for the organization of Grid services. In this model, called the Open Grid Service

---

[1] This research was supported by NSF grant ASC 9619019, NCSA Alliance

M. Parashar (Ed.): GRID 2002, LNCS 2536, pp. 169–180, 2002.
© Springer-Verlag Berlin Heidelberg 2002

Architecture (OGSA) [5], [23], a Grid service is described by extensions to the Web Services Description Language [6] and accessed by protocols like the Simple Object Access Protocol (SOAP). The second technology driving this work is an application construction framework called the Common Component Architecture (CCA) that was originally developed by the DOE for large-scale parallel computation. An implementation of the CCA specification, called XCAT [7], has been built using the same web service technology as used in OGSA. While OGSA provides a model for building Grid Services, XCAT provides a model for building Grid applications by composing components that are located on remote resources on the Grid. These applications may be distributed, coupled multidisciplinary simulations, or dynamic networks of data-mining agents. Unlike the persistent Grid services such as a directory service, these distributed applications are stateful, transient services that are executing on behalf of a single user or a group of users. The users can steer the application by adjusting the parameters at run-time and monitor the application by examining its output stream. Also, users can create a persistent service, called an application factory, which can be used by collaborators to launch instances of other applications. In this context, the security problem can be stated as follows:

- What mechanisms can a group of scientists use to control access to running Grid computations that expose a Grid service interface?

Typically, authentication of Grid users is handled using GSI. It was designed with the notion of a global identity and a robust security scheme based on Public Key Infrastructure that allows the mapping of global identities to local identities. It enables single sign-on for multiple connected resources, while maintaining local institutional control over the individual resources. In this paper we discuss the use of existing technology to provide authentication and propose a solution for handling authorization for the problem described above.

2   Requirements

2.1   User and Developer Roles

Application scientists have helped us identify the people involved in the lifecycle of applications. Individuals may fall into multiple groups. These groups have different requirements on how and why they need to specify access control.

Component Architects: These are the developers who provide mechanisms as part of a framework (library that implements the component specification) for the application developers, primary collaborators, users and resource/service providers to describe and implement authorization control for their resources.

Application Developers: These are the application scientists who develop application code and use the library developed by Component Architects to incorporate a security system in their code.

Primary Collaborator: The primary collaborator is the person who owns the process for the application code. He/she instantiates components in the framework and uses an authorization system to set access control policies for the instantiated components.

Users: These secondary collaborators use the software components to gain access to codes and data.

Resource/Service providers: This includes the class of people who own the physical resources that the component requires. They may have constraints on who can use their resources.

2.2   Application Security Requirements

The following are some characteristics that are important for running applications on the Grid.

- Different levels of security may be required depending on the sensitivity of the application.
  - Security may not be important for all applications and there may be some components with no restrictions.
  - Sensitive data and computations have greater security considerations.
- The authorization framework should not impact performance when it is not needed.
- Different versions of digital certificates or various identity mechanisms are used on the Grid. An authorization scheme has to account for these differences.

2.3   Policy Management Requirements

A basic authorization framework should have the following capabilities:

- Policy Representation and Management: It is necessary to be able to express and manage policy about trusted users and their allowed actions.
- Policy Evaluation: The policy needs to be evaluated at the time the action is requested. The result of the evaluation is based on the user's identity and the security policy governing the use of the resources.

Policy management in an authorization framework can be either distributed or centralized and the choice is dictated by the characteristics of the application and the environment. Consider the drawbacks in each case: first, in the case of distributed policy management/evaluation, where an access control list is associated with each individual component in an application, a change in policy needs to be propagated across each component. This would impose a large administrative overhead. Secondly, in the case of a centralized policy management/evaluation system a large number of requests for authorization can negatively affect the system performance.

3   Common Component Architecture

3.1   Component Framework Overview

The Common Component Architecture (CCA) [8], [9], [10], [11] is an architecture that describes how to compose, create and connect applications that are wrapped as components in a distributed environment. The external interfaces of CCA components are called ports. A component provides and uses services through ports. According to the CCA specifications there are two types of ports:

Provides Port: A provides port is the interface through which the component makes available a set of services that can be used by other components.

Uses Port: A uses port acts as a reference to the remote service from the component using the service.

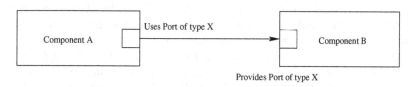

Fig. 1. A uses port of type X is connected to a provides port of the same type.

As shown in Figure 1, a component with a uses port type "X" can use the services provided by a provides port of the same type of another component.

3.2   Grid Tools - XCAT and XSOAP

XCAT [12], [7] is a component system that wraps high performance application code and provides an elegant scripting based programming model to compose and run applications on the Grid. XCAT components can be represented as web services, which facilitates easy, standards-based access to the components. The XML descriptions of the component and port characteristics are parsed to extract the information pertaining to the instantiation environment.

The component framework provides creation, connection, registry and directory services that allow standard mechanisms that an instance can use to discover, instantiate, connect and advertise other component instances. To facilitate code reusability, the framework provides these services as "pseudo-components" that exist either as a separate, remote component or within the process that owns the component instance. We intend to add authorization to this list of services provided by the component framework.

The communication protocol between the ports is based on XSOAP [13]. XSOAP is an RMI system implemented both in Java and C++ that is based on SOAP-RPC. SOAP [14] defines XML based communication and SOAP RPC states the protocol for using XML as the data format and HTTP as the network protocol. XSOAP uses GSI [1] to handle authentication [15].

4   Related Work

GSI enables secure authentication using public key encryption. It uses X.509 certificates as mechanism for identity and Secure Sockets Layer (SSL) as the communication protocol. Delegation of credentials and single sign-on is supported as part of GSI. In the Community Authorization Service (CAS) [3], resources and users are classified into groups called communities. Communities run CAS servers, which keep track of fine-grained access control information and grant restricted proxies to community members.

Akenti [2] is a security model based on a distributed access control mechanism. The policy engine gathers the use-condition certificates from the various stakeholders and the attribute certificates from trusted directories and grants access to a resource based on the matching of the attributes in these two certificates. Legion [16] is an object based system used to access resources on the Grid. In Legion an object has a MayI layer [4] that verifies the credentials received with a method call using the access control list stored as part of the object to determine if access to the resource may be granted.

The Oasis Security Assertion Markup Language (SAML) [24] defines a protocol by which clients can request and receive assertions from SAML authorities concerning authenticated identities [17] and receive information regarding the authorization of the client attempting to access the component. XACML is an XML policy language from OASIS that expresses policies for information access over the internet [18]. The XML Trust Assertion Service (XTASS) is designed to manage long-term trust relations between principals [19]. In the XTASS architecture, authorization data is bound to a cryptographic key by means of a URI that corresponds to a set of resources for which access is granted. An assertion service can be queried to determine authorization. WS-Security from Microsoft and IBM provides mechanisms for transferring credentials through SOAP and ensuring the integrity and confidentiality of SOAP messages [20]. The digital signature security extension to SOAP allows SOAP messages to be signed [21]. In addition, XKMS and XML Signature Syntax and Processing deal with the representation and processing of digital signatures in XML [22]. The Object Management Group (OMG) Security Specifications [25] describes the service needed to acquire authorization tokens to access a target system. These tokens are used to gain access to a CORBA invocation on the target.

We have mentioned the related security work in the Grid and Web services. We believe that these and other systems can be used with our model for security in the component framework.

5   Authorization Framework

We have designed an authorization framework that is tailored for Grid based component systems. Our authorization framework contains the following

- A standard way to intercept method invocations on components that require authorization checks.

– A standard mechanism for a component to indicate choice of an internal or
external authorization service.
– A mechanism for using authorization services that evaluates the policy once
method invocations have been intercepted.
– Standard information the authorization services can expect to receive in
order to make authorization decisions.

5.1   Authorization Model

The architecture of our framework can be described using the stack abstraction
shown in Fig 2. Our system employs a simple request response protocol.
Communication Layer: The communication layer is analogous to the transport layer in the network model. The communication layer handles the authentication when it receives a request.
Framework Layer: The framework layer is an abstraction of the implementation of an architecture for instantiating applications. The authorization sub-layer
embedded in this layer, intercepts the incoming call, checks authorization, and
either allows (Fig 2b) or denies (Fig 2c) the call to the method in the component.
Fig 2a shows the request-response path without authorization.
Application Layer: The application layer contains components that manage
applications. It has hooks to the framework layer, so that the application can
dynamically affect the information stored by the authorization sub-layer.

The implementation of the policy management and evaluation are abstracted
into an authorization service which may be an internal implementation or an
external authorization service, as can be seen in Figure 3. The authorization
service provides the following features for policy management and evaluation.

– A method to dynamically add a credential or list of credentials that can be
trusted for a particular action.
– A method to dynamically delete a credential that is not allowed to perform
an action.

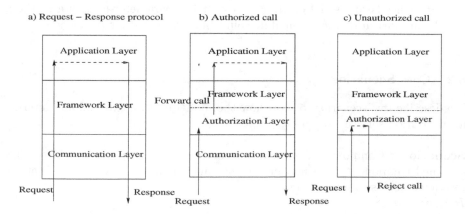

Fig. 2. Stack Abstractions in our Component Framework

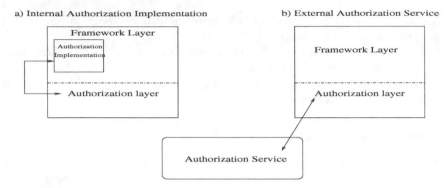

Fig. 3. Details of Authorization Layer.

- The ability to verify that the presented credential allows the user to access the requested resource.

The internal structure of the authorization layer is separated from the details of the implementation of the authorization service. This layer need not evaluate the policy, but just needs to know which authorization service to contact that will perform the policy check during the request-response protocol. The advantages of the model are:

- The authorization model is pluggable into existing applications thus allowing for the flexibility of having secure and un-secure applications
- The authorization service acts as a bridge between the diverse security subsystems that may exist on the Grid.
- The intricacies of the policy representation, management and evaluation are abstracted away from the application.
- The model provides the user the flexibility to choose between existing security or an application-specific security mechanism. For example if an application needs to restrict or grant access at the parameter level of a method, the authorization service module could be customized for the same.

5.2   Case Scenarios

We describe two scenarios to show how the model uses an external and internal authorization service.

Scenario 1: Component A provides a service. The component architect has designed component A to use an external authorization service X to manage restricted access to its methods.
Initialization

1. Component A registers a provides port for the service being provided.

2. Component A registers a uses port that it can use to contact the authorization service.
3. Component A's uses port is connected to the authorization service.
4. The policy information about trust relations in the environment is initialized with the authorization service X.

Policy Check

1. The call received from the communication layer is intercepted and information (target method, port and component, identity of the caller) is extracted.
2. The authorization layer recognizes that an external authorization service needs to be contacted for policy evaluation.
3. The authorization layer invokes the policy evaluation method on the external service including the information required for the authorization check.
4. The authorization layer forwards or rejects the intercepted call depending on the result of the policy check.

Policy Management
An external authorization service dictates that the changes to the policy management are done by interacting with the authorization service.

Scenario 2: Component A provides a service. The component architect has designed component A to use an internal authorization service
Initialization

1. Component A registers a provides port for the service being provided.
2. Component A registers the internal authorization service with the authorization layer.
3. Component A registers a policy management provides port.
4. The policy information about trusted users is initialized.

Policy Check

1. The call received from the communication layer is intercepted and required information (target method, port and component, identity of the caller) is extracted.
2. The authorization layer identifies that an internal authorization service exists.
3. In this case the authorization layer invokes an internal authorization method. The information required for the authorization check is included in the call.
4. The authorization layer forwards or rejects the intercepted call depending on the result of the policy check.

Policy Management
Policy Management is done by making method calls on the policy management port. These calls have authorization policies set and controlled in the same fashion as any other provides port.

5.3   Implementation of Authorization Model in XCAT

We have a prototype implementation of the model with an internal authorization service in the XCAT framework. Some of the elements in our prototype are
Identity: We obtain the user's credential and use the Distinguished Name from the user's credential for policy information.
Policy type: We use a simple access control list.
Policy initialization: We can specify the initial policy, which includes information about the identity of the user and the actions he is allowed to perform, in XML. In our prototype the information specifies the trusted user's Distinguished Name and the methods he/she is allowed to access. This information is parsed when the component is instantiated and an access control list is initialized.
Policy check: When a method is invoked on the provides port of a component, the interceptor in the XCAT framework intercepts the method call. It parses the method name and parameters and forwards the call to the corresponding method on the provides port of the component. We have introduced some additional functionality to the interceptor by having it enforce a policy check before the call is forwarded, thus making it equivalent to the authorization layer of the stack abstraction. The user credentials required to evaluate the policy is extracted from the communication layer. The interceptor calls the authorization method and accepts or rejects the method call based on the result of the policy check. The interceptor also has the ability to exercise various levels of access control - at the method, port and parameter level. For example: if sensitive parameters are being passed to a method, the interceptor can authorize the call based on the actual values to those parameters according to the policy access information. Furthermore, the interceptor detects the presence of an external authorization service or an internal authorization service for the policy check by determining whether the component has registered a uses port for an external authorization service, or has registered its use of an internal authorization service.

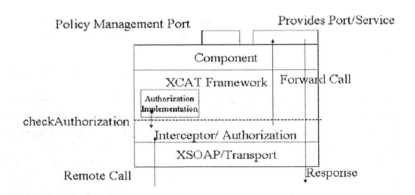

Fig. 4. Schematic of XCAT Implementation

Policy Management: The policy management port is a provides port with methods to add and delete credentials from the access control list. By specifying the policy information for these methods, tasks of policy management are restricted to authorized users. This port allows the access control to be modified to reflect the changes in trust relations during the lifetime of a component.

5.4 Authorization as an External Service

The service providers make available their resources or services on the Grid. So when authorization is presented as a service it abstracts away the details of the implementation of the authorization mechanism, from the component framework. Some of the characteristics of an authorization service are

- The authorization service will be registered at a well-known location. WSDL [5] references for the service will help in the discovery of this service.
- The service will be authenticated to discourage impostors. GSI's authentication protocol in the communication layer will satisfy this requirement.
- Important information such as credentials and the results of the policy evaluation will be exchanged between the service provider and the user. Encryption technologies that are part of GSI will be vital to protect this information.
- The authorization service will need to have its own scheme of authentication and authorization for allowing access to its services.
- There maybe different security sub-systems running on the Grid. The authorization system could act as the middle-ware to allow interaction between these sub-systems by doing credential conversion. A client may use Kerberos credentials while the service provider's security system may use X.509 certificates. The authorization service will match the Kerberos credential with the X.509 certificate expected by the service provider.

The authorization service may or may not be designed as a component in the framework. An authorization service component would provide its services, i.e. policy management and policy evaluation, through a provides port. The services would thus have authorized access as the calls to a provides port would pass through the interceptor or authorization layer.

6 Future Work

The OGSA specification will incorporate standard interfaces for authorization and policy management required by applications. We plan to make the required changes in our design so that our authorization model can be presented as an OGSA compliant service.

The use of Akenti and CAS in the given framework will give rise to interesting possibilities. For our initial implementation we are using a simple policy language specified in XML. We would like to experiment with other policy languages. We are also working towards authorization as a service with WSDL references. Currently the user needs to explicitly specify the authorization service or implementation to use. We propose to use the ongoing research on dynamic discovery services to be able to automate this process to some extent. The applicability of the model to other component models eg: CORBA Component Model (CCM) [26], Enterprise JavaBeans (EJB) [27] needs to be studied.

Authorizing every call has an effect on performance. We need to measure the overhead and look at schemes to improve this. The possibility of using caching or buffering to improve performance needs to be investigated in greater detail.

7   Conclusions

We present an authorization model for a Grid based component system. The model concentrates on the authorization infrastructure in a distributed component environment. It allows the use of various levels of security. Apart from simple access or denial of access to components, it allows the establishment of fine grained access control at the method, port and parameter levels.

The design allows the use of internal or external authorization services. The model is flexible to allow the use of various existing policy languages and authorization systems to take care of advanced security needs of the user.

References

1. I. Foster, C. Kesselman, G. Tsudik, S. Tuecke: A Security Architecture for Computational Grids ACM Conference on Computer and Communications Security Conference, pp. 83-92, 1998
2. W. Johnston, S. Mudumbai, M. Thompson: Authorization and Attribute Certificates for Widely Distributed Access Control Proceedings of the IEEE 7th International Workshops on Enabling Technologies: Infrastructure for Collaborative Enterprises, WETICE '98
3. L. Pearlman, V. Welch, I. Foster, C. Kesselman, S. Tuecke: A Community Authorization Service for Group Collaboration. Submitted to IEEE 3rd International Workshop on Policies for Distributed Systems and Networks, 2001. http://www.globus.org/research/papers/CAS_2002_Submitted.pdf
4. A. Ferrari, F. Knabe, M. Humphrey, S. Chapin, A. Grimshaw: A Flexible Security System for Metacomputing Environments. TR CS-98-36. January 1998.
5. S. Tuecke, K. Czajkowski, I. Foster, J. Frey, S. Graham, C. Kesselman: Grid Service Specification. February 2002. http://www.globus.org/research/papers/gsspec.pdf
6. Christenser E., Curbera, F., Meredith, G. and Weerawarana.,S.: Web Services Description Language (WSDL) 1.1 W3C, Note 15,2001, http://www.w3.org/TR/wsdl
7. Madhusudhan Govindaraju, Sriram Krishnan , Kenneth Chiu, Aleksander Slominski, Dennis Gannon, Randall Bramley: XCAT 2.0: Design and Implementation Technical Report 562. Department of Computer Science, Indiana University. June 2002.
8. R. Armstrong, D. Gannon, A. Geist, K. Keahey, S. Kohn, L. McInnes, S. Parker and B. Smolinski: Toward a Common Component Architecture for High-Performance Scientific Computing. In Proceedings of the 8th IEEE International Symposium on High Performance Distributed Computation, August 1999.

9. B. A. Allan, R. C. Armstrong, A. P. Wolfe, J. Ray, D. E. Bernholdt and J. A. Kohl: The CCA Core Specification In a Distributed Memory SPMD Framework submitted to Concurrency: Practice and Experience.
10. The Common Component Architecture Technical Specification, Version 0.5. See http://www.cca-forum.org.
11. R. Bramley, K. Chiu, S. Diwan, D. Gannon, M.Govindaraju, N. Mukhi, B. Temko, and M. Yechuri: A component based services architecture for building distributed applications In Proceedings of Ninth IEEE International Symposium on High Performance Distributed Computing Conference,Pittsburgh, August 1-4 2000.
12. J. Villacis, M. Govindaraju, D. Stern, A. Whitaker, F. Breg, P. Deuskar, B. Temko, D. Gannon, R. Bramley: CAT: A High Performance, Distributed Component Architecture Toolkit for the Grid Proceedings of Eighth IEEE International Symposium on High Performance Distributed Computing Conference. August 3-6 1999.
13. Indiana Extreme Lab. XSOAP Toolkit.
    http://www.extreme.indiana.edu/xgws/xsoap/
14. D. Box, et al Simple Object Access Protocol (SOAP) 1.1. W3C Note.
    http://www.w3.org/TR/SOAP/
15. DOE Science Grid's GSI Enabled Java SOAP client/server project.
    http://doesciencegrid.org/Grid/projects/soap/index.html
16. A. S. Grimshaw, W. A. Wulf, J. C. French, A. C. Weaver, P. F. Reynolds Jr. Legion: The Next Logical Step Toward a Nationwide Virtual Computer. Technical Report CS-94-21. August 1994.
17. OASIS. Assertions and Protocol for the OASIS Security Assertion Markup Language (SAML). Technical Specification.
    http://www.oasis-open.org/committees/security/docs
18. OASIS. Extensible Access Control Markup Language.
    http://www.oasisopen.org/committees/xacml/index.shtml
19. P. Hallam-Baker: X-TASS: XML Trust Assertion Service Specification. 2001.
20. B. Atkinson, et al: Web Services Security (WS-Security). Version 1.0. April 5, 2002.
    http://msdn.microsoft.com/library/en-us/ dnglobspec/html/ws-security.asp
21. M. Bartel, J. Boyer, B. Fox, B. LaMacchia, E. Simon: XML-Signature Syntax and Processing. W3C Recommendation. http://www.w3.org/TR/xmldsig-core/.
22. W. Ford, P. Hallam-Baker, B. Fox, B. Dillaway, B. LaMacchia, J. Epstein, J.Lapp.: XML Key Management Specification (XKMS). 2001.
    http://www.w3.org/TR/xkms/
23. Argonne National Lab. Globus. http://www.globus.org
24. D. Platt: Oasis Security Services Use Cases and Requirements. Oasis SSTC. 30 May 2001.
    http://www.oasis-open.org/committees/security/docs/draft-sstc-saml-reqs-01.pdf
25. OMG Security:
    http://www.omg.org/technology/documents/formal/omg_security.htm
26. Diego Sevilla Ruiz: CORBA and CORBA Component Model (CCM).
    http://ditec.um.es/ dsevilla/ccm/
27. Eneterprise JavaBeans (EJB). http://java.sun.com/products/ejb/
28. T. Bray et al: Extensible Markup Language (XML) 1.0 (Second Edition). W3C Recommendation. 6 October 2000. http://www.w3.org/TR/REC-xml
29. Xuhui Ao, Naftaly Minsky, Thu Nguyen, Victoria Ungureanu: Law-Governed Communities Over the Internet. In Proc. of Coordination' 2000: Fourth International Conference on Coordination Models and Languages, Sept 2000

Supporting Secure Ad-hoc User Collaboration in Grid Environments*

Markus Lorch and Dennis Kafura

Department of Computer Science, Virginia Tech
Blacksburg, VA 24061, U.S.A.
{mlorch, kafura}@cs.vt.edu
http://zuni.cs.vt.edu/grid-security

Abstract. We envision that many grid usage scenarios will be based on small, dynamic working groups for which the ability to establish transient collaboration is a key requirement. Current grid security mechanisms support individual users as members of well-defined virtual organizations. Recent research seeks to provide manageable grid security services for self-regulating, stable communities. Our prior work with component-based systems for grid computation demonstrated a need to support spontaneous, limited, short-lived collaborations which rely on shared or delegated fine grained access privileges. Our mechanisms enable the high-level management of such fine grained privileges based on PKIX attribute certificates and enforce resulting access policies through readily available POSIX operating system extensions. In combination, our mechanisms leverage other work in the grid computing and security communities, reduce administrative costs to resource providers, enable ad-hoc collaboration through incremental trust relationships and can be used to provide improved security service to long-lived communities.

1. Introduction

This paper describes two complementary mechanisms to support secure collaboration among ad-hoc, transient groups of grid users with minimal overhead imposed on resource administrators. Currently deployed grid security services support stable, well defined collaboratories [1] and virtual organizations [2]. Often only coarse grained access decisions are made by these grid authorization services (e.g. the mapping of authenticated global users to local user accounts as in [3] and [4]). The resulting requirement for existing local user accounts on the grid resources for every grid entity poses a scalability problem and hinders ad-hoc collaboration.

Current research aims at supporting long-lived communities in which the allocation of access rights is separated into two levels: the allocation of rights to a community as a whole by resource providers (resource administration) and the allocation of rights to individual members of the community by community administrators (community administration). This separation reduces the administrative costs for resource owners and enables community-specific, fine grained security policies. Our work seeks to further extend this line of research by supporting collaborations that are unanticipated

---

*This research is funded by the Virginia Commonwealth Information Security Center (CISC)

M. Parashar (Ed.): GRID 2002, LNCS 2536, pp. 181–193, 2002.

(achieved by dynamic discovery or synchronous interaction), short-lived (perhaps only days or even a single session), and involving a small number (perhaps only two) of grid users. Our goal is it to provide a mechanism for the management of fine grained rights (e.g. read access to a single file) through the grid middleware and a mechanism to enforce access with fine grained rights at the resource. The mechanisms we develop can also be used to provide improved security services to virtual organizations and other longer-lived communities.

The focus on ad-hoc groups arose from our earlier work with Symphony [5], a component-based system for collaboration and sharing. Symphony enables users to integrate components representing grid computations or data made available by others. The integrated components can be accumulated through resource discovery (asynchronous sharing) or through real-time interaction (synchronous sharing).

An ad-hoc collaboration is illustrated by the following scenario: A university researcher, Bob, has developed an experimental network protocol emulator that runs on his special purpose compute cluster. Joan, a corporate researcher, would like to use Bob's emulator to simulate a proprietary protocol. She asks Bob for permission to use the simulator. Bob agrees, creates a privilege credential bound to Joan's identity which grants short-lived access and execute permissions, and sends it to Joan. Joan can now contact Bob's compute cluster, authenticate with her own identity credential and provide the privilege credential for authorization. The resource will validate that the privilege credential came from an authoritative user (Bob) and grant access for the validity period of the privilege credential. In a traditional grid environment such a scenario would require the following steps by a system administrator: (1) creation of a user and a group account, (2) modification of a grid access control list, (3) changing of group membership for the simulator executable (expressiveness limitations of the operating system might prevent the executable from being a member several groups), and (4) the revocation of access privileges after the collaboration ends.

In practice, shared accounts and universal group accounts are often used to reduce the administrative overhead. This reduces overall system security and hinders ad-hoc collaboration due to the high level of trust required before such a large set of permissions can be granted and the associated administrative costs justified. We envision that on computational grids many collaboration scenarios will be based on small, ad-hoc working groups for which the ability to establish transient groups with little or no intervention from site administrators is a key requirement.

The next section presents in more detail the management and enforcement issues and gives an overview of related projects. Section 3 explains our approach to privilege management and enforcement. Section 4 is a description and evaluation of a prototype implementation of the developed mechanisms. Section 5 identifies research issues for future work. Section 6 concludes with a summary.

2. Issues and Related Work

Management of fine grained privileges comprises functionality for the administration of privileges and their secure association (binding) with entities. This includes the specification, assignment, delegation, composition, and revocation of fine grained security privileges in a platform independent manner. The scope of such privileges can range from single grid objects (e.g. files) to multiple grid resources and entities.

The enforcement of fine grained access rights is defined as the limitation of operations performed on resources by a user to those permitted by an authoritative entity. Enforcement mechanisms need to be able to cope with expressiveness limitations of prevalent operating system security mechanisms. Portability, support for legacy applications and acceptable overhead are other key factors.

The most widely deployed grid security systems do not provide privilege management mechanisms but rather require privileges to be administrated using legacy operating system commands and tools. These systems rely on standard OS enforcement mechanisms which are not meant to support users from separate administrative domains nor do these mechanisms provide adequate support for temporary users with only a very constrained set of fine grained rights. For example it is not easily possible in traditional UNIX based systems to have two groups of users share access to a specific file unless access is permitted for all users of the system. It is also not possible to give file access permissions to an additional single user without that user being a member of a user group that has access. These expressiveness limitations [1] prevent many collaborative usage scenarios. More flexible and scalable means for privilege management and more powerful, fine grained enforcement mechanisms with support for legacy codes are needed to provide support for various forms of team collaborations on grid systems.

Two projects that have addressed these issues to varying extents and with different aims are the Community Authorization Service CAS [1] and Akenti [6]. Privilege management is handled differently in CAS and Akenti. CAS incorporates authorization information into restricted GSI [3] proxy certificates (PCs). The PCs specify an entity's subset of rights from the set of rights assigned to the CAS community. Such a PC is generated at the request of an authenticated user by a CAS server and subsequently used by the user to provide for authentication and authorization when accessing grid resources (a user never authenticates directly to a resource but rather uses the restricted community identity known to the resource). In CAS the applicable access policy for a specific request is defined by the rights granted to the community account by the resource owner less the restrictions for this access specified by the CAS administrator and embedded in the PC by the CAS server. The main goal and advantage of CAS is scalability: each resource owner assigns only coarse grained rights to a single community group account, CAS administrators manage the assignment of fine-grained privileges to community members via the CAS server. Akenti binds user attributes (e.g. a user's role and group membership) and privileges through attribute certificates (ACs) and thus separates authentication from authorization. Akenti uses X.509 identity certificates for authentication and a set of proprietary ASCII ACs that hold policy information for privilege management. Long-lived ACs convey group and role membership status. Short-lived ACs are used to cache and share authorization decisions among processes. So called "use-case" ACs are generated by resource owners to define usage policies for their resources. In Akenti the applicable access policy for a specific request results from the intersection of use-policies defined by the resource owners and the group and role assignments made in attribute certificates by user managers. Akenti's main goal is the ability for often multiple resource owners (in Akenti referred to as stakeholders) and administrative parties to define fine-grained and flexible usage policies in a widely distributed system.

Both CAS and Akenti use policy languages that allow arbitrarily fine grained specification of privileges. Akenti relies on its own policy language [24] to specify privileges, use-cases and attributes. While the current CAS implementation uses a simple proprietary policy language, the CAS architecture is independent of a specific language. A variety of policy languages exist which can be used to specify privileges and user attributes ranging from basic privilege lists to sophisticated languages [7, 8].

For enforcement, both CAS and Akenti rely on the software providing the requested service to self-regulate system access. The CAS team developed an implementation of the Generic Authorization and Access-Control API (GAA API) [9] to provide a defined interface for the service to query authorization data from CAS independent of the used policy language. Akenti provides proprietary means by which an Akenti service can query for authorization information and then make access decision. The resource server (e.g. an ftp server or a scientific application) that accepts and serves a request enforces the applicable access policy.

The solutions presented by CAS and Akenti are aimed at long-lived collaborative environments that change in size and composition rather slowly and use code specifically developed for, or ported to their security mechanisms. CAS reduces the administrative overhead that basic GSI mechanisms impose on large collaborative grid communities. Akenti allows multiple resource owners to specify flexible usage policies and supports role based access control. The use of policy languages in both projects provides for the necessary granularity in the specification of privileges.

However, both CAS and Akenti have two shortcomings. First, neither system provides the flexibility in their privilege management mechanisms that is required by ad-hoc, short lived collaborations. Second, both systems use an incorrect layering of the enforcement mechanisms: to solve the expressiveness limitations they do not rely on operating system enforcement but rather require fine-grained enforcement of access rules at the grid-middleware and application layer. This layering violates the fundamental design principles of "separation of concerns" and "least privilege access". As a result the usage of legacy applications and standard system services is not supported. Moreover, there is lower overall security due to the need for fully trusted application code which performs enforcement.

To further promote the evolution of grid security mechanisms to support short-lived, ad-hoc collaborations additional mechanisms for privilege management and enforcement are needed. It is these mechanisms at which our work is aimed.

3. Support for Ad-hoc Collaboration

We focus on a privilege management scheme based on attribute certificates that allows for flexible assignment, delegation, composition and revocation of fine-grained rights directly by users, and a portable, low-overhead enforcement scheme for fine-grained security policies that provides support for legacy applications. Both mechanisms can be used independently of each other and can interoperate with existing security solutions. We have implemented a first prototype by extending our Symphony framework which is discussed in section 4. Currently we are working on interfacing our mechanisms with the Grid Security Infrastructure (GSI) and Globus services [10]. Our evaluation of the security mechanisms implemented by other projects, such as UNICORE and Legion [11], suggests that our schemes can also be incorporated into those projects.

Our privilege management scheme employs privilege credentials in the form of standardized X509v2 attribute certificates [12] to convey privileges separately from identity credentials used for authentication. The separation of authentication from authorization, as shown by the Akenti project, allows for very flexible delegation and the combination of privileges from different sources and with variable lifetimes. By delegating and trading such credentials, users can form and dissolve groups directly through user-to-user interaction and peer trust relationships without the need for administrator intervention.

Our novel enforcement mechanism enacts fine-grained access policies through the use of commonly available operating system extensions providing access control lists. This mechanism enables the secure execution of legacy codes, imposes significantly less overhead than mechanisms which make access decisions on a call-by-call basis (e.g. sandboxing), and provides a simple and thus reliable means to protect system resources. By linking the grid access control services to the security services provided by the underlying resource operating systems our mechanism satisfies a security requirement stated in the recent work on an Open Grid Services Architecture [13].

3.1 Privilege Management

In our mechanism privileges are specified in a platform independent policy language and are securely assigned or delegated to entities by embedding them in attribute certificates (ACs, see Fig. 1). We use ACs to bind privileges to a distinguished name, the privilege holder. The grantor (issuer) of the privilege will sign the AC. Given the identity certificate of the issuer a resource can check if the issuer is authoritative for the embedded privilege (i.e. the owner of the corresponding system object) and determine whether the delegation is valid. The use of X.509v2 attribute certificates as defined in [12] allows us to create and process such certificates with standard tools.

```
Holder: EntityName: [CN=Dennis Kafura, O=VT, C=us]
Issuer: IssuerName: [CN=VT Campus Grid Admin, O=VT, C=us]
Signature: SHA1withRSA, OID = 1.2.840.113549.1.1.5
SerialNumber: SerialNumber: [    05]
AttrCertValidityPeriod:
    NotBeforeTime: Sat May 11 09:27:16 EDT 2002
    NotAfterTime: Sat May 18 09:27:16 EDT 2002
Attributes: 1
    [1]: Type: ObjectId: 1.3.6.1.4.1.6760.8.1.1  Values: 1
    Values[0]: AccessPrivilege://zuni.cs.vt.edu
```

Fig. 1. Essential fields of an attribute certificate which conveys a temporary privilege

The separation of privilege credentials from identity credentials avoids the limitations of impersonation. Impersonation, as used by the GSI through proxy certificates, allows an entity to delegate all or a subset of its own privileges to an agent that then acts on the delegating entity's behalf. Impersonation schemes implement a subtractive security solution – the delegated rights are obtained by reduction from the set of all rights possessed by the grantor. This solution bears the danger of violating the least privilege principle [14]. As with all subtractive security schemes, it is problematic to ensure that only the minimum subset of required privileges is delegated (the entity's total rights need to be known and accurately restricted). Furthermore it may be difficult to audit who is actually using a specific resource as delegated identities are being used for authentication (e.g. a collaborator authenticates with the identity of the privilege grantor, the collaborator's own identity is not supplied to the remote resource).

With separate credentials for privileges and identities, privileges from arbitrary sources can be securely combined to create a list of minimal privileges supplied with a specific access, which is consistent with the least privilege principle. This is a much needed feature which is not supported by impersonation schemes. An entity in a user-to-user collaboration scenario needs the ability to combine a subset of its own rights with rights received from collaborating entities. Collaboration may start with a low level of trust and minimal shared privileges. As the entities continue to work together the trust level increases and additional privileges may be granted. The ability to create flexible and dynamic combinations of privileges models more accurately the actual relations between the collaborating entities.

Several mechanisms can be used for revoking attribute certificates. Certificate revocation lists (CRLs) are a common way to distribute information on certificate validity. The Online Certificate Status Protocol OCSP [15] provides an alternative mechanism for revocation. In order to apply these means to a large number of possible issuers (as every user is authoritative for his own resource objects and thus can issue access privileges) a centralized certificate status server is needed which acts as a repository for CRLs and can answer OCSP queries. To revoke an attribute certificate, a user creates and submits a new CRL to the certificate status server. Alternatively, if the revocation is for an attribute certificate that only applies to a small number of resources, the authoritative user can push the revocation information by sending unsolicited OCSP responses directly to the affected resources.

3.2 Enforcement

Enforcement strategies can be characterized in one of three ways depending on how the identity credentials and the privilege credentials (if any) are combined to determine the effective privileges applicable to authorize a request. The three strategies are:

- *Credential Mapping:* Basic or restricted identity credentials are mapped to local user accounts. This grants all permissions associated with the local user account less the optional restrictions to the request if restricted credentials are being used. The GSI and CAS use this scheme.
- *Mixed Mode Authorization:* Credential mapping is used to define an initial set of privileges. Additional privileges based on presented privilege credentials are applied to the specific local user account before the request is served. After a resource access is completed the resource server revokes the additional privileges. Alternatively the privileges could remain assigned to the local user id for the lifetime of the presented privilege credentials.
- *Full Credential Combination:* A user requests services from a resource where she has no local account. The resource accumulates all the presented privileges and applies them to a generic, initially very restricted, user account; the request can then be served. After completion the privileges are removed and the account returned into its original, restricted state. Keeping the account assigned for subsequent re-

quests based on the credential lifetimes is an alternative and can be combined with a demand-driven user allocation scheme as suggested in [16].

The enforcement of complex security policies which cannot be translated into credential mapping is a challenging task. CAS and Akenti deal with this issue by requiring a grid service to implement self-policing mechanisms that perform access control based on provided policy information. The underlying operating system no longer performs fine grained authorization of system access as these services run with a large set of OS privileges. Legacy services cannot be accommodated as they are unable to make the necessary authorization decisions (they rely on the OS restricting their access) and would thus pose a significant security risk.

We have investigated the use of file system access control lists (ACLs) on a number of UNIX operating systems, specifically Linux, Solaris, and IRIX. On these systems ACLs are implemented following the POSIX.1E [17] recommendation. The application of shared access privileges in many Unix based operating systems traditionally involves the creation of user group accounts and the changing of group membership for users as well as resource objects (i.e. files). File system ACLs extend the standard file permissions to allow finer control on a user-by-user basis. Figure 2 shows a typical ACL listing specifying additional permissions for users abazaz, kafura and akarnik for a file owned by user mlorch.

ACLs can be modified dynamically by the resource gatekeeper during the authorization of an incoming request to reflect permissions stated in privilege credentials. The requested service can then be provided by a legacy program. After the request has been served the additional privileges can be revoked. This scheme provides the means necessary to assign transient access privileges to entities and support scenarios where several users have access to a single file without being members of the same user group. Dynamic, collaborative access to resource objects with a minimal set of rights assigned on demand is thus possible.

```
# file: data/simparam
# owner: mlorch
# group: users
user::rw-
user:abazaz:rw-
user:kafura:rw-
user:akarnik:rw-
group::r--
mask::rw-
other::r-
```

Fig. 2. A file system ACL

Additional privileges or restrictions that limit the use of system wide resources can also be applied and enforced by the operating system through portable and commonly available operating system tools. Quota mechanisms can be handled in this way. For example, storage space can be allocated based on conveyed ACs.

The combined use of credential mapping mechanisms together with authorization mechanisms based on cumulative privileges conveyed through ACs from possibly different issuers allows for very flexible and efficient authorization services that can operate within existing infrastructures. Two strengths of this approach are: (1) the low overhead due to enforcement within the operating system kernel, and (2) the ability to execute legacy code without modifications or wrappers. Unfortunately, the POSIX.1E recommendations have never been formally completed. Interfaces and implementations differ slightly. A portable and unified API is required to set and modify entries through grid gatekeepers. We have implemented such a library for the Linux and IRIX operating systems and will soon be able to support Solaris platforms.

Two other mechanisms to enforce fine grained system access with support for legacy applications are "sandboxing" and the redirection of library calls. While it would be possible to replace our ACL based enforcement mechanism with either one of these two approaches, we prefer the ACL approach for the reasons given below.

Sandboxing of applications is another way for resources to enforce fine-grained security policies for legacy codes. Tools like Janus [18] or the Virtual Execution Environment VXE [19] provide a constrained environment that monitors and evaluates all system access (e.g. through system call interception). Arbitrarily fine grained access policies can be enforced using such mechanisms. However, this flexibility comes at the price of considerable overhead which is often unacceptable for high-performance applications. In addition, it may be a significant effort to configure minimal access permissions for complex codes. Finally, sandboxing environments are often closely tied to vendor specific operating system mechanisms and not portable.

Redirection of library calls through dynamically injected shadow libraries is another mechanism that can be used to enforce security policies without application support. Bypass [20] uses such an approach as part of the Condor [21] project. This approach is more promising than sandboxing as the shadow libraries are likely to be more portable. However, it requires a mechanism to ensure that the application is not using any system calls that are not "shadowed" and thus not controlled.

4. Implementation

Symphony [5] is a component-based framework for creating, sharing, composing and executing grid applications and elements thereof. Fig. 3 shows a sample meta program in Symphony. An input data file is read by a simulator component which generates a simulation result file which in turn is eventually processed by a visualization component. The Java CoG Kit [22] facilitates access to grid services in addition to access provided by a proprietary resource server. We extended the framework with

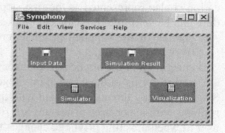

Fig. 3. A Symphony meta program

our mechanisms for privilege management and enforcement. Extensions include new tools for the creation and management of attribute certificates, the ability to attach ACs to Symphony components, and modifications of the Symphony resource server to parse and apply those ACs.

A graphical user tool to create attribute certificates that convey specific file and general system access permissions to another entity (see Figure 4), has been implemented. The "Issuer" and "Holder" entities are defined through their X.500 distinguished names (DN). The issuer can use existing GSI proxy credentials for the signing. In this case the issuer field holds the proxy credential DN and the proxy certificate path identifying the issuing end entity is stored with the AC. The holder DN can either be acquired by searching an LDAP server, or through direct interaction between the users (e.g. through e-mail). A validity period states the time frame during which the AC will be accepted by grid resources for authorization. Of course, the identity credentials used to sign the AC also determine the AC's lifetime. If a short-lived proxy credential is used for signing the AC lifetime is significantly constrained.

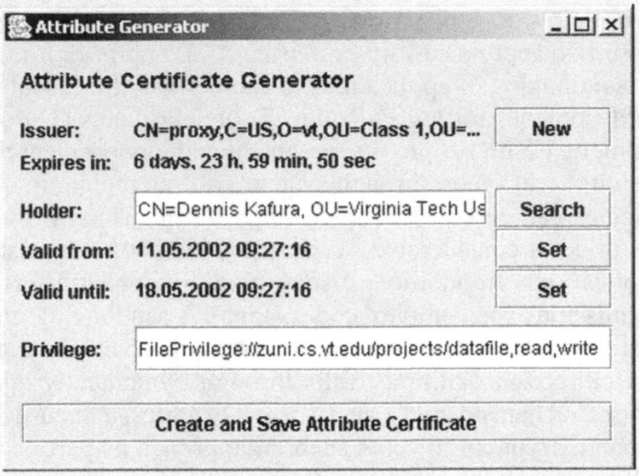

Conveyed privileges are specified as an embedded ASCII text string. A URL like naming scheme is used, which denotes the type of privilege (File-Privilege or AccessPrivilege), the host to which this privilege applies and, for file privileges the path to the file and a comma separated list of possible access rights (read, write, and execute). In future implementations this scheme will be extended to include a more power-

Fig. 4. The Symphony attribute certificate generator GUI

ful policy language. Created ACs are saved in a PEM formatted file [23] together with the certificate path of the issuer. AC paths are associated with and supplied during grid resource access.

On the remote resources our prototype employs a proprietary server based on Java RMI. Figure 5 shows the simplified logical program flow for authorization (authentication is also represented as the first step for completeness). The authorization procedure can be split into three logical blocks:

1. parsing of the supplied privilege credentials (ACs) and validation of authoritativeness of the issuer,
2. enactment of the applicable changes to the file system ACLs,
3. and restoring of the original privilege state (after the request has been served).

System security threats associated with the changing of system privileges by a process running with super user privileges are reduced through the changing of the effective user id when enacting privilege changes to the user id of the validated privilege issuer. Privileges are applied on the behalf of the issuing entity and thus modifications of privileges should be performed with only the set of rights that the issuing entity holds.

Our server supports authorization based on credential mapping, mixed mode, and full credential combination. If an authenticated user has a local account the mapping will be performed and optional privileges credentials are evaluated and applied. If a user has no local account at the resource from which a service is requested an access privilege credential needs to be presented with the request. The resource will check if the issuer of the access privilege is authoritative to permit additional users to access the system. This capability can be given to a user by the system administrator through an entry in a server configuration file. If the access privilege is valid the server maps the requesting user to a temporary, very restricted account. The "nobody" account is an example. Additional privileges need also be present in the request such that the actual service requested from the resource can be accessed (e.g. execute permission on a specific program).

A native C library is used to access POSIX system calls to modify file system ACLs and to change the effective user ID from within the Symphony server, which is implemented in Java. In order to have a portable implementation, only those system calls to modify ACL entries that are available on multiple platforms are being used by the library. The current implementation supports ACLs on Linux 2.4 and IRIX 6.5. Solaris implements ACL system calls based on an older draft standard of POSIX.1E which requires a redundant implementation of the functions in our library to cope with a different syntax for the system calls and ACL data structures.

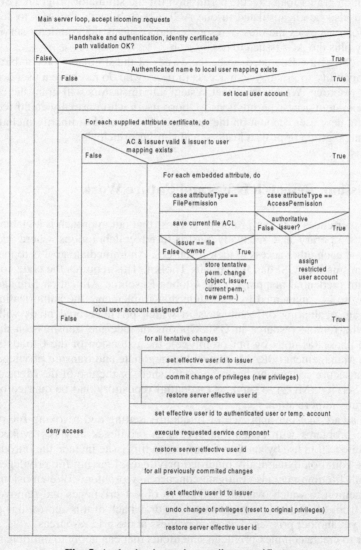

Fig. 5. Authorization using attribute certificates

The native library includes functions to query and set the existing ACL associated with files and directories. The library also provides access to functions that convert ACLs between the system representation and a text representation (Fig. 2). POSIX does not define mechanisms to add or remove ACL entries but rather only provides means to load and write complete access control lists. It was thus necessary to implement mechanisms that parse ACLs and insert, delete or replace specific entries.

In our initial scenario example in which Bob, a university researcher, wanted to grant access to his simulator program to Joan, the following simple steps need to be performed when using our prototype: (1) Bob creates an attribute certificate for Joan, permitting her to access the cluster while not having a local user account, plus a second AC which grants Joan execute permission for the simulator program. (Both privileges could also be encapsulated in one AC); (2) Bob sends the ACs to Joan by e-mail; (3) Joan accesses the cluster resource and requests the simulator service using her identity plus the ACs issued to her by Bob.

For this delegation Bob needs to be the owner of the simulator executable and also hold the capability to grant system access to users who do not have a user account on the cluster resource. We envision that system administrators will grant the capability to delegate system access permissions to those users who normally could request the creation of a new user account on the resource. This would ordinarily include the resource owners, group or project leaders, and similar principals.

5. Discussion, Research Issues and Future Work

The first experiences with our prototype suggest that our approach is a viable solution for small, temporary and relatively unstructured collaborations where individuals need to grant each other access to their resources. An immediate goal is to incorporate our mechanisms into GSI and the Globus Toolkit. This requires the code component dealing with credential mapping in the Globus Resource Allocation Manager (a.k.a. gatekeeper) to be augmented by a module that implements the authorization procedure. We are evaluating different ways in which privilege credentials will be presented to the remote resource in GSI. Options include the transmission during the handshake phase (as done by our prototype), the extension of the Globus Resource Allocation Management (GRAM) protocol to negotiate and transmit privilege credentials after a secure connection has been established, or the use of the Metacomputing Directory Service (MDS) to serve as credential repository and be queried by the resource during authorization.

We are aware that our approach of frequently setting and revoking file privileges may cause problems with concurrent access as privileges may be revoked by one process while still in use by another. Solutions to this issue include the introduction of a reference count on dynamically modified privileges. Leaving file privileges applied for their full lifetime may also mitigate concurrency problems. We envision an ACL monitor daemon to watch over all changes to object privileges and remove expired privileges from file ACLs to achieve this. One drawback of this approach is the introduction of yet another privileged daemon process at the grid resources.

In order to create complex privilege statements that can apply to multiple resources a more powerful policy language is needed. The Akenti policy language with its hierarchical resource naming scheme as well as the Extended Access Control Markup Language (XACML) appear to be promising choices. The CAS project is also experimenting with different policy languages. We will closely monitor their results and investigate the feasibility to employ an implementation of the GAA-API and thus have a policy language independent security service as done by CAS.

Experiences with the Akenti system have shown that policy languages are too complex to be used directly by the end user to specify fine grained permissions. A user interface needs to be developed that enables an arbitrary user to specify attribute certificates which convey the minimum amount of privileges needed for a specific service. The user needs to be guided through the process of AC generation by the software tool. Furthermore, a protocol for entities to negotiate the necessary capabilities for a certain request would enable automatic credential selection. Legacy applications may require a security description that clearly states what system components and user files are accessed as a basis for privilege selection. We have looked at automatically evaluating system call traces from sample application runs. However, often access to system resources depends on dynamic decisions during the program execution. Currently the most promising way to specify such access requirements is through a programmer or experienced user. This issue is not unique to our mechanisms but rather present in any system that aims to achieve least privilege access. In Akenti privilege problems can be debugged by an experienced user via extensive log files. In the case of legacy applications our experiences show that it may be difficult for an arbitrary user to infer which privileges are missing from the often unrelated errors a legacy application reports in the case of insufficient privileges. Legacy applications often assume an open, relatively unrestricted system.

Our mechanism for privilege management provides better support for accounting of system usage than impersonation schemes as the resource knows from the presented credentials who requests a specific accesses and who authorized the access. When impersonation is used the identity of the requesting entity, which is impersonating the authenticating user, is typically unknown.

A resource gatekeeper authorizing requests using our enforcement mechanism requires super user privileges to assume the user identities of privilege credential issuers and of the authenticated user to perform tasks on their behalf (setting and revoking of privileges, execution of legacy programs). We have not found a way to ease this requirement. However, existing resource gatekeepers that can change their effective user id to the requesting entities local user id (credential mapping) have the same requirement.

6. Conclusion

This paper reports on our approach to provide enhanced grid security services that support a variety of collaborative scenarios. These services enable low-overhead transient collaboration and improve the abilities of systems that focus on more static collaborative structures. More flexible binding of rights is achieved through the use of standard attribute certificates. Low-overhead enforcement mechanisms for file access rights enable efficient realization of fine-grain access policies while supporting legacy software. The ability to securely run legacy codes with fine-grained access permissions using existing operating system extensions is a much-needed feature in grids. User-to-user delegation without administrative intervention may prove to be the enabling mechanism for transient ad-hoc collaboration. Our work complements that of GSI and CAS, and incorporates experiences from the Akenti project.

References

1. L. Pearlman et al., "A Community Authorization Service for Group Collaboration", 2002 IEEE Workshop on Policies for Distributed Systems and Networks
2. I. Foster, C. Kesselman, and S. Tuecke, "The Anatomy of the Grid: Enabling Scalable Virtual Organizations," International Journal of Supercomputer Applications, 2001.
3. I. Foster et al, "A Security Architecture for Computational Grids", ACM Conference Proceedings, Computers and Security, ACM Press, NY, pp. 83-91, 1998
4. M. Romberg "UNICORE: Beyond Web-based Job-Submission" Proceedings of the 42nd Cray User Group Conference, May 22-26,2000, Noordwijk
5. M. Lorch, D. Kafura, "Symphony – A Java-Based Composition and Manipulation Framework for Computational Grids", In Proc. Second Int. Symposium on Cluster Computing and the Grid, Berlin, Germany, May 2002
6. M. Thompson et al., "Certificate based Access Control for Widely Distributed Resources", Proceedings of the 8th Usenix Security Symposium, 1999
7. OASIS, "extensible Access Control Markup Language", http://www.oasis-open.org/committees/xacml/index.shtml, visited August 10th, 2002
8. "XrML - The Digital Rights Language for Trusted Content and Services", http://www.xrml.org, visited August 10th, 2002
9. T.V. Ryutov, G. Gheorghiu and B.C. Neuman, "An Authorization Framework for Metacomputing Applications", Cluster Computing Journal, Vol. 2 Nr. 2, 1999, pp. 15-175
10. I. Foster, C. Kesselman, "Globus: A Toolkit-Based Grid Architecture", The Grid, Blueprint for a Future Computing Infrastructure, Morgan Kaufmann, San Francisco, 1999, 259-278
11. A. Grimshaw et al., "Legion: An Operating System for Wide-Area Computing", IEEE Computer, 32:5, May 1999: pp. 29-37.
12. S. Farrell, R. Housley, "An Internet Attribute Certificate Profile for Authorization", IETF RFC, April 2002
13. I. Foster et al, "The Physiology of the Grid – An Open Grid Services Architecture for Distributed Systems Integration", presented at the Global Grid Forum 4, February 2002, http://www.globus.org/research/papers/ogsa.pdf, visited August 10th, 2002
14. J. R. Salzer and M. D. Schroeder, "The Protection of Information in Computer Systems", Proceedings of the IEEE, Sept. 1975
15. M Myers et al. "Online Certificate Status Protocol, Version 2 ", IETF PKIX Working Group draft, March 2001, http://www.ietf.org/internet-drafts/draft-ietf-pkix-ocspv2-02.txt
16. T. Hacker, B. Athey, "A Methodology for Account Management in Grid Computing Environments", In Proc. 2nd Int. Workshop on Grid Computing, Denver, USA, Nov. 2001
17. "IEEE standard portable operating system interface for computer environments", IEEE Std 1003.1-1988 , Sept. 1988
18. I. Goldberg et. al, "A secure environment for untrusted helper applications" Proceedings of the Sixth USENIX UNIX Security Symposium, July 1996
19. "Virtual Executing Environment", http://www.intes.odessa.ua/vxe, visited August 10th, 2002
20. D. Thain, M. Livny, "Multiple Bypass: Interposition Agents for Distributed Computing", Journal of Cluster Computing, Volume 4, pp. 39-47, 2001
21. J. Basney, M. Livny, T. Tannenbaum, "High Throughput Computing with Condor", HPCU news, Volume 1(2), June 1997.
22. G. von Laszewski et al., "A Java Commodity Grid Kit", Concurrency and Computation: Practice and Experience, Volume 13, Issue 8-9, pp. 643-662, 2001.
23. J. Linn „Privacy Enhancement for Internet Electronic Mail: Part I: Message Encryption and Authentication Procedures ", IETF RFC, February 1993
24. M. Thompson, "Akenti Policy Language", White paper, http://www-itg.lbl.gov/Akenti/Papers/, visited August 10th, 2002

XML-Based Policy Engine Framework for Usage Policy Management in Grids

Babu Sundaram and Barbara M. Chapman

Department of Computer Science, University of Houston, Houston TX 77204, USA
babu,chapman@cs.uh.edu

Abstract. We have implemented a XML-based usage policy framework that provides authorization and cost-based accounting in the EZGrid system, a resource broker for grid computing. Primarily, this framework allows the resource owners to exercise more control over their resources by dictating usage permissions in a grid environment. The usage policies and associated rules are expressed as attribute-value pairs in XML. Interfaces are developed for administrators to set these rules and tools are designed to help the users and client-side brokerage systems to examine these policies while making resource choices. Globus toolkit's middleware services are used for authentication and data transport.

1 Introduction

Controlled and coordinated resource sharing is a principal requirement in any sufficiently complex distributed problem solving effort. Grids [7] present a new paradigm to enable such efforts through virtual organizations [8]. Existing middleware such as the Globus toolkit [6]assist us to construct grids to collaboratively share isolated compute resources. By virtue of their very widely distributed nature, grids would typically be composed of resources domains controlled by varied authorities and administrators. Each participating resource might be governed by varied usage policies. Enforcing coordinated and controlled resource sharing in such an environment is an extremely complicated task.

Resource providers need absolute control over their resources while committing them to a grid. Also, mechanisms are needed to allow them to specify usage policies that indicate how other users gain access to and use the resources. On the other hand, for grid users, the task of evaluating and managing such policies of grid resources is a non-trivial challenge. Hence, frameworks need to be developed to address this issue of policy specification and evaluation.

2 Overview of the EZGrid System and Policy Framework

The EZGrid project [4] at the University of Houston aims at promoting controlled resource sharing and efficient job execution in a grid environment. This is achieved by constructing high-level services such as resource brokerage systems coupled with information sub systems, policy frameworks and user interfaces.

M. Parashar (Ed.): GRID 2002, LNCS 2536, pp. 194–198, 2002.

Policy Engine [11] is an automated framework that facilitates policy-based authorization and accounting as part of the EZGrid system. It allows for policy specification in the form of attribute-value pairs. In the initial vesion, we used standard Unix text files to store the usage policies. The client-side module transparently checks the remote usage policy file and evaluates the resource availability. It uses Globus toolkit for middleware services such as Grid Security Infrastructure (GSI) [3] for security, Globus Resource Allocation Manager (GRAM) [5]for resource management and Globus Access Secondary Storage (GASS) [2] for data transport. For platform independence, the entire framework was implemented in Java. Globus toolkit's services are accessed from within the framework using the CoG kit's [9] Java libraries.

3   Deficiencies in the Initial Version of Policy Model

Though our model was flexible enough to accommodate arbitrary policies, it was a significant burden to modify the user-side framework to accommodate evaluation of such new policies. Huge coordination efforts between the resource-side and the user-side frameworks when user acquires access to new grid resources. So, a promising approach would be to make the remote resources' policy files self contained in that they hold information not only pertaining to the policies, but also rules or expressions about how to handle the policies.

Such a redesign of the model would then require no modification of the userside framework, when new policies or attribute-value pairs are introduced. Employing a suitable policy language with rich functionalities and that is supported by standards and widespread acceptance would solve this issue. Also, there was concern about the lack of tool support and utilities for administrators to easily specify, edit and manage policies. Additional methods such as GSI-FTP were required to be supported for data transport.

4   Improvements to the Implementation of Policy Engine

In this paper, we discuss our efforts with the redesigning of the policy framework to overcome the above shortcomings. We have chosen to employ XML[13] as the language for policy specification and evaluation. Policies and the associated rules or expressions that indicate how to handle the policies would also be framed in XML itself. Availability of Java libraries and other related APIs such as Java API for XML Processing(JAXP)[14] to parse and manage XML tags and files highly simplifies the evaluation framework on the client side. Also, it enables us to accommodate multiple-level rules such as a chain of rules with "AND" or "OR" relation to one another. Multiple levels of hierarchies in expressing rules can also be achieved. Utilities and interfaces have been developed that would require only minimal effort from the administrators to generate XML policy files. Thus, the resource providers are isolated from the complexities of translating the usage policies into XML. Support for GSI-FTP is added to transfer policy and rule files.

5   Services and Tools for Resource Providers

The resource-side utilities include the following major modules: Tools that enable usage policy specification, editing and managing Services that evaluate the user's job requests to ensure that policies are satisfied before granting resource access through GRAM We now discuss these components in detail.

5.1   Policy and Rule Specification in XML

Earlier implementation of the policy framework lacked server-side support for easy specification and managing of usage permissions or restrictions. We have developed server-side utilities that isolate the policy makers from expressing policies in XML and hence require only minimal effort from administrators to set policies. The interfaces have been implemented using Java swing components. The following list explains the terminology used in the formation of a policy as well as the corresponding rule while specifying usage permissions/restrictions.

1. **type** - indicates the nature of the rule. For instance, administrators might prefer to enforce usage policies at site-level (that apply to all users, also termed global policies) or at the user-level (that apply only to a specific user).
2. **attribute** - denotes a parameter in policy formation, such as CPU, memory, allowed resource usage periods , priorities and so on.
3. **operator** - identifies the operation to be performed during the evaluation of policies. Typically, it includes arithmetic operators such as $\geq, \leq, \neq, ==$ and so on. Other operations such as "AND" and "OR" can also be supported.
4. **value** - reference value in the rule or allowed limits for the user, which are used during the policy evaluation. For instance, value would be 20 if a policy states that a user cannot access more than 20 processors at any given time.
5. **true , false** - indicate the change in the rank value if the policy evaluation is successful or unsuccessful respectively

The above set indicates the sufficient set of parameters to express a complete rule in our framework. Let us discuss an example scenario in the "nanogrid" which is being used as the test bed for the EZGrid software being developed by the HPCTools group at the University of Houston.

Sample Policy. The user 'janedoe' of the "nanogrid" will have an initial usage limit of 1000 credits, where the "credit" is an accounting metric to reflect resource usage. (This permits us to employ flexible cost and accounting models in the future. The available credits are managed by the EZGrid job monitoring subsystem discussing which is beyond the scope of this paper.) Also, the user cannot have more than 15 jobs in the scheduler queue at any given time. She belongs to the group 'users'. The above policy is generated as shown:

```
<?xml version="1.0" encoding="utf-8" ?>
<policy_u458>
<initCrediti>1000</initCredit> <availCredit>1000</availCredit>
<maxJobs>15</maxJobs> <group>users</group>
</policy_u458>
```

where the u458 indicates that the user 'janedoe' has the user ID 458. Also, the grid-mapfile of the Globus toolkit can be enhanced in order to include the policy details together with the certificate subject name to local identity mapping.

Sample Rule. The global rules are used to enforce usage control over all the users. For instance, the administrator might want to enforce a policy that permits the grid users to access the resources only during weekends. However, users belonging to group 'research' might be granted uncontrolled access to resources irrespective of time. The above rule would be generated by the utility as shown:

```
<?xml version="1.0" encoding="utf-8" ?> <rule>
<rule1> <type>global</type> <attribute>group</attribute>
<condition>=</condition> <value>research</value>
<operator>OR</operator> <true>TRUE</true>
<false>FALSE</false> </rule1>
<rule2> <type>global</type> <attribute>submitTime</attribute>
<condition>=</condition> <value>3</value>
<operator>OR</operator> <true>TRUE</true>
<false>FALSE</false> </rule2> </rule>
```

6 Policy Evaluation Mechanism

This XML rule file will be evaluated against the user's policy file when resource requests are obtained from users. Policy evaluation is performed on client side prior to making resource choices. Also, evaluation on the resource side needs to be done in order to to prevent the clients from circumventing their local policy framework. In the above example, if a job request is made anytime other than a weekend (represented by integer 3 in our model) it would deny of access as per rule 2. Further, the rule 1 would always result in FALSE since the group of 'janedoe' is 'users' as mentioned by her policy file.

7 Conclusions and Summary

Enforcing absolute control is a major requirement for resource providers that commit their resources to grid environments. In this paper, we have discussed the XML-based Policy framework that supports resource usage policy specification and evaluation mechanisms. We have extended our earlier framework to provide support for expressing policies as XML tags and values. Also, the new design makes the policy files self-contained in that they are complemented by rule files that dictate how the policies are to be evaluated. However, no modification is required on the client side evaluation mechanism to accommodate any new policies. Also, the design is scalable to manage very high number of resources, typical to computational grids. Support for GSI-FTP has been introduced to enable policy file fetching by the client if policy changes are detected.

Acknowledgements

The authors would like to thank the people of Globus Project, especially Steven Tuecke for pointing us in this research direction. Also, we acknowledge the following graduate students for contributing to the implementation: Bo Liu, Zhenying Liu, Eric Shafer and Chandler Wilkerson.

References

1. W. Allcock, J. Bester, J. Bresnahan, A. Chervenak, I. Foster, C. Kesselman, S. Meder, V. Nefedova, D. Quesnel, and S. Tuecke, "Data Management and Transfer in High-Performance Computational Grid Environments," Parallel Computing 2001.
2. J. Bester, I. Foster, C. Kesselman, J. Tedesco, S. Tuecke, "GASS: A Data Movement and Access Service for Wide Area Computing Systems," Sixth Workshop on I/O in Parallel and Distributed Systems, May 5, 1999.
3. R. Butler, D. Engert, I. Foster, C. Kesselman, S. Tuecke, J. Volmer, V. Welch, "A National-Scale Authentication Infrastructure," IEEE Computer, 2000.
4. B. M. Chapman, B. Sundaram, K. Thyagaraja, S.W. Masood, P. Narayanasamy, "EZGrid: A Resource Brokerage System for Grids," http://www.cs.uh.edu/ ezgrid.
5. K. Czajkowski, I. Foster, N. Karonis, C. Kesselman, S. Martin, W. Smith, S. Tuecke, "A Resource Management Architecture for Metacomputing Systems," Proc. IPPS/SPDP '98 Workshop on Job Scheduling Strategies for Parallel Processing, 1998.
6. I. Foster and C. Kesselman, "Globus: A Metacomputing Infrastructure Toolkit," International Journal of Supercomputer Applications, Summer 1997.
7. I. Foster and C. Kesselman, "The GRID: Blueprint for a New Computing Infrastructure," Morgan Kauffman Publishers, 1999.
8. I. Foster, C. Kesselman and S. Tuecke, "The Anatomy of the Grid: Enabling Scalable Virtual Organizations," International Journal of Supercomputing Applications, 15(3), 2001.
9. G. von Laszewski, I. Foster, J. Gawor, W. Smith, and S. Tuecke, "CoG Kits: A Bridge between Commodity Distributed Computing and High-Performance Grids," ACM 2000 Java Grande Conference, 2000.
10. L. Pearlman, V. Welch, I. Foster, C. Kesselman, S. Tuecke, "A Community Authorization Service for Group Collaboration," IEEE 3rd International Workshop on Policies for Distributed Systems and Networks, 2001.
11. B. Sundaram, B. M. Chapman, "Policy Engine: A Framework for Authorization, Accounting Policy Specification and Evaluation in Grids," 2nd International Conference on Grid Computing, Nov 2001.
12. B. Sundaram, C. Nebergall, S. Tuecke, "Policy Specification and Restricted Delegation in Globus Proxies," Research Gem, Super Computing 2000, Dallas, TX, November 2000.
13. "Extensible Markup Language," http://www.w3c.org/XML
14. "Java API for XML Processing," http://java.sun.com/xml/jaxp/index.html

Fine-Grain Authorization for Resource Management in the Grid Environment

Kate Keahey[1] and Von Welch[2]

[1] Argonne National Laboratory, Argonne, IL, USA
keahy@mcs.anl.gov
[2] U. of Chicago, Chicago, IL, USA
welch@mcs.anl.gov

Abstract. In this document we describe our work-in-progress for enabling fine-grain authorization of resource management. In particular we address the needs of Virtual Organizations (VOs) to enforce their own polices in addition to those of the resource owners[1].

1 Introduction

In some Virtual Organizations (VOs) [1] the primary motivation for using the Grid is remote sharing of application services deployed on community resources, rather directly sharing those hardware resources themselves [2]. Since hardware resources are shared only through the agency of the VO, and the community is large and dynamically changing, the traditional mode of operation requiring each user to obtain an account from the owner of each resource participating in the VO is no longer satisfactory. Instead, we see an increasing trend to allow the use of both hardware and software resources based on VO credentials. In addition, sharing VO-owned application services requires VO-wide (as opposed to resource-specific) mechanisms for managing both these services and the VO's resource usage rights related to their execution. In this paper, we present an architecture relying on VO credential for service and resource management and allowing us to specify and enforce VO-wide service and resource usage policies.

We propose changes and extensions to the current Globus Toolkit's (GT2) resource management mechanism [3] to support this enforcement of rich VO policies. We describe how we can combine policies that are *resource-specific*, that is, determined by the resource owner, and *community-wide*, that is set by the VO. The goal of our work is to provide an architecture that allows a Virtual Organization to express policy on by whom and how its allocation is consumed, while at the same time ensuring that the resource provider's policies are still honored. Further, we consider two kinds of policy targets: application services, and traditional computing resources.

---

[1] This work was supported by the Mathematical, Information, and Computational Sciences Division subprogram of the Office of Advanced Scientific Computing Research, U.S. Department of Energy, and by the Scientific Discovery Through Advanced Computing (SciDAC) Initiative

In the remainder of this paper we will propose a set of mechanisms enabling VOs to realize the scenarios described above for resource management. We discuss this architecture in the context of the current capabilities of the Globus Toolkit's (GT2) resource management mechanism [3] and propose extensions. We are currently implementing this architecture using GRAM and the Grid Security Infrastructure [4] mechanisms.

2   Use Scenarios and Requirements

VOs are often interested in setting policies on its member's use of community resources, not only in terms of *who* can use *what* resource, but *how* they are used. In this section we describe scenarios driving our work and illustrating the kinds of authorization required.

1. *Combining policies from different sources.* A supercomputing center decides to give allocations on some of its resources to several VOs specifying how much resource each of the VOs is allowed to use. The VOs can then decide: (1) which services can be run on these resources by which of their members and (2) how much of the community allocation can be used by individual members. This scenario requires combining policies coming from 2 different sources: the resource owner, and the VO. These policies can be expressed in different languages, and can contain dependencies necessary to resolve for full evaluation.

2. *Fine-grain control of how resources are used.* A VO has two groups of users: one group has the role of developing, installing and debugging the application services used by the VO to perform their scientific computation and the second group runs analysis using the application services. The first group may need a large degree of freedom in the types of applications they can run (e.g. compilers, debuggers, the applications themselves) in order to debug and deploy the VO application services, but should only be consuming small amounts of traditional computing resources (e.g. CPU, disk and bandwidth) in doing so. The second group may need the ability to consume large amounts of resources in order to perform science, but should only be doing so using application services approved by the VO. Furthermore, VO may wish to specify policies that certain users may use more or less resources than others and that certain applications may consume more or less resources than others.

3. *VO-wide management of jobs and resource allocations.* Currently, the only users who are allows to manage (e.g. suspend, kill) a job are: the user who instantiated it and any administrators on the resource on which it is running. However, for jobs using VO resource allocations it is often desirable for the VO to be able specify policy on who can manage a job. For example, users in a particular VO often have long-running computational jobs using VO resources and this same VO often has short-notice high-priority jobs that can't wait until other jobs are finished. Since it is often difficult to quickly find the users who submitted the original jobs, the VO wants to give a groups of it's members the ability to manage any jobs on VO resources so they can instantiate high-priority jobs on short notice.

Although we express our requirements in terms of authorization properties, and important aspect of our work deriving from these requirements involves creating enforcement mechanisms suitable for fine-grain authorization enforcement.

3   Problem Statement, Requirements, and General Approach

In order to support the use cases described in the previous section, we need to provide resource management mechanisms that allow the specification and consistent enforcement of authorization and usage policies set by a VO in addition to policies specified by the resource providers. In addition to allowing the VO to specify policies on standard computational resources, like processor time and storage, we want to allow the VO to specify policies on application services that it deploys as well as long-running computational jobs instantiated by community members.

In our work we will assume the following interaction model: An interaction is initiated by a user submitting a request, composed of the action of starting a job and the job's description, accompanied by the user's Grid credentials. This request is then evaluated against both resource and VO policies at different policy evaluation points (PEPs) located in the resource management facilities. If the request is authorized, it is carried out by local enforcement mechanisms operating based on local credentials. During the job execution, a VO user may submit management requests composed of a management action (e.g. request information, suspend or resume a job, cancel a job, etc.) In other words, following a pattern generally present in the Grid architecture, the enforcement module is an intermediary that translates grid-specific capabilities into local capabilities.

4   Overview of Current GRAM System

The current Globus Toolkit GRAM (Grid Resource Acquisition and Management) [3] system has two major software components: the Gatekeeper and the Job Manager. The Gatekeeper is responsible for creating a Grid service requested by the user. The Job Manager Instance (JMI) is a Grid service providing resource management and job control. This section will analyze the current system and explain its limitations.

4.1   Gatekeeper

The Gatekeeper is responsible for authenticating and authorizing a Grid user. The authorization is based on the user's grid credential and an access control list contained in a configuration file called grid-mapfile. This file is also used to map the user's Grid identity to a local account effectively translating the user's Grid credential into a local credential. Finally, the Gatekeeper starts up a Job Manage Instance (JMI), executing with the user's local credential. This mode of operation requires the user to have an account on the resource and implements enforcement only to the extent defined by privileges on this account.

4.2   Job Manager Instance (JMI)

The JMI parses the user's job startup request, and interfaces with the resource's job control system (e.g. LSF) to initiate the user's job. During the job's execution the JMI monitors its progress, and handles job management requests from the user. As the JMI is run under the user's local credential as defined by the user's account, the OS and local job control system are able to enforce local policy tied to that account on the JMI and user job.

The JMI does no authorization on job startup. However, once the job has been started, the JMI accepts, authenticates and authorizes management requests (e.g. suspend, stop, query, etc.) on the job. The authorization policy on these management requests is that the user making the request must be the same user who initiated the job. There is no provision for modifying this policy.

4.3   GRAM Shortcomings

The current GRAM architecture has a number of shortcomings when matched up with the requirements we laid out in Section 0:

1.   Authorization of Grid service and user job startup is coarse-grained and not up to the expressiveness required.

2.   Authorization on job management is coarse-grained and fixed to allow only the user who initiated a job to manage it.

3.   Enforcement is implemented chiefly through the medium of privileges tied to a statically configured local account (JMI runs under local user credential) and therefore useless for enforcing fine-grained policy or policy coming from sources external to the resource (such as a VO).

4.   Local enforcement depends on the rights attached to the user's account, not on the rights associated with a specific request and Grid credential accompanying that request.

5.   A local account must exist for a user; this creates an undue burden on system administrators and users alike and prevents wide adoption of the network services model in large and dynamically changing communities.

These problems can, and have been, in some measure alleviated by clever setup. For example, the impact of (4) can be alleviated by mapping a grid identity to several different local accounts with different capabilities. (5) is often coped with by working with "shared accounts" (which however introduces many security, audit, accounting and other problems) or by providing a limited implementation of dynamic accounts [5].

5   Proposed Authorization and Enforcement Extensions to GRAM

In this section we describe our work in progress on implementing extensions to GRAM intended to overcome the shortcomings described above. Our works targets extensions to GRAM for policy evaluation including the design of a policy language for resource management, and strategies suitable for fine-grain policy enforcement.

5.1   Authorization System Extensions

Our requirements bring forth the need to replace the authorization methods currently used in GRAM by systems that are capable of evaluating complex fine-grain policies coming from multiple sources; in our case specifically the resource provider and the VO. We are currently working with two systems that meet these requirements: Akenti [6] and the Community Authorization Service (CAS) [7]. Both of these systems allow for multiple policies sources, but have significant differences, both in terms of architecture (Akenti uses a pull model to query outside sources while CAS uses a push model where the user gets credentials from outside sources and pushes them to the resource) and programming APIs. We are in the process of experimenting with using either, or both of these systems (to combine different policy sources).

In order to retain flexibility in the choice of an authorization system, we defined a generic policy evaluation API that could be called by the PEP. This API will include passing, at a minimum, the following elements to the authorization system: the user's grid credentials, the name(s) of the policy target, and a description of the action the user is requesting.

5.2   Policy Language

GRAM allows user to start and manage jobs by submitting requests composed of an *action*, describing what is to be done with a job (start, cancel, provide status, change priority, etc.) and a job description. The job description is formulated in terms of attributes specified by the Resource Specification Language (RSL)[3]. RSL consists of attribute value pairs specifying job parameters such as executable description (name, location, etc.), and resource requirements (number of CPUs to be used, maximum allowable memory, etc.).

We are currently designing a policy language that allows for specification of the contents of the job description in terms of RSL and concepts related to job management such as actions, job ownership, and jobtags (see below). This allows a policy to limit not only the usage of traditional computational resources, but to dictate the executables they are allowed to invoke, allowing a VO to limit the way in which they can consume resources.

In order to specify VO-wide job management policies we introduce the notion of job tags. By requiring that a job have a certain jobtag we define a group of jobs that we can write policy about. This allows us to make policy about those jobs, for example to grant a set of users, who have an administrative role within a VO the right to manage those jobs. In order to implement it we extended RSL to accept a jobtag as a parameter; a VO user can then be required to submit a job with a specific jobtag (or any jobtag depending on the policy) and a user with administrative privileges can be given the right to use the jobtag to manage the jobs tagged by it. At present, jobtags are defined statically by a policy administrator, but we envision an approach in which the users will define them dynamically.

In the current implementation we experiment with the following assertions in our policy language:

- The job request can contain a particular attribute with the following values (e.g. enumerated list, range, regular expression or combination)
- The job request must/must not contain a particular attribute with one of the following values (e.g. it must specify the following queue, or a single processor, etc.)
- The job request must/must not contain a particular attribute (e.g. a jobtag must be specified)
- The job request must not contain any attributes not specified in this policy (in other words unless something is specified it is assumed to be forbidden)

So far we have found that these assertions cover the range of semantics we need to express.

5.3   Policy Enforcement

The current enforcement methods relied on by GRAM are unsuitable for enforcement of dynamically changing, fine-grained policies coming from sources external to the resource such as present in our requirements. In order to improve them we are working on thrusts in two areas: (1) implementing an enforcement gateway in GRAM itself and associated resource management tools, (2) implementing dynamic accounts, and sandboxing technologies. Combined together these approaches allow us to control external job initiation and management, securely support users who do not have an account on they system, and control locally operations of a job which we believe to be necessary and sufficient to securely implement our policies.

5.3.1   Implementing Enforcement in GRAM

Implementing enforcement in GRAM means creating a gateway controlling all external access to a resource; an action is authorized or not depending on decision yielded by a gateway. Policy can be enforced in GRAM at multiple PEPs corresponding to different decision domains; for example a PEP placed in the Gatekeeper can allow or disallow the creation of a Grid service. Since our work focuses on job and resource management we established a PEP in the JM where user requests are parsed and can therefore be evaluated. The PEP evaluates a request in the context of user credentials and policies from multiple sources and, if authorized, carries out the action. Since the PEP can deal with the full range of actions implemented by GRAM, it also allows users other than the initiator of a job to manage a job. We are working on a set of resource management tools to deal with situations where the user's local credential (carried by JMI) is not sufficient to carry out the request.

The weakness of this approach is that once the resource gateway decides to allow an action (for example a job execution), it has no control over subsequent actions of the job including actions specifically forbidden by the gateway. This places much responsibility in the hands of policy administrator, code developers and screeners, etc. who have to ensure that no undesirable actions will be taken by the code itself. In short, the gateway solution is similar to firewalls in that it places severe limitations on how initial connections to resources can be made, but unlike firewalls it depends on a wide range of variables that will be hard to control (such deep understanding of the implications of the actions of a complex code).

5.3.2   Dynamic Accounts and Sandboxing

A sandbox is an environment that imposes restrictions on resource usage [8]. Sandboxing represents a strong enforcement solution, having the resource operating system act as the policy evaluation and enforcement modules and is largely complementary to the gateway approach. It is usually implemented by using platform-specific tools such as the Java Virtual Machine, or operating system specific capabilities. While they provide a solution with relatively high degree of security, they are hard to implement portably and introduce a degree of inconsistency across different platforms. At present our focus in this area is to tie our sandboxing needs to the dynamic accounts.

Dynamic Accounts are accounts that are created and configured on the fly by a resource management facility. This enables the resource management system to run jobs on a system for users that do not have an account at that system, and it also enables account configuration relevant to policies for a particular resource management request as opposed to a static user's configuration. Because of that, a dynamic account configuration can be also used as a sandbox on the user's rights. For example, by modifying user's group membership to control file system access, the account's quotas and other limits on resource usage, we can ensure that the user does not use more resources than authorized. On the other hand, accounts allow the user to modify only very few configuration parameters, and hence the enforcement implemented in an account is coarse-grained and may need to be supplemented by sandboxing technologies in order to implement fine-grained enforcement.

6   Summary

We described a work in progress aiming to provide mechanisms for VO-wide authorization and enforcement. The purpose of this work is to make VO-based trust model acceptable to resource owners and also to provide mechanisms enabling making and enforcing policies related to VO-wide operations such as resource management. Our system is designed to support fine-grain authorization on job startup and management, VO-wide job as well as resource allocation management. We are also working on strategies suitable for fine-grain policy enforcement

References

[1] The Anatomy of the Grid: Enabling Scalable Virtual Organizations. I. Foster, C. Kesselman, S. Tuecke. International J. Supercomputer Applications, 15(3), 2001.

[2] Computational Grids in Action: The National Fusion Collaboratory, K. Keahey, T. Fredian, Q. Peng, D. P. Schissel, M. Thompson, I. Foster, M. Greenwald, D. McCune, to be published in Journal of Future Generation Computer Systems

[3] A Resource Management Architecture for Metacomputing Systems. K. Czajkowski, I. Foster, N. Karonis, C. Kesselman, S. Martin, W. Smith, S. Tuecke. Proc. IPPS/SPDP '98 Workshop on Job Scheduling Strategies for Parallel Processing, po. 62-82, 1998.

[4] A National-Scale Authentication Infrastructure. R. Butler, D. Engert, I. Foster, C. Kesselman, S. Tuecke, J. Volmer, V. Welch. IEEE Computer, 33(12):60-66, 2000.

[5] http://www.gridpp.ac.uk/gridmapdir/

[6] Certificate-based Access Control for Widely Distributed Systems, M. Thompson, et. al., Proceedings of the 8th Usenix Security Symposium, 1999.

[7] A Community Authorization Service for Group Collaboration. L. Pearlman, V. Welch, I. Foster, C. Kesselman, S. Tuecke. IEEE 3rd International Workshop on Policies for Distributed Systems and Networks, 2001.

[8] User-level Resource-constrained Sandboxing, F. Chang, A. Itzkovitz, and V. Karamcheti, *Proceedings of the USENIX Windows Systems Symposium* (previously *USENIX-NT*), August 2000.

Adaptive Resource Scheduling for Network Services

Byoung-Dai Lee and Jon B. Weissman

Department of Computer Science and Engineering, University of Minnesota,
Minneapolis MN, U.S.A.
{blee, jon}@cs.umn.edu

Abstract. Recently, there has been considerable interest in providing high performance codes as network services. In particular, high performance network services provide improved performance by executing complex and time-consuming applications (or part of an application) on remote high performance resources. However, since service providers resources are limited, without effective resource scheduling, end-users will not experience performance improvement. In this paper, we propose adaptive resource harvesting algorithms to schedule multiple concurrent service requests within network services. The preliminary results show that our approach can achieve service time improvement up to 40% for a prototypical parallel service.

1 Introduction

Recently, there has been considerable interest in providing high performance codes as network services. High performance applications such as data mining [4], theorem proving and logic [3], parallel numerical computation [2], [6] are example services that are all going on-line. Network services allow the end-users to focus on their applications and obtain remote services when needed simply by invoking remote services across the network. The primary advantages of using network services, in particular high performance network services, are:

- by executing complex and time-consuming applications (or part of an application) on remote sites that provide high performance resources, the end-users will experience significantly reduced service time.
- the end-users need not be involved with maintaining low-level infrastructure to run service codes because such activities are taken care of by the service providers.

Network services imply the potential of multiple concurrent users across the network. Moreover, since service providers' resources are limited, effective resource management is essential to providing acceptable performance. To address this problem, our approach for scheduling multiple concurrent service requests within network services is based on *Resource Harvesting*, where resources are dynamically added/removed to/from active service requests to support high performance.

The paper is organized as follow: Section 2 gives the related work and Section 3 describes the system model. Section 4 presents the resource harvesting algorithms and Section 5 shows the experimental results. Finally, we conclude in Section 6.

M. Parashar (Ed.): GRID 2002, LNCS 2536, pp. 207–218, 2002.
© Springer-Verlag Berlin Heidelberg 2002

2   Related Work

Much research has been conducted on efficient resource management for executing high performance applications on multiple resources. However, most of them are limited to scheduling a single application using shared resources whereas in our model, the resource management system schedules multiple concurrent service requests to meet the performance objective.

[1] provides convenient tools for parametric computation experiments. Users can vary parameters related to the experiment by using a simple declarative parametric modeling language and the parametric engine manages and maintains the whole experiment. The scheduling scheme employed in the system is based on an economic model, which selects resources that meet the deadline and minimize the cost of computation. [2] and [6] are two representative network service infrastructures and they bear strong similarities both in motivation and general design. For each user request, a scheduler (or an agent in [2]) selects a set of servers that can handle the computation and ranks them based on the minimum completion time. [5] proposed local learning algorithms for the prediction of run-specific resource usage on the basis of run-time input parameters. Our run-time prediction technique is similar to their approach. However, they did not consider parallel applications. [7] proposed deadline scheduling that uses a load correction mechanism and a fallback mechanism to minimize the overall occurrence of deadline misses as well as their magnitudes. Unlike other works mentioned above, its goal is to schedule multi-client requests on multi-server environments.

In contrast to our work, none of these works support dynamic resource addition and removal to user requests. For example, once a server is allocated to the user request, it remains until the request completes or the server fails.

3   System Model for Network Services

We believe that some classes of high performance services are not appropriate for the resource harvesting technique. For example, network services with complex workflows may suffer from increased overhead for saving and redistributing their states when new resources are added in the middle of their execution. Therefore, the target classes of high performance network services that we are considering are data parallel and distributed services, which are common to high performance computing. Data parallel services are those that require communication between the constituent processors and the communication patterns are symmetric. Examples include numeric servers, N-body simulator, parallel CFD, etc. Distributed services are similar to data parallel services, but do not require communication among the distributed processes. Examples include stochastic simulation (e.g. monte carlo), parameter studies, etc.

Fig. 1 shows the general run-time infrastructure for network services. It consists of three primary components: scheduler, run-time predictor and service instances. The scheduler contacts the run-time predictor to acquire the estimated run-time of the service requests for resource scheduling. If it is needed to add/remove resources to/from active service instances, the scheduler contacts corresponding service instances, where adaptive actions are actually implemented. In addition, the service

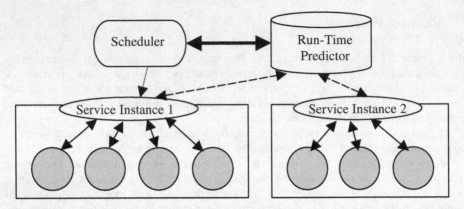

Fig. 1. General run-time infrastructure for network services: service instance 1 is using four resources and service instance 2 is using three resources.

instances are responsible for reporting performance information to the run-time predictor so that the run-time predictor can maintain up-to-date performance information.

4   Adaptive Resource Management

Network services imply the potential of multiple concurrent users across the network and heterogeneous service requests (e.g. requests with different input parameters). Therefore, the run-time infrastructure must provide acceptable performance for a wide-spectrum of users. Our approach for scheduling multiple concurrent service requests is based on resource harvesting, where resources are dynamically added/removed to/from the active service requests to support high performance. For example, a scheduler may initially allocate a large number of resources to a request because there are no other requests pending. But when competing requests start to arrive and insufficient resources are available to run them, the scheduler may choose to harvest resources from running service requests. Therefore, performance prediction is crucial to adaptive resource management because deciding how to best allocate resources dynamically depends on the estimation of service execution time. The overhead of harvesting must be measured within the service and made available as part of the decision process. Resource harvesting raises two fundamental questions that should be addressed.

- *From which service requests should resources be harvested?*
- *How many resources should be harvested?*

One way to address the first question is the service provider establishes priority classes of its user base so that higher priority requests can harvest resources from lower priority requests. The second question is more complex because performance gain achieved by resource harvesting must be able to amortize the performance loss experienced by requests from which resources are taken away.

4.1 Performance Prediction

Performance prediction is needed by the scheduler to estimate the cost of executing a specific instance of a service request on a given amount of resources. The service execution time depends on not only the number of resources but also the input parameters to the service. For example, the time to solve NxN system of equations on K resources may be different from the time required to solve the system on L resources or to solve MxM system of equations on N resources. For simple services such as matrix multiplication, it is possible to predict run-time accurately using static cost functions. However, for complex services, we believe that static specification of detailed cost functions is not always possible. For the latter case, we use local linear regression and clustering technique to predict run-time, where local linear regression is applied using a subset of prior performance data that are clustered near the new data point. Performance history is organized in a two dimensional matrix, where each column represents the resource set and each row represents performance of the service given a set of input parameters on each resource set. To fill in the matrix, a configurable parameter, *cluster range*, is used. It determines whether or not two different input parameters can be regarded as similar in terms of the performance when the same resource set is used. For example, we might say that the run-time for 10000x10000 matrix multiplication is the same as the time for 10001x10001 matrix multiplication if the same resource set is used. When a triple < input parameter, resource set, performance> is known after finishing a service request, the corresponding cell in the matrix is located and the following condition is tested:

$$\alpha \le \beta \pm (\beta \times cluster\ range)$$
α :new performance data, β :the average value of the performance in the cell

If the condition is satisfied, then the new performance data is stored into the cell. Otherwise, a new row for the input parameters is created. Note that each cell can maintain several performance data with different input parameters values.

To predict the performance of the service given (input parameters: i, resource set: j), the scheduler first locates the corresponding cell in the performance history matrix indexed by (i, j). If it is populated, then it simply returns the average value of the performance data in the cell. Otherwise, it finds the nearest two cells on the same row as the cell and applies local linear regression using the performance data in the two cells (row-wise prediction). After that, it finds the nearest two cells on the same column as the cell and does the same operation (column-wise prediction). Finally, the average value of the two estimated values are returned as estimated run-time. Row-wise prediction reflects the performance change depending on resource set given the input parameters, whereas column-wise prediction reflects the performance change depending on input parameters given the same resource set.

4.2 Shortest-Remaining-Time Harvesting

The idea behind shortest-remaining-time harvesting (SRT_Harvest) is only when a new service request, S, can finish earlier than other service requests that are currently running, then S can harvest resources from those service requests to enable it to run. The behavior of the algorithm is determined by two configurable parameters:

- *HP (Harvesting Parameter)*: controls how aggressively the system can harvest resources from running requests.
- *WP (Wait Time Parameter)*: defines the maximum wait time threshold for each request. It is proportional to the minimum run-time of the request.

Fig. 2 describes the algorithm. If the run-time of a service request is long, its resources are frequently taken away for shorter requests, which sometimes results in the request not making any progress. To prevent the starvation of longer requests, whenever resources are available, the scheduler checks if there are any pending requests whose total wait time exceeds the maximum threshold, defined by *(EstimatedMimimumRunTime * WP)*. If so, resources are allocated to those requests and the resources are marked as *"Non-Harvestable"* so that no requests can take resources away from them (line 1).

Before harvesting resources, the scheduler contacts each of the active requests to acquire the current status information as to progress. For example, iterative services will return information on how many iterations has been done and the average iteration time. Using this information, the scheduler computes the available time of the resources that are currently being used by the active requests. Then, for each request in the wait queue, the scheduler computes the best performance achievable using resource harvesting (line 3-7). It can harvest resources from request R for request S, only when the following condition is satisfied:

$Run-Time of S \times HP < Remaining Time of R, (HP \geq 1.0)$

This condition determines the candidate requests from which resources will be taken away and the number of resources from those requests. Thus, as long as a request S can finish earlier than R, S can harvest resources from R. If not, it can harvest none of the resources of R. If only a subset of resources of a request are

---

```
SRT_Harvest () {
1.    Find pending requests of which wait time exceeds the maximum wait time
          threshold. Assign resources to those requests and mark the resources as "Non-
          Harvestable".
2.    Contact active service instances and compute the available time of resources
          that they are using.
3.    while (!done)    {
4.    Find a pending request whose run-time is smallest through resource
          harvesting.
5.    Start the request using selected resources; if the resources are being used by
          other requests, then send "resource removal" messages to them;
6.    If there is change in the wait queue due to resource harvesting, then go to 3.
7.    }
8.    for (each active request r that only a subset of resources are harvested) {
9.        Check if there is any pending request that can finish earlier than r using the
              remaining resources of r.
10.       If s is such request, assign the remaining resources of r to s and put r into the
              wait queue.
11.   }
}
```

Fig. 2. Pseudo-code for shortest-remaining-time harvesting algorithm.

```
IB_Harvest ()    {
1.       Contact active service instances and compute the available time of resources
            that they are using.
2.       for (each active service instance)      {
3.           compute the number of harvestable resources. If it is greater than zero, then
                mark the instance as "Harvestable"
4.       }
5.       m = the number of resources to harvest.
6.       while (m    > 0)    {
7.           for (i = 0; i < the number of harvestable instances; ++i)      {
8.               collect k resources from instance(i), where k is randomly generated.
9.               send "resource removal" message to instance(i).
10.              m = m − k;
11.          }
12.      }
}
```

Fig. 3. Pseudo-code for impact-based harvesting algorithm.

harvested, then there could be requests in the wait queue that can finish earlier than the request using the remaining resource set. Since the algorithm favors shorter requests, in such case, the active request should relinquish its resources to the one in the wait queue. If there are multiple requests in the wait queue that satisfy the requirement, the one that can finish the earliest is selected (line 8-11).

4.3   Impact-Based Harvesting

In contrast to shortest-remaining-time harvesting, impact-based harvesting (IB_Harvest) focuses on resource lenders rather than resource borrowers (Fig. 3). For example, resources of an active service request, R, can be harvested for a new service request, S, only when the impact of resource harvesting that R will experience is below a threshold. The impact is defined in terms of service time. In order to compute the service time threshold for each request, we use a configurable parameter, *IP (Impact Parameter)* and the optimal run-time of the request. The optimal run-time is defined as the minimum run-time achievable.

If there are not enough resources available for a new request, for each active service request, the scheduler computes the number of resources that can be harvested from each of them (line 2-4). The number of harvestable resources of each active request is defined as follow:

$\max\{n : ElapsedTime + RemainingTime(n) < Service\ Time\ Threshold\}$

$ElaspedTime : CurrentTime - Service\ StartTime$

$RemainingTime(n) : estimated\ remaining\ run-time\ when\ n\ resources\ are\ used$

The number of resources that will be allocated to the new request is the minimum number of resources with which it can finish earlier than the service time threshold. Once the harvestable service requests and the number of resources to harvest for the new request are determined, the scheduler collects resources randomly from each of the selected service requests until the desired number of resources is collected (line5-12).

When a service request finishes, it returns the harvested resources to service requests where the resources are collected. If the requests have already finished, instead of assigning the resources to active requests whose remaining time are small as in shortest-remaining-time harvesting, those resources are allocated to requests in the wait queue to reduce wait time of the requests.

5   Experimental Results

We have deployed an N-body simulation service to test the performance of the proposed scheduling policies. The objective of N-body simulation is to find the positions and movements of the bodies in space that are subject to gravitational forces from other bodies using Newtonian laws of physics [8].

In the prototype, the N-body simulation is implemented using Master/Slave paradigm, where the master maintain a bag of tasks and slaves repeatedly get tasks, update the bodies, then return the result to the master. Given n bodies and p slaves, the master divides the bodies into m blocks of size n/p and the slaves compute the forces between bodies in block i and those in block j. However, the computed forces do not reflect the effects of bodies in block k $(k\ != i, j)$, once the slaves finish computing forces of bodies in every pair of blocks, the master computes the total forces of each body. To use the N-body simulation service, the users submit four parameters: start time, end time, delta time (the length of the time interval), and input bodies. The first three parameters control the number of iterations. We deployed the prototype service on a Linux cluster consisting of 10 dual CPU PCs and the cluster is dedicated to the service.

5.1   Performance Prediction

Accurate prediction of run-time is important in the resource harvesting algorithms we presented. For this experiment, we generated input parameters to the service randomly and cluster range is set to 0.05. The experimental results show that our prediction system can achieve estimation accuracy to within 4% (Fig. 4). Since initially there are not enough data in the performance history matrix, the error rates of the first few predictions are high. However, as clients requests are served, the prediction system

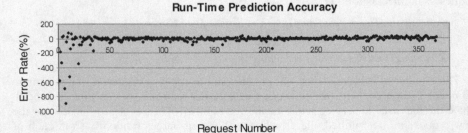

Fig. 4. Accuracy of Run-Time Prediction.

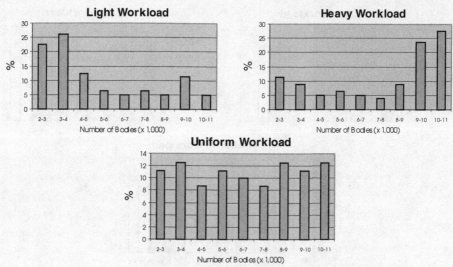

Fig. 5. Synthetic workloads.

learns the relationship among input parameters, resource set and the run-time. Therefore, after the learning phase, it can predict the run-time accurately.

5.2   Performance Comparison

To assess the performance of our scheduling policies, we generated three synthetic workloads: light workload, uniform workload and heavy workload (Fig. 5). The X-axis in the graph represents the number of bodies submitted to the service to compute movement. Note that since we fixed the three time-related parameters (start time, end time, delta time), which determine the number of iterations, the number of bodies controls the run-time. For example, the more bodies requested, the longer it takes to compute the result.

We compare performance against two simple scheduling policies: MOLDABLE and IDEAL (Fig. 6). MOLDABLE assigns idle resources up to the optimal number of resources for each request. If there are no available resources, the request is queued. Otherwise, the request is "molded" to the available number of resources. In IDEAL, only the optimal number of resources are assigned to the request. Therefore, if the number of available resources is less than the optimal number of resources, the request waits until the optimal number of resources are available. Both scheduling do not use resource harvesting. Table 1 shows configurable parameters of SRT_Harvest and IB_Harves used in the experiments.

Table 1. Configurable parameters for resource harvesting algorithms.

	Light workload	Uniform Workload	Heavy Workload
Cluster Range	0.05	0.05	0.05
HP	1.5	1.8	1.2
WP	12.0	8.0	12.0
IP	1.7	1.1	1.3

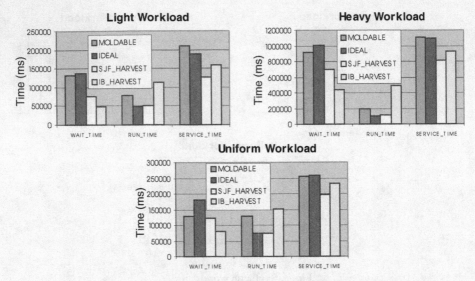

Fig. 6. Comparative performance for different resource scheduling policies.

For each workload, we measured average values of wait time, run-time, and service time of requests under different resource scheduling policies. Wait time of a request denotes a period of time in the wait queue, whereas run-time represents the time consumed to process the request. The service time is the sum of wait time and run-time. As IDEAL always waits until the optimal number of resources are available, its wait time is the highest but the average run-time of IDEAL is the smallest for the same reason. In SRT_Harvest, by executing shorter requests earlier than longer ones, the wait time is decreased significantly. In addition, because requests may not always run using the optimal number of resources, its average run-time is higher than that of IDEAL. However, if there is no shorter requests pending in the wait queue, instead of assigning idle resources to requests in the wait queue, it assigns as many resources as the optimal number of resources to the active requests. Therefore, the average run-time can be reduced. In this experiment, SRT_Harvest achieved service time improvement up to 40%, 27% and 20% for light workload, heavy workload and uniform workload, respectively. As in SRT_Harvest, IB_Harvest also dynamically collects resources for new requests whenever there are not enough resources for them. Therefore, its average wait time is also smaller than those of simple policies. Moreover, unlike SRT_Harvest, since IB_Harvest favors requests in the wait queue, the average wait time is even smaller than that of SRT_Harvest. However, due to resource harvesting, each request can use only the minimum number of resources, which leads to increased run-time.

5.3 Sensitivity to Configurable Parameters

In theory, running shortest requests first always reduces the average wait time. Therefore, in shortest-remaining-time harvesting, $HP=1.0$ should provide the best performance. However, due to WP, shorter requests may wait until non-harvestable requests finish. Furthermore, smaller HP makes the wait time of longer requests reach

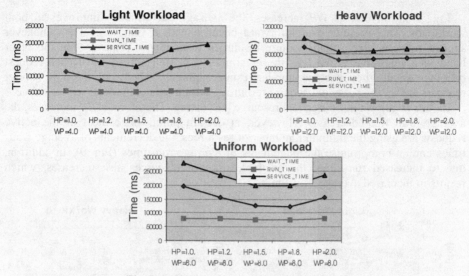

Fig. 7. Sensitivity to harvesting parameter.

the maximum wait time threshold faster because longer requests either may not be selected for execution or may relinquish all of their resources frequently to shorter requests. These two behaviors make the wait time of shorter requests longer if they arrive when non-harvestable requests are using all of the system resources (Fig. 7). However, as *HP* increases, the total wait time also increases because shorter requests may not be executed even though longer requests are using resources. The reason for choosing a larger value as *WP* for a heavy workload is as the run-time of each request is relatively high in the heavy workload, small *WP* makes the total wait time of each request exceed the maximum wait time threshold quickly. Therefore, it may not take advantage of resource harvesting. This behavior is explained in Fig. 8.

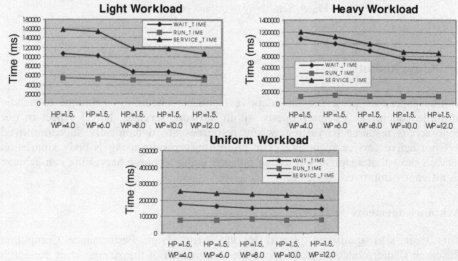

Fig. 8. Sensitivity to wait time parameter.

Fig. 8 shows that as *WP* increases, the average performance improves in both workloads. This is quite straightforward because with a very large *WP*, whenever shorter requests arrive, they acquire resources from longer requests. On the other hand, if a small *WP* is used, as the maximum wait time threshold of each request becomes small, they become non-harvestable quickly. Therefore, even if shorter requests arrive, they may not acquire resources, which results in increased wait time.

Larger *IP* allows more frequent resource harvesting. Therefore, as *IP* increases, the average wait time decreases. However, at certain point, since most of the active requests are using the minimum number of resources, the decrements of average wait-times cannot compromise the increments of average run-times (Fig. 9). In addition, due to increased run-times, the available time of resources also increases, which results in increased average wait-times.

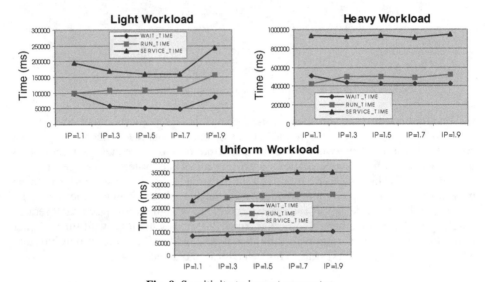

Fig. 9. Sensitivity to impact parameter.

6   Conclusions

In this paper, we presented the adaptive resource scheduling technique to handle multiple concurrent service requests within network services. Novel aspect of our approach is resource harvesting, where resources are dynamically added/removed to/from active service requests.   The preliminary results using N-body simulation service show that adaptive scheduling policies using resource harvesting can achieve significantly improved service time.

Acknowledgements

This work was sponsored in part by the Army High Performance Computing Research Center under the auspices of the Department of the Army, Army Research Laboratory cooperative agreement number DAAD19-01-20014

References

1. R. Buyya, D. Abramson, J. Giddy: Nimrod/G: An Architecture for a Resource Management and Scheduling System in a Global Computational Grid, Proceedings of 4th High Performance Computing in Asia-Pacific Region (2000)
2. H. Casanova, J. Dongarra: Netsolve: A Network Server for Solving Computational Science Problems, International Journal of Supercomputing Applications and High Performance Computing. Vol. 11(3). (1997)
3. D. Dill: SVC: The Standard Validity Checker, http://www.sprout.standford.edu/SVC
4. R.L. Grossman, S. Kasif, D. Mon, A. Ramu, B. Malhi: The Preliminary Desgin of Papyrus: A System for High Performance, Distributed Data Mining over Clusters, Meta-Clusters and Super-Clusters, Proceedings of KDD-98 Workshop on Distributed Data Mining (1998)
5. N. H. Kapadia, J. Fortes, C. Brodley: Predictive Application-Performance Modeling in a Computational Grid Environment, Proceedings of 8th International Symposium on High Performance Distributed Computing (1999)
6. H. Nakada, M. Sato, S. Sekiguchi: Design and Implementation of Ninf: Towards a Global Computing Infrastructure, Journal of Future Generation Systems, Metacomputing Issue (1999)
7. A. Takefusa, H. Casanova, S. Matsouka, F. Berman: A Study of Deadline Scheduling for Client-Server Systems on Computational Grid, Proceedings of 10th International Symposium on High Performance Distributed Computing (2001)
8. B. Wilkinson, M. Allen: Parallel Programming, Prentice Hall (1999)

Enhanced Algorithms for Multi-site Scheduling

Carsten Ernemann[1], Volker Hamscher[1], Achim Streit[2], and Ramin Yahyapour[1]

[1] Computer Engineering Institute, University of Dortmund, 44221 Dortmund, Germany, ({carsten.ernemann,volker.hamscher,ramin.yahyapour}@udo.edu)
[2] Paderborn Center for Parallel Computing, University of Paderborn, 33102 Paderborn, Germany, (streit@upb.de)

Abstract. This paper discusses two approaches to enhance multi-site scheduling for grid environments. First the potential improvements of multi-site scheduling by applying constraints for the job fragmentation are presented. Subsequently, an adaptive multi-site scheduling algorithm is pointed out and evaluated. The adaptive multi-site scheduling uses a simple decision rule whether to use or not to use multi-site scheduling. To this end, several machine configurations have been simulated with different parallel job workloads which were extracted from real traces. The adaptive system improves the scheduling results in terms of a short average response time significantly.

1 Introduction

Computational grids gained much attention in recent years as shown by current initiatives like the Global Grid Forum [14] or the implementations of the Globus project [11] or Legion [2]. The idea of joining resources that are geographically distributed leads to the expectation to enable access to limited resources. In addition, potentially a larger number of resources is available for a single job. This is assumed to result in a reduction of the average job response time. Moreover, the utilization of the grid computers and the job-throughput is likely to improve due to load-balancing effects between the participating systems.

The management of the grid environment, especially the scheduling of the computational tasks, becomes a rather complex problem. The computational resources in a grid are often high-performance computers as for example parallel machines or clusters. Without grid computing local users are typically only working on the local resources. These resources have their own local management systems. Job scheduling for parallel computers has been subject to research for a long time. However, most real systems still use some kind of list scheduling, as e.g. backfilling [10]. It is the task of a grid scheduler to utilize the local management systems for scheduling jobs on a machine. Previous works discussed several strategies for such a grid scheduler. One approach is the transition and modification of conventional list scheduling strategies for grid usage [15,4].

The usage of multi-site applications [1] for the grid scenario has been examined in previous works. Multi-site computing is the execution of a job in parallel at different sites. Under the condition of a limited communication overhead, the

M. Parashar (Ed.): GRID 2002, LNCS 2536, pp. 219–231, 2002.

results from [4] showed that for distinct workloads derived from real machine traces multi-site applications improve the overall average response time. This overhead mainly results from the communication between the job parts. It has been modelled by extending the execution time of a job by a certain percentage.

If a single site job start was possible immediately the applied algorithm always tried to initiate a multi-site execution. In this paper we examine whether the potential benefit of multi-site can be improved by applying heuristics and limitations on the multi-site scheduling and adding a first approach of an adaptive decision process to our algorithm. As in [5], discrete event simulations on the basis of workload traces have been executed for sample configurations. The results show that the proposed strategy is a significant improvement in terms of average weighted response time.

The following sections are organized as follows. In section 2 a short overview on our model for the grid scenario is given. Then the applied algorithm is presented in section 3. The evaluation is presented in Section 4. The paper ends with a brief conclusion in Section 5.

2   Model

In this work our scenario is based on independent computing sites with existing local workload and management system. We examine the impact from a job scheduling point of view if the computing sites participate in a grid environment [4,5,12]. The sites combine their resources and share incoming jobs. That is, job submissions of all sites are redirected to and then distributed by a grid scheduler. This scheduler exclusively controls all grid resources.

The local scheduler is only responsible for starting the jobs after allocation by the grid scheduler. Note, that we use a central grid scheduler for our study. In a real implementation the architecture of the grid scheduler can differ as single central instances usually lead to drawbacks in performance, fail-safety or acceptance of resource users and owners. Nevertheless, distributed architectures can be designed that act similar as a central grid scheduler. For example, this can be achieved by deploying an information service about queued jobs, using several distributed grid schedulers which query for idle times.

We assume that each participating site in the computational grid has a single MPP (Massive Parallel Processor system), which consists of several nodes. Nodes (resources) are single-processor systems with local memory and disc. The nodes are linked with a fast interconnect that does not favor any specific communication pattern inside the machine [9]. The actual mapping of a job on the nodes is neglected. The machines support space-sharing and run the jobs in an exclusive fashion. Moreover, the jobs are not preempted nor time-sharing is used. Therefore, once started a job runs until completion. Furthermore, a job that exceeds its allocated time is cancelled.

Typically a preselection phase takes place ahead of the actual scheduling process and generates a reduced set of resources, that are all suitable for executing the job request. In our study we neglect this preselection and focus on the job scheduling process. Therefore, sites only differ in the number of nodes and all resources are of the same type and all jobs can be executed on all nodes.

The jobs are executed without further user interaction. In our grid computing scenario, a job can be transmitted and executed at a remote site without any additional overhead. In real implementations the transport of data requires additional time which is taken into account in our model as part of the communication overhead, that extents the job's run time. This effect can often be hidden by pre- and postfetching before and after the execution. In this case the resulting overhead is not necessarily part of the scheduling process. The data management is subject to further research.

Jobs are submitted by independent users on the local sites. This produces an incoming stream of jobs over time. Therefore, the scheduling problem is an on-line scenario without any knowledge on future job submissions. Our evaluations are restricted to batch jobs, as this job type is dominant on most MPP systems. Interactive jobs are often executed on dedicated partitions of the system, where the effects of scheduling algorithms are limited [16]. A job request consists of several parameters as e.g. the requested run time and the requested number of resources. After submission a job requests a fixed number of resources that are necessary for starting the job. This number is not changed during the execution of the job. That is jobs are not moldable or malleable [6,7]. It is the task of the scheduling system to allocate the jobs to resources and determine the starting time. Newly submitted jobs are executed on the grid either on a single site/machine or they are split up into several job fragments for *multi-site* execution. These job fragments are executed synchronously. That means a job can run in parallel on a set of nodes distributed over more than one site. This allows the execution of large jobs requiring more nodes than available on a single machine. In this case the impact of bandwidth and latency has to be considered as wide area networks are involved. For our modelling, we summarize the overheads caused by communication and data migration as an increase of the job's run time.

3   Algorithm

In previous research [4,5,15] we have examined the potential benefits of using multi-site scheduling in detail. The algorithms used within these projects were extended for this study.

Earlier, the effects of using multi-site in comparison to single site scheduling and job sharing have been analyzed [4]. The single site scenario describes the case that all local submitted jobs have to be calculated on the local resources. The job sharing scenario described an environment where jobs can be exchanged between a collection of sites. The results clearly indicated that using multi-site scheduling improves the scheduling results in terms of a better average weighted response time significantly. The analysis was extended in order to study the effects of an increasing run time for multi-site scheduling resulting from the overhead due to data management and communication [5].

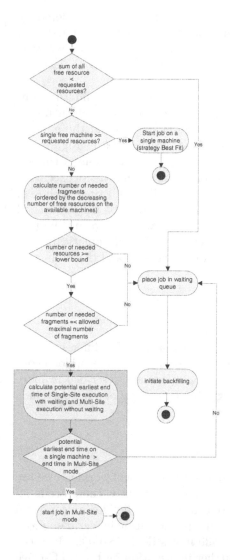

Fig. 1. Algorithm for Multi-Site Scheduling.

If a job is executed in multi-site, the run time of the job is extended by the overhead which is specified by a parameter **p**. Therefore the new run time r^* is: $r^* = (1 + p) \cdot r$

Where r is the run time for the job running on a single machine. This modelling of the communication overhead is used within this work in all multi-site cases. The results showed that considering the communication overhead multi-site scheduling is still advantageous if the overhead is limited to about 40 % of the run time. Alternative modelings of the overhead calculations were presented in [15]. In the work presented in this paper, we examined the multi-site scheduling behavior by applying constraints for the job fragmentation during the multi-site scheduling. To this end two parameters are introduced for the scheduling process. The first parameter *lower bound* restricted the jobs that can be fragmented during the multi-site scheduling by a minimal number of necessary requested processors. The second parameter was implemented as a vector describing the maximal number of job fragments for certain intervals of processor numbers. This lead to a further improvement of the scheduling process. Based on those results the algorithm was extended by the ability to react on the current status of the system.

The basic scheduling process in the grid scheduler works as described in Figure 1. In a first step the algorithm determines whether or not there are enough free resources at this point in time. If the job cannot be started in single nor multi-site mode immediately the job is added to a waiting queue. Jobs are scheduled from this queue by a First-Come-First-Serve algorithm in combination with Backfilling ([17,13]) where each step consists of the method described above. Otherwise a single machine with enough free resource is searched. Upon a successful search the job is started on this machine, which is chosen by using the BestFit-strategy [8], immediately. A search failure leads to the check of the parameter *lower bound* e.g. a value of 8 implies that only jobs requesting more than 8 resources may be split up. Next, the needed number of fragments is calculated by using a machine list ordered by the decreasing number of free resources. This allows to minimize the number of fragments (job parts running multi-site) for a job. If the number of fragments is larger than a given maximal allowed number of fragments the job is placed in the waiting queue and again backfilling is initiated.

In the following we must distinguish between the adaptive and the non-adaptive case. The non-adaptive algorithm directly executes the job in multi-site mode. In the adaptive case the *lower bound* is set to zero and the number of fragments is not limited. Additionally the boxed, greyed area in Figure 1 is inserted. In this part of the algorithm an earliest potential end time of the job running on a single machine is compared to the end time of a multi-site execution with its additional overhead. The solution with the earliest end time is chosen. Note that the real starting time of the job may vary depending on the jobs ahead in the queue. The algorithm is adaptive as the decision whether to run the jobs in multi-site mode or to wait for a single site execution is done automatically and depends on the given situations in terms of machine schedules and the submitted jobs.

4 Evaluation

For the comprehensive evaluation of the described algorithms for different structures a discrete event simulation was performed. The machine and workload configurations that were examined during these simulations are described in more detailed in [5,15]. For a better understanding a brief overview of our notation is given in the following two subsections.

4.1 Job Configurations

For our scenario with different independent machines with local workload we use real traces of MPP systems to model this workload. Currently, there are is no real grid workload traces or grid workload model available. Therefore, we use real traces to emulate the workload of single machines participating in a grid environment. To this end workload traces from the 430 nodes IBM RS/6000 SP of the Cornell Theory Center (CTC) are used. Further information on the CTC-trace are available in [20]. The used workloads and their identifiers are summarized in Table 1. Note that the actual workload in future grid environments may vary in the consistence and characteristics. Nevertheless, the used workloads give a good impression of the nowadays demand on computing resources at a MPP.

Table 1. Job Configurations

identifier	description
10_20k_org	An extract of the original CTC traces from job 10000 to 19999.
30_40k_org	An extract of the original CTC traces from job 30000 to 39999.
60_70k_org	An extract of the original CTC traces from job 60000 to 69999.
CTC-syn	The synthetically generated workload derived from the CTC workload traces.

4.2   Resource Configuration

The resource configuration is highly influenced by the job model. As we use workload traces that are derived from a real machine installation with 430 nodes, the resources configuration has to be selected accordingly. The partitioning of the simulated configurations is shown in Table 2. We use configurations with a total of 512 resources (nodes) in order to ensure comparability. A larger grid environment would require additional scaling of the workload without improving the evaluation validity. Note, that the combination of workload and resource configuration impacts the backlog by submitted and not yet started jobs. The existence of this backlog is important for the achievable scheduling quality; e.g. the backfilling strategy relies on the availability of queued jobs to choose from.

Table 2. Resource Configurations

identifier	configuration	max. size	number of machines	sum
m64	$4 \cdot 64 + 6 \cdot 32 + 8 \cdot 8$	64	18	512
m64-8	$8 \cdot 64$	64	8	512
m128	$4 \cdot 128$	128	4	512
m256	$2 \cdot 256$	256	2	512
m256-5	$1 \cdot 256 + 4 \cdot 64$	256	5	512
m384	$1 \cdot 384 + 1 \cdot 64 + 4 \cdot 16$	384	6	512
m512	$1 \cdot 512$	512	1	512

4.3   Performance Metrics

The resource consumption of a job can be described as the product of the job's run time and the number of requested resources. Therefore large jobs have a larger resource consumption than smaller jobs. The resource consumption of a single job j is defined as follows:

$$\text{Resource\_Consumption}_j = (\text{reqResources}_j \cdot (\text{endTime}_j - \text{startTime}_j))$$

One measure for the schedule quality is the average response time weighted by the job's resource consumption [18]. We define it as follows:

$$\text{AWRT} = \frac{\sum_{j \in \text{Jobs}} (\text{Resource\_Consumption}_j \cdot (\text{endTime}_j - \text{submitTime}_j))}{\sum_{j \in \text{Jobs}} \text{Resource\_Consumption}_j}$$

With weighting the response time of each job with its resource consumption, therefore all jobs with the same resource consumption have the same influence on the schedule quality. Otherwise a small, often insignificant job would have the same impact on this metric as a big job with the same response time.

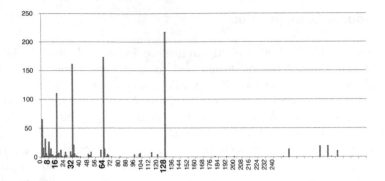

Fig. 2. Resource consumption of jobs in the CTC-syn workload, sorted by requested resources.

4.4 Fragmentation Parameters

The analysis of the used workloads shows a tendency of jobs to size with the power of 2 [3], as seen in Figure 2. Herein the resource consumption is summed up for all jobs of a specific width (i.e. the number of requested resources) for the ctc_syn workload. The other workloads show a similar behavior. Because of this "power of 2" focus we also used power of 2 values for the *lower bound* parameter. Jobs that fall short of this *lower bound* can only be scheduled on a single machine and cannot be distributed across several sites. For the maximum number of job fragments we use a function defined over several intervals. We define two configurations with different values for each interval:

1. a *limited* configuration, wherein only necessary fragmentation of a job is allowed and
2. an *unlimited* configuration, which does not restrict the fragmentation process at all.

For the *unlimited* case the number of fragments is only limited by the maximum number of machines in these configurations and the maximum number of requested resources for a specific job, as shown in Table 3.

Table 3. Maximal fragmentation for the *limited* and *unlimited* configuration

requested resources		maximal number of fragments	
lower limit	upper limit	limited configuration	unlimited configuration
1	4	1	4
5	8	1	8
9	16	1	16
17	32	1	18
33	64	1	18
65	128	2	18
129	512	8	18

4.5   Evaluation Results

All displayed results were achieved using the CTC_syn workload. As mentioned earlier this workload represents the average behavior of all used data sets. The results vary depending on the used workload, but only within close ranges.

Impact of Lower Bounds.   The influence of the *lower bound* is highly dependent on the additional run time caused by the overhead. Obviously, without any overhead a multi-site execution would be beneficial in any case. Jobs which run unnecessarily in multi-site mode can be forced to run on a single machine. This reduces the impact of the overhead on the overall performance. Up to a certain level of overhead the use of multi-site (besides mandatory fragmentation to execute the job at all) leads to a better average weighted response time in our simulations.

This correlation can be observed for the *m384* configuration and a *lower bound* of 128 presented in Figure 3: a decrease of the average weighted response time by 16,3% for p = 80%, and by 29,9% for p = 120%. Here the *limited* and the *unlimited* configurations show no difference with regard to the average weighted response time. Similar results can be achieved for the *m256* configuration. Here a *lower bound* of 128 proves to be beneficial compared to any other values. In this configuration 128 is half the size of the biggest machine, which verifies the theorem, that it is beneficial for the scheduling that the job size stays below half the machine size, mentioned in [19]. For an overhead of 80% a reduction of about 12% is reached and for 120% even 32%.

For the *m384* configuration, it can be seen that choosing an unappropriate *lower bound* may lead to a performance decrease, e.g. a *lower bound* of 256 results in an increased average weighted response time of 16% and a *lower bound* of 96 increases the average weighted response time by at least 29 % compared to a *lower bound* of 128 in the *m384* configuration, as shown in Figure 3.

An optimal lower bound can not be specified as it varies between the different machine configurations. In our simulations a lower bound of half the machine size

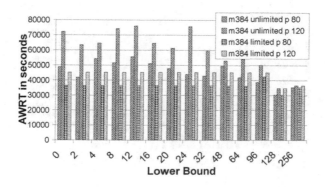

Fig. 3. Influence of the *lower bound* in a *m384* configuration.

proved to be beneficial in most cases. Exceptions are the configurations *m384* and the small configuration *m64*.

Comparison of *Limited* and *Unlimited* Fragmentation. In configurations with smaller machines e.g. *m64* and an overhead up to 60% the *unlimited* multi-site strategy is superior to the *limited* fragmentation strategy, as shown by the first 4 bars of each group in Figure 4. In [5] we have presented a study of the impact of machine configurations on strategies, where multi-site execution is not limited. In comparison, in this paper we evaluate enhancements of those strategies by using constraints and an additional new adaptive scheduler. We present the different machine configurations only very briefly as they are based on [5].

Applying a higher number of fragments is beneficial. This can be seen in Figure 4, where the average weighted response time is decreased by about 60% for the *unlimited* scenario compared to the *limited* scenario for an overhead up to 60%. Whereas the *m64_8* configuration with equally sized machines shows a decrease of the average weighted response time of only around 10% for a higher fragmentation. In this scenario the *lower bound* has an higher impact. Especially in resource configurations with smaller machines the average weighted response time scales directly with the overhead parameter p, as major parts of the workload can only be scheduled in multi-site mode, as shown earlier in Figure 2. Figure 4 underlines the advantages of unlimited fragmentation under the condition of a *lower bound* of 64 and an overhead of up to 180% for small machine configurations. Note, that in this case the average weighted response time may reach values up to twelve times as high as the average weighted response time on a single large machine of 512 nodes.

The Adaptive Multi-site Algorithm. In the following we show only the lower bound for each configuration presenting the best achieved results. In Figure 5 the average weighted response time for the resource configurations *m512*

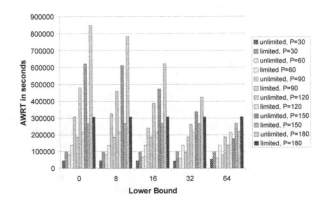

Fig. 4. Comparison of *m64*

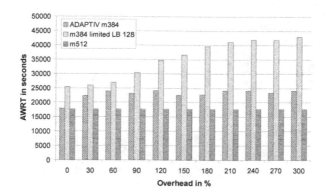

Fig. 5. Comparison of adaptive and best non-adaptive schedules for m384

and *m384* for the best non-adaptive and the adaptive scheduling results are given. The improvements by using adaptive scheduling in comparison to the non-adaptive case can clearly be identified. The average weighted response time using the adaptive scheduling process increases only about 35% in comparison to the single site machine *m512* using an overhead of 300%. In opposite, the average weighted response time of the non-adaptive scheduling system increases about 244% with the same overhead of 300%.

Note, that using the resource configuration *m384* even for the largest jobs, multi-site scheduling is not necessary, as the largest job within the workload requests only 336 nodes and can therefore be executed on the largest machine which consists of 384 nodes. Even with an overhead of 300% using resource configuration *m384* the adaptive scheduling system executes about 4% of all jobs in multi-site mode. This is only a 42% reduction compared to an overhead of 30% in the same configuration. Whereas the resource consumption of the multi-site jobs decreases to 30% in the same case. This indicates a shift towards the use of jobs with a smaller resource consumption for multi-site scheduling. Overall, increasing the overhead ten times from 30% to 300% only results in an increase of the average weighted response time of about 7% in this configuration.

In the best non-adaptive case increasing the overhead from 30% to 300% results in a by 66% higher average weighted response time. Note, that in the *m384* configuration with any or even without overhead the best non-adaptive multi-site scheduling system performs worse than the adaptive system with an overhead of 300% as seen in Figure 5. A similar behavior can be observed in all other resource configurations as shown in Table 4.

In Figure 6 all resource configurations with the adaptive scheduling system are compared. The average weighted response time for the resource configuration *m512*, given as a reference, is always constant as no multi-site scheduling is invoked. The results of configurations *m64* and *m64_8* show an increasing disadvantage which almost scales with the overhead from 30% to 300% up to a factor

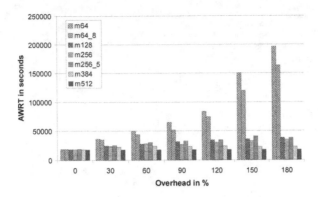

Fig. 6. Comparison of Adaptive Schedules.

of about 15. Whereas the influence of the overhead on the overall performance for all other resource configurations is not as significant. The configurations *m128*, *m256*, and *m256_5* show a similar behavior in terms of performance. For overheads between 30% and 300%, none of these three configurations clearly outperforms any of the other two in the adaptive case as shown in Figure 6.

This figure also displays the influence of different machine configurations. The equal partitioned configuration *m64_8* outperforms its non-balanced counterpart *m64*. This is due to the fact that more larger machines are available for the execution of large jobs, leading to more flexibility for the overall scheduling process. The most significant impact of the adaptive scheduling system can be observed in the results of the resource configuration *m384* as most resources are combined in a single machine and therefore no multi-site scheduling is necessary. Here the multi-site scheduling is only used to enhance the quality of the overall schedule.

5 Conclusion

In this paper we examined three enhancements to a multi-site scheduler for grid computing environments. If a job cannot be placed directly on a single machine,

Table 4. Comparison of adaptive configurations with overheads of 30 % to 300 % in regard to the alternation of the number and the resource consumption of multi-site jobs

resource configuration	number of multi-site jobs		Δ Jobs	Δ resource consumption
	overhead 30 %	overhead 300 %	in %	in %
m64	1069	430	-60	+176
m64-8	815	387	-53	+132
m128	478	337	-29	+88
m256	336	189	-44	≈ 0
m256-5	589	411	-30	+90
m384	637	368	-42	-71

the multi-site scheduler splits the original job in several fragments which are then started synchronously on multiple sites/machines. The communication between job fragments and the additional effort of data migration is considered in extending the jobs runtime by a given percentage. We used a simulation environment to evaluate and compare the performance of different multi-site grid scheduling strategies in terms of average weighted completion time. As job input we extracted job sets from real trace logs. Additionally different machine configurations were evaluated in order to measure the impact of different machine sizes on the way multi-site jobs are distributed across the grid.

In the first enhancements a *lower bound* parameter has been introduced restricting the multi-site execution to jobs requiring at least a certain number of resources. Setting the *lower bound* resulted in a significant improvement of up to 30% in the average weighted response time for certain scenarios. Additionally we restricted the number of fragments to be generated by the multi-site scheduler. For communication overheads with over 60% of the original execution time it proved to be beneficial to limit the fragmentation process.

A different approach was examined using an adaptive version of the multi-site scheduler. Here the scheduler compares the completion times of single- and multi-site execution. For single-site execution the waiting time until the job can be started has to be considered, whereas for multi-site the overhead has to be added to the runtime. Depending on the result the job either is added to the queue or is directly started in multi-site mode. The evaluation showed that the adaptive version substantially improved the performance of the multi-site scheduler, regardless what overhead percentage for the multi-site execution is chosen. Therefore adaptive multi-site scheduler seem to be the best algorithm for a multi-site environment. As the presented adaptive algorithm is a basic implementation, more sophisticated adaptive algorithms may further increase the performance.

Generally, the results indicate that the usage of small systems in combination with multi-site scheduling can not perform as well as single large machines with the same amount of resources. The presented algorithms decrease this difference significantly. In any case the participation in a grid environment seems to be beneficial, as the usage of multi-site computing enables the execution of jobs that consume more resources than available on the largest single machine in such a grid environment.

References

1. M. Brune, J. Gehring, A. Keller, and A. Reinefeld. Managing clusters of geographically distributed high-performance computers. *Concurrency - Practice and Experience*, 11(15):887–911, 1999.
2. S. J. Chapin, D. Katramatos, J. Karpovich, and A. Grimshaw. Resource management in Legion. *Future Generation Computer Systems*, 15(5–6):583–594, 1999.
3. A. B. Downey and D. G. Feitelson. The Elusive Goal of Workload Characterization. Technical report, Hebrew University, Jerusalem, March 1999.

4. C. Ernemann, V. Hamscher, U. Schwiegelshohn, A. Streit, and R. Yahyapour. On Advantages of Grid Computing for Parallel Job Scheduling. In *Proceedings of the 2nd IEEE International Symposium on Cluster Computing and the Grid (CC-GRID 2002)*, pages 39–46, 2002.
5. C. Ernemann, V. Hamscher, A. Streit, and R. Yahyapour. On Effects of Machine Configurations on Parallel Job Scheduling in Computational Grids. In *International Conference on Architecture of Computing Systems, (ARCS 2002)*, pages 169–179. VDE-Verlag, April 2002.
6. D. G. Feitelson, L. Rudolph, U. Schwiegelshohn, and K. C. Sevcik. Theory and Practice in Parallel Job Scheduling. *Lecture Notes in Computer Science*, 1291:1–34, 1997.
7. D.G. Feitelson. A Survey of Scheduling in Multiprogrammed Parallel Systems. Research report rc 19790 (87657), IBM T.J. Watson Research Center, Yorktown Heights, NY, February 1995.
8. D.G. Feitelson. Packing Schemes for Gang Scheduling. *Lecture Notes in Computer Science*, 1162:89–101, 1996.
9. D.G. Feitelson and L. Rudolph. Parallel job scheduling: Issues and approaches. In *IPPS'95 Workshop: Job Scheduling Strategies for Parallel Processing, pages 1-18. Springer Verlag, Lecture Notes in Computer Science LNCS 949, 1995.*, 1995.
10. D.G. Feitelson and A.M. Weil. Utilization and Predictabillity in Scheduling the IBM SP2 with Backfilling. In *Proceedings of IPPS/SPDP 1998*, IEEE Computer Society, pages 542–546, 1998.
11. I. Foster and C. Kesselman. Globus: A Metacomputing Infrastructure Toolkit. *The International Journal of Supercomputer Applications and High Performance Computing*, 11(2):115–128, Summer 1997.
12. I. Foster and C. Kesselman, editors. *The GRID: Blueprint for a New Computing Infrastructure*. Morgan Kaufmann, 1998.
13. R. Gibbons. A Historical Application Profiler for Use by Parallel Schedulers. In *Job Scheduling Strategies for Parallel Processing*, pages 58–77. Springer, Berlin, Lecture Notes in Computer Science LNCS 1291, 1997.
14. The Grid Forum, http://www.gridforum.org, June 2002.
15. V. Hamscher, U. Schwiegelshohn, A. Streit, and R. Yahyapour. Evaluation of Job-Scheduling Strategies for Grid Computing. *Lecture Notes in Computer Science*, 1971:191–202, 2000.
16. S. Hotovy. Workload Evolution on the Cornell Theory Center IBM SP2. In D.G. Feitelson and L. Rudolph, editors, *IPPS'96 Workshop: Job Scheduling Strategies for Parallel Processing*, pages 27–40. Springer–Verlag, Lecture Notes in Computer Science LNCS 1162, 1996.
17. D. A. Lifka. The ANL/IBM SP Scheduling System. In D. G. Feitelson and L. Rudolph, editors, *IPPS'95 Workshop: Job Scheduling Strategies for Parallel Processing*, pages 295–303. Springer, Berlin, Lecture Notes in Computer Science LNCS 949, 1995.
18. U. Schwiegelshohn and R. Yahyapour. Analysis of First-Come-First-Serve Parallel Job Scheduling. In *Proceedings of the 9th SIAM Symposium on Discrete Algorithms*, pages 629–638, January 1998.
19. U. Schwiegelshohn and R. Yahyapour. Fairness in parallel job scheduling. *Journal of Scheduling, 3(5):297-320. John Wiley*, 2000.
20. Parallel Workloads Archive. http://www.cs.huji.ac.il/labs/parallel/workload/, June 2002.

Experiments with Scheduling Using Simulated Annealing in a Grid Environment*

Asim YarKhan and Jack J. Dongarra

Computer Science Department
University of Tennessee, Knoxville, TN
{yarkhan, dongarra}@cs.utk.edu

Abstract. Generating high quality schedules for distributed applications on a Computational Grid is a challenging problem. Some experiments using Simulated Annealing as a scheduling mechanism for a ScaLAPACK LU solver on a Grid are described. The Simulated Annealing scheduler is compared to a Ad-Hoc Greedy scheduler used in earlier experiments. The Simulated Annealing scheduler exposes some assumptions built into the Ad-Hoc scheduler and some problems with the Performance Model being used.

1 Scheduling in the GrADS Project

Despite of the existence of several Grid infrastructure projects such as Globus [6] and Legion [8], programming, executing and monitoring applications on a Computational Grid remains a user intensive process. The goal of the *Grid Application Development Software (GrADS)* [2] project is to simplify distributed heterogeneous computing in the same way that the World Wide Web simplified information sharing. The GrADS project intends to provide tools and technologies for the development and execution of applications in a Grid environment. This includes tasks such as locating available resources on the Grid and scheduling an application on an appropriate subset of the resources.

The naive approach of testing all possible machine schedules to select the best schedule quickly becomes intractable as the number of machines grows. When N machines are available, the naive approach would require checking approximately 2^N possible subsets of machines. This *minimum execution-time multiprocessor scheduling problem* is known to be NP-hard in its generalized form, and is NP-hard even in some restricted forms [13]. Many heuristics exist that can be used to reduce the search space, and search strategies such as greedy searches (which rank order the machines using some criteria), and (non)-linear programming searches (which seek to minimize an objective function given certain constraints) can be used to find solutions. However, these techniques generally do not contain mechanisms to avoid local minima.

* This work is supported in part by the National Science Foundation contract GRANT #E81-9975020, SC R36505-29200099, R011030-09, "Next Generation Software: Grid Application Development Software (GrADS)".

M. Parashar (Ed.): GRID 2002, LNCS 2536, pp. 232–242, 2002.

There are many research efforts aimed at scheduling strategies for the Grid, see Berman [1] for an overview of scheduling on the Grid and a summary of alternative approaches. Berman argues that a successful scheduling strategy for the Grid has to produce time-frame specific performance predictions, has to use dynamic information, and has to adapt to a variety of potential computational environments. Scheduling in the GrADS project takes dynamic resource information about a distributed, heterogeneous Grid environment, and tries to generate a schedule to minimize the execution time.

The GrADS project is developing generic tools to perform application scheduling, using greedy orderings and application specific performance models to select machines. Experiment have shown certain situations where greedy orderings can return an undesirably sub-optimal schedule. In order to avoid these situation, and to handle arbitrary applications that have varying requirements, we are experimenting with a scheduler based on simulated annealing.

This paper will present some experiments on automated scheduling in a Grid environment. The scheduling is done over a non-homogeneous set of Grid resources residing at geographically disparate locations, and uses dynamic machine status and connectivity information from the Globus Metacomputing Directory Service (MDS) [6, 7] and the Network Weather System (NWS) [14].

1.1   Numerical Libraries and the Grid

As part of an earlier GrADS project demonstration [11], a ScaLAPACK [3] numerical solver routine (i.e., the LU solver routine PDGESV) was analyzed to obtain an accurate *Performance Model* for the routine. This Performance Model is used to predict the execution time for the routine given the current machine characteristics (i.e., CPU load, free memory) and their current connection characteristics (i.e., bandwidth and latency). The information from the Performance Model can be used to schedule the routine on a subset of the available resources to execute in the minimum time. Scheduling the LU solver routine is somewhat complicated by the fact that the minimum per-machine memory requirements change as the number of machines chosen varies. This means, if the selection or removal of a machine changes the number of chosen machines, all the other currently selected machines may need to be reevaluated.

An Ad-Hoc greedy approach was used for scheduling in the earlier GrADS project demonstration [11], a slightly modified version of this scheduler is described in this document. Experiments in a simplistic, homogeneous, single cluster environment have shown that this scheduler can make better than 95% accurate predictions of the execution time.

1.2   Ad-hoc Greedy Scheduler Used in the ScaLAPACK Experiment

The scheduling algorithm used in the ScaLAPACK LU solver demonstration [11] uses an Ad-Hoc greedy technique in conjunction with a hand-crafted Performance Model to select the machines on which to schedule the execution. The list of all qualified, currently available machines is obtained from the Globus

Metacomputing Directory Service (MDS); it may contain machines from several geographically distributed clusters. The Network Weather Service (NWS) is contacted to obtain details pertaining to each machine (i.e., the CPU load, the available memory) and the latency and bandwidth between machines. This detailed resource information is used by the Performance Model to estimate the execution time for the ScaLAPACK routine. The Ad-Hoc scheduling algorithm can be approximated as shown below.

```
FOR {each cluster, starting a new search in the cluster}
  select fastest machine in the cluster to initialize
  REPEAT
    find a new machine which has highest average bandwidth to
      the machines that are already selected and add it to the
      selected machines
    ensure that memory constraints are met by all machines
    use the Performance Model with detailed machine and
      network information to predict the execution time
  UNTIL {the Performance Model shows that execution time is
    no longer decreasing}
  track the best solution
ENDFOR
```

In this algorithm, new machines are ordered by their average bandwidth with already selected machines, and they are added to the selection in this order. This technique returns a good set of machines for the application, but it assumes that communication is the major factor determining the execution time of the algorithm. Other greedy techniques using different orderings have been implemented within the GrADS resource selection process, for example, using CPU load to order the machines [5].

2   Global Scheduling Strategies

The scheduling problem can be viewed as an multivariate optimization problem, where the application is being assigned to a set of machines so as to optimize some metric (i.e., the overall execution time). Techniques exist for finding locally optimal solutions for multivariate optimization problems, such as gradient descent techniques, linear programming, or greedy techniques. However, these techniques only search some local space, and will not find the global optimum if it is not contained in that local space. For example, the Ad-Hoc greedy method orders the machines by communication, and thus will not find the optimal solution if it is not contained in that ordering.

A globally optimal schedule for the application is desirable, however, most classes of global optimization problems are NP-hard. There are several stochastic and heuristic approaches to optimization that attempt to avoid most local minima, such as Monte Carlo methods, simulated annealing, genetic algorithms, and branch-and-bound methods. This paper details experiments using Simulated

Annealing as a global optimization technique for selecting the set of machines for scheduling the GrADS ScaLAPACK application.

2.1 Quick Overview of Simulated Annealing

Simulated Annealing [10] is a generalization of a Monte Carlo method for statistically finding the global optimum for multivariate functions. The concept originates from the way in which crystalline structures are brought to more ordered states by a *annealing process* of repeated heating and slowly cooling the structures.

In Simulated Annealing, a system is initialized at a temperature T with some configuration whose energy is evaluated to be E. A new configuration is constructed by applying a random change, and the change in energy dE is computed. The new configuration is unconditionally accepted if it lowers the energy of the system. If the energy of the system is increased by the change, the new configuration is accepted with some random probability. In the original Metropolis scheme [10], the probability is given by the Boltzmann factor $exp(-dE/kT)$. This process is repeated sufficient times at the current temperature to sample the search space, and then the temperature is decreased. The process is repeated at the successively lower temperatures until a frozen state is achieved. This procedure allows the system to move to lower energy states, while still jumping out of local minima (especially at higher temperatures) due to the probabilistic acceptance of some upward moves.

Simulated Annealing has been used in Operations Research to successfully solve a large number of optimization problems [9] such as the Traveling Salesman problem and various scheduling problems [12]. Here, it is applied to the problem of application scheduling in a Grid environment.

3 Scheduling in GrADS Using Simulated Annealing

The scheduler uses the Metacomputing Directory Service to get a list of the available machines, and uses the Network Weather Service to get CPU load, memory and communication details for the machine. The Simulated Annealing scheduler is outlined below, however various simple heuristics used to speed up the search process and avoid unnecessary searches are not shown.

```
given N available machines from MDS with NWS information
FOR {each possible virtual machine size vmsize = 1...N}
  find all R machines having sufficient resources (i.e. free
    memory)
  IF {number of machines with sufficient resources R < vmsize}
    continue to next vmsize
  ELSE [select vmsize machines from R using Simulated Annealing]
    create an initial schedule using random n from the R
      eligible machines
```

```
evaluate the Performance Model on the n selected machines
  using the dynamic NWS information
REPEAT [at each temperature]
  FOR {a number of steps, breaking loop if energy stabilizes}
    perturb the schedule randomly, remove a machine, add
      another machine, and swap their order
    evaluate the Performance Model on the new schedule
    IF {energy (execution time) is decreased }
      accept new schedule unconditionally
    ELSE
      accept new schedule if a random number < exp(-dE/kT)
        [Metropolis step]
    ENDIF
  ENDFOR
  decrease temperature
  UNTIL {energy does not change or temperature is at minimum}
  ENDIF
ENDFOR
```

Each virtual machine size (from $1..N$) is searched separately because in the LU solver application the minimum per-processor memory requirements vary with the number of machines used in the schedule. Trying to search over all the machine sizes simultaneously would disrupt the search process, because the addition (or subtraction) of a machine, leading to a different number of machines in the schedule, might cause other machines to become qualified (or disqualified) because of the memory requirements. Searching each virtual machine size separately allows the minimization process to work smoothly at that size.

3.1 Comparing Generated Schedules
for the Annealing and Ad-hoc Schedulers

In this experiment, the Annealing Scheduler is compared to the Ad-Hoc scheduler to see which one produces better *estimated* schedules when given the same information. The list of available machines obtained from MDS and their characteristics obtained from NWS are cached, so that the scheduling is done using consistent information. The experimental testbed consisted of x86 CPUS running Linux; there were 3 machines from the University of Tennessee (UTK) TORC cluster (550 MHz PIII, 512 MB memory), 3 machines from the UTK MSC cluster (933 MHz PIII, 512 MB memory), and 9 machines from the University of Illinois (UIUC) OPUS cluster (450 MHz PII, 256 MB memory).

The schedules that were generated were not actually run in this experiment since consistent machine information was required to test the schedulers, this information would have been stale by the time the runs were performed. The best schedules and their predicted execution times are shown in Fig. 1. This testbed of 12 machines was not able to handle matrices of size 15000 or larger, so the largest problem that was scheduled was of size 14000. The annealing

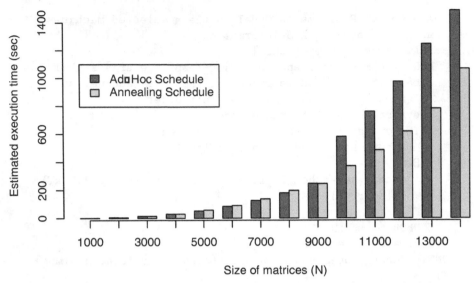

Fig. 1. Estimated execution times for Simulated Annealing and Ad-Hoc schedules using static network information

scheduler is usually able to find a schedule having a better estimated execution time than the Ad-Hoc scheduler. This trend is stronger for the larger matrix sizes. However, this estimated schedule depends on how accurately the Performance Model reflects reality.

3.2   Accuracy of the Generated Schedules

In this experiment we want to determine how accurately the estimated execution time matches the actual execution time for the two schedulers. The difficulty is that the estimated schedules measure the accuracy of the Performance Model far more than the accuracy of the Scheduler. However, since the same Performance Model is used for both the Simulated Annealing scheduler as well as the Ad-Hoc scheduler, the comparison of the two schedulers shows how well they perform given the current Performance Model.

If the Performance Model is not correct, we expect that the Ad-Hoc scheduler will perform somewhat better than the Simulated Annealing scheduler, since it includes some implicit knowledge of the application and the environment. For example, the Ad-Hoc greedy scheduler uses bandwidth as a major factor for ordering its selection of machines and generating a good schedule for the ScaLAPACK example. Also, it assumes that it is better to use machines within a cluster (having high connectivity) before using remote machines. These assumptions, though valid for the ScaLAPACK application, may not be valid in all cases.

The Simulated Annealing scheduler is application agnostic; it creates the schedule without any knowledge of the application. The scheduler depends purely on the Performance Model, so if the Performance Model is accurate, the annealing scheduler will return accurate results.

For this experiment, 25 machines from three Linux clusters at the were used as the testbed. Nine machines were from the UTK/TORC cluster (550 MHz PIII, 512 MB memory), 8 machines were from the UTK/MSC cluster (933 MHz PIII, 512 MB memory), and 8 machines were from the UIUC/OPUS cluster (450 MHz PII, 256 MB memory) . Figure 2 shows that estimated execution times for the runs using dynamic network (NWS) information. The difference between the estimated execution times for the two scheduling techniques is not as dramatic as in Fig. 1, however, these measurements were taken at different times and under different network and load conditions, and the Ad-Hoc scheduler did not get caught in a bad local minima in this example as it did in Fig. 1. Figure 3 shows the measured execution time when the generated schedules were run, and here we see that the measured times are generally larger than the estimated times. This exposes a problem with the current Performance Model, which does not properly account for the communication costs. The Simulated Annealing schedule generally takes a little less time than the Ad-Hoc schedule, however this trend is not totally consistent.

Figure 4 shows the ratio of the measured execution time to the estimated execution time. If the Performance Model was fully accurate and execution environment was perfectly known, the ideal ratio in Fig. 4 would be a 1.0 across all the matrix sizes. However, both the schedulers differ substantially from the ideal, implying that the Performance Model is not estimating the time required for execution accurately for a distributed set of machines. There could be several reasons why this is happening, however the current belief is that the Performance Model does not properly account for the communication costs.

3.3   Overhead of the Scheduling Strategies

The Ad-Hoc scheduler has very little overhead associated with it. The number of times it has to evaluate the Performance Model for different machine configurations is at most (number of clusters × total number of available machines). This takes a negligible amount of time given the size of the current testbeds.

The Simulated Annealing scheduler is has a higher overhead; however, it is still relatively small in comparison to the time required for most of the problems that would solved in a Grid environment. The time taken by simulated annealing is dependent on some of algorithm parameters, like the temperature reduction schedule and the desired number of iterations at each temperature, as well as the size of the space that is being searched. In our experiments, when the testbed consists of 38 machines, we got the maximum overhead of 57 seconds from the Simulated Annealing scheduling process (on a 500MHz PIII machine). This is still relatively small compared to execution time for most of the ScaLAPACK problems.

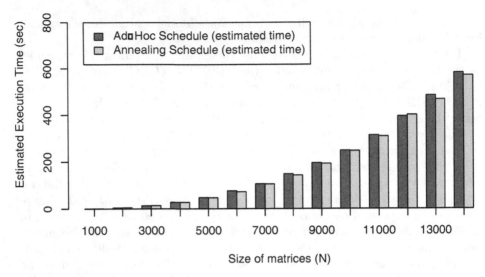

Fig. 2. Estimated execution time for the Ad-Hoc and Simulated Annealing schedules using dynamic network information

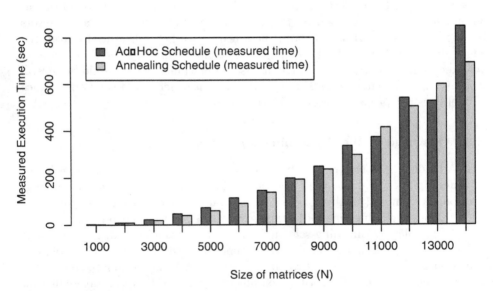

Fig. 3. Measured execution time for the Ad-Hoc and Simulated Annealing schedules using dynamic network information

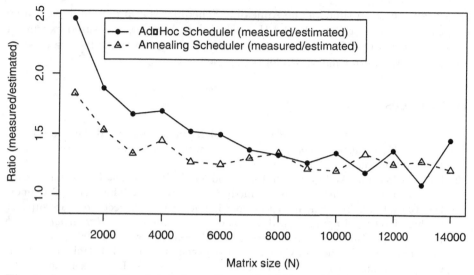

Fig. 4. Accuracy of Simulated Annealing and Ad-Hoc scheduling shown as ratio of measured execution time to estimated execution time

4   Future Research

Firstly, the Performance Model needs to be examined, to see if it can be improved. Also, the performance of the schedulers has to be verified on larger testbeds. In order to construct large, repeatable experiments, a simulation environment designed to examine application scheduling on the Grid such as SimGrid [4] could be used. Additional scheduling algorithms (using non-linear programming techniques, genetic algorithms, etc.) should also be evaluated.

A possible improvement to the scheduling process might be to combine the Ad-Hoc and Simulated Annealing schedulers. The Ad-Hoc scheduler could be used to determine the approximate space where the optimal solution can be found (e.g., returning the approximate number N of machines to be used), and the Annealing Scheduler could be used to search that space more thoroughly (e.g., search using $N-1$, N, $N+1$ machines). This would combine the speed of the Ad-Hoc approach and retain elements of the global search process.

5   Summary

The Simulated Annealing scheduler generates schedules that have a better *estimated* execution time than those returned by the Ad-Hoc greedy scheduler. This is because the Simulated Annealing scheduler can avoid some of the local minima that are not anticipated in the ordering imposed in the Ad-Hoc techniques greedy search. When the generated schedules are actually executed, the measured execution time for the Annealing Scheduler is approximately the same or just a little better than the Ad-Hoc scheduler. Also, the measured execution time is sufficiently different from the estimated execution time that we need to re-examine the Performance Model being used.

References

1. Francine Berman. High-performance schedulers. In Ian Foster and Carl Kesselman, editors, *The Grid: Blueprint for a New Computing Infrastructure*, pages 279–309. Morgan Kaufmann, San Francisco, CA, 1999.
2. Francine Berman, Andrew Chien, Keith Cooper, Jack Dongarra, Ian Foster, Dennis Gannon, Lennart Johnsson, Ken Kennedy, Carl Kesselman, John Mellor-Crummey, Dan Reed, Linda Torczon, and Rich Wolski. The GrADS Project: Software support for high-level Grid application development. *The International Journal of High Performance Computing Applications*, 15(4):327–344, November 2001.
3. L. S. Blackford, J. Choi, A. Cleary, E. D'Azevedo, J. Demmel, I. Dhillon, J. Dongarra, S. Hammarling, G. Henry, A. Petitet, K. Stanley, D. Walker, and R. C. Whaley. ScaLAPACK: a linear algebra library for message-passing computers. In *Proceedings of the Eighth SIAM Conference on Parallel Processing for Scientific Computing (Minneapolis, MN, 1997)*, page 15 (electronic), Philadelphia, PA, USA, 1997. Society for Industrial and Applied Mathematics.
4. Henri Casanova. Simgrid: A Toolkit for the Simulation of Application Scheduling. In *Proceedings of the First IEEE/ACM International Symposium on Cluster Computing and the Grid (CCGrid 2001)*, Brisbane, Australia, May 15–18 2001.
5. Holly Dail. A Modular Framework for Adaptive Scheduling in Grid Application Development Environments. Master's thesis, University of California, San Diego, 2002.
6. I. Foster and C. Kesselman. Globus: A Metacomputing Infrastructure Toolkit. *The International Journal of Supercomputer Applications and High Performance Computing*, 11(2):115–128, Summer 1997.
7. Ian Foster and Carl Kesselman. The Globus Toolkit. In Ian Foster and Carl Kesselman, editors, *The Grid: Blueprint for a New Computing Infrastructure*, pages 259–278. Morgan Kaufmann, San Francisco, CA, 1999. Chap. 11.
8. Andrew S. Grimshaw, William A. Wulf, and the Legion team. The Legion Vision of a Worldwide Virtual Computer. *Communications of the ACM*, 40(1):39–45, January 1997.
9. Scott Kirkpatrick. Optimization by Simulated Annealing: Quantitative Studies. *Journal of Statistical Physics*, 34(5-6):975–986, 1984.
10. N. Metropolis, A. W. Rosenbluth, M. N. Rosenbluth, A. H. Teller, and E. Teller. Equations of state calculations by fast computing machines. *J. Chem. Phys.*, 21:1087–1091, 1953.
11. Antoine Petitet, Susan Blackford, Jack Dongarra, Brett Ellis, Graham Fagg, Kenneth Roche, and Sathish Vadhiyar. Numerical libraries and the Grid. *The International Journal of High Performance Computing Applications*, 15(4):359–374, November 2001.
12. Tindell, Burns, and Wellings. Allocating hard real-time tasks: An NP-hard problem made easy. *RTSYSTS: Real-Time Systems*, 4, 1992.
13. J Ullman. NP-Complete Scheduling Problems. *Journal of Computer and System Sciences*, 10:384–393, 1975.

14. Rich Wolski, Neil T. Spring, and Jim Hayes. The Network Weather Service: a Distributed Resource Performance Forecasting Service for Metacomputing. *Future Generation Computer Systems*, 15(5–6):757–768, October 1999.

A Policy Service for GRID Computing

Dinesh Verma, Sambit Sahu, Seraphin Calo, Manid Beigi, and Isabella Chang

IBM TJ Watson Research Center
PO Box 704
Yorktown Heights, NY 10598
{dverma, sambits, scalo, mandis, ichang}@us.ibm.com

Abstract. In a distributed multi-institute environment like the GRID, each participating institute may want to enforce some limits on how its resources are being used by other institutes. We discuss how the concept of resource allocation policies can assist in this task. We then present an architecture for policy based resource management in the case of a single institute, and how a policy server based on GRID concepts can be developed. We then show how to extend the policy server to support virtual organizations.

1 Introduction

One of the key aspects of the GRID architecture is the ability to share resources across multiple institutes, leading to the creation of abstractions such as virtual organizations [1]. A virtual organization (VO) is a dynamic entity created by machines and resources belonging to several different institutes. A VO may be created to perform a complex scientific simulation, or for several members of a group to come together to handle an emergency like an oil spill. Each member institute in the VO offers some of its computing resources for the computational needs of the VO. A single institute may participate in many different virtual organizations, each with a potential different set of partner institutes.

While the concept of resource sharing enables many new functions, it introduces new issues associated with security and resource control. From a resource control perspective, each institute may want to enforce some constraints on how its resources are to be shared among the different virtual organizations. An institute may want to: share some resources only on weekends/evenings; limit the amount of network traffic/resources external members are allowed to use; ensure that communication with external machines is authenticated; and, maintain an adequate level of security by mandating a minimum set of intrusion detection tools. The participants in a VO may also have their own unique needs which would require them to define their own set of intrusion detection schemes, or authenticate the communication among the different institutes that are members of the VO. In other words, both the VO and the participating institutes may want to install and implement policies related to resource usage and security on their computing resources. Some recent work in the literature has looked at GRID security policy issues [2] [3] [18]. In contrast, we propose a general extensible architecture that can handle a wide variety of policy needs, with a special focus on policies governing resource allocation. Some of the issues arising with resource accounting and allocation policies for the Globus toolkit have been

M. Parashar (Ed.): GRID 2002, LNCS 2536, pp. 243–255, 2002.

examined in [4]. We take a more comprehensive approach towards general policy specification, leveraging the existing policy framework in standards organizations such as the IETF [5] and DMTF [6]. We also extend the policy framework to encompass the concept of virtual organizations.

In this paper, we present a policy server that would be appropriate for the distributed virtual organizations enabled by GRID based services. We begin the paper with a brief overview of the policy framework developed within the IETF/DMTF for enforcement of network policies. We then look at the GRID environment and the requirements that the GRID environment imposes on a policy system. We then present a policy architecture for the GRID environment, showing how a virtual organization would use a policy based service. Finally, we summarize our work and present future areas of activity.

2   IETF/DMTF Policy Framework

A *policy* is defined as an administrator-specified directive which manages certain aspects of the desired *outcome* of interactions among users, applications and services in a distributed system [7]. The policy provides guidelines for how the different system elements should handle the work resulting from different users and applications. As an example, a resource allocation policy may place limits on how much traffic within a network can be used by a class of applications, e.g., multicast UDP traffic may not take more than 10% of total network capacity. Policies are applicable to different aspects of a distributed environment, including (but not limited to): access to network and system resources by different users/applications, restrictions on the set of applications accessible by a user, or support for different service levels and performance targets within the network or server.

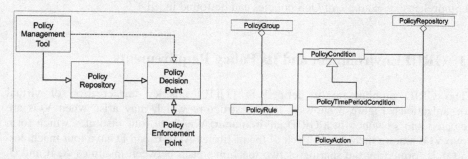

Fig. 1. IETF Policy Architecture   **Fig. 2.** Policy Common Information Model

The policy framework defined by the IETF consists of four basic elements as shown in Figure 1. The basic elements are: the policy manager, the policy repository, the policy enforcement point (PEP), and the policy decision point (PDP). The *policy management tool* is used by an administrator to input the different policies that are to be active in the network. The devices that can apply and execute the different policies are known as the *policy enforcement points* (PEPs). The preferred way for the management tool and policy targets to communicate is through a policy repository. The *policy repository* is used to store the policies generated by the management tool.

Instead of communicating directly with the repository, a policy enforcement point can also use an intermediary known as the policy decision point. The *policy decision point* (PDP) is responsible for interpreting the policies stored in the repository and communicating them to the policy enforcement point.

Each PDP/PEP in the system may be operating in one or more roles within the system, the role defining the set of policies that would need to be implemented for a particular service. As an example, in a Differentiated Services network, all access routers have the role of "Edge" while all internal routers have the role of "Core", and they retrieve their respective policies depending on their roles.

The specification of policy rules within the repository is key to obtaining interoperability. An information model for the rules to be specified is defined by the IETF and DMTF. The underlying premise in the information model is that each policy should be considered as an expression of the form "if condition then action". Here, the conditional part describes a specific situation that can be encountered by a system, and the action component specifies the action that is to be performed by the system in that situation. The Policy Common Information Model [8] is an information model that defines the structure of the policies that are to be stored in the policy repository. The important classes and their attributes from the common information model are shown in the UML diagram in Figure 2.

For any discipline to which policies can be applied, the common information model can be refined to define a discipline-specific information model. The discipline-specific information model would typically subclass PolicyConditions and PolicyActions. A very simple application of the model to Differentiated Services in a network can be obtained by defining a PolicyCondition that deals with attributes in the TCP/IP header fields (source/destination IP addresses, protocol, incoming ToS byte, etc.); and, by defining a related PolicyAction in which are specified the rate constraints that are to be associated with each flow matching the condition, as well as the value to be put into the outgoing ToS byte of each packet for such flows. A more comprehensive example of QoS policies can be found in [9].

3 GRID Environment and Its Policy Requirements

The GRID architecture as defined in [1][10] enables the creation of virtual organizations. Figure 3 shows a typical structure which may arise when VOs are created and sustained in a GRID environment. We show four institutes which form two VOs among themselves. Each of the institutes A, B, C and D have four machines. VO1 is formed by the sharing of two machines each between institutes A, B and C, while VO2 is formed by the sharing of one machine each from institutes B and C, and two machines from institute D. Each of the institutes has some machines that are not part of any VO and are being used for their own internal purposes. VOs are dynamic entities that are formed when needed and discontinued when their function is completed.

The setting up of a GRID virtual organization requires each institute to offer certain resources (such as machines and network connections) to the shared environment. Each institute may want to control the access to resources within its own computing infrastructure in ways that it deems appropriate. Some examples of resource usage policies that an institute may want to put into place include:

Access to multicast UDP traffic is denied due to higher loads on the network.
• No machine should support more than 1000 concurrent TCP connections to avoid thrashing.
• Intrusion detection systems must be active against known patterns of hacker attacks.

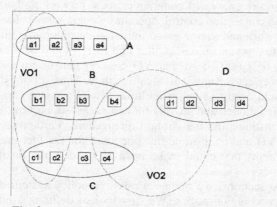

Fig. 3. Virtual Organizations in a Grid Environment

These policies reflect the needs of each institute to protect its network and machines from excessive unproductive or possibly disruptive usage. When participating in virtual organizations, each institute may want to put in further policies restricting how the virtual organizations may access or share resources. These policies would reflect the needs of each institute to restrict the amount of resources that VOs could use, as well as the need to contain the impact VO usage may have on the other resources within the institute. Examples of such policies may include:
• No VO may use more than 5 machines from the institute concurrently.
• VO machines are not allowed to communicate with any other machines within the institute.
• VO traffic into the institute's domain may not exceed 400 Mbps between 9:00 AM - 5:00 PM on weekdays.

A virtual organization in turn would need to install policies on the usage of the machines that are running within itself. The policies may take the form of:
• VO machines communication must be encrypted using specific levels of encryption.
• VO machines should not support more than 500 concurrent TCP connections to avoid thrashing.
• VO machines should not support more than 600 concurrent processes to avoid thrashing.
The resource usage policies expressed by a VO must coexist with the policies used by each of the institutes that contributes machines to the VO.

While our allocation example has shown the allocation of resources in a virtual organization at the granularity of a machine, different GRID toolkits [11] [12] may enable the allocation of resources at different levels. Some Grid toolkits may enable many concurrent VOs to share resources on the same machines, other toolkits may enable the allocation of multiple machines in a cluster, while yet others may use virtualization technologies to support different levels of resource sharing. However, the policy issues that we have outlined above would remain valid for each of these scenarios.

The support of the policies as expressed above would require the consistent inter operation of many different areas of networking and operating systems, including the use of IPSec for secure encrypted communications, networking QoS mechanisms to provide for rate and connection control, operating system support for process controls, and the use of network and server based intrusion detection systems. Moreover, the creation of the virtual organizations implies that there should be a single point where such policies can be specified so that VO creators can be aware of the different policies that are in effect for any individual institute. Thus, a policy server for GRID based systems would need to support multiple disciplines in a common site using a common information model, and provide for concurrent support of the enforcement of policies from the institute and the virtual organizations. Furthermore, the support of policies within a VO and/or institute must account for the fact that there are many heterogeneous systems that could make up a VO and/or the institute's computing infrastructure.

In the next two sections, we outline a possible policy system that can meet the needs of GRID based organizations. We first look at defining a policy server for a single institute, which mostly handles issues related to support of multiple disciplines over heterogeneous systems in an efficient manner. The second section looks at extending the same framework to the support of the disciplines across different virtual organizations.

4   Policy Service for a Single Institute

In this section, we describe the policy service for a single institute. We first delineate the different levels of policy definitions that may exist in the system, present the policy architecture for a single institute, define the policy information needed at the policy service, discuss the interfaces exported by the policy service, and show the operational scheme for the single-institute policy service.

4.1 Policy Levels

In order to support policies in a single institute, we define three distinct levels of policies. Each of the different disciplines that require resource allocation policies have their own definition of policies. The IPSec discipline defines an IPSec level policy [13], the networking QoS Discipline has its own QoS level policy [9], the intrusion detection system would have its own definition of policies, etc. The definition of a discipline policy at this level follows the DisciplineSchema. The DisciplineSchema provides a vendor-neutral and platform-neutral description of the technology.

Each platform implements the policies for a discipline in a different manner. The Linux operating system supports a different mechanism for creating IP-security policies than the IBM mainframe z/OS platform, even though they may both support the same semantics. The PlatformSchema captures the platform-specific definition of policies in the system. All PEPs would accept policy information expressed in the

PlatformSchema. The PlatformSchema is an expression of the support for a specific discipline on a platform, and need not conform to the information model described in Figure 2. The policy system as we present does not interpret the format of platform schema, but it does require that a translation function exist to map policies expressed in accordance with the DisciplineSchema to policies in accordance with the PlatformSchema.

One of the frustrating issues facing many IT operators is that the DisciplineSchemas and PlatformSchemas are quite complex and require a deep understanding of the underlying technology to provide the right set of policies. While the complexity is necessary due to the wide flexibility offered by each discipline, the configuration and control of the system operations can be simplified significantly by presenting a simpler interface to the administrator defining the policies. The simpler presentation language is provided by the Presentation Schema.

An administrator defines the policies (presentation policies) using the constructs provided by the PresentationSchema. The policy service translates these policies into a format (discipline policies) according to the DisciplineSchema and stores the presentation policies and the discipline policies in its local repository. The information is translated into the platform-specific policies when a PEP retrieves it. The translation rules for mapping presentation policies to discipline policies are associated with a discipline, and the translation rules for mapping discipline policies to platform-specific policies are associated with each combination of a discipline and a platform supporting that discipline.

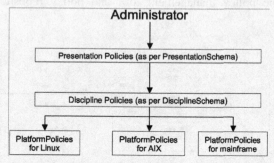

Fig. 4. Levels of Policy Specification

The relationship between the different levels of policy specification is shown in Figure 4. An administrator in the institute defines presentation-level policies, which are specified using a PresentationSchema. The presentation level policies are translated into discipline level policies specified using the DisciplineSchema. A second step of translation is used to obtain the configuration of a specific platform according to the PlatformSchema.

4.2 Single Institute Policy Architecture

We envision the computational GRID infrastructure offered by a single institute to have a policy architecture as shown in Figure 5. The GRID infrastructure enables sharing at the level of a Virtual Resource (VR). The VR could be a single machine, a virtual partition on the same machine, or a cluster of machines. Each GRID institute has several VRs that it is willing to share with other participants. At any given time, some of the VRs would be shared as part of a VO, while other VRs may be available for possible sharing in the future. Each VR runs a policy agent, and one or more PEPs. The PEPs are software entities that are responsible for the control and allocation of specific resources. As shown in Figure 5, each VR is running three PEPs, a PEP for network QoS control, a PEP for IP-security control, and a PEP for server based intrusion detection systems. Other PEPs that manage a machine's server and CPU processing resources are also likely to be active at a VR.

The policy server offers a policy service interface in accordance with the GRID services specification [14]. GRID services are a specialization of web-services, hence the policy server would be a web-service that publishes the set of services that it can provide for an institute into the GRID registry. The set of operations provided by the policy server is exported as a WSDL specification. For remote access, the policy server supports a SOAP/HTTP protocol binding. In order to exchange documents easily over SOAP, the policy documents conforming to the specification of the common information model are encoded in XML. The Policy Agent can be viewed as an instance of the PDP defined by the IETF architecture, and the Policy Server as a combination of the policy management tool and policy repository as shown in Figure 1.

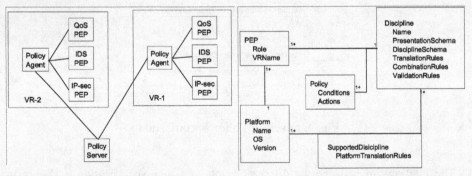

Fig. 5. Single Domain Policy Architecture   **Fig. 6.** Structure of Policy Entities

The administrator defines and stores presentation policies at the Policy Server. Policy Agents register with the Policy Server, providing information regarding the platform upon which they are running, and designating notification sources for listening to policy changes related to their VRs. A Policy Agent also retrieves and caches the set of policies relevant to its associated PEPs at the local machine. The Policy Agent notifies the PEPs when its set of active policies change, e.g. when the time-of-day condition for a specific policy activates or deactivates the policy. The policy agent exports the same WSDL interface as the policy server to its local PEPs.

However, the binding exported by the policy agent can be a local platform-specific binding instead of a SOAP/HTTP binding.

4.3 Policy Data Model and Interfaces

The policy server itself is responsible for maintaining the information about policies and policy-related entities within the system. The functions it exports are related to manipulating the structure of policy related entities, which are shown in the UML diagram in Figure 6. The explanation of several attributes of these entities is provided in the next subsection.

For a single institute, the policy related data entities are the following:

• *Disciplines*: A discipline is a specific area for which policies can be defined. Examples of disciplines would include the IPSec protocol suite for secure communications, intrusion detection systems, network QoS controls, operating system resource controls, etc.

• *PEPs* : A PEP is an entity within the institute responsible for enforcing policies for a specific discipline.

• *Platforms*: A platform represents an individual system (machine with its operating system) within the institute. A Linux server or a mainframe would be an example of a platform. Since different platforms may potentially have different methods to support a given discipline, they need to be accounted for by the policy server.

• *Policies*: These are collections of policy statements for specific disciplines.

As shown in Figure 5, each discipline may be associated with one or more platforms, and a platform may support multiple disciplines. On each association between a platform and a discipline, a platform-specific schema is defined and translation rules for that platform are specified. The different levels of schema and their relationships were explained in section 4.1 above. The platform simply describes the operational environment of a VR, and there may be many VRs on the same platform in the VO.

For each of the four policy related entities, the policy server would need to maintain the following sets of information:

• Discipline: A discipline can only be modified and created by institute administrators. The information about each discipline would include its name, the schema representing its presentation policies, the schema representing its discipline-specific policies, the description of the policy conditions and actions which enable the consistency and dominance checks to be run [11], and the translation rules by which the presentation policies can be transformed into the discipline policies. Furthermore, the discipline registration also includes the set of rules by which two policies in that discipline can be combined together.

• Platform: The information about the platform consists of its set of supported disciplines (the association in Figure 5), and for each supported discipline, a transform to map policies expressed in accordance with DisciplineSchema to platform-specific representation of discipline policies. Platforms can only be created and modified by institute administrators.

- PEP: Each PEP registers itself when it becomes active on the system. The information about each PEP includes the platform it is running upon, the notification mechanism the PEP could use for receiving changes to the policies, and the set of disciplines that it supports. Each PEP needs to know its role so that is can retrieve the policies associated with that role

- Policy: Policies are defined by the administrators, and include specific values for the conditions and actions as specified by them.

The policy schemas are instances of XML schemas [15] where each discipline needs to only identify the conditions and action elements that it is defining to subclass the core information model. The validation tests are specified by identifying the set of actions that are mutually inconsistent, and the type of constraints imposed by each condition attribute. Algorithms for running these tests are described in [16]. The translation rules are instances of XSLT scripts [17] which allow XML policy definitions to be mapped into other formats.

4.4 Policy Roles and Policy Definition

The policy service ought to enable the PEPs to automatically obtain their policies from the repository. In order to support an automatic distribution of policies to different PEPs, the Policy Service includes support for a special Discipline called the RoleDefinition Discipline. Each Policy Agent in the system supports an implicit RoleDefiniton PEP.

The role is an attribute assigned by an administrator to different machines/VRs in the system. In a tiered web-based environment, a machine may have the role of "caching-proxy" while another machine would have a role of "backend-database". The resource allocation policies provided to each machine would be determined by its role within the system.

The condition part of the Role-Discipline includes filters that can identify a VR or a machine in the system. Thus, the condition part of the system would include attributes such as the IP address of a machine, a specific subnet or domain name for the machine, the port at which a VR runs (in those environments where resources are shared on a port basis), etc. The condition also includes the discipline within which a role is defined, and the action part of the Role-Discipline simply contains the roles that are to be assigned to a PEP running on specified machines or ports. The administrator defines the role allocation policies at the policy server, as well as defining any role-specific policies for the different PEPs.

When a PEP registers with the Policy Agent, the Policy Agent on the system obtains the role-definition policies for that PEP by matching policies using the PEP discipline and VR-identifier of the PEP. The Policy Agent then notifies the PEP of its roles, and the PEP can retrieve its policies according to the roles and disciplines from the schema. The PEP now knows the set of policies it needs to enforce and can then continue with its normal execution. Policy Agent and Policy Server are GRID services and can be discovered by exploiting the GRID registry service. Thus, the bundling of a RoleDefinition PEP with the Policy Agent eliminates any need for manual configuration of the PEPs or Policy Agents on the system.

5 VO Policy Architecture

When a GRID policy service is available, the resource allocation entities responsible for creating virtual organizations would need to discover and take the policies of different organizations as part of their resource publishing and matching process. Once formed, it is likely that many VOs would not need to define any refinements of the policies that are installed at the physical institutes. Some VOs, however, may need to define their own policies in addition to those installed by the physical institutes. In this section, we discuss how the architecture can be extended to handle the needs of such virtual organizations.

5.1 VO Policy Levels

When a virtual organization defines its own policies, the policies need to be communicated and relayed to the individual PEPs that are running on the VRs assigned to that virtual organization. However, allowing PEPs to obtain policy directives from entities outside their physical institute exposes them to several security vulnerabilities. In order to avoid this situation, we require that each PEP remain under the sole administrative control of the policy server in its physical institute, and that the policies defined for a virtual organization be relayed via the policy servers to the PEP.

The introduction of the virtual organizations introduces another level of policies as shown in Figure 7. The VO policies are shown at the top level policies of the domain. These policies are communicated to the policy server at each of the institutes participating in the VO. Figure 7 shows only one such institute. The institute policy servers may already have some policies defined by the administrator of the institute, shown as physical institute policies. The institute policy servers combine the policies from the institute administrator and the policies from the VO to obtain the effective set of policies for VRs belonging to that VO. The effective set of policies are the ones seen by the Policy Agents running on each VR assigned to that VO in the grid. A VR that is not assigned to any VO is subject only to the policies defined by the institute.

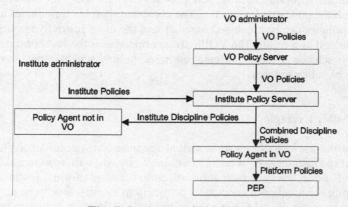

Fig. 7. Institute and VO Policies

The VO administrator defines its policies using the presentation schema. Thus, the policy server at the institute always receives the policies specified according to the presentation schema. The institute policy server combines the policies and translates them to obtain the discipline-level policies, expressed in the discipline schema. The policies in accordance with the discipline schema would be provided to the policy agents, who then translate them to the platform specific discipline.

5.2 VO Policy Architecture

Each Virtual Organization is assumed to have its own Virtual Organization Policy Server (VOPS) which is the central point where a VO administrator can define the policies for machines belonging to the Virtual Organization. The VOPS exports the same WSDL interface as the Policy Server for a single institute described in Section 4.

The VOPS does not have any policy agents that directly access it. Instead, a VOPS acts as a proxy for the Policy Servers that run at each of the different institutes. VOPS are responsible for relaying any requests from the VO administrator to the Policy Servers at each of the different institutes. In the figure, the Policy Servers for each of the institutes is labeled as IPS (Institute Policy Servers). The PEPs running at each institute simply communicate with their respective IPS, and are unaware of the presence of the VOPS.

The IPS at each institute, however, has to provide support for the VOPS. This support is provided by adding a VO entity to the data model of the single institute policy server. The information about a VO consists of the set of disciplines supported by the VO, the set of machines allocated to the VO, and for each discipline, the VO specific policies that are defined by the administrator of the VO. The WSDL exported by each single institute policy server includes the creation, retrieval, update and deletion of VO entities. Only the administrator (or the entity creating VOs in a specific GRID implementation) is allowed to invoke the VO related operations.

The policy manipulation routines are also extended to include an additional optional parameter, the identity of the VO which is requesting a new policy addition/deletion to any discipline policy. The IPS take the policy update requests, and combine the requests to define new policies only for the VRs that belong to the VO for which the policy update occurs. The combination rules for policies are defined so that two policies can be combined together and the more restrictive policies among them be obtained as a result. The VOPS always operates at the level of the discipline-level policy schema or the presentation-level policy schema, but never at the platform-level policy schema.

5.3 A VO Policy Example

To illustrate the use of policies for a virtual organization, , consider a VO which is formed by three institutes, A, B and C. For simplicity, we will assume a single policy schema at all three levels, presentation, discipline and platform. Institute A has a policy limiting the number of concurrent connections per machine to be no more than 1000, while institutes B and C have the same limit defined by policy to be less than 500. Consider a VO administrator that defines a new policy that the connection control limit be no more than 750. The VO policy server relays this information to each of its member institute policy servers. On receiving this limit, the institute policy servers combine the new policy with the existing policy and send the resulting policy definition to the policy agents that are active on each machine belonging to the VO. The machines belonging to the VO in institute A would have the limit set to 750, while the machines belonging to institute B and C in the VO would have the limit set to 500.

The example illustrates that the effect of a VO-defined policy could be quite different in different institutes due to interactions with the institute's policies. If this difference in implementation is not acceptable, then the VO administrator should query the policies in each of the member institutes and use them to determine the right threshold to use in his/her policy definition. Defining a VO policy constraint to be more restrictive than that of any institute's policy would ensure a common operating policy across all the machines of a VO

6 Summary and Future Work

We have presented an architecture for policy based resource management in the GRID environment that supports virtual organizations. This architecture is being prototyped, and assessments of its effectiveness are being made by comparison with existing systems in the networking area. More extensive evaluation through experimentation will be performed once the initial implementation is complete.

Future work will focus on multi-dimensional resource allocation. We have already considered the interaction of policies for server workload management and networking resources. This is being extended to include storage policies as well. Conceptually, one would like to take a high level specification of an application or service and automatically determine the sets of computing resources, their configuration, and the policies necessary for its implementation.

Acknowledgments

The authors would like to acknowledge the following for their many helpful insights on policies and GRID related issues: Lap Huynh, Lee Rafalow, Bob Moore, Brad Topol, Linwood Overby, Steve Graham, Mike Baskey, John Rofrano and Donna Dillenberger.

References

[1] I. Foster, C. Kesselman, S. Tuecke, *The Anatomy of the Grid: Enabling Scalable VOs* International J. Supercomputer Applications, 15(3), 2001, http://www.globus.org/ research/ papers/ anatomy.pdf
[2] T. Ryutov and B. Neuman, *Representation and Evaluation of Security Policies for Distributed System Services*, Proceedings of the DARPA Information Survivability Conference and Exposition, January 2000.

[3] B. Sundaram, C. Nebergall and S. Tuecke, *Policy Specification and Restricted Delegation in Globus proxies*, SuperComputing 2000, Dallas, TX. November 2000.

[4] B. Sundaram and B.Chapman, *Policy Engine: A Framework for Authorization, Accounting Policy Specification and Evaluation in Grids*, 2nd International WorkShop on Grid Computing, Denver, Colorado, November 2001

[5] The IETF Policy Framework Working Group: Charter available at the URL http://www.ietf.org/html.charters/policy-charter.html

[6] Distributed Management Task Force Policy Working Group, Charter available at URL http://www.dmtf.org/about/working/sla.php.

[7] D . Verma, *Policy enabled Networking*, New Riders Publications, 2000.

[8] B. Moore et. al., *Policy Core Information Model -- Version 1 Specification*, RFC 3060, February 2001.

[9] Y. Snir et. al, *Policy QoS Information Model*, IETF Internet Draft .November 2001, http://www.ietf.org/internet-drafts/draft-ietf-policy-qos-info-model-04.txt.

[10] I. Foster, C. Kesselman, J. Nick, S. Tuecke, *The Physiology of the Grid: An Open Grid Services Architecture for Distributed Systems Integration*, January, 2002. http://www.globus.org/ research/ papers/ ogsa.pdf..

[11] The Globus toolkit, http://www.globus.org/ toolkit

[12] The Gridlab project. Http://www.gridlab.org.

[13] J. Jason, L.Rafalow and E. Vyncke, *IPsec Configuration Policy Model*, February 2002, URL http://www.ietf.org/internet-drafts/draft-ietf-ipsp-config-policy-model-05.txt.

[14] S. Tuecke et. al., *Grid Service Specification*, http://www.globus.org/ research/ papers/gsspec.pdf.

[15] XML Schema, Description available at http://www.w3.org/XML/Schema.

[16] D. Verma, *Simplifying Network Management using Policies*, IEEE Network Magazine, February 2002.

[17] XSLT. Description available at http://www.w3.org/Style/xsl.

[18] L. Pearlman, et. al., *A Community Authorization Service for Group Collaboration*, Policy WorkShop 2002, Monterey, California, June 2002.

DYNAMO – DirectorY, Net Archiver and MOver

Mark Silberstein, Michael Factor, and Dean Lorenz

IBM Haifa Research Laboratories
{marks,factor,dean}@il.ibm.com

Abstract. The Grid communities efforts on managing and transporting data have focused on very large data sets consisting of very large elements. We are interested in leveraging the benefits of solutions such GridFTP, in particular with respect to parallel data transfer and restartability (as well as security, third party control, *etc.*), for moving large data sets consisting of very large numbers of small objects, *e.g.*, moving a file system subtree. In addition, we require a solution that 1) imposes constant memory overhead on the client and server systems, 2) is independent of the actual transfer mechanism used so we can easily take advantage of advances in technologies for transferring large files, 3) works well even for very large collections of very small files and 4) is a complete solution, *i.e.*, reproduces the directory tree at the server. In this paper, we present DYNAMO which is our tool built on GridFTP for transferring directory subtrees. In addition to describing the architecture and implementation of DYNAMO, we present performance results on a range of networks showing that we have met our goals.

1 Introduction

The Grid community has invested much thought and effort on how to manage and transport data. Such work is seen in the underlying infrastructure (*e.g.*, [1], [2], etc.), in the development of higher level frameworks for managing data in a grid setting (*e.g.*, [3], [4], [5], [6]) and in the large number of application data grids [7]. This work has focused on very large data sets, particularly those generated by the scientific community [8], [9]. Not only are these data sets themselves very large, but each element is also very large.

We are interested in the related but somewhat different scenario of moving large data sets consisting of very large numbers of small objects. The particular instantiation of the problem which we address is moving a directory subtree of a file system. We present DYNAMO which is our tool built on top of GridFTP [1] to address this problem.

There are many reasons to move a directory subtree. Our initial motivation was to provide support for migrating user directories in a storage service provider (SSP) environment. In such a setting, the ability to move a user's directory is a critical building block for advanced load balancing and capacity management. The data movement could be used either for purposes of replication or migration.

Such functionality is useful, however, even outside of the context of an SSP. Many large enterprises have multiple, widely distributed, and independently administered data centers; the same problems and motivations for moving data that occur in an SSP setting can also occur in this environment. For instance, a facility that replicates modified files to a remote site for purposes of disaster recovery (*e.g.*, [10]) has similar data movement requirements. Whatever its use, we assume that the task is to move an entire subtree,

M. Parashar (Ed.): GRID 2002, LNCS 2536, pp. 256–267, 2002.

including the directory structure and attributes, and that the task is only complete when the directory is reconstructed and available at the destination.

Our focus on small data objects, albeit very large numbers of such objects, is a significant difference from prior work. Mechanisms such as GridFTP are very useful for moving large files. GridFTP can take advantage of multiple data streams to allow parallel transfer and provides restartability in the event of a failure while transferring an individual file. Similar functionality is seen in the Web download accelerators.

However, for small files, there is no performance benefit from using multiple streams; the overhead of managing the multiple streams can easily outweigh any benefit. In addition, restartability for small files is not very interesting since it is simple and cheap enough to resend the entire file. Thus, the most naive approach of using a facility such as GridFTP to transfer an subtree of small files, namely transferring each individual file with GridFTP, is not appropriate. Another naive way we might be able to take advantage of GridFTP for moving a directory subtree would be to package all of the tree in a single file (*e.g.*, via `tar`). This approach however requires significant free space to hold the package file and it serializes the steps of creating the pack file, transferring the file and opening the archive. While we could use the operating systems piping facilities to address the space and serialization issues by redirecting the output of the packaging command directly into the data transfer interface, this would raise restartability problems. Since the client is not transferring a true file, if the server asks the client to restart transmission from a certain byte offset, the client will need to reconstruct the entire package file from the beginning to find the offset.

In addition to requiring a solution which has the benefits of GridFTP, in particular with respect to parallel data transfer and restartability (as well as security, third party control, *etc.*), we make additional constraints on the solution. First, the solution must impose a fixed memory overhead on both the client and server systems, independent of the total amount of data transferred. Second, the solution must build on existing mechanisms for transferring large amounts of data and should be independent of the actual transfer mechanism used; this way, we can easily take advantage of advances in technologies for transferring large files. Third, the solution must work well for very large collections of very small files. Finally, we are interested in a complete solution; it is important that both sides know when the directory tree has been reconstructed at the server. Note that the object replication described in [6] addresses a similar problem; in this case, GridFTP is used with GDMP to replicate objects selected from multiple Objectivity data base files and packaged into a single larger file for transport to enable obtaining the advantages of GridFTP for large files.

Our main contribution is a mechanism which meets all of these goals. In our approach, described in the next section, we provide both client-side and server-side agents. These agents sit on top of a transfer mechanism, such as GridFTP, which provides high performance and restartability for transferring large data objects. The agents package the files at the client into (relatively) fixed-sized *chunks* which are transferred to the server using the transfer mechanism; the chunk size is picked to be large enough to gain the benefits of the mechanism for transferring large files. The server agent unpacks the chunks and notifies the client agent which chunks have been successfully processed. The client agent generates new chunks, in a pipelined fashion, based upon the rate at which the server agent receives and processes the chunks. Section 2 describes the initial implementation of DYNAMO on top of Globus [11] and GridFTP.

Section 4 presents performance results on a range of networks; we show that our mechanism achieves the benefits GridFTP gives for transferring large data objects when we transfer subtrees composed of small files. We compare the performance of DYNAMO to several other approaches, including transferring a single large tar file up front and 'piping' multiple independent executions of tar into multiple instances of GridFTP. In the concluding section, we summarize our results and present some other ideas on how this work might be leveraged.

2 Approach

We designed a tool on top of GridFTP that supports high performance reliable transfer of a directory structures consisting of a a very large collection of small files. There are several other desired features (except high performance), which we take into account.

Resource usage. We want a configurable limit on the temporary space required at both client and server, which is independent of the total amount of data being transfered.

Fault tolerance. We want to be able to efficiently recover from both failed communication and failed processes. This means that a partial transfer can be resumed from the point of failure even if both sides and the network were down. Furthermore, we require end-to-end reliability, namely, the transfer is complete only when the entire directory structure has been reconstructed at the receiving end.

Standardization. An important design guideline is to make use of existing tools, and thus, take advantage of technology advances. In particular, we want to use existing file transfer utilities, and the "standard" Grid security facilities.

In order to meet those requirements we chose to build upon GridFTP. GridFTP provides a standard transport mechanism that conforms to the grid security requirements, and it is constantly being improved. However, GridFTP is tailored for large file transfer. The challenge is to maintain its performance, reliability, and restartability features while applying it for transfer of large numbers of small files organized in a directory.

2.1 Optimal File Size

The GridFTP protocol supports high throughput transfer for very large files over broadband connections by using parallel TCP streams and optimally setting TCP parameters (*e.g.*, buffer and window sizes). GridFTP sends files sequentially, waiting for the completions of each transfer before starting the next one; therefore, maximal throughput is bounded by the ratio between file size and round trip delay. For small files this is the dominating factor and there is hardly any performance gain from using parallel streams or larger TCP buffers. Furthermore, breaking files over parallel streams adds overhead for each transfer, which, for small files, more than outweighs its benefits. Indeed, there is a minimal file size required by GridFTP for optimal performance, and (as shown in Section 4) the throughput of GridFTP sharply decreases when used with smaller files.

In order to get around this problem, we aggregate small files into larger data blocks which we term *chunks*. Since GridFTP is used to send these large chunks, it is kept at an optimal "work point", achieving peek performance throughout the transfer.

If a maximal file size threshold is required (*e.g.*, to avoid disk thrashing and save temporary space) then very large files can be broken down into optimal sized chunks.

2.2 Fault Tolerance and Recovery

An important feature of GridFTP is its ability to recover from failed transfers, by salvaging partial transfers and resuming from mid-file. However, GridFTP does not support a recovery mechanism for multiple files. We can utilize GridFTP recovery to resume each chunk transfer, but we must also implement an external recovery mechanism to track which files have been successfully transferred and which files still need to be packed and sent. Partial transfer recovery is not important for small files, since resending the entire file can actually take less time than figuring out where to resume transfer.

We keep persistent state information on disk to be capable of resuming transfer even if both client and server were down. We use a three-way handshake to acknowledge successful reception of each chunk, and append a small signature at the end of each chunk, so a partial chunk transfer can be easily detected. We also need to make sure that the complete directory structure is reconstructed at the server. Our control process indicates a complete chunk transfer only after the server successfully unpacks the chunk. We use `tar` to pack an unpack the chunks and catch any errors.

DYNAMO supports data manipulations (*e.g.*, packing and compression) before and after the transfer. Some applications may require other useful operations (*e.g.*, database interaction [6], encryption, version control, etc). This requirement was also partially addressed in the GridFTP protocol specification by the *extended retrieve* and *extended store* modes. When adding such processing to the transfer, it is important to provide separate acknowledgements, since processing failures (*e.g.*, disk quota exceeded) are different than communication failures and require different recovery actions (*e.g.*, issue a request to increase the allocated space). We require end-to-end reliability mechanisms, which, combined with modular design, allow for easy integration of user-defined plug-ins that implement pre/post-processing.

The end-to-end application level control also allows for more flexibility in the transport layer. For example, performing data transfer via intermediate sites (*e.g.*, [12]), which may provide better performance or may be used to overcome firewall restriction. The intermediary can utilize GridFTP to provide reliable transfer for each hop, while the DYNAMO framework provides end-to-end reliability, flow control, and restartability.

2.3 Temporary Space

An important requirement is limiting the size of temporary space consumed during transfer. The amount of temporary space is proportional to the size of the chunks. The server can open each chunk only after it is completely received. The client can delete a sent chunk only after it is successfully opened on the server. In order to further improve performance, it may be necessary to prepare a new chunk while sending another. In this case, there is a "window" of chunks in mid-transfer state, and the temporary space required would be the size of this window. Temporary space is minimal when chunks are small (*e.g.*, when sending each file separately), but performance is poor. The throughput increases with the chunk size, however, as shown in Section 4, beyond a certain threshold, there is no further significant performance gain.

The client may reduce temporary space by pipelining some of the operations, rather than creating a complete chunk and then sending it. It could use `tar` through a Unix pipe and send the chunks directly from the pipe, consuming as little as the buffer size. On the other hand, if we use GridFTP as an independent transport layer then the server must receive a whole chunk before it can pipe it to an external program (*i.e.*, the temporary space used is at least as large as a chunk). Furthermore, if we do not want to block incoming GridFTP connections until the chunk is opened and deleted, the temporary space must be several chunks in size.

One simple approach to sending a directory structure is to package all of it into a single file and send the whole file by GridFTP. The GridFTP protocol is well suited for sending such large files and would even support recovery for failed connections. On the other hand, this approach effectively duplicates the space required for the directory structure, and may require a huge amount of temporary space. Also, this approach would require the serialization of the pack-send-unpack sequence.

DYNAMO can compress chunks during their creation to reduce file sizes and increase effective throughput. On the other hand, the minimal chunk size required for GridFTP is independent of any compression (although more files can be put in each chunk), therefore the temporary space is not reduced by compression. Furthermore, compression may actually degrade performance when the bottleneck is not the network, since it slows processing which decreases overall throughput.

3   The Dynamo Tool

In this section we give a high level view of the DYNAMO tool. The tool includes two components: a client and a server, and currently supports transfers from client to server. It provides a reliable directory transport mechanism over the GridFTP protocol.[1]

The server may receive concurrently from several clients. It keeps a separate transfer session with each client and allocates temporary disk space for each. The client uses GridFTP to deliver packed directory chunks to the DYNAMO server and stores them in the allocated temporary space. The client then alerts the server when each chunk transfer is complete and is ready for unpacking. The server, in turn, sends back an indication after a chunk is successfully unpacked. The DYNAMO server is completely independent of the file transport mechanism and does not communicate with the GridFTP server.

The normal message flow between the server and client is summarized in Fig. 1. The client is responsible for session lifetime management, for flow control, and for restarting failed transfers. The client establishes a connection and receives from the server a session ID and temporary space location. It creates chunks and sends them using a local GridFTP client. When GridFTP indicates transfer is done, the DYNAMO client sends a message to the DYNAMO server requesting unpacking. After unpacking is complete the DYNAMO

---

[1] We use the `globus_ftp_client` libraries that come with the Globus 2.0 distribution.

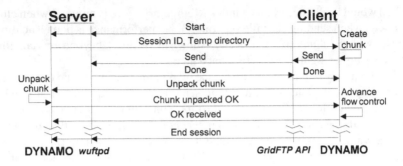

Fig. 1. Message flow between DYNAMO client and server.

server sends an OK message back to the client, which, in turn, advances the flow control window and sends an acknowledgement back to the server.

3.1   Chunk Creation and Flow Control

The DYNAMO client packs together several small files and sends them as one large file (chunk). The DYNAMO tool allows tuning of chunk size and supports configuration of the GridFTP parameters. The current DYNAMO implementation does not set these parameters automatically. DYNAMO goes over the directory listing and creates the list of files for each chunk based on the desired chunk size. The chunks are created with `tar` and are optionally compressed with `gzip`. The chunks are not created on disk but rather `tar`-ed into buffers and sent directly from memory.[2]

Chunks are created and sent to the server in a pipeline, new chunks are prepared while previous ones are GridFTP transfered. A new chunk is sent immediately upon GridFTP completing the transfer of the previous one, even before the DYNAMO server unpacks the received chunk. The DYNAMO client maintains a flow-control "window" of chunks that are in mid-transfer. The size of this window is configurable and is restricted by the amount of the temporary space available both on the server and on the client.

3.2   Fault Tolerance and Recovery

Each individual chunk file is reliably transferred using the GridFTP protocol, and DY-NAMO catches any errors that are produces by `tar` while unpacking. DYNAMO encodes critical chunk meta-data (*e.g.*, session ID and serial number) in the chunk file name and appends a signature to the end of each chunk (for easy detection of partial transfer).

We use application level end-to-end reliability for each chunk, namely chunk delivery is complete only after a chunk is unpacked successfully. The DYNAMO server sends an error message if unpacking fails, and specifies the reason of failure. Persistent session information is stored on disk at both the DYNAMO client and the DYNAMO server. In order to save disk space, only chunk meta-data is stored and the chunks themselves are not stored on disk. The DYNAMO client keeps, on disk, the state and file listing for every

---

[2] If there is not enough memory, chunks are prepared on the disk and reloaded before transfer.

Table 1. IBM Intra-grid Configuration

Site	Hardware Configuration			Connectivity to Yorktown			
	CPU (PIII)	RAM	Disk (SCSI)	Network Type	Hops	RT Delay	Rate
Yorktown	1.2GHz	1 GB	160MB/s	Local	–	–	–
Hawthorne	1GHz	512MB	160MB/s	MAN	5	0.17ms	93.8Mb/s
Toronto	2×1.2GHz	2GB	160MB/s	Broadband WAN	13	63ms	39Mb/s
Haifa	600MHz	128MB	40MB/s	Intercontinen. WAN	15	200ms	1.1Mb/s

chunk, from its creation and for the duration of the session. The chunk's state changes when GridFTP returns after delivery is complete and again upon the DYNAMO server indication of successful unpacking. The DYNAMO server also keeps on disk the sate records of all chunks.

This persistent data allows for recovery of failed sessions not only in the case of connection failure, but even if both client and server were down. When a failed session is restarted the DYNAMO client issues a restart request to the the server. The server then checks the persistent state information and examines the session's temporary space for chunks for which GridFTP delivery was not complete and for chunks that were not yet unpacked. When the DYNAMO client receives the state information it uses GridFTP restart mechanism for partially delivered chunks and resends entire chunks when necessary. It also resends any needed flow control messages to resynchronize with the server.

4 Results

The main goal of our performance tests is to understand the performance of DYNAMO when used to transfer large collections of small files. Another goal is to study the impact of file size on the performance of GridFTP.

We conducted our tests on the IBM Intra-grid – a geographically distributed Globus based grid linking IBM research and development labs in the United States, Switzerland, Japan, Israel, Germany, France, England, China, and Canada. The tests were performed between the IBM Intra-grid node at Yorktown (NY) and three other IBM Intra-grid nodes – Hawthorne (NY), Toronto (Canada), and Haifa (Israel). The connections between these sites offer a variety of network conditions. All grid nodes that participated in the tests run Globus 2.0 Beta for Linux on an Intel $PIII$ with 100Mb Ethernet. Table 1 lists the hardware configuration for each site and its connectivity with Yorktown.

We used grid-enabled `wuftpd` as the GridFTP server and `globus-url-copy` (GUC) as the GridFTP client. Both are part of the standard Globus kit distribution and implement most of the GridFTP protocol. The TCP buffer size and the FTP block size were fixed at 256KB for all experiments.

4.1   File Size Dependency

We first studied the connection between file size and GUC performance. We measured the total transfer time required to transfer a single file for different files sizes and with different setting to the numbers of parallel streams which GridFTP can use. The whole

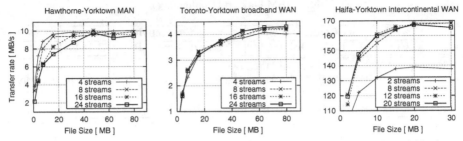

Fig. 2. `globus-url-copy` throughput over different networks as a function of file size.

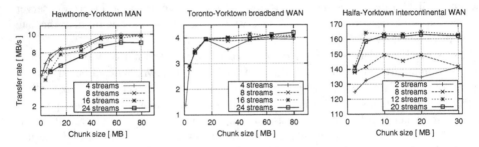

Fig. 3. DYNAMO throughput over different networks as a function of chunk size.

experiment was repeated nine times, with six consecutive runs for each setting, and the results were averaged. In order to remove the effects of sharp, short-lived swings in network conditions, we discarded batches that were very far from the average. Less than 10% of runs were discarded this way.

The results (Fig. 2) show that throughput increases with file size, with a much sharper increase for small file sizes than for larger ones. The same throughput characteristics hold for all connection types and for any number of streams, while the minimal file size for which 90% of optimal performance is reached depends on both parameters.

For the MAN, few streams produce the best results, which suggests that the bottleneck is not the network but rather the disk or CPU. The overhead of managing multiple streams degrades performance. The affect of small file sizes on performance is more significant for this type of connection by almost an order of magnitude. Throughput of within 90% of the optimum is reached for file size of less than 20MB. On the broadband WAN the number of streams is less significant, although more streams produce slightly better results. File sizes of about 50MB achieve 90% of optimal performance. On the slower Intercontinental WAN performance can be greatly improved by adding more streams, although the affect is significantly lessened for over 12 streams. File sizes of 10–15MB are enough to achieve 90% of optimal performance.

4.2   Chunk Size Dependency

In the second set of experiments, we studied the connection between chunk size and DYNAMO performance. We sent random directory structures (that contained files of various sizes) using the DYNAMO tool with different chunk sizes and with different numbers of streams.[3] Unlike GUC performance measurements, the calculated throughput for DYNAMO, includes chunk creation time (tar-ing of the files), but does not include unpacking time on the server (untar-ing). The experiment was repeated nine times, with two consecutive runs for each setting, and the results were averaged.[4]

The results (Fig. 3) are very similar to the results obtained by the corresponding experiment with GUC. Throughput increases with the chunk size, with a sharp increase for small sizes and less significant one for larger values. In general we see that the optimal performance of DYNAMO is similar to that of GUC. A more detailed comparison is given in the next section.

For the MAN, again, a few streams produce the best results. The DYNAMO tool does more processing so the performance degradation due to large number of streams is more significant. Throughput of 90% the optimum is reached for chunk size of about 40MB. On the broadband WAN the number of streams is less significant and chunk sizes of 50MB achieve 90% of optimal performance. On the Intercontinental WAN 90% of optimal performance is achieved for chunk sizes of only 5MB.

4.3   Comparison of Dynamo and globus-url-copy

In the main test set, we compared the performance of GUC and DYNAMO for directory transfer. We used a directory structure made of a large collection of files from a range of sizes as described in Section 4.2.

A straightforward method of sending the directory is calling GridFTP sequentially for each file. This method uses very small temporary space on both client and server and can be easily extended to support restartability for failed sessions (by using GridFTP partial transfer recovery mechanism or just resending each failed file). In order to avoid having to establish a new connection for each file, we modified the GUC code to allow transfer of multiple files without closing the connection. We still expected low throughput, since this method is inherently serial and since (as seen in Fig. 2) GUC performs poorly for small files (most of the files in our directory were below 1MB). Indeed, the tested throughput was so low that for the intercontinental WAN, we could not even complete a significantly sized directory transfer because it literally took hours.

An alternative method for sending a whole directory is to create a single file for the entire directory structure (using tar), send it using GUC, and unpack it on the server (using untar via a globus-job-run script). Since this method uses GridFTP the way it was intended (to send a single very large file), it can benefit from both high transfer rates and restartability capabilities. On the other hand it requires a very large temporary space on both client and server (large enough to contain a full copy of the directory structure) and also, tar-ing and untar-ing are executed sequentially.

The tar operation can be pipelined on the client by piping tar output into GUC instead of creating a file. This pipelining cannot be done on the server, since the whole tar file is received before unpacking starts. This *piped*-GUC saves time and space on the client but on the server still requires large temporary space and untar-ing is still sequential. Also, restartability is much more complicated in this case. The experiments

---

[3] The structures were generated by replicating the Linux /usr/sbin directory. The size of the structure was $1.5GB$ for the broadband networks and 100MB for the intercontinental WAN.

[4] As was done with the GUC experiments, outlying batches were removed.

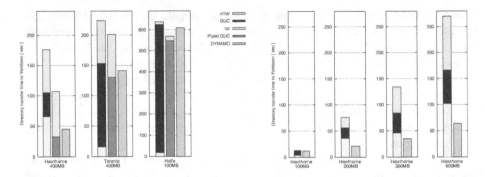

Fig. 4. Performance comparison of DYNAMO and globus-url-copy by network type for directory transfer to Yorktown.

Fig. 5. Comparison of DYNAMO and globus-url-copy by transfer size for directory transfer from Hawthorn to Yorktown.

with the piped-GUC proved to be unstable when GUC uses parallel streams.[5] In order to overcome this problem we split the directory structure into even sized parts. Each part was tar-ed and piped into a separate GUC session with a single stream setting. All sessions were run in parallel, each in a separate process (and a separate TCP stream).

We conducted experiments for GUC, piped-GUC, and DYNAMO, using the optimal setting for the number of streams and chunk size. Each experiment was repeated ten times and the results were averaged. The results (Fig. 4) show the total time required for a directory transfer over each of the three networks, including tar-ing and untar-ing.[6] The bars for GUC show the time spent on untar-ing the structure on the server. The non-piped version shows also how long it took to tar the structure at the client.

The sequential execution of the non-piped GUC is most apparent for the MAN connection. For this case tar and untar are the bottleneck and not the network. Since DYNAMO is able to perform operations in a pipelined fashion it significantly outperforms the other methods. We also see that there is hardly any performance hit due to the extra processing. Results for the broadband WAN are similar. The shorter time required for tar-ing is probably due to the better hardware available at the Toronto site.

Note, that it takes more time to perform untar alone, than for DYNAMO to complete the whole process of directory structure transfer (pack, send, unpack). This is due to the fact that in the GUC configurations untar is run on very large files (as large as the entire directory structure). The file system cannot cache the entire tar file, which is first written (by wuftpd) and then read again (by untar). This in effect causes thrashing of the file system buffer, which is enhanced by the fact that at the same time the file system is busy writing the directory structure as it is being unpacked. The DYNAMO server does not suffer from this problem because chunks are relatively small, and are unpacked and deleted immediately after their arrival. The file system is capable to fit the entire chunk in its buffers and is able to delete it before it is ever physically written to disk. A similar behavior is observed at the client side.

---

[5] We experienced difficulties with the currently installed GUC implementation when using standard input and more than one stream.

[6] We sent a 400MB directory on the broadband networks 100MB on the intercontinental WAN.

We verified this result by conducting additional performance comparisons between the non-piped GUC and DYNAMO for different sized directories over the MAN. The results (Fig. 5) show that there is indeed a performance hit for large files. We also used iostat[13] to measure disk throughput and disk activity on the server. With the non-piped GUC, there is intensive disk read activity and relatively low write rate, while the DYNAMO server never reads from disk and almost triples the disk write rate.

On the intercontinental WAN, the DYNAMO and GUC have similar performance. In this case the network is clearly the bottleneck, so using compression may improve throughput. We were able to double the overall throughput of DYNAMO with the gzip flag turned on. Interestingly, the network throughput of our "hacked" parallel, piped GUC is the best. It even outperformed the single file transfer for which GUC was built. Note, that both the single file tar setting and DYNAMO use the same GridFTP client implementation for parallel streams usage. The performance gain of the parallel piped-GUC is more significant for slower networks, but is apparent on the MAN too. There is reason to believe that it would outperform DYNAMO if we could invoke untar-ing on the server in a pipelined manner. This suggests that the Linux OS is more efficient in utilizing parallel TCP streams than the current GUC implementation of GridFTP.

We can conclude that DYNAMO is able to achieve better performance than straight-forward combinations of tar, GUC, and untar over broadband connections. Also, remember that the GUC transfers required a huge amount of extra space on the server (as big as the entire directory structure), and the single tar file setting (non-piped GUC) requires the same space also on the client.

5   Conclusions

We address the question of moving large data sets which consist of very large numbers of small objects. The particular instantiation of the problem which we address is moving a directory subtree of a file system. In this paper, we present DYNAMO which is our tool built on top of GridFTP [1] to address this problem.

The main contribution of this work is a mechanism which provides a high performance directory transfer mechanism for large collections of small files. The tool, called DYNAMO, provides an end-to-end reliable directory transfer using the existing GridFTP protocol as a transport layer. It consumes only a limited and controllable amount of temporary space on both sender and receiver and supports recovery of partial transfers.

We show that GridFTP performs better for large files and throughput degrades strongly for small files (a few MBytes). In DYNAMO we pack the small files into fixed-sized *chunks*, which are then transferred through GridFTP and unpacked. The size of the chunks is chosen to be large enough to gain the benefits of the GridFTP mechanism for transferring large files. Chunk preparation, sending and unpacking is done in a pipeline, which allows us to save temporary space and perform operations in parallel. We also show that the DYNAMO pipelined approach achieves much better overall throughput than the straightforward approach of packing an entire directory structure into a single large file, sending, and unpacking.

We have tested the DYNAMO tool over the IBM Intra-grid – a geographically distributed Globus based grid linking IBM research and development labs all over the world. We have conducted extensive experiments over different networks types. DY-

NAMO achieves significantly better performance than the naive approach of sending all files separately with GridFTP. Its network throughput when transferring a collection of small files is similar to the throughput that GridFTP achieves for large files. On broadband connections, DYNAMO is capable of sending and rebuilding an entire directory structure in less time than it takes just to unpack it, when sent as a single file. This is due to the fact that the file system is less efficient in manipulating very large files.

The DYNAMO tool supports optional compression of data, which can increase effective bandwidth on slower networks. It manages end-to-end reliable transfer including any pre/post-processing, and can be easily extended to support user-supplied plug-ins. For example DYNAMO can be used in conjunction with incremental update and backup utilities. It can also be implemented over more complex transfer mechanisms (*e.g.*, through an intermediary).

References

1. W. Allcock, J. Bester, J. Bresnahan, A. Chernevak, I. Foster, C. Kesselman, S. Meder, V. Nefedova, D. Quesnal, and S. Tuecke, "Data management and transfer in high performance computational grid environments," *Journal of Parallel Computing*, 2002.
2. A. Hanushevsky, A. Trunov, and L. Cottrell, "Peer-to-peer computing for secure high performance data copying," Tech. Rep., Stanford University, 2001.
3. C. Baru, R. Moore, A. Rajasekar, and M. Wan, "The sdsc storage resource broker," in *Proc. CASCON'98 Conference*, Toronto, Canada, November 1998.
4. W. Hoschek, J. Jaen-Martinez, A. Samar, H. Stockinger, , and K. Stockinger, "Data management in an international data grid project," in *Proceedings of the first IEEE/ACM International Workshop on Grid Computing*, Banglore, India, Dec. 2000, Springer Verlag Press.
5. A. Shoshani, A. Sinm, and J. Gu, "Storage resource managers: Middleware components for grid stroage," in *Tenth Goddard Conference on Mass Storage Systems and Technologies in cooperation with the Nineteenth IEEE Symposium on Mass Storage Systems*, B. Kolber and P. C. Hariharanan, Eds., College Park, MD, April 2002, NASA, p. 209.
6. H. Stockinger, A. Samar, B. Allcock, I. Foster, K. Holtman, and B. Tierney, "File and object replication in data grids," in *Proceedings of the Tenth International Symposium on High Performance Distributed Computing (HPDC-10)*. Aug. 2001, IEEE Press.
7. R. Oldfield, "Summary of existing and developing data grids," White paper for the Remote Data Access group of the Global Grid Forum, Mar. 2001.
8. "European datagrid," http://eu-datagrid.web.cern.ch/eu-datagrid/.
9. "Griphyn," http://griphyn.org.
10. H. Patterson, S. Manley, M. Federwisch, D. Hitz, S. Kleiman, , and S. Owara, "Snapmirror : File system based asynchronous mirroring for disaster recovery," in *Proceedings of the FAST 2002 Conference on File and Storage Technologies*, Monterey, CA, Jan. 2002.
11. I. Foster and C. Kesselman, "Globus: A metacomputing infrastructure toolkit," *International Journal of Supercomputer Applications*, vol. 11, no. 2, pp. 115–128, 1997.
12. D. Thain, J. Basney, S.-C. Son, and M. Livny, "The kangaroo approach to data movement on the grid," in *Proceedings of the Tenth IEEE Symposium on High Performance Distributed Computing (HPDC10)*, August 2001.
13. M. Loukides, *System Performance Tuning*, Nutshell Handbook Series. O'Reilly & Associates Inc, Dec. 1992, ISBN 0-937175-60-9.

GridRM: A Resource Monitoring Architecture
for the Grid

Mark Baker and Garry Smith

The Distributed Systems Group,
University of Portsmouth, Portsmouth UK.
{mark.baker, garry.smith} @computer.org

Abstract. Monitoring resources is an important aspect of the overall efficient usage and control of any distributed system. In this paper, we describe a generic open-source resource monitoring architecture that has been specifically designed for the Grid. The paper consists of three main sections. In the first section, we outline our motivation and briefly detail similar work in the area. In the second section, we describe the general monitoring architecture and its components. In the final section of the paper, we summarise the experiences so far and outline our future work.

1. Introduction

A wide-area distributed system such as a Grid requires that a broad range of data be monitored and collected for a variety of tasks such as fault detection and performance monitoring, analysis, prediction and tuning. In this paper, we present and describe a generic open-source resource monitoring architecture that has been specifically designed for the Grid. The system we describe here, called GridRM, is based on the Global Grid Forum's [1] Grid Monitoring Architecture [2], Java technologies (applets, servlets and JDBC) a SQL database and SNMP (agents and objects). Unlike many other monitoring systems, GridRM is designed to monitor Grid resources, rather than the applications that execute on a Grid. The GridRM is capable of registering interest in events, remotely observing devices, as well as gathering and displaying monitoring data.

2. Related Work

The following systems were reviewed in the process of researching GridRM.
- The Globus Heartbeat Monitor (HBM) [3],
- The Network Weather Service (NWS) [4],
- The NetLogger (Networked Application Logger) toolkit [5],
- The Autopilot project, based on the Pablo Toolkit [6],

M. Parashar (Ed.): GRID 2002, LNCS 2536, pp. 268–273, 2002.

- The Remos (REsource MOnitoring System) [7],
- Java Agents for Monitoring and Management (JAMM) [8].

Details of these projects can be found elsewhere [9]. In summary, we found a variety of different systems exist for monitoring and managing distributed Grid-based resources and applications. However, for resource monitoring and management, we believe that none fulfil the criteria that are desired in today's Grid-based environments. That of using standard and open components (Java applets, servlets, JDBC, and an SQL database), being scalable, requiring no additional modification or installation of additional software on the monitored resources (SNMP agents and MIBs), taking advantage of the GGF advocated architecture to bind together the monitored resources (GMA) and security.

3. GridRM Architecture

3.1 Introduction

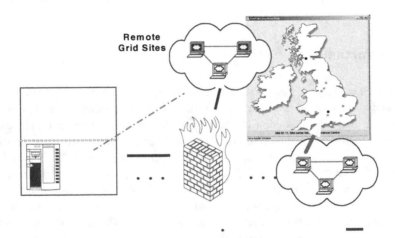

Fig, 1. Grid Resource Monitoring Architecture

The GridRM architecture is shown in **Fig, 1**. Each Grid site within a virtual organisation is viewed as an island of resources, with a GridRM Gateway providing; controlled access to local resource information and a mechanism for the user to query the status of remote resources.

Each GridRM Gateway provides a web-based user interface allowing users to observe monitored resources at the local and remote sites; geographic maps present the 'islands of resources' as colour coded icons. These icons are then selected to reveal information about a site's monitored resources. A hierarchical approach is envisioned, whereby a user may proceed from global, to country, to organisational views. Users are free to connect to any GridRM Gateway and retrieve the user interface, however access to monitored resource information is controlled by sites access policy. Mechanisms will be implemented for distributed session management to ensure the user's view of the Grid is consistent, regardless of the Gateway serving the user interface.

The GridRM architecture has two hierarchical layers, the global layer (Fig. 2), and the local layer. The global layer of GridRM uses GMA software to bind together the local islands that are Grid-enabled sites. These islands interact with the GMA via a GridRM Gateway. The Gateway is used internally to configure, manage and monitor SNMP-enabled resources. The gateway provides a type of firewall that ensures there is controlled access to resource information. Finally, specific devices have their SNMP agents and MIBs configured in standard way to provide resource information.

3.2 The Global Layer of GridRM

The global layer of GridRM is shown in **Fig. 2**. This layer functions in the following way:
1. The GridRM Gateways register with the GMA as compound information providers/consumers.
2. A Web client connects to a particular GridRM Gateway and downloads a Java applet; on applet initialisation the GMA directory is utilised to locate other GridRM Gateways. Summary information from each site is used to compose the applet graphical display.
3. The client can now instruct the local Gateway to return monitoring information from its own Grid site resources, or any of the remote sites (assuming valid user credentials). Information requests and notifications are fulfilled between remote Gateways using GMA events.

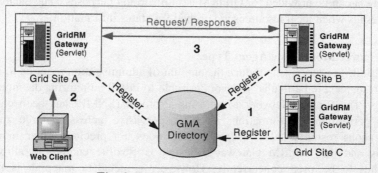

Fig. 2. The Global GridRM Layer

3.3 The Local GridRM Layer

The GridRM Gateway monitors local resources and provides both real-time and historical performance information to authenticated consumers. The Gateway comprises of a Web server, servlets, a relational database, and a monitoring and event APIs.

3.3.1 The Web Server and Servlets

Java servlets are used to monitor resources, provide client access control and perform request processing. Clients connect to a Gateway Web server and download the GridRM user interface. The Gateway coordinates the necessary information to construct a graphical Grid site status map.

3.3.2 Interaction with SNMP Agents

Three mechanisms are used for resource monitoring at the GridRM Gateway:
1. The direct result of a consumer request; if the request was for real-time information, resources are queried directly. Results are cached and returned to the requester.
2. Resource monitoring by polling. This implies repeated queries of resource attributes over some time period at a specific frequency. The user can choose to store polled results in the Gateway's database (for later viewing) and/or receive results directly as they are obtained from the resource.
3. Events produced by monitored resources. These are captured in a database for later analysis. Users must subscribe to events in order to receive specific resource event-notifications, within their user interface, in real-time.

3.3.3 The SQL Database

The Gateway is configured with a relational database for storing resource monitoring information, and general site metadata. The availability of remote Gateways and other general runtime conditions are logged within the database so that an event trace of the environment can be provided for GridRM administration purposes. The database also caches results when local resources are probed for status information.

3.3.4 Resource Monitoring Agent Types

A key GridRM criterion is to reduce the amount of administration required to monitor diverse resources; in particular, it is not desirable to install monitoring daemons on all resources. The Simple Network Monitoring Protocol (SNMP) has been chosen to provide performance information, as it is pervasive across a large range of heterogeneous resources. The use of SNMP does not preclude other monitoring protocols and the GridRM Gateway's design is flexible enough to allow other approaches to be used concurrently. However, a metadata mapping is required between different monitoring protocols, so that regardless of the source, data meaning and equivalence are consistent.

3.3.5 The GridRM User Interface

The GridRM interface uses a Java Swing-based Applet to provide a seamless view of monitored data across the Grid. Any number of clients can use the GridRM concurrently and the user interface can be downloaded from any GridRM Gateway within the virtual organisation (if the nearest Gateway is unavailable, a user can simply choose another server to download the user interface from).

After initialisation, users are presented with a graphical map showing the status of GridRM Gateways. Examples of a prototype user interface can be found at [10][11]. A coloured icon represents each site's location and shows the status of Gateways and other key resources. Selecting an icon reveals detailed monitoring information for the chosen site. A hierarchy of maps will present different views from the global to local level.

The user interface allows resources to be monitored in real-time. The user can directly probe resources, register for event notifications and schedule historical data capture for analysis later.

3.4 Security

At the global GridRM level, security is based on the GSA security model. At the local GridRM level the user interface communicates with the Gateway using encrypted HTTP connections. Users are required to enter a password/certificate when logging into the user interface.

4. Conclusions

GridRM is an open source, generic, distributed, resource-monitoring system for Grid environments. GridRM is composed of a global and local layer. The global layer permits GridRM Gateways to exchange monitoring data between Grid sites in a scalable and secure manner, using a combination of subscription based event notification and direct requests for information. The local layer operates within an individual Grid site providing a mechanism to monitor management and performance information from local site resources. Gateways collaborate (at the global level) to provide a consistent view of the performance of the Grid.

The complexity of gathering resource information from diverse Grid sites is hidden behind a Web-based (Java applet) interface that seamlessly combines monitoring information from remote sites. The user interface combines all site information within a consistent view; a user can connect to any GridRM Gateway within the virtual organisation and always see a consistent representation of all related Grid resources.

To date an early Grid monitoring prototype has been produced. Based on these experiences, and the architecture described in this paper, an enhanced GridRM prototype is under construction. Details of our experiences with the new prototype (for example, request processing performance, distributed session management and failure recovery issues) will be reported in later papers.

References

[1] Global Grid Forum, http://www.gridforum.org/
[2] B. Tierney, et al, Grid Monitoring Architecture, Working Document, January 2002, http://www-didc.lbl.gov/GGF-PERF/GMA-WG/papers/GWD-GP-16-2.pdf
[3] The Globus Heartbeat Monitor, http://www-fp.globus.org/hbm/heartbeat_spec.html
[4] Network Weather Service, http://nws.cs.ucsb.edu/, 7th June 2002.
[5] The NetLogger Toolkit: End-to-End Monitoring and Analysis of Distributed Systems, DIDC, Lawrence Berkley National Laboratory http://www-didc.lbl.gov/NetLogger/, 5th June 2002.
[6] Scalable Performance Tools (Pablo Toolkit), Department of Computer Science, University of Illinois at Urbana-Champaign, USA, http://www-pablo.cs.uiuc.edu/Project/Pablo/ScalPerfToolsOverview.htm, June 29th 1999.
[7] Remos: Resource Monitoring for Network-Aware Applications, http://www-2.cs.cmu.edu/~cmcl/remulac/remos.html, April 2002.
[8] Java Agents for Monitoring and Management, DIDCG, Lawrence Berkeley National Laboratory, http://www-didc.lbl.gov/JAMM/, 6th July 2000.
[9] M.A. Baker and G. Smith, GridRM: A Resource Monitoring System for the Grid, DSG Preprint, August 2002, http://homer.csm.port.ac.uk/publications/research/gridrm/gridrm-arch.pdf.
[10] M.A. Baker and G. Smith, A Prototype Grid-site Monitoring System, Version 1, DSG Technical Report 2002.01, http://homer.csm.port.ac.uk/publications/ technical/reports /grid/DSGmonitoring.pdf, January 2002.
[11] M.A. Baker and G. Smith, Grid Monitor Applet: Prototype 1, online demonstration, http://homer.csm.port.ac.uk:8088/MonitorServlet/GridMonitorApplet.html,   November 2002.

Overview of GridRPC: A Remote Procedure Call API for Grid Computing [*]

Keith Seymour[1], Hidemoto Nakada[5,6], Satoshi Matsuoka[6,7], Jack Dongarra[1], Craig Lee[4], and Henri Casanova[2,3]

[1] Department of Computer Science, University of Tennessee, Knoxville
[2] San Diego Supercomputer Center
[3] Dept. of Computer Science and Engineering, University of California, San Diego
[4] Computer Systems Research Dept., The Aerospace Corp., El Segundo, California
[5] National Institute of Advanced Industrial Science and Technology (AIST)
[6] Tokyo Institute of Technology
[7] National Institute of Informatics

Abstract. This paper discusses preliminary work on standardizing and implementing a remote procedure call (RPC) mechanism for grid computing. The GridRPC API is designed to address the lack of a standardized, portable, and simple programming interface. Our initial work on GridRPC shows that client access to existing grid computing systems such as NetSolve and Ninf can be unified via a common API, a task that has proven to be problematic in the past.

1 Introduction

Although Grid computing is regarded as a viable next-generation computing infrastructure, its widespread adoption is still hindered by several factors, one of which is the question "how do we program on the Grid (in an easy manner)". By all means there have been various attempts to provide a programming model and a corresponding system or a language appropriate for the Grid. Many such efforts have been collected and catalogued by the Advanced Programming Models Research Group of the Global Grid Forum [1]. One particular programming model that has proven to be viable is an RPC mechanism tailored for the Grid, or "GridRPC". Although at a very high level view the programming model provided by GridRPC is that of standard RPC plus asynchronous coarse-grained parallel tasking, in practice there are a variety of features that will largely hide the dynamicity, insecurity, and instability of the Grid from the programmers. As such, GridRPC allows not only enabling individual applications to be distributed, but also can serve as the basis for even higher-level software substrates such as distributed, scientific components on the Grid. Moreover, recent work [2] has shown that GridRPC could be effectively built upon future Grid software based on Web Services such as OGSA [3].

[*] This work funded in part by a grant from the NSF EIA-9975015.

M. Parashar (Ed.): GRID 2002, LNCS 2536, pp. 274–278, 2002.

This work was motivated by earlier attempts to achieve interoperability between by two systems that provide *network-enabled services*, namely NetSolve [4] and Ninf [5]. This proved to be difficult, indicating the need for a more unified effort to understand the requirements of a GridRPC model and API. This is reported in the next section.

2   The GridRPC Model and API

Function Handles and Session IDs. Two fundamental objects in the GridRPC model are *function handles* and the *session IDs*. The function handle represents a mapping from a function name to an instance of that function on a particular server. Once a particular function-to-server mapping has been established all RPC calls using that function handle will be executed on the server specified in that binding. A session ID is an identifier representing a particular non-blocking RPC call.

Initializing and Finalizing Functions. The initialize and finalize functions are similar to the MPI initialize and finalize calls. Client GridRPC calls before initialization or after finalization will fail.

– grpc_initialize reads the configuration file and initializes the modules.
– grpc_finalize releases any resources being used by GridRPC.

Remote Function Handle Management Functions. The *function handle management* group of functions allows creating and destroying function handles.

– grpc_function_handle_default creates a handle using the default server.
– grpc_function_handle_init creates a handle with a user-specified server.
– grpc_function_handle_destruct frees the memory for the specified handle.
– grpc_get_handle returns the handle corresponding to the given session ID.

GridRPC Call Functions. The four GridRPC call functions may be categorized by a combination of two properties: blocking behavior and calling sequence. A call may be either blocking (synchronous) or non-blocking (asynchronous) and it may use either a variable number of arguments (like printf) or an *argument stack* calling sequence (see Section 2).

– grpc_call makes a blocking call (variable argument list).
– grpc_call_async makes a non-blocking call (variable argument list).
– grpc_call_argstack makes a blocking call (argument stack).
– grpc_call_argstack_async makes a non-blocking call (argument stack).

Asynchronous GridRPC Control and Wait Functions. The following functions allow probing the status or waiting for completion of previously submitted non-blocking requests. The wait calls allow an application to express desired non-deterministic completion semantics to the underlying system, rather than repeatedly polling on a set of sessions IDs.

- grpc_probe checks whether the asynchronous GridRPC call has completed.
- grpc_cancel cancels the specified asynchronous GridRPC call.
- grpc_wait blocks until the specified non-blocking request completes.
- grpc_wait_and waits for *all* of the non-blocking requests in a given set.
- grpc_wait_or waits for *any* of the non-blocking requests in a given set.
- grpc_wait_all waits for *all* previously issued non-blocking requests.
- grpc_wait_any waits for *any* previously issued non-blocking request.

Error Reporting Functions. The following error reporting functions provide error codes and human-readable error descriptions.

- grpc_perror prints the error string associated with the last GridRPC call.
- grpc_error_string returns the error description string, given an error code.
- grpc_get_error returns the error code for a given non-blocking request.
- grpc_get_last_error returns the error code for the last invoked call.

Argument Stack Functions. With the following argument stack interface it is possible to construct the arguments to a function call at run-time.

- grpc_arg_stack_new creates a new argument stack.
- grpc_arg_stack_push_arg pushes the specified argument onto the stack.
- grpc_arg_stack_pop_arg removes the top element from the stack.
- grpc_arg_stack_destruct frees the memory for the specified argument stack.

3   Implementations

3.1   GridRPC over NetSolve

NetSolve [4] is a client-server system which provides remote access to hardware and software resources through a variety of client interfaces, such as C, Fortran, and Matlab. Since NetSolve's mode of operation is in terms of RPC-style function calls, it provides much of the infrastructure needed to implement GridRPC.

Overview of NetSolve. A NetSolve system consists of three entities, as illustrated in Figure 1. The *Client*, which requests remote execution of some function (through C, Fortran, or an interactive program such as Matlab or Mathematica). The *Server* executes functions on behalf of the clients. The server hardware can range in complexity from a uniprocessor to a MPP system and similarly the functions executed by the server can be arbitrarily complex. The *Agent* is the focal point of the NetSolve system. It maintains a list of all available servers and performs resource selection for all client requests as well as ensuring load balancing of the servers.

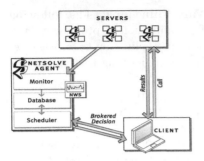

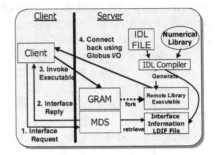

Fig. 1. Overview of NetSolve.   **Fig. 2. Overview of Ninf-G.**

Using NetSolve to Implement GridRPC. Currently we have a full implementation of the GridRPC API running on top of the NetSolve system. An important factor in enabling the implementation of GridRPC in NetSolve is the strong similarity of their APIs. Besides this similarity, NetSolve has several properties that make it an attractive choice for implementing GridRPC: fault-tolerance, load-balancing, and security.

3.2   GridRPC over Ninf

Overview of Ninf-G. Ninf-G is a re-implementation of the Ninf system [5] on top of the Globus Toolkit. The Globus toolkit provides a reference implementation of standard (or subject to proposed standardization) protocols and APIs for Grid computing. Globus serves as a solid and common platform for implementing higher-level middleware and programming tools, etc., ensuring interoperability amongst such high-level components, one of which is Ninf-G. Figure 2 shows an overview of the Ninf-G system in this regard.

Ninf-G is designed focusing on simplicity. In contrast with NetSolve, Ninf-G does not provide fault detection, recovery or load-balancing by itself. Instead, Ninf-G assumes that backend queuing system, such as Condor, takes responsibility for these functionality. Ninf-G fully deploys Globus Security Infrastructure. It means that not only all the components are protected properly, but also they can utilize other Globus components, such as GridFTP servers, seamlessly and securely.

Using Ninf-G to Implement GridRPC. As in NetSolve, the Ninf-G design allows direct support for the GridRPC model and API. The steps in making an actual Ninf-G GridRPC call can be broken down into those shown in Figure 2.

1. *Retrieval of interface information and executable pathname.*
2. *MDS sends back the requested information.*
3. *Invoking remote executable.*
4. *Remote executable callbacks to the client.*

4 Related Work and Conclusions

We have presented preliminary work in defining a model and API for a grid-aware RPC mechanism. The concept of Remote Procedure Call (RPC) has been widely used in distributed computing and distributed systems for many years. Previous work in this area has focused on RPC mechanisms for single processors, tightly-coupled homogeneous processors, and also distributed objects, such as CORBA and Java RMI. The work reported here focuses on RPC functionality that meets the needs of scientific computing among loosely-coupled heterogeneous systems over wide-area networks, while allowing multiple implementations. While the NetSolve and Ninf implementations are reported here, the GridRPC API does not preclude the internal use of XML-based protocols since this is not exposed through the API. Since a more complete discussion is beyond the scope of this short paper, the interested reader is referred to [6].

While the model and API presented here is a first-step towards a general GridRPC capability, there are certainly a number of outstanding issues regarding wide-spread deployment and use. Quite briefly these include *discovery, metadata schemas, scheduling* (including the *co-scheduling* of multiple GridRPCs), and *workflow management* among multiple servers. Transitive and composible *fault-tolerance* and *security* will also have to be provided across a potentially distributed call-tree of GridRPCs. The development of a practical, basic GridRPC capability, however, will produce a body of experience that will establish the priorities for such future work.

References

1. C. Lee, S. Matsuoka, D. Talia, A. Sussman, M. Mueller, G. Allen, and J. Saltz. A Grid Programming Primer. http://www.gridforum.org/7_APM/APS.htm, submitted to the Global Grid Forum, August 2001.
2. Satoshi Shirasuna, Hidemoto Nakada, Satoshi Matsuoka, and Satoshi Sekiguchi. Evaluating Web Services Based Implementations of GridRPC. In *Proc. of HPDC11*, pages 237–245, 2002.
3. Ian Foster, Carl Kesselman, Jeffrey Nick, and Steven Tuecke. The Physiology of the Grid: An Open Grid Services Architecture for Distributed Systems Integration. http://www.globus.org/ogsa, January 2002.
4. D. Arnold, S. Agrawal, S. Blackford, J. Dongarra, M. Miller, K. Sagi, Z. Shi, and S. Vadhiyar. Users' Guide to NetSolve V1.4. Computer Science Dept. Technical Report CS-01-467, University of Tennessee, Knoxville, TN, July 2001. See also http://icl.cs.utk.edu/netsolve.
5. Hidemoto Nakada, Mitsuhisa Sato, and Satoshi Sekiguchi. Design and Implementations of Ninf: towards a Global Computing Infrastructure. In *Future Generation Computing Systems, Metacomputing Issue*, volume 15, pages 649–658, 1999. See also http://ninf.apgrid.org.
6. K. Seymour, N. Hakada, S. Matsuoka, J. Dongarra, C. Lee, and H. Casanova. GridRPC: A Remote Procedure Call API for Grid Computing (long version). http://www.eece.unm.edu/~apm/docs/APM_GridRPC_0702.pdf, July 2002.

Distributed Query Processing on the Grid

Jim Smith[1], Anastasios Gounaris[2], Paul Watson[1], Norman W. Paton[2],
Alvaro A.A. Fernandes[2], and Rizos Sakellariou[2]

[1] Department of Computing Science, University of Newcastle upon Tyne,
Newcastle, NE1 7RU, UK
{Jim.Smith, Paul.Watson}@newcastle.ac.uk
[2] Department of Computer Science, University of Manchester,
Manchester, M13 9PL, UK
{gounaris, norm, alvaro, rizos}@cs.man.ac.uk

Abstract. Distributed query processing (DQP) has been widely used
in data intensive applications where data of relevance to users is stored
in multiple locations. This paper argues: (i) that DQP can be important
in the Grid, as a means of providing high-level, declarative languages
for integrating data access and analysis; and (ii) that the Grid provides
resource management facilities that are useful to developers of DQP systems. As well as discussing and illustrating how DQP technologies can
be deployed within the Grid, the paper describes a prototype implementation of a DQP system running over Globus.

1   Introduction

To date, most work on data storage, access and transfer on the Grid has focused
on files. We do not take issue with this – files are clearly central to many applications, and it is reasonable for Grid middleware developers to seek to put in
place effective facilities for file management and archiving. However, database
management systems provide many facilities that are recognised as being important to Grid environments, both for managing Grid metadata (e.g., [3]) and for
supporting the storage and analysis of application data (e.g., [18]).

In any distributed environment there are inevitably multiple related data
resources, which, for example, provide complementary or alternative capabilities. Where there is more than one database supported within a distributed
environment, it is straightforward to envisage higher-level services that assist
users in making use of several databases within a single application. For example, in bioinformatics, it is commonly the case that different kinds of data (e.g.,
DNA sequence, protein sequence, protein structure, transcriptome) are stored
in different, specialist repositories, even though they are often inter-related in
analyses.

There are perhaps two principal functionalities associated with distributed
database access and use – distributed transaction management and distributed
query processing (DQP) [12]. This paper is concerned with DQP on the Grid,

M. Parashar (Ed.): GRID 2002, LNCS 2536, pp. 279–290, 2002.

and both: (i) discusses the role that DQP might play within the Grid; and (ii) describes a prototype infrastructure for supporting distributed query optimisation and evaluation within a Grid setting.

There is no universally accepted classification of DQP systems. However, with a view to categorising previous work, we note that DQP is found in several contexts: in distributed database systems, where an infrastructure supports the deliberate distribution of a database with some measure of central control [13]; in federated database systems, which allow multiple autonomous databases to be integrated for use within an application [11]; and in query-based middlewares, where a query language is used as the programming mechanism for expressing requests over multiple wrapped data sources (e.g., [9]). This paper is most closely related to the third category, in that we consider the user of DQP for integrating various Grid resources, including (but not exclusively) database systems.

Another important class of system in which queries run over data that is distributed over a number of physical resources is parallel databases. In a parallel database, the most common pattern is that data from a centrally controlled database is distributed over the nodes of a parallel machine. Parallel databases are now a mature technology, and experience shows that parallel query processing techniques are able to provide cost-effective scaleability for data-intensive applications (e.g., [15]). This paper, as well as advocating DQP as a data integration mechanism for the Grid, also shows that techniques from parallel database systems can be applied in support of data access and analysis for Grid applications.

The claims of this paper with respect to DQP and the Grid are as follows:

1. In providing integrated access to multiple data resources, DQP in and of itself is an important functionality for data intensive Grid applications.
2. The fact that certain database languages can integrate operation calls with data access and combination operations means that DQP can provide a mechanism for integrating data and computational Grid services.
3. Given (1) and (2), DQP can be seen to provide a generic, declarative, high-level language interface for the Grid.
4. By extending technologies from parallel databases, implicit parallelism can be provided within DQP environments on the Grid.

The paper makes concrete how these claims can be supported in practice by describing a prototype DQP system, Polar*, which runs over the Globus toolkit, and illustrates the prototype using an application from bioinformatics.

The remainder of this paper is structured as follows. Section 2 presents the principal components of a DQP system for the Grid, in particular indicating how this relates to other Grid services. Sections 3 and 4 describe, respectively, how queries are planned and evaluated within the architecture. Section 5 illustrates the proposal using an example involving bioinformatics databases and analysis tools. Finally, Section 6 presents some conclusions and pointers to future work.

2   Architecture

The two key functions of any DQP system are query compilation and query execution. In the Polar* system described in this paper, both these components are based on those designed for the Polar project [16]. Polar is a parallel object database server that runs on a shared-nothing parallel machine. Polar* exploits Polar software components where possible, but as Polar* must provide DQP over data repositories distributed across a Grid, there are a number of key differences between query processing in the two systems. These include:

1. The data dictionary must describe remote data storage and analysis resources available on the Grid – queries act over a diverse collection of application stores and analysis programs.
2. The scheduler must take account of the computational facilities available on the Grid, along with their variable capabilities – queries are evaluated over a diverse collection of computational resources.
3. The data stores and analysis tools over which queries are expressed must be wrapped so that they look consistent to the query evaluator.
4. The query evaluator must use Grid authentication, resource allocation and communication protocols – Polar* runs over Globus, using MPICH-G [5].

A representative query over bioinformatics resources is used as a running example throughout the paper. The query accesses two databases: the Gene Ontology Database *GO* (*www.geneontology.org*) stored in a MySQL (*www.mysql.com*) RDBMS; and *GIMS* [2], a genome database running on a Polar parallel object database server. The query also calls a local installation of the BLAST sequence similarity program (*www.ncbi.nlm.nih.gov/BLAST/*) which, given a protein sequence, returns a set of structs containing protein IDs and similarity scores. The query identifies proteins that are similar to human proteins with the GO term *8372*:

```
select p.proteinId, Blast(p.sequence)
from   p in protein, t in proteinTerm
where  t.termID='8372' and p.proteinId=t.proteinId
```

In the query, *protein* is a class extent in *GIMS*, while *proteinTerm* is a table in *GO*. Therefore, as illustrated in Figure 1, the infrastructure initiates two sub-queries: one on GIMS, and the other on GO. The results of these sub-queries are then joined in a computation running on the Grid. Finally, each protein in the result is used as a parameter to the call to BLAST.

One key opportunity created by the Grid is in the flexibility it offers on resource allocation decisions. In the example in Figure 1, machines need to be found to run both the join operator, and the operation call. If there is a danger that the join will be the bottleneck in the query, then it could be allocated to a system with large amounts of main memory so as to reduce IO costs associated with the management of intermediate results. Further, a parallel algorithm could be used to implement the join, and so a set of machines acquired on the Grid

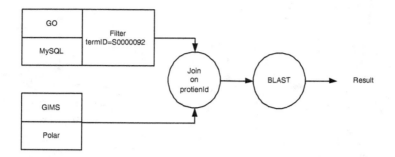

Fig. 1. Evaluating the example query.

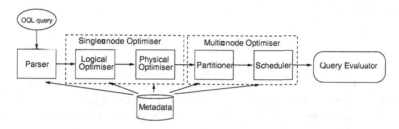

Fig. 2. The components of Polar* query compiler.

could each contribute to its execution. Similarly, the BLAST calls could be speeded-up by allocating a set of machines, each of which can run BLAST on a subset of the proteins.

The information needed to make these resource allocation decisions comes from two sources. Firstly, the query optimiser estimates the cost of executing each part of a query and so identifies performance critical operations. Secondly, the Globus Grid infrastructure provides information on available resources. Once a mapping of operations to resources has been chosen, the single sign-on capabilities of the Grid Security Infrastructure simplify the task of gaining access to those resources.

3   Query Planning

Polar* adopts the model and query language of the ODMG object database standard [1]. As such, all resource wrappers must return data using structures that are consistent with the ODMG model. Queries are written using the ODMG standard query language, OQL.

The main components of the query compiler are shown in Figure 2. The Polar* optimiser has responsibility for generating an efficient execution plan for the declarative OQL query which may access data and operations stored on many nodes. To do this, it follows the two-step optimisation paradigm, which is popular for both parallel and distributed database systems [12]. In the first phase, the single node optimiser produces a query plan as if it was to run on one

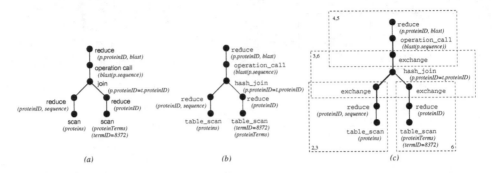

Fig. 3. Example query: (a) single-node logical plan, (b) single-node physical plan (c) multi-node physical plan.

processor. In the second phase, the sequential query plan is divided into several partitions or subplans which are allocated machine resources by the scheduler.

Figure 3(a) depicts a plan for the example query expressed in the logical algebra of Fegaras and Maier [4], which is the basis for query optimisation and evaluation in Polar*. The logical optimiser performs various transformations on the query, such as fusion of multiple selection operations and pushing *project*s (called *reduce* in [4] and in the figures) as close to *scan*s as possible.

The physical optimiser transforms the optimised logical expressions into physical plans by selecting algorithms that implement each of the operations in the logical plan (Figure 3(b)). For example, in the presence of indices, the optimiser prefers *index_scans* to *seq_scans*. Operation calls, like the call to BLAST, are encapsulated by the *operation_call* physical operator. For each OQL query, many physical plans are produced, and the physical optimiser ranks these according to a cost model.

A single-node plan is transformed into a multi-node one by inserting parallelisation operators into the query plan, i.e., Polar* follows the operator model of parallelisation [7]. The *exchange* operator encapsulates flow control, data distribution and inter-process communication. The partitioner firstly identifies whether an operator requires its input data to be partitioned by a specific attribute when executed on multiple processors (for example, so that the potentially matching tuples from the operands of a join can be compared [10]). Secondly, it checks whether data repartitioning is required, i.e., whether data needs to be exchanged among the processors, for example for joining or for submitting to an *operation_call* on a specific machine.

The *exchange*s are placed immediately below the operators that require the data to be repartitioned. For each *exchange* operator, a data distribution policy needs to be defined. Currently, the policies Polar* supports include *round_robin*, *hash_distribution* and *range_partitioning*. A multi-node query plan is shown in Figure 3(c), where the *exchange*s partition the initial plan into many subplans. The physical algebra extended with *exchange* constitutes the parallel algebra used by Polar*.

The final phase of query optimisation is to allocate machine resources to each of the subplans derived from the partitioner, a task carried out by the scheduler in Figure 2 using an algorithm based on that of Rahm and Marek [14]. For running the example query, six machines were available. Three of the machines host databases (numbers *2* and *3* for the GIMS database, and *6* for the GO database). For the *hash_join*, the scheduler tries to ensure that the relation used to construct the hash table can fit into main memory, for example, by allocating more nodes to the join until predicted memory requirements are satisfied. In the example, nodes *3* and *6* are allocated to run the *hash_join*. As some of the data is already on these nodes, this helps to reduce the total network traffic.

The data dictionary records which nodes support BLAST, and thus the scheduler is able to place the *operation_call* for BLAST on suitable nodes (*4* and *5* in Figure 3(c)). The scheduler uses a heuristic that may choose not to use an available evaluator if the reduction in computation time would be less than the increase in the time required to transfer data (e.g., it has decided not to use machine *1* in the example).

4   Query Evaluation

4.1   Evaluating the Parallel Algebra

The Polar* evaluator uses the *iterator* model of Graefe [8], which is widely seen as the model of choice for parallel query processing. In this model, each operator in the physical algebra implements an interface comprising three operations: *open()*, *next()* and *close()*. These operations form the glue between the nodes of a query plan. An individual node calls *open()* on each of its input nodes to prompt them to begin generating their result collections. Successive calls to *next()* retrieve every tuple from that result collection. A special *eof* tuple marks the end of a result collection. After receiving an *eof* from an input, a node calls *close()* on that input to prompt it to shut itself down.

We note that although the term *tuple* is used to describe the result of a call to *next()*, a tuple in this case is not a flat structure, but rather a recursive structure whose attributes can themselves be structured and/or collection valued.

To illustrate the iterator model, Figure 4 sketches an iterator-based implementation of a *hash_join* operator. *open()* retrieves the whole of the left hand operand of the join and builds a hash table, by hashing on the attributes for which equality is tested in the join condition. In *next()*, tuples are received from the right input collection and used to probe the hash table until a match is found and all predicates applying to the join result are satisfied, whereupon the tuple is returned as a result.

The iterator model can support a high degree of parallelism. Sequences of operators can support *pipeline parallelism*, i.e., when two operators in the same query plan are independent, they can execute concurrently. Furthermore, when invocations of an operation on separate tuples in a collection are independent, the operation can be partitioned over multiple machines.

```
class HashJoin: public Operator {
private:
    Tuple *t; HashTable h; Predicate predicate;
    Operator *left; set<Attribute> hash_atts_left;
    Operator *right; set<Attribute> hash_atts_right;
public:
    virtual void open() {
        left->open(); t = left->next();
        while (! t->is_eof()) {
            h.insert(t, hash_atts_left); t = left->next();
        }
        left->close(); right->open(); t = right->next();
    }
    virtual Tuple *next() {
        while (! t->is_eof()) {
            if (h.probe(t, hash_atts_right) && t->satisfies(predicate))
                return t;
            delete t; t = right->next();
        }
        return t;
    }
    virtual void close() {
        right->close(); h.clear();
    }
};
```

Fig. 4. Implementing hash-join as an *iterator*.

Whereas data manipulation operators tend to run in a request-response mode, *exchange* differs in that, once *open()* has been called on it, the producers can run independently of the consumers. Because tuples are complex structures, they are flattened for communication into buffers whose size can be configured. Underlying an instance of *exchange* is a collection of threads managing pools of such buffers so as to constrain flow to a lagging consumer, but to permit flow to a quicker consumer, within the constraints of the buffer pools. This policy is very conveniently implemented in MPI [17] where the tightly defined message completion semantics permit the actual feedback to be hidden within its layer. This use of MPI has enabled the Polar *exchange* to port easily to MPICH-G [5], for use with Globus.

Since MPICH-G is layered above Globus, a parallel query can be run as a parallel MPI program over a collection of wide area distributed machines, oblivious of the difficulties inherent in such meta-computing, which are handled by the underlying Globus services. A parallel program running over such a Grid environment has to find suitable computational resources, achieve concurrent login, transfer of executables and other required files, and startup of processes on the separate resources. In the Polar* prototype, concurrent login to separate accounts is achieved through GSI, and executable staging across wide

```
class PhysicalOperationCall: public PhysicalOperator {
private:
    string signature;                // operation to call
    list<expr*> expression;          // select args from tuple
    list<genform*> *predicate;       // predicate on output tuple
    int key;                         // from cross ref in oplib
    vector<concrete_object*> arg;    // sized appropriately
    class operation_library_stub;    // functions etc in shared library
    operation_library_stub *stub;
public:
    virtual void open() {
        input->open();          // input is pointer to operator
        const d_Operation *oper = search_metadata(signature);
        stub = load_operation_library(oper->operation_library_name());
        key = stub->xref(signature);
    }
    virtual tuple_object *next() {
        while (! t->eof()) {
            tuple_object *t = input->next();
            for (list<expr>::iterator it = expression.begin();
                 it != expression.end(); it++)
                arg[i+1] = t->evaluate(*it);  // leave arg[0] for result
            stub->call_operation(key, arg); t->insert(arg[0]);
            if (t->evaluate(predicate)) return t;
        }
        return t;
    }
    virtual void close() {
        unload_operation_library(stub); input->close();
    }
}
```

Fig. 5. The iterator-based implementation of external operation calls.

area connections through GASS, but all these features are accessed through the
MPICH-G interface rather than in a lower level way.

4.2 Accessing Computational and Data Resources during Query Evaluation

From the point of view of the evaluator, both database and analysis operations
referred to within a query are external resources, which must be wrapped to
enable consistent passing of parameters and returning of results during query
evaluation.

To support access to external tools such as BLAST, Polar* implements, in
iterator style, the *operation_call* operator in Figure 5. While concerns regarding
the integrity of the evaluator lead to an isolation of such an operation call within
a separate user context in some databases, the view taken so far in Polar* is that

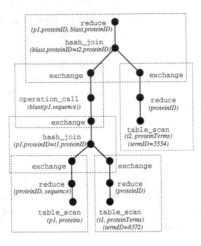

Fig. 6. Query plan for the example in Section 5.

higher performance is achievable when a user can in good faith code an operation to be executed in the server's own context. Thus, such operations are linked into dynamically loadable modules, with stub code generated by the Polar* system to perform the translation of types between tuple format and the format of the programming language used to implement the operation. At runtime, *operation_call* loads the appropriate module in its *open()* call and unloads it in *close()*. Within *next()*, the operator passes attributes from the current tuple to the stub code which assembles required parameters, makes the call and translates the result, which may be collection valued and/or of structured type, back to tuple format before passing it back as the result of the operator.

By making such an application available for use in a Polar* schema, the owner does not provide unrestricted, and thereby unmanageable, access on the internet. By contrast, since Polar* sits above Globus, a resource provider must have granted access rights to a user, in the form of a local login, which they can revoke. Subsequent accesses, while convenient to the user through the single sign-on support of Globus, are authenticated through the GSI.

A specific case that requires access to external operations is the provision of access to external, i.e. non Polar*, repositories. For example, the runtime interface to a repository includes an *external_scan* operator, which exports an *iterator* style interface in common with other operators. However, below the level of *external_scan* the interface to an arbitrary external repository requires special coding. When an external collection is defined in the schema, the system generates the definition of a class, which has the three operations of the *iterator* interface plus other operations to gather statistics and set attributes of the interface such as a query language and the syntax of results generated by the external repository.

The generated class is the template within which a user can implement an *iterator* style interface to the external repository. The mechanisms used are at the discretion of the user, but the pattern in which the operations of this system-defined class are called is defined by the Polar* system. Fixed attributes, such as the syntax of result tuples returned, are set at the time the completed access class is registered with the Polar* system. Because the access class contains in its instance state a reference to the specification of the wrapped collection in the data dictionary, application data statistics gathered from the particular external store can be written into the data dictionary. The *open()*, *next()* and *close()* operations are simply called by *external_scan* in the usual iterator-based style. However, the results returned by the *next()* operation are translated from the selected syntax into Polar* tuples.

In the running example, the *GO* database is implemented using MySQL, so access to it is through such a system-specified user-defined class of operations. A delegated sub-query such as the access to *proteinTerm* tuples is expressed in SQL, and the results are formatted within the *MySQLAccess* class in Object Interchange Format (OIF)[1]. The *next()* operation of the *external_scan* operator parses each OIF instance to construct tuples which that returned as results to the evaluator.

5   Example from Bioinformatics

The example query introduced in Section 2 is straightforward, but has illustrated how DQP can be used to provide optimisation and evaluation of declarative requests over resources on the Grid. We note that the alternative of writing such a request using lower-level programming models, such as MPICII-G or a COG kit [19] could be quite time consuming. We note also that as the complexity of a request increases, it becomes increasingly difficult for a programmer to make decisions as to the most efficient way to express a request.

For example, a more complex request over the same resources as before could request information about the proteins with the GO term *5554* which are similar to the proteins with the GO term *8372*. In Polar*, such a request can be expressed as follows:

```
select p1.proteinId, p2.proteinId
from   p1 in protein, t1 in proteinTerm,
       p2 in Blast(p1.sequence), t2 in proteinTerm
where  p1.proteinId=t1.proteinId and t1.termID='8372' and
       p2.proteinId=t2.proteinId and t2.termID='5554'
```

This query is compiled into the parallel algebraic expression illustrated in Figure 6. The query plan is decomposed into 6 subplans, each of which is allocated to many nodes, in particular the data and CPU intensive operators like *hash-join* and *operation_call*, for which it is important to exploit parallelism. While retrieving the data from the GO database, the Polar* engine checks whether the data satisfies the condition on the *termID*. In addition, *reduce* operators are inserted before data is communicated over the network. These features are key to reducing the communication cost.

---

[1] OIF is a standard textual representation for ODMG objects.

6   Conclusions

One of the main hopes for the Grid is that it will encourage the publication of scientific and other data in a more open manner than is currently the case. If this occurs then it is likely that some of the greatest advances will be made by combining data from separate, distributed sources to produce new results. The data that applications wish to combine will have been created by different researchers or organisations that will often have made local, independent decisions about both the best database paradigm and design for their data. The role of DQP in such a setting is to provide high-level, declarative facilities for describing requests over multiple data stores and analysis facilities.

The ease with which DQP allows such requests to be phrased has been illustrated through example queries in Sections 2 and 5. Developing efficient execution plans for such tasks using existing Grid programming environments would take a skilled developer a significant time. We believe that DQP can serve an important role in Grid environments by: (i) increasing the variety of people who can form requests over multiple Grid resources; (ii) reducing development times for certain categories of Grid programming task; and (iii) enabling typical requests to be evaluated efficiently as a result of system-supported query optimisation and support for implicit parallelism.

This paper has described the Polar* prototype DQP system for the Grid. The prototype has been implemented over Globus middleware using MPICH-G, and experiments have been conducted over bioinformatics databases and analysis tools at the authors' geographically remote sites. Future work will: (i) extend the range of physical operators in the algebra; (ii) increase the amount of system information used by the scheduler in query planning; (iii) explore the development of more powerful scheduling algorithms; and (iv) conduct performance evaluations over more and larger databases. We also plan to evolve the Polar* system to be compliant with the emerging Open Grid Services Architecture [6], and to make use of standard service interfaces to databases [20] to reduce the cost of wrapper development.

Acknowledgements

This work was funded by the EPSRC Distributed Information Management Initiative and the UK e-Science Core Programme, whose support we are pleased to acknowledge. We are also grateful for the contribution of Sandra Sampaio, whose work on Polar has been built upon extensively in Polar*.

References

1. R.G.G. Cattell and D.K. Barry. *The Object Database Standard: ODMG 3.0*. Morgan Kaufmann, 2000.
2. M. Cornell, N.W. Paton, S. Wu, C.A. Goble, C.J. Miller, P. Kirby, K. Eilbeck, A. Brass, A. Hayes, and S.G. Oliver. GIMS – A Data Warehouse for Storage and Analysis of Genome Sequence and Functional Data. In *Proc. 2nd IEEE Symposium on Bioinformatics and Bioengineering (BIBE)*, pages 15–22. IEEE Press, 2001.

3. P. Dinda and B. Plale. A unified relational approach to grid information services. Technical Report GWD-GIS-012-1, Global Grid Forum, 2001.
4. L. Fegaras and D. Maier. Optimizing object queries using an effective calculus. *ACM Transactions on Database Systems*, 24(4):457–516, December 2000.
5. I Foster and N. T. Karonis. A Grid-Enabled MPI: Message Passing in Heterogeneous Distributed Computing Systems. In *Proc. Supercomputing (SC)*. IEEE Computer Society, 1998. Online at: http://www.supercomp.org/sc98/proceedings/.
6. I. Foster, C. Kesselman, J. Nick, and S. Tuecke. Grid Services for Distributed System Integration. *IEEE Computer*, 35:37–46, 2002.
7. G. Graefe. Encapsulation of parallelism in the Volcano query processing system. In *ACM SIGMOD*, pages 102–111, 1990.
8. G. Graefe. Query evaluation techniques for large databases. *ACM Computing Surveys*, 25(2):73–170, June 1993.
9. L. Haas, D. Kossmann, E.L. Wimmers, and J. Yang. Optimizing Queries Across Diverse Data Sources. In *Proc. VLDB*, pages 276–285. Morgan-Kaufmann, 1997.
10. W. Hasan and R. Motwani. Coloring away communication in parallel query optimization. In *Proceedings of the 21th VLDB Conference*, 1995.
11. D. Hsiao. Tutorial on Federated Databases and Systems. *The VLDB Journal*, 1(1):127–179, 1992.
12. D. Kossmann. The State of the Art in Distributed Query Processing. *ACM Computing Surveys*, 32(4):422–469, 2000.
13. M.T. Ozsu and P. Valduriez, editors. *Principles of Distributed Database Systems (Second Edition)*. Prentice-Hall, 1999.
14. E. Rahm and R. Marek. Dynamic multi-resource load balancing in parallel database systems. In *Proc. 21st VLDB Conf.*, pages 395–406, 1995.
15. S.F.M. Sampaio, J. Smith, N.W. Paton, and P. Watson. An Experimental Performance Evaluation of Join Algorithms for Parallel Object Databases. In R. Sakellariou et al., editors, *Proc. 7th Intl. Euro-Par Conference*, pages 280–291. Springer-Verlag, 2001.
16. J. Smith, S. F. M. Sampaio, P. Watson, and N. W. Paton. Polar: An architecture for a parallel ODMG compliant object database. In *Conference on Information and Knowledge Management (CIKM)*, pages 352–359. ACM press, 2000.
17. M. Snir, S. Otto, S. Huss-Lederman, D. Walker, and J. Dongarra. *MPI - The Complete Reference*. The MIT Press, Cambridge, Massachusetts, 1998. ISBN: 0-262-69215-5.
18. A. Szalay, P. Z. Kunszt, A. Thakar, J. Gray, and D. R. Slut. Designing and mining multi-terabyte astronomy archives: The sloan digital sky survey. In *Proc. ACM SIGMOD*, pages 451–462. ACM Press, 2000.
19. G. von Laszewski, I. Foster, J. Gawor, and P. Lane. A Java Commodity Grid Kit. *Concurrency and Computation: Practice and Experience*, 13(8-9):643–662, 2001.
20. P. Watson. Databases and the Grid. Technical Report CS-TR-755, University of Newcastle, 2001.

Using Disk Throughput Data
in Predictions of End-to-End Grid Data Transfers

Sudharshan Vazhkudai[1,2] and Jennifer M. Schopf[1]

[1] Mathematics and Computer Science Division, Argonne National Laboratory
[2] Department of Computer and Information Science, The University of Mississippi
{vazhkuda, jms}@mcs.anl.gov

Abstract. Data grids provide an environment for communities of researchers to share, replicate, and manage access to copies of large datasets. In such environments, fetching data from one of the several replica locations requires accurate predictions of end-to-end transfer times. Predicting transfer time is significantly complicated because of the involvement of several shared components, including networks and disks in the end-to-end data path, each of which experiences load variations that can significantly affect the throughput. Of these, disk accesses are rapidly growing in cost and have not been previously considered, although on some machines they can be up to 30% of the transfer time. In this paper, we present techniques to combine observations of end-to-end application behavior and disk I/O throughput load data. We develop a set of regression models to derive predictions that characterize the effect of disk load variations on file transfer times. We also include network component variations and apply these techniques to the logs of transfer data using the GridFTP server, part of the Globus Toolkit™. We observe up to 9% improvement in prediction accuracy when compared with approaches based on past system behavior in isolation.

1 Introduction

Increasingly, scientific discovery is driven by computationally intensive analyses of massive data collections. This recent trend has encouraged the research and development of sophisticated infrastructures for maintaining large data collections in a distributed, secure fashion and for improving the rapid access of large subsets of data files.

One example is in high-energy physics experiments, such as ATLAS [MMR+01] and CMS [HSS00], that have agreed on a tiered architecture [HJS+00, Holtman00] for managing and replicating the petascale data generated by the LHC experiment at CERN beginning 2006. The current architecture proposes to manage these petabytes of data, generated at CERN (Tier 0), by replicating subsets (approximately an order of magnitude reduction) across national (Tier 1) and regional (Tier 2) centers.

As data grid environments begin to be deployed and used, the amount of replication of data will likely grow rapidly as more users cache copies of datasets nearby for

M. Parashar (Ed.): GRID 2002, LNCS 2536, pp. 291–304, 2002.
© Springer-Verlag Berlin Heidelberg 2002

292   Sudharshan Vazhkudai and Jennifer M. Schopf

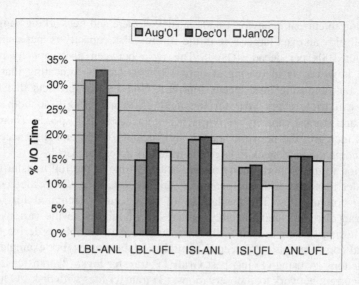

Fig. 1. Disk I/O time as a percentage of the total data transfer time for our experiments. Sites include Argonne National Laboratory (ANL), Lawrence Berkeley National Laboratory (LBL), University of Southern California's Information Sciences Institute (ISI), and University of Florida at Gainesville (UFL). Transfers include several file sizes ranging from 10 MB to 1 GB. Transfers were conducted over three distinct two-week periods.

better performance. Thus, a particular copy of a dataset will reside at multiple locations, and a choice of site to retrieve it from must be made.

In previous work [VS02, VSF02], we addressed this replica selection problem by having replica locations expose transfer performance estimates. Estimates were derived from past history of transfers (using the GridFTP server, part of the Globus Toolkit™) between sources and sinks, and by also factoring in the network link load to account for the sporadic nature of data grid transfers using regressive techniques. Our results showed prediction accuracy hovered around 15-24% error for predictors solely based on past transfer behavior, but improved 5-10% when network load variations were factored in. In this paper, we consider the effects of disk I/O as well.

The addition of disk I/O behavior in our predictions is motivated by three main factors: (1) disk I/O currently plays a large role, up to 30% on our testbed, in large data transfer times (as detailed below); (2) this role will become more important as a result of trends in disk size and network behavior; (3) and having access to additional data streams become more important as Grid environments grow, and not all resources will have the same information available about them.

In fact, we observe that disk I/O can account for up to 30% of the transfer time. In Figure 1, we show the percentage of I/O time spent on an average data transfer. We compare the cost of performing a local GridFTP read/write (source disk to device abstraction at source, essentially eliminating the network) with the wide-area transfer cost (source disk to device abstraction at sink). For these experiments, the disks on the source ends were all high-end RAID servers. On lower-end disk systems the effect would be even more significant.

In addition to current behavior, trends in disk storage and networking suggest that disk I/O will play an even larger role in the future. Disk capacity is increasing at the rate of about 100x per decade [GS00]. The ratio between disk capacity and disk throughput, however, is increasing at only 10x per decade, indicating that storage capacity is far outpacing disk speeds. Further, Gilder's law predicts that network bandwidth will triple every year for the next 25 years [GS00], so both network throughput and storage capacity are outpacing advances in disk speeds. Therefore, as link speeds increase, the network latency significantly drops and disk accesses are likely to become the bottleneck in large file transfers across the Grid.

In addition to the proportionality of the disk I/O time to the full transfer time, we must consider that data grids are potentially highly dynamic, with resources joining and leaving communities. The availability of data sources (required for obtaining forecasts) can also vary unpredictably as a result of failures in the various components, monitoring sensors and so forth. Thus, we need to be able to derive forecasts from several combinations of "currently available" data sources. For example, we can build predictions by using (1) just past GridFTP transfer logs, (2) transfer logs combined with current network load observations, (3) transfer logs with disk I/O load data, or (4) a combination of past transfer logs, network, and disk load traces. In our previous work, we investigated (1) and (2), this paper explores techniques to derive predictions for the (3) and (4).

In this paper, we extend our previous work to combine transfer log data with disk throughput data. Specifically, we develop multiple regression models, deriving predictions from past transfer logs, disk I/O, and network load data combined. Our results denote an improvement in prediction accuracy of up to 4% when using regression techniques between GridFTP transfers and disk I/O throughput data when compared with predictions based on past GridFTP behavior in isolation; we achieved a 9% improvement when combining all three data sources.

In the remainder of the paper we present related and previous work (Section 2), our prediction model (in Section 3), an evaluation of our techniques (in Section 4), and suggestions for future work (Section 5).

2 Related and Previous Work

Our goal is to obtain an accurate prediction of file transfer times between a storage system and a client. Achieving this can be challenging because numerous devices are involved in the end-to-end path between the source and the client, and the performance of each (shared) device along the end-to-end path may vary in unpredictable ways.

One approach to predicting this information is to construct performance models for each system component (CPUs at the level of cache hits and disk access, networks at the level of the individual routers, etc.) and then use these models to determine a schedule for all data transfers [SC00], similar to classical scheduling [Adve93, Cole89, CQ93, Crovella99, ML90, Schopf97, TB86, ZLP96]. In practice, however, it is often unclear how to combine this data to achieve accurate end-to-end measurements.

Also, since system components are shared, their behavior can vary in unpredictable ways [SB98]. Further, modeling individual components in a system will not capture the significant effects these components have on each other, thereby leading to inaccuracies [GT99].

Alternatively, observations from past application performance of the entire system can be used to predict end-to-end behavior, which is typically what is of interest to the user. This technique is used by Downey [Downey97] and Smith et al. [SFT98] to predict queue wait times and by numerous tools (Network Weather Service [Wolski98], NetLogger [NetLogger02], Web100 [Web100Project02], iperf [TF01], and Netperf [Jones02]) to predict the network behavior of small file transfers. We used this technique in [VSF02] but found that it had large errors because of the sporadic nature of GridFTP transfers and that we needed to be able to include additional data about current system conditions in order to improve the predictions.

In our previous work [VS02], we combined end-to-end throughput observations from past GridFTP data transfers and current network load variations, using regression models to obtain better predictions. Faerman et al. [FSW+99] addressed the issue using the NWS and adaptive linear regression models for the Storage Resource Broker [BMR+98] and SARA [SARA02]. That work compared transfer times obtained from a raw bandwidth model (*Transfer-Time=ApplicationDataSize/NWS-Probe-Bandwidth*, with 64 KB NWS probes) with predictions from regression models and observed accuracy improvements ranging from 20% to almost 100% for the sites examined. Swany and Wolski have also approached the problem by constructing cumulative distribution functions (CDF) of past history and deriving predictions from them as an alternative to regressive models. This has been demonstrated for 16 MB HTTP transfers with improved prediction accuracy when compared with their univariate prediction approach [SW02].

3   Prediction Model

In this section, we examine the various data sources we used, their relations, regressive models and our prediction algorithm.

3.1   Data Transfer Logs and Component Data

Our three data sources are GridFTP, NWS and iostat. We use a GridFTP server [AFN+01] to perform the data transfers and to log the behavior every time a transfer is made, thereby recording the end-to-end transfer behavior. Since these events are very sporadic, however, we also need to capture data about the current environment to have accurate predictions. We use the iostat disk throughput data to measure disk behavior and the Network Weather Service network probe data as an estimate of bandwidth for small data transfers.

GridFTP [AFN+01] is part of the Globus Toolkit™ [FK98, Globus02] and is widely used as a secure, high-performance data transfer protocol [ACF+02, AFN+01,

DataGrid02, GriPhyN02]. It extends standard FTP implementations with several features needed in Grid environments, such as security, parallel transfers, partial file transfers, and third party transfers. We instrumented the GT 2.0 wuftp-based GridFTP server to log the source address, file name, file size, number of parallel streams, stripes, TCP buffer size for the transfer, start and end timestamps, nature of the operation (read/write), and logical volume to/from which file was transferred. [VSF02].

The iostat tool is part of the sysstat [SYSSTAT02] system-monitoring suite. It collects disk I/O throughput data. Iostat can be configured to periodically monitor disk transfer rates, block read/write rates and so forth of all physically connected disks. We are particularly interested in the disk transfer rate that represents the throughput of a disk.

The Network Weather Service [Wolski98] monitors the behavior of various resource components by sending out lightweight probes or querying system files at regular intervals. NWS sensors exist for components such as CPU, disk, and network. We used the network bandwidth sensor with 64 KB probes to estimate the current network throughput.

In subsequent sections, we see how forecasts can be derived from these correlated data streams by using regressive techniques.

3.2   Correlation

Correlation gives a measure of the linear strength of the relationship between two variables and is often used as a test of significance before linear regression analysis is performed [Edwards84]. For our data sources, namely, GridFTP logs, iostat load, and NWS traces we computed rank-order correlation (a distribution free test) and observed moderate correlation between the variables from 0.2 to 0.7 (95% confidence interval for the correlation).

3.3   Algorithm

Our three data sources (GridFTP, disk I/O, and NWS network data) are collected exclusive of each other and rarely had same timestamps. To use common statistical techniques on the data streams, however, we need to line up the values to be considered. Hence, we must match values from these three sets such that, for each GridFTP value, we find disk I/O and network observations that were made around the same time.

For each GridFTP data point (T_G, G), we match a corresponding disk load (T_D, D) and NWS data point (T_N, N) such that T_N and T_D are the closest to T_G. By doing this, the triplet (N_i, D_j, G_k) represents an observed end-to-end GridFTP throughput (G_k) resulting from a data transfer that occurred with the disk load (D_j) and network probe value (N_i). At the end of the matching process the sequence looks like the following:

$$(N_i, D_j, G_k)(N_{i+1}, D_{j+1}, \_)...(N_{i+m}, D_{j+m}, G_{k+1}),$$

where G_k, and G_{k+1} are two successive GridFTP file transfers, N_i and N_{i+m} are NWS measurements, and D_j and D_{j+m} are disk load values that occurred in the same time-frame as the two GridFTP transfers. The sequence also consists of a number of disk load and NWS measurements between the two transfers for which there are no equivalent GridFTP values, such as $(N_{i+p}, D_{j+p}, \_)$. Note that these interspersed network and disk load values also need to be time aligned, as they seldom have same timestamps.

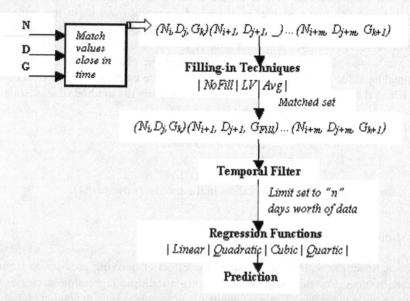

Fig. 2. Algorithm for deriving predictions from GridFTP (G), disk load (D), and NWS (N) data streams by using regression techniques.

After matching the data streams we need to address the tuples that do not have G values. Because of the sporadic nature of data grid transfers we will have more disk I/O and network data than GridFTP data. Regression models expect a one-to-one mapping between the data values, so we can either discard unaccounted network and I/O data (for which there are no equivalent GridFTP data) or fill in synthetic transfer values for the unaccounted data. We use three strategies to fill in missing values. These filling-in strategies are as follows: discard unaccounted disk I/O and network data (NoFill), use last GridFTP transfer values as a filling (LV) for unaccounted data, and use average of previous transfers as a filling (Avg) for unaccounted data. After the G values are filled in, these datasets are fed to the regression models (Figure 2).

3.4   Regressive Techniques

To predict the end-to-end GridFTP throughput and study the effect of the disk I/O component, we use standard regressive techniques. Regression provides the necessary mechanisms to analyze the impact of several independent variables (in our case, I/O traces or NWS bandwidth data) on the dependent variable (GridFTP throughput).

3.4.1 Simple Regression

In our previous work, we developed simple regression techniques between GridFTP (G) and NWS network data (N). We built a set of linear and nonlinear regression models between the two variables and derived forecasts from it. In this paper, we employ similar techniques to analyze the effect of disk I/O variations (D) on end-to-end GridFTP bandwidth. We construct a linear model between two variables D and G as follows: $G^|=a+bD$, where $G^|$ is the prediction of the observed value of G for the corresponding value of D. The coefficients, a and b, are calculated based on a regression function that accounts for previous Ds and Gs, using the method of least squares,

$$a = \text{Mean}(G) - b * \text{Mean}(D),$$

while the coefficient b is calculated by using the formula

$$b = \frac{\sum DG - (\sum D \sum G/size)}{\sum G^2 - (\sum G)^2/size},$$

where "size" is the total number of values in the dataset [Edwards84].

3.4.2 Multiple Regression

In addition to simple regression, we study the effect of deriving predictions from all three data sources. For this purpose, we construct multiple regression strategies that allow us to study the effect of several independent variables on a dependent variable.

We construct multiple regression models by adding terms corresponding to various components to the simple regression equation. Similar to the disk component discussed earlier, to include network variations into the equation, we add a network load term. Thus, the multiple regression model is as follows: $G^|=a+b_1D+b_2N$, where $G^|$ is the prediction of the observed value of G for the corresponding values of N and D. The regression coefficients are calculated [Edwards84] as follows

$$a = \text{Mean}(G) - (b_1*\text{Mean}(D)) - (b_2*\text{Mean}(N))$$

$$b_1 = \frac{(\sum DG \; \sum N^2) - (\sum NG \; \sum DN)}{(\sum D^2 \; \sum N^2) - (\sum DN)^2}$$

$$b_2 = \frac{(\sum NG \; \sum D^2) - (\sum DG \; \sum DN)}{(\sum D^2 \; \sum N^2) - (\sum DN)^2}$$

Including further components (which contribute to the end-to-end data path) would mean adding terms to the multiple regression equation, whose coefficients can then be computed by using the method of least squares [Edwards84]. To summarize, we are interested in predicting the performance of the dependent variable, GridFTP, by studying the impact of adding independent components such as disk and network link loads to the regression model.

4   Evaluation

To analyze the performance of our predictors, we conducted several wide-area experiments between our testbed sites comprising resources from Argonne National Laboratory (ANL), Lawrence Berkeley National Laboratory (LBL), University of Southern California's Information Sciences Institute (ISI) and University of Florida at Gainesville.

First, we set up GridFTP experiments between these sites, transferring files ranging from 10 MB to 1 GB at random intervals in twelve-hour durations for a two-week period (during August 2001, December 2001 and January 2002). All transfers were made with tuned TCP buffers size of 1 MB and eight parallel streams. Disk I/O throughput data was collected by using the iostat tool logging transfer rates every five minutes. NWS was set up to monitor network bandwidth between these sites at five-minute intervals using 64 KB probes. All logs were maintained at the respective sites.

We analyze the performance of our regressive techniques in the following cases: (1) regression between GridFTP transfer data and disk I/O trace data, and (2) regression between GridFTP, disk I/O, and NWS network data. We compare the results from these approaches with predictions based on GridFTP data in isolation [VSF02] and predictions based on regressing GridFTP and NWS data [VS02]. In all of the above, we compare several of our filling strategies.

4.1   Metrics

We calculate the prediction accuracy using the normalized percentage error calculation

$$\% \ \text{Error} = \frac{\sum | \text{Measured}_{BW} - \text{Predicted}_{BW} |}{(\text{size} * \text{Mean}_{BW})} * 100 \, ,$$

where "size" is the total number of predictions and the Mean is the average measured GridFTP throughput. We show our results based on the August 2001 dataset. Results for all our datasets can be found at [Traces02].

In addition to evaluating the error of our predictions, we evaluate information about the variance. Depending on the use case, a user may be more interested in selecting a site that has reasonable performance bandwidth estimates with a relatively low prediction error instead of a resource with higher performance estimates and a possibly much higher error in prediction. In such cases, it can be useful if the forecasting error can be stated with some confidence and with a maximum/minimum variation range. These limits can also, in theory, be used as catalysts for corrective measures in case of performance degradation.

In our case, we can also use these limits to verify the inherent cost of accuracy of the predictors. Comparing the confidence intervals of these prediction error rates, we can determine whether the accuracy achieved is at the cost of greater variability, in which case there is little gain in increasing the component complexity of our prediction approach.

Thus, for any predictor (for any site pair), the information denoted by the following triplet can be used as a metric to gauge its accuracy:

Accuracy-Metric = [Throughput, % Error-Rate, Confidence],

where *Throughput* is the predicted GridFTP value (higher the better), with a certain percentage error (lower the better) and a percentage confidence interval (smaller the better). Interested parties can use a function of this accuracy metric to choose one site from the other.

4.2 Results

Table 1 presents the average normalized percent error based on all transfers for the site pairs we examined. They are classified as follows: MovingAvg corresponds to prediction based on GridFTP in isolation [VSF02]; G+N corresponds to regression between GridFTP and NWS network data [VS02]; G+D corresponds to regression between GridFTP and disk I/O; and G+N+D corresponds to regressing all three datasets. We have shown all results in the interest of continuity.

Table 1. Normalized percent prediction error rates for the various site pairs for the August 2001 dataset. The figure denotes four categories: (1) prediction based on GridFTP data in isolation (Moving Avg), (2) regression between GridFTP and NWS network data with the three filling in techniques (G+N), (3) regression between GridFTP and disk I/O data with the three filling in techniques (G+D), and (4) regression based on all three data sources (G+N+D). Shaded portions indicate a comparison between our approaches.

	GidFTP Logs [VSF02]	Linear Regression between GridFTP Logs and Network Load [VS02]			Linear Regression between GridFTP Logs and Disk Load			Linear Regression Using All Three Data Sources		
	Moving Avg	G+N NoFill	G+N LV	G+N Avg	G+D NoFill	G+D LV	G+D Avg	G+N+D NoFill	G+N+D LV	G+N+D Avg
LBL-ANL	24.4	22.4	20.6	20	25.2	21.7	21.4	22.3	17.7	17.5
LBL-UFL	15	18.8	11.1	11	20.1	11.6	11.9	11.1	8.7	8
ISI-ANL	15	12	9.5	9	13.1	13	11.4	11	8.9	8.3
ISI-UFL	21	21.9	16	14.5	22.7	19.7	18.8	14.7	13	12
ANL-UFL	20	21	20	16	21.8	19.9	19.3	15.3	16.7	15.5

From Table 1, we can observe that including disk I/O component load variations in the regression model provides us with gains of up to 4% (G+D Avg) when compared with MovingAvg (first and third shaded columns in Table 1). Different filling techniques (G+D Avg and G+D LV) perform similarly.

Further, from Table 1, we see that all variations of G+N perform better than G+D in general, that is, regression using network data performs better than regression using disk I/O data. This observation agrees with our initial measurements that only 15-30% of the total transfer time is spent in I/O, while the majority of the transfer time (in our experiments) is spent in network transport.

When we include both disk I/O and NWS network data in the regression model (G+N+D) along with GridFTP transfer data, we see that the prediction error drops up to 3% when compared with G+N (second and fourth shaded columns in Table 1). Overall, we see up to 9% improvement when we compare G+N+D with our original prediction based on Moving Avg. As disk sizes grow and speeds stay the same, we believe this will be even more significant.

Figure 3a compares the forecasting error in Moving Avg, G+D Avg, G+N Avg, and G+N+D Avg for all of our site pairs (the shaded columns in Table 1) and also presents 95% confidence limits for our prediction error rates. The forecasting accuracy trend is as follows:

$$Moving\ Avg < (G+D\ Avg) < (G+N\ Avg) < (G+N+D\ Avg).$$

From Figure 3b we can observe that the interval does in fact reduce with more accurate predictors, but the reduction is not significant for our datasets.

Figure 4 depicts the performance of predictors G+D Avg and G+N+D Avg. Graphs show the relevant data sources and the associated predictions. We can see how predictors closely track the measured GridFTP values. Predictions were obtained by using regression equations that were computed for each observed network or disk throughput value. Sample regression equations with computed coefficients (based on discussion from Section 3.4) for the last observed N and D values in Figures 4a and 4b are as follows:

$$G^{|} = 6.9 - 0.18 * D$$

for the simple regression case and

$$G^{|} = 7 - 0.38 * N - 0.18 * D$$

for the multiple regression.

5   Conclusion

In this paper, we present techniques to combine observations of end-to-end application behavior and disk I/O throughput load data. We develop a set of regression models to derive predictions that characterize the effect of disk load variations on file transfer times. For deriving predictions we use simple statistical tools that are reasonably straightforward and easy to implement and therefore easy to apply to other datasets.

Using disk I/O data improves prediction accuracy by up to 4% when compared with predictions based on past GridFTP behavior. Similarly, predicting based on I/O, NWS, and GridFTP data improved accuracy further, by up to 9%. By adding additional data streams, each of which describing a piece of the end-to-end GridFTP transfer path, we see improvements in the accuracy of the predictions generated. For our datasets, we observe no improvements in using polynomial regression.

Future work includes exploring rank functions to evaluate the accuracy of predictors and using the variance information of predictors to perform scheduling decisions.

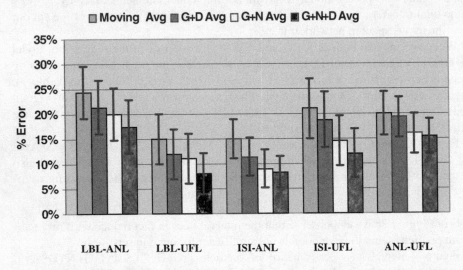

(a) **Comparison of normalized percent errors for the predictors with 95% confidence limits**

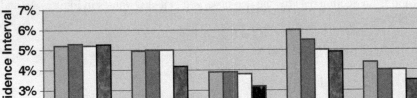

(b) **Comparison of intervals for the predictors**

Fig. 3. (a) Normalized percent prediction error and 95% confidence limits for August 2001 dataset from (1) prediction based on GridFTP in isolation (MovingAvg), (2) regression between GridFTP and disk I/O with Avg filling strategy (G+D Avg), (3) regression between GridFTP and NWS network data with Avg filling strategy (G+N Avg), and (4) regressing all three datasets (G+N+D Avg). Confidence Limits denote the upper and lower bounds of prediction error. For instance, the LBL-ANL pair had a prediction range of 17.3% ± 5.2%. (b) Comparison of the percentage of variability among the predictors.

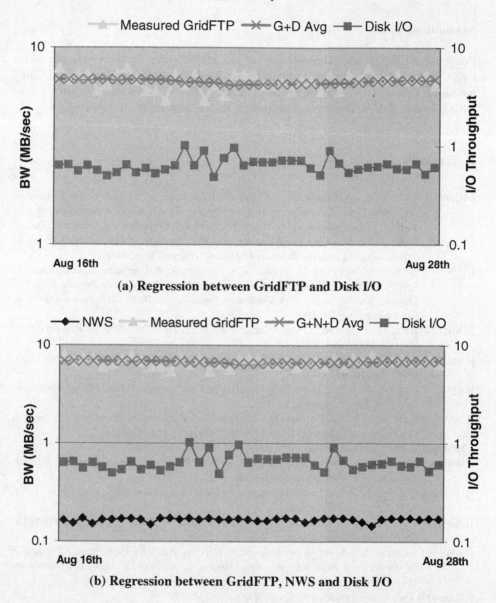

(a) Regression between GridFTP and Disk I/O

(b) Regression between GridFTP, NWS and Disk I/O

Fig. 4. Predictors for 100 MB transfers between ISI and ANL for August 2001 dataset. In both graphs, GridFTP, G+D Avg, G+N+D Avg, and NWS are plotted on the primary y-axis; while Disk I/O is plotted on the secondary y-axis. I/O throughput denotes transfers per second.

Acknowledgments

We thank all the system administrators of our testbed sites for their valuable assistance. This work was supported in part by the Mathematical, Information, and Computational Sciences Division subprogram of the Office of Advanced Scientific Computing Research, U.S. Department of Energy, under contract W-31-109-Eng-38.

References

[ACF+02] Allcock, W., A. Chervenak, I. Foster, C. Kesselman, C. Salisbury, and S. Tuecke, *The Data Grid: Towards an Architecture for the Distributed Management and Analysis of Large Scientific Datasets.* Network and Computer Applications, 2002.

[Adve93] Adve, V.S., *Analyzing the Behavior and Performance of Parallel Programs*, in *Department of Computer Science.* 1993, University of Wisconsin.

[AFN+01] Allcock, W., I. Foster, V. Nefedova, A. Chevrenak, E. Deelman, C. Kesselman, A. Sim, A. Shoshani, B. Drach, and D. Williams. *High-Performance Remote Access to Climate Simulation Data: A Challenge Problem for Data Grid Technologies.* in *Supercomputing' 01.* 2001.

[BMR+98] Baru, C., R. Moore, A. Rajasekar, and M. Wan. *The SDSC Storage Resource Broker.* in *CASCON'98.* 1998.

[Cole89] Cole, M., *Algorithmic Skeletons: Structured Management of Parallel Computation.* 1989: Pitman/MIT Press.

[CQ93] Clement, M.J. and M.J. Quinn. *Analytical Performance Prediction on Multicomputers.* in *Supercomputing'93.* 1993.

[Crovella99] Crovella, M.E., *Performance Prediction and Tuning of Parallel Programs*, in *Department of Computer Science.* 1999, University of Rochester.

[DataGrid02] *The Data Grid Project, http://www.eu-datagrid.org, 2002.*

[Downey97] Downey, A. *Queue Times on Space-Sharing Parallel Computers.* in *11th International Parallel Processing Symposium.* 1997.

[Edwards84] Edwards, A.L., *An Introduction to Linear Regression and Correlation.* 1984: W.H. Freeman and Company.

[FK98] Foster, I. and C. Kesselman. *The Globus Project: A Status Report.* in *IPPS/SPDP '98 Heterogeneous Computing Workshop.* 1998.

[FSW+99] Faerman, M., A. Su, R. Wolski, and F. Berman. *Adaptive Performance Prediction for Distributed Data-Intensive Applications.* in *ACM/IEEE SC99 Conference on High Performance Networking and Computing.* 1999. Portland, Oregon.

[Globus02] *The Globus Project, http://www.globus.org, 2002.*

[GriPhyN02] *The GriPhyN Project, http://www.griphyn.org, 2002.*

[GS00] Gray, J. and P. Shenoy. *Rules of Thumb in Data Engineering.* in *International Conference on Data Engineering ICDE2000.* 2000. San Diego: IEEE Press.

[GT99] Geisler, J. and V. Taylor. *Performance Coupling: Case Studies for Measuring the Interactions of Kernels in Modern Applications.* in *SPEC Workshop on Performance Evaluation with Realistic Applications.* 1999.

[HJS+00] Hoschek, W., J. Jaen-Martinez, A. Samar, and H. Stockinger. *Data Management in an International Grid Project.* in *2000 Internationsl Workshop on Grid Computing (GRID 2000).* 2000. Bangalore, India.

[Holtman00] Holtman, K. *Object Level Replication for Physics*. in *4th Annual Globus Retreat*. 2000. Pittsburgh.

[HSS00] Hafeez, M., A. Samar, and H. Stockinger. *Prototype for Distributed Data Production in CMS*. in *7th International Workshop on Advanced Computing and Analysis Techniques in Physics Research (ACAT2000)*. 2000.

[Jones02] Jones, R. *The Public Netperf Homepage, http://www.netperf.org/netperf/NetperfPage.html*. 2002.

[ML90] Mak, V.W. and S.F. Lundstrom, *Predicting the Performance of Parallel Computations*. IEEE Transactions on Parallel and Distributed Systems, 1990: pp. 106-113.

[MMR+01] Malon, D., E. May, S. Resconi, J. Shank, A. Vaniachine, T. Wenaus, and S. Youssef. *Grid-enabled Data Access in the ATLAS Athena Framework*. in *Computing and High Energy Physics 2001 (CHEP'01) Conference*. 2001.

[NetLogger02] *NetLogger: A Methodology for Monitoring and Analysis of Distributed Systems*. 2002.

[SARA02] *SARA: The Synthetic Aperture Radar Atlas, http://sara.unile.it/sara/*, 2002.

[SB98] Schopf, J.M. and F. Berman. *Performance Predictions in Production Environments*. In *IPPS/SPDP'98*. 1998.

[SC00] Shen, X. and A. Choudhary. *A Multi-Storage Resource Architecture and I/O, Performance Prediction for Scientific Computing*. in *9th IEEE Symposium on High Performance Distributed Computing*. 2000: IEEE Press.

[Schopf97] Schopf, J.M. *Structural Prediction Models for High Performance Distributed Applications*. in *Cluster Computing (CCC'97)*. 1997.

[SFT98] Smith, W., I. Foster, and V. Taylor. *Predicting Application Run Times Using Historical Information*. in *IPPS/SPDP '98 Workshop on Job Scheduling Strategies for Parallel Processing*. 1998.

[SW02] Swany, M. and R. Wolski. *Multivariate Resource Performance Forecasting in the Network Weather Service*. in *Supercomputing'02*. 2002.

[SYSSTAT02] *SYSSTAT Utilities Homepage, http://perso.wanadoo.fr/sebastien.godard/*, 2002.

[TB86] Thomasian, A. and P.F. Bay, *Queuing Network Models for Parallel Processing of Task Systems*. IEEE Transactions on Computers, 1986. **35**(12).

[TF01] Tirumala, A. and J. Ferguson. *Iperf 1.2 - The TCP/UDP Bandwidth Measurement Tool, http://dast.nlanr.net/Projects/Iperf*. 2001.

[Traces02] *GridFTP predictor Trace Data, http://www.mcs.anl.gov/~vazhkuda/Traces*, 2002.

[VS02] Vazhkudai, S. and J. Schopf. *Predicting Sporadic Grid Data Transfers*. in *11th IEEE High Performance Distributed Computing (HPDC-11)*. 2002. Edinburgh, Scotland: IEEE Press.

[VSF02] Vazhkudai, S., J. Schopf, and I. Foster. *Predicting the Performance Wide-Area Data Transfers*. in *16th International Parallel and Distributed Processing Symposium (IPDPS)*. 2002. Fort Lauderdale, Florida: IEEE Press.

[Web100Project02] *The Web100 Project, http://www.web100.org*, 2002.

[Wolski98] Wolski, R., *Dynamically Forecasting Network Performance Using the Network Weather Service*. Cluster Computing, 1998.

[ZLP96] Zaki, M.J., W. Li, and S. Parthasarathy. *Customized Dynaimic Lad Balancing for Network of Workstations*. in *High Performance Distributed Computing (HPDC'96)*. 1996.

Improving the Throughput of Remote Storage Access through Pipelining

Elsie Nallipogu[1], Füsun Özgüner [1], and Mario Lauria[2]

[1] Dept of Electrical Engineering, The Ohio State University,
2015 Neil Ave, Columbus, OH 43210, USA
{nallipogu, ozguner}@ee.eng.ohio-state.edu
[2] Dept. of Computer and Information Science, The Ohio State University,
2015 Neil Ave, Columbus, OH 43210, USA
lauria@cis.ohio-state.edu

Abstract. Data intensive applications constitute a large and increasing share of Grid computing. However there are relatively few results on how to improve the efficiency of the basic data transfer mechanisms used to move large data set in and out of Grid nodes. In this paper we describe a simple and general technique to improve the throughput of data transfer protocols and we demonstrate it on the SDSC Storage Resource Broker (SRB), a remote storage access middleware for supercomputer applications. We achieve a maximum performance improvement of 43%/52% for remote reads/writes larger than 1MB with a few changes to the original SRB protocol. The protocol was restructured by introducing a notion of pipelining that enables the overlapping of the various stages of the data processing, such as network transfer and disk access. We present a detailed analysis of the pipelined SRB implementation and of the pipeline cost model we used to drive our design.

1. Introduction

In recent years there has been an increasing interest in large data set applications. An increasingly number of applications in domains such as genomics/proteomics, astrophysics, physics, computational neuroscience, or volume rendering, need to archive, retrieve, and compute on increasingly large datasets. NPACI projects like the Digital Sky Survey project and the Neuro Imaging repository are representative of HPC applications developed from start to use terabyte-sized datasets. Typically, the data for these applications is distributed across remote repositories, is the result of multi-institutional collaborations, and it is shared with a large community of users worldwide. The combination of data set size, geographic distribution of resources, and computationally intensive analysis results in performance requirements that are not satisfied by the current network and data management infrastructure.

In a computational grid, a data-intensive application will require high-bandwidth data access all the way to the remote data repository. The most commonly used approach to move data between machines is the remote storage access model. Tools such as SRB, GASS, RIO provide a way for applications to transparently access data stored in a variety of storage servers. These tools present to the application an interface that is very close to the standard Unix I/O API (i.e. with primitives such as open,

M. Parashar (Ed.): GRID 2002, LNCS 2536, pp. 305-316, 2002.

read, write, close), which means they are simple to use and only minimal modifications are required to existing applications. These tools are typically implemented as a library of I/O primitives in which calls performed by the application are remotely executed on a server using a RPC-like model.

In this paper we study how to improve this basic mechanism by transferring the data in several small blocks as opposed to one single large block, so to enable the overlapping of different phases of the operation such as network transfer and disk access. By pipelining the different phases of the remote disk access operation a substantial benefit can be gained for large transfers in most conditions. In the simplest scenario, the network transfer can be overlapped with the disk access on the server, leading to an almost twofold performance improvement in the ideal case of disk and network with comparable throughput. A larger improvement can be derived if there are more than two overlappable stages, for example in the case of multiple network hops, or of intermediate processing steps along the data path to the disks.

We use clusters as the reference architecture for our study because of their increasing role as a platform not only for high performance computation but also as storage servers. We choose SRB for our study because of its frequent use in connection with data-intensive computing applications. With a simple restructuring of the SRB protocol, we demonstrate a maximum performance improvement of 43%/52% for remote reads/writes larger than 1MB on our platform. The main contributions of this work are the demonstration of the effectiveness of the pipelining concept for data transfers of practical size, and the description of a design procedure based on a simple analytical model of the pipeline.

The rest of the paper is organized as follows. Section 2 describes some related work. Section 3 gives an overview of SRB. Section 4 describes the pipeline model we use for our design and for determining the optimal chunk size. Section 5 details the changes we made to implement the pipelined protocol. Section 6 describes the experimental setup and the results we achieved. In section 7 we discuss the results obtained on the two testbeds. Finally section 8 concludes the paper.

2.   Related Work

The closest system to SRB in terms of functionality is the Global Access to Secondary Storage (GASS) package, which is a part of the GLOBUS [17] toolkit. The optimizations made in GASS for remote file access concentrate on using a number of caching schemes as opposed to overlapping of communication and disk transfer at the remote site [2].

In the Condor high-throughput computing system, application codes are linked with a runtime library that replaces I/O system calls with remote procedure calls back to the remote client that submitted the job. While this approach provides transparent access to remote files, it transfers only requested data and does not require access to local storage on the remote machine; it provides no support for caching or pipelining [14]. The Legion system provides global access only for files that have been copied to the "Legion space" through specialized I/O methods [15].

Kernel-level implementations such as the Andrew File System (AFS) [16] and the Distributed File System (DFS) provide UNIX file system operations in a wide area environment. In these systems, typical users cannot control performance because the services provided are kernel-level. These data-handling systems aim to provide improved remote access by various means mentioned above such as caching, single initial copy etc. However, none of these systems seem to incorporate pipelining into file access. Presumably pipelining can easily be incorporated in these systems, especially GASS, but the papers do not describe such optimizations.

The type of messaging layers prevalent in cluster computing today, e.g. Active Messages (AM) [11], Fast Messages (FM) [9], Trapeze [10], Virtual Memory Management Communication (VMMC) [12], and BIP [13] do use some form of pipelining with fragmentation of messages. However, these optimizations are carried out at much lower protocol layers and are not dedicated to data-intensive applications. The strategies studied on user-level messaging protocols can be extended to provide the same form of optimizations in higher-level data-handling protocols such as the SRB. The main point to note here is that data-handling systems are geared towards applications run over Wide Area Networks, as opposed to user-level protocols that were optimized mainly for localized clusters (using Local Area Networks, LANs).

3.   The Storage Resource Broker (SRB)

The San Diego Supercomputer Center (SDSC) is involved in developing an infrastructure for a high performance distributed computing environment for its National Partnership for Advanced Computational Infrastructure (NPACI). One of the key objectives of the NPACI effort is to provide support for data-intensive computing, which involves providing high performance I/O to massive data and providing digital library capabilities for storage, search and retrieval of scientific data [1,3,6-8].

The Storage Resource Broker (SRB) was developed as part of that infrastructure to provide seamless access to data stored on a variety of storage resources. The SRB provides an Application Program Interface (API) which enables applications executing in the distributed NPACI environment to access data stored at any of the distributed storage sites. The SRB API provides the capability for information discovery, identify data collections, and select and retrieve data items that may be distributed across a Wide Area Network (WAN). The design of the SRB is based on a network-connected client/server model. The model consists of three components: the metadata catalog (MCAT) service, SRB servers and SRB clients connected together over a network. The catalog is not used in our experiments so it is not described here.

The SRB server consists of one or more SRB Master Daemon Processes with SRB agent processes that are associated with each Master. Each SRB Master is identified uniquely by its (hostname, port number). Each Master controls a distinct set of storage resources. The Master listens to its well-known ports for connection requests from clients using TCP/IP connections. A distinct SRB agent is spawned each time a client opens a connection to the master

Two types of API are provided on the client side: high-level API and low-level API. The high-level API includes functions like query, update metadata, connecting to a server and creation of data items. Low-level APIs are direct storage operations like open, read, write & delete which do not involve the MCAT service (however, deleting of data items requires updates to the MCAT service). In all our experiments we have used the low level API. The SRB was developed with a goal of providing an easy-to-use interface and was not geared for high performance. In particular, the low-level API (e.g., srbFileRead and srbFileWrite) has no particular optimizations for large data transfers.

4.   Performance Model

A two-step analysis was applied to the pipelined SRB. In the first step of the analysis we derived an abstract pipeline model in which each stage is characterized in terms of two simple parameters, fixed overhead and per-byte cost. Next the values of each of these two parameters for each stage were measured borrowing techniques developed for the measurement of the LogP model parameters of a system [4]. In this section we describe the model we used; the measurement of the pipeline parameters discussed in this section is described in the section 6.

Our pipeline model is based on generalization and models studied by Wang et. al. in the context of user level messaging protocols [5]. According to this model, a system can be represented as a sequence of store-and-forward pipeline stages, which can be characterized by the following parameters: n, the number of pipeline stages; g_i, fixed per-chunk overhead for stage i; G_i, per-byte overhead (inverse bandwidth) for stage i. For the optimization of a general pipeline we will also be using the following variables: B, size of file or packet; k, number of chunks; T, latency of entire file or message.

The contribution of the slowest pipeline stage is a key issue in developing optimal fragmentation algorithms. The bottleneck, or slowest stage, is denoted as the bth stage. If the bottleneck stage is kept busy at all steps but at the beginning and at the end, then the total latency can be represented as follows:

$$T = T_f + T_b + T_l$$

where T_f is the time the first chunk takes to reach the bottleneck, T_b is the time the entire piece of data spends in the bottleneck, T_l is the time the last chunk takes to leave the pipeline from the time it leaves the bottleneck.

To minimize T, we must minimize $(T_f + T_b + T_l)$. Minimizing $(T_f + T_l)$ requires small fragments; as we decrease the size of the fragments, we decrease the time the first fragment takes to reach the bottleneck (T_f) and the time the last fragment takes to leave the bottleneck (T_l). On the other hand, minimizing T_b requires large fragments, because the total overhead experienced at the bottleneck is lowered with fewer fragments. If we assume chunks have the same size, the optimal size can be found by expressing T as a function of k and annulling the derivative of the resulting function. As shown by Wang et. al. [5] the optimal chunk size is:

$$\text{Optimal chunk size} = \sqrt{\frac{B \bullet g_b}{\sum_{j \neq b} G_j}} \tag{1}$$

It is interesting to note that factors such as the overheads of the non-bottleneck stages and the bandwidth of the bottleneck stage (G_b) do not affect the chunking strategy. The overheads of the non-bottleneck stages are masked by the overhead of the bottleneck stage, and the bandwidth of the bottleneck stage is masked by the total time all the chunks spend in the non-bottleneck stages ($\sum_{j \neq b} Gj$).

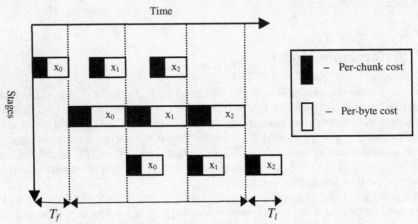

Fig. 1. Example of 3-stage pipeline

5. Pipelined Protocol Implementation

To maintain compatibility with the existing implementations of SRB and to keep the changes to the existing code to a minimum we decided to add two new functions to implement the pipelined protocol. The new function calls, srbFileChunkWrite and srbFileChunkRead, correspond to pipelined operation for writes and reads respectively.

The function srbFileChunkRead sends a read request to the server with information on the file size, and the number of portions, or chunks, that it should be split into for the pipelining. The server queues the appropriate number of asynchronous reads on its local disk.. The server maintains a circular queue of buffers, one buffer for each outstanding read.

The buffer queue is statically created at compile time to minimize the overhead associated with dynamic allocation of large amounts of memory. Once any one of the reads completes, the server sends the data from the appropriate buffer back to the client. This continues until all the outstanding chunk reads and hence the total amount of data requested has been read from disk, in other words the srbFileChunkRead only returns when all the data has been sent.

After sending the initial read request, the client application waits until it receives the first chunk of data. The client continues listening to its socket port until it receives its data from the server. On receipt of a chunk, the client copies this data to the appropriate location in the file. When the total amount of data has been received, the function returns. Figure 2(a) shows the sequence of requests between the client and the server.

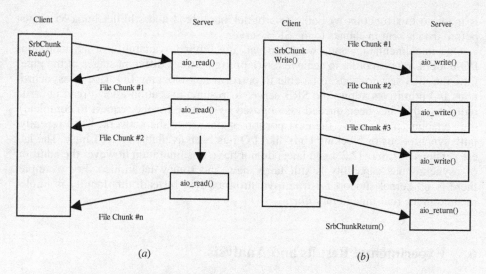

Fig. 2. Sequence of protocol messages for srbChunkRead (*a*) and srbChunkWrite (b)

In calling the srbFileChunkWrite function the user specifies the name of the file, the size of the file, and can choose the number of chunks or pieces that should be used to split the total data. The function, when executed by the SRB client application, sends a portion of the data, or chunk, of a size equal to that specified by the user. It sends each sequentially, until all chunks have been sent. A chunk is sent only after the previous one has been sent and received by the server. After the client has sent all its data, it sends a blocking srbFileChunkReturn call, which basically blocks until the disk I/O on the server side completes.

On the server side, when the data is received it is copied from the receive buffer to disk using an asynchronous write command. A circular queue is used to keep track of outstanding writes. Figure 2(b) shows the sequence of requests between the client and the server. For both the srbFileChunkRead and srbFileChunkWrite functions, the size of the chunks can be specified by the user, or if not specified, then an optimal size is selected.

A critical aspect of the implementation was the automatic selection of the optimal chunk size. When the data to be read or written is split into pieces or chunks the processing of each chunk within the different pipeline stages affects the amount of overlapping and thus the pipeline performance. Optimal chunk size in general depends not only on the characteristics of the system but also on the total size of the transfer. Experimental evidence confirmed that the optimal chunk size is not constant for a given system, that is, one-size does not fit all.

The choice of the optimal chunk size is obtained through the formula described in the previous section. For the measurements described in this paper, the pipeline parameters, namely fixed overhead (g_i) and the inverse bandwidth of each stage (G_i), were measured manually and then hard-coded in the SRB code prior to each experiment. The values for each of the four stages (ClientProc, NetCom, DiskIO and ServerProc) are stored in an array. The details of how these stages were defined and how their parameters were measured are discussed in the next section. The function FindFixedOptimal computes the optimal chunk size according to equation (1). A call is made to this function by both the srbFileChunkRead and srbFileChunkWrite just before data is sent in chunks to the SRB Server.

One implementation issue we faced was the limited availability of asynchronous I/O under Linux. In order to achieve overlapping between different stages of the pipeline, the SRB server needs to be able to perform non-blocking I/O. Use of asynchronous I/O primitives allows the SRB server to resume execution after a read or write request to disk has been queued (as opposed to waiting for the request to complete), thus enabling it to receive the next portion of data from the network. Until recently, only synchronous or blocking Unix-like I/O has been available under Linux. The latest versions of Linux (2.2.4 and later) do not have this limitation however the addition of asynchronous capability is still fairly new and somewhat limited. For example, there is no kernel support for true asynchronous I/O. Instead, this facility is implemented in the real-time library *librt*.

6. Experimental Results and Analysis

This section is divided into four parts: the first part reports the experimental testbed configuration, the second contains a description of the methods used to measure pipeline parameters, the third describes the performance measurements and their results, and the last is a discussion of the results.

Testbed Configuration. All the measurements were performed with the SRB client and server running on two nodes of the same cluster. We repeated the measurements on the following two systems. The NowLab cluster is a 16 node PentiumPro 200MHz cluster, with 128MB physical memory and one 6GB IDE disk per node, and a 100MBit Ethernet interconnection network. The cluster has Linux 2.2.4 installed on it. The Blitz Cluster is a 8 node cluster running Redhat 6.2 (Linux kernel 2.2.4). Each node is a Dell PowerEdge 1400 with dual 1GHz Pentium III processor, 1GB of physical memory, 18 GB SCSI disk, two 60 GB IBM Deskstar 75GXP IDE disks connected to a 3Ware controller in RAID 0 (disk striped) configuration. Each node is also configured with both a 100Mbit/s Ethernet card and 1.2Gbit/s Myrinet card.

Measurement of Pipeline Parameters. Tuning the performance of the pipelining mechanism requires conceptually two steps: i) identification of the number of potential stages of the pipeline, and then ii) measurements of the g_i and G_i parameters for each stage. The first step requires identifying the exact stage boundaries and the extent to which these stages can be overlapped, and both of these pieces of information can be non trivial to obtain directly. Therefore, the two steps were performed concurrently, using results from the parameter measurement phase to help in determining the number of effective stages.

Initially, the system was broken down into all active entities i.e. entities such as CPU, network processors, disk controllers with independent processing capabilities. Such entities correspond to the following four processing stages: client protocol processing (SRBClient), network transport (NetCom), protocol processin on SRB server (SRBServer), disk access on the server (DiskIO). We then proceeded to measure the parameters of these stages. Based on the measurement results, we obtained pipeline models that differ for the two clusters with respect to which of these stages were actually relevant.

In the NowLab cluster all four stages were found to be significant; the pipeline parameters for these stages are shown in Table I. In the Blitz cluster the client and server processing overheads were so small and that the system could be reduced to essentially a two-stage model. These two stages thus comprise the following operations: i) network communication time that includes both TCP/IP protocol-processing times and raw network transmission time, and ii) disk access time that includes time to copy data to or from the local hard disk on the server. This is a result of the high speed of the processors on the Blitz cluster (1GHz) that makes the processing overhead very small compared to the other stages. Also, the experiments were run over Myrinet, which allows DMA transfers to/from the network card thereby freeing the CPU from part of the protocol processing. In the Nowlab cluster, where each node has slower CPU and no Myrinet card, all stages had a non zero latency and thus all four were needed to model the system.

The pipeline parameters G_i and g_i were obtained by measuring the latency of each stage in the pipeline. First, files of various sizes are accessed through the data path without pipelining to obtain the timing vector. G_i was obtained by measuring the latencies of each stage for large file sizes and applying regression analysis to this data. The slope of the straight-line fit curve thus obtained gave G_i. The fixed overhead, g_i, was obtained by measuring the latency for small file transfers and taking the average of these values. The values of these parameters are shown in the tables below.

Table 1. Pipeline parameters for the NowLab cluster.

	Writes		Reads	
	g_i (ms)	G_i (ms/MB)	g_i (ms)	G_i (ms/MB)
SRBClient	15.86	0	13.97	0
NetCom	5.62	440	0.01	640
DiskIO	68.50	350	0.02	190
SRBServer	0.06	0	15.99	0

Table 2. Pipeline Parameters for the Blitz cluster

	Writes		Reads	
	g_i (ms)	G_i (ms/MB)	g_i (ms)	G_i (ms/MB)
NetCom	5.984	25.1	5.155	27.1
DiskIO	1.014	22.5	0.007	22.7

Performance Results. In the first set of experiments the chunk sizes were fixed, and manually set at predetermined values. Figure 3 shows the performance of the pipelined operation for a number of chunk sizes on the Blitz cluster.

These experiments were run to identify empirically the optimal chunk size and the corresponding amount of performance improvement. As expected from the analysis presented in Section 4, the optimal chunk size is not constant for either system, and is dependent on the file size (or the total amount of data to be sent). The selection of a chunk size is more critical on the Nowlab (not shown) than on the Blitz cluster, where the bandwidth and overhead of the two stages are approximately equal.

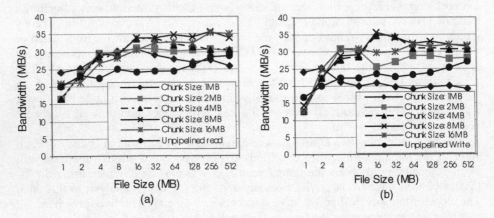

Fig. 3. Performance of preset size chunking on Blitz cluster: (a) Reads (b) Writes.

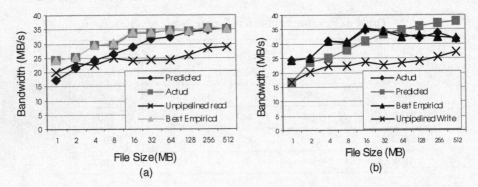

Fig. 4. Performance of adaptive size chunking on Blitz cluster; (a) Reads (b) Writes.

In a second set of experiments the chunk size for each file size (or total data size) was calculated by the pipelining protocol according to the formula given in Section 4. Figures 4 and 5 show the performance of the chunking algorithm on both the Nowlab cluster and the Blitz cluster. The Blitz graphs also show the bandwidth predicted by the algorithm and the best empirically obtained bandwidth. The empirically obtained bandwidth is compared to the bandwidth predicted by the algorithm, thereby showing the accuracy of the model developed and also of the measured parameters. The bandwidth predicted by the model converges with the experimentally obtained bandwidth for large data sizes, but is less accurate in predicting the performance for lower data sizes for both reads and writes. The slope of the predicted curve will decrease (and thereby converge with the experimental results) if the fixed-overhead of the stages increases. This implies that the measured fixed-overhead could be higher than that measured. However, the model developed does predict optimal chunk sizes, which achieve performance close to the maximum empirically obtained bandwidths.

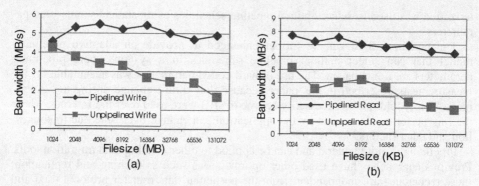

Fig. 5. Performance of adaptive size chunking on the NowLab cluster; (a) Reads, (b) Writes.

7. Discussion

In the Nowlab cluster the maximum performance improvement was 230% for reads and 195.18% for writes. On average the performance for both read and write more than doubled. In this system, where disk access is clearly a bottleneck, performance is greatly affected by slow disk access.

In the Blitz cluster, a maximum of 52.73% for writes and 43.48% for reads performance improvement was achieved. On average, performance increased by a third. In this cluster, where all stages have similar bandwidths (that is, there is no obvious single bottleneck stage), the performance can still benefit from pipelining. A even larger performance improvement would be theoretically possible in this case; we attribute this discrepancy to the imperfect overlapping of the two stages, possibly due to a significant involvement of the operating system in the operation of both stages on the server side.

The performance improvement was greater in the Nowlab cluster mainly because the disk access in that system is one order of magnitude lower than the network bandwidth. The disk access rate is actually five times lower than the network speed for large data transfers. On the other hand, in the Blitz cluster there is no significant difference between network speeds and disk access. This implies that there is a greater room for improvement in the Nowlab cluster than in the Blitz cluster.

8. Conclusion and Future Work

In this paper we have shown that pipelining provide significant performance improvement when applied to a tool like SRB. The performance gain varied from 230% for reads and 195.18% for writes on Nowlab cluster, and from 43.48% for reads and 52.73% for writes on the Blitz cluster. Various models and approaches were studied to characterize the behavior of the SRB. A performance model was developed that involved breaking down the system into overlappable stages each characterized with a fixed-overhead and a variable per-byte overhead (or inverse bandwidth). This characterization was used to select optimal pipeline schedules using statically measured parameters.

The pipelined SRB can be further enhanced to provide an adaptive pipelining model that can select optimal pipeline schedules in a system where pipelining parameters are not constant. The use of hard coded parameters was acceptable for the measurements described in this paper because they didn't change during the experiment. This would not be necessarily be true if SRB were used over the Internet, where the link performance as seen by the application can change over time due to congestion and other factors.

Pipelining is quite general and can be applied to other existing data migration tools. Previous approaches have used other optimizations such as caching and replication; these techniques are independent from the particular data transfer protocol used and thus can coexist with and benefit from pipelining. We are considering experimenting with other data migration tools such as IBP and GASS to study the interaction of different throughput enhancement techniques.

Acknowledgments

We wish to thank Arcot Rajasekar and Reagan Moore at SDSC for giving us access to the SRB source, and D.K. Panda at OSU for allowing us to use the NowLab cluster for our experiments.

References

1. C. Baru, R. Moore, A. Rajasekar, M. Wan, "The SDSC Storage Resource Broker,"   Proc. CASCON'98 Conference, Nov.30-Dec.3, 1998, Toronto, Canada.
2. J. Bester, I. Foster, C. Kesselman, J. Tedesco, S. Tuecke, "GASS: A Data Movement and Access Service for Wide Area Computing Systems", Sixth Workshop on I/O in Parallel and Distributed Systems, May 1999.
3. The SDSC Storage Resource Broker Homepage": http://www.npaci.edu/DICE/SRB/
4. D.E. Culler, R. Karp, D.A. Patterson, A. Sahay, K.E. Schauser, E. Santos, R. Subramonian, and T. von Eicken, "LogP: towards a realistic model of parallel computation", Procs. of the 4th SIGPLAN Symp. on Principles and Practices of Parallel Programming, ACM, May 1993.
5. R. Wang, A. Krishnamurthy, R. Martin, T. Anderson & D. E. Culler, "Modeling Communication Pipeline Latency", Procs. Of ACM International Conference on Measurement and Modeling of Computer Systems (SIGMETRICS '98), June 1998.
6. X. Shen, W. Liao and A. Choudhary. "Remote I/O Optimization and Evaluation for Tertiary Storage Systems through Storage Resource Broker" to appear in IASTED Applied Informatics, Innsbruck, Austria, Febuary, 2001
7. T. Kurc, M. Beynon, A. Sussman, J. Saltz, " DataCutter and a Client Interface for the Storage Resource Broker with DataCutter services".
8. Ian Foster and Carl Kesselman, The Grid, Blueprint for a New Computing   Infrastructure, Morgan Kaufmann Publishers Inc., 1999.
9. S. Pakin, M. Lauria, A. Chien "High Performance Messaging on Workstations: Illinois Fast Messages (FM) for Myrinet" Supercomputing '95.
10. J. Chase, D. Anderson, A. Gallatin, A. Lebeck, K. Yocum, "Network I/O with Trapeze", 1999 Hot Interconnects Symposium, August 1999.

11. T. von Eicken, .D. Culler, S. Goldstein, K. E. Schauser, "Active Messages: A mechanism for Integrated, Communication and Computation:, Proceedings ASPLOS-V, May 1992, pp. 256-266.
12. C. Dubnicki, A. Bilas, Y. Chen, S. Damianakis, and Kai Li," VMMC-2: Efficient Support for Reliable, Connection-Oriented Communication", Hot Interconnects V, August 1997.
13. L. Prylli, B. Tourancheau,"BIP: A new protocol designed for high performance networking on Myrinet", Workshop PC-NOW IPPS/SPDP98, 1998.
14. M. Litzkow, M. Livny, M. Mutka, "Condor – a hunter of idle workstations", Proc. of the 8th International Conference on Distributed Computing Systems", April 1988, pp. 104-111.
15. A. Grimshaw, W. Wulf, J. French, A. Weaver and P. Reynolds Jr., "Legion: The next logical step toward a nationwide virtual computer", Technical Report CS-94-21, Department of Computer Science, University of Virginia, 1994.
16. J. Morris, M. Satyanarayanan, M. Conner, J. Howard, D. Rosenthal and F. Smith,", Andrew: A distributed personal computing environment", Communications of the ACM, 1986, pp. 184-201.
17. I. Foster, C. Kesselman, "Globus: A Metacomputing Infrastructure Toolkit", Intl J. Supercomputer Applications, 11(2):115-128, 1997.

Author Index